Effective onscreen editing: new tools for an old profession (3rd edition)

"No p^assion in *the worl~~l~~d is equal~~t~~*
to the p^assion *to al~~t~~ter some~~o~~ne*
else's dr^aft." —*H.G. Well~~l~~s*

The "a" on your typewriter seems to be stuck!

[GH1] The "o" on your keyboard isn't working, and the "l" is stuck!

D1372574

by Geoff Hart

Dedication

Even after three editions, this book is still dedicated to Shoshanna Green, wife and fellow word geek, for partnership in all things editorial and in the more important things that make life worth living and books worth writing.

Copyright © 2016 by Geoffrey J.S. Hart.

Library and Archives Canada Cataloguing in Publication
Hart, Geoff, 1962-, author
Effective onscreen editing : new tools for an old profession / Geoffrey Hart. -- 3rd edition.
Includes bibliographical references and index.
Issued in print and electronic formats.
ISBN   978-1-927972-04-5   (paperback).—ISBN   978-1-927972-05-2 (pdf).—ISBN 978-1-927972-06-9 (epub)
1. Editing--Data processing. 2. Text processing (Computer science). 3. Word processing. 4. Microsoft Word (Computer file). I. Title.
PN162.H37 2016   808'.027028553684
C2016-902476-8   C2016-902477-6

Diaskeuasis Publishing
112 Chestnut Ave.
Pointe-Claire, Quebec
H9R 3B1 Canada
www.geoff-hart.com

Diskeuasis Publishing

Acknowledgments

"Think not those faithful who praise all thy words and actions; but those who kindly reprove thy faults."—Socrates, philosopher (469?–399 B.C.)

"For what I have published, I can only hope to be pardoned; but for what I have burned, I deserve to be praised."—Alexander Pope

A book of this scope would have been impossible without the assistance of many individuals. First and foremost, I thank the many authors who worked with me so patiently while I learned the tools of my (onscreen) trade. Second, my thanks to the many kind and sometimes lost souls who belong to two e-mail discussion groups: Copyediting-L and Techwhirl. Much of what I've presented in this book comes from my own explorations of the nooks and crannies of my computer while fighting with Word and other software. But I've also learned much from many experts who selflessly gave hours of their time helping amateurs. Third, thanks to Woody Leonard for helping me begin my long and often strange journey in Microsoft Word well-armed and confident Word's many idiosyncrasies had solutions, even if they weren't obvious. Subscribe to Woody's free *Office Watch* newsletters via his site, and buy his books; they're great resources for coping with all things Microsoft. You'll be thanking Woody and his team for their tireless efforts to make Microsoft software usable by mere mortals.

This book began as a quarterly column on onscreen editing for the Society for Technical Communication's *Intercom* magazine. Maurice Martin, Cate Nielan, and Ed Rutkowski provided a valuable second set of eyes and reality check on what I'd written. This book has evolved greatly over more than a decade, but their dedicated editorial efforts provided a sound basis on which to build. Jane Lyle and Hilary Powers provided a crucial reality check on the first edition of this book, and many suggestions for improvement. Since I've continued tinkering with the contents for nearly 10 years, any remaining issues are my fault, not theirs. Thanks also to Brian Doonan and Karen Loftstrom for copyediting the 3rd edition; blame any remaining errors on my refusal to stop tinkering with the text after their edits.

Last but not least, a vote of thanks to the Microsoft Word development team. Microsoft Word has quirks, bugs, and outright disastrous features, but on the whole, not significantly more than most other software I've used over the years. Moreover, since you folks aren't the ones who decide what problems to fix and when to fix them, it's time we stopped blaming you for these problems. A note to your managers, however: Isn't it time you folks stopped adding useless new features and breaking existing features that used to work just fine? Instead, please spend some time making Word more stable and fixing existing features. It's inexcusable that well-known bugs persist for years before being fixed.

Griping aside—a very long aside some days—Word is an indispensable tool, and one that lets me quickly and efficiently earn a very good living doing what I love. For that, my congratulations and my thanks.

A Word on Copyright

If you're reading this book and you didn't pay for it, please read on. I promise I'll be brief and not overly moralistic.

If a friend gave you the e-book and you printed a copy, or if you photocopied someone else's copy of the printed version, that's not okay. I earn part of my living selling it. (Two hungry kids, and all that—are we feeling guilty yet?) I've priced the book low enough that price shouldn't be a barrier. If you're working as an editor (who else would read this book?), you'll repay your investment after about 10 minutes of applying the tips. Plus, the cost is tax-deductible—make that 5 minutes of work.

If you're a teacher or a trainer, *fair use* does not give you the right to distribute copies of this book to your students. Instead, contact me to discuss academic pricing. Teachers get a free review copy, and students get a substantial discount. If you're living somewhere that wages are below what's necessary to afford the book, please contact me to see if we can negotiate a more affordable price. I'm willing to be reasonable.

Preface to the 3rd edition

The first edition of *Effective Onscreen Editing* appeared nearly 10 years ago, and the reception has been better than I expected. For the 3rd edition, I thought it would be interesting to look back on the previous editions and consider where we're going from here.

Why You Should Read This Book

Over the years, I've been consistently surprised by how reluctant editors are to invest the time required to improve their use of computer technologies in editing. That's mystifying because the whole point of this book is to teach you how to think about using software to improve your work life by making editing faster, easier, and more effective. Investing 5 minutes once to learn a new skill can save you more than 5 minutes per day every day for the rest of your career. Why wouldn't you invest that time?

My goal is to teach you the thought process involved in editing using a word processor. The goal is NOT to teach you Microsoft Word; Word is just one of many possible tools. I've provided Word-specific examples because just about every editor uses Word these days; it's what our clients demand. Moreover, my teaching experience suggests that it's necessary to make the editing strategies concrete, and (despite its many blemishes) Word lets you implement those editing strategies easily. Having reached a *modus vivendi* with Word, I can't imagine doing my work without it.

But here's the important thing: you can accomplish the same things with other word processors. You'll just have to invest the time to learn how they implement the features I've described for Word.

Before you ask: I'd love to expand this book to include other word processors, but the demand simply isn't there. Nor the time. It's hard enough keeping up with Microsoft.

To reinforce that message, I've split the book into two parts. The part you're reading now focuses on how to think about editing on a computer. In it, I'll describe strategies and overall approaches. Then I'll briefly describe the software basics to get you started. For the details, you'll need to consult the second part, which is available exclusively online (http://www.geoff-hart.com/books/eoe/eoe3/eoe3.html). In that part, freed from the constraints of the printed page, I'll illustrate how these editing tools work using annotated screenshots from Word. Time permitting, I'll add videos.

My rationale for this design is simple: You won't be using those illustrations unless you're sitting at the computer, ready to try out the instructions in Word, so why clutter the book with visuals that will quickly become outdated? Instead, display the instructions in a Web browser window beside your word processor and follow them while you work. I've provided separate Web pages for each version of Word. As time permits, I'll update the book by adding new Web pages to account for newer versions of Word without requiring you to buy a new version of the book.

Look ma, no Web! Since you won't always have Internet access, the book's Web page provides a downloadable version of the Web site that you can use off-line. Display the Web page cited at the start of each chapter to find the download link.

Word for Macintosh

For more than a decade, I've harshly criticized Microsoft for their Macintosh versions of Word. Sadly, MacWord remains a half-baked piece of work that would earn you an F in most undergraduate programming courses. The interface is clumsy and the implementation is consistently buggy—for Word 2011, it's still buggy and unreliable as I write this, more than 5 years after the original release. Despite having been a Mac evangelist for more than 20 years, my advice to onscreen editors is to avoid MacWord and use the Windows version: you'll be happier and more productive. It's easy and inexpensive to install Windows on your Mac using software such as Parallels, VMWare Fusion, or VirtualBox. See the book's software Web page (http://www.geoff-hart.com/books/eoe/eoe3/software.htm) for links to these and other products.

An additional problem is that learning Word for either Macintosh or Windows provides surprisingly little help in learning the other version: the interface differs egregiously, and many software features behave differently, in unpredictable ways. That's annoying for people like me who write "how to" books, but it's a complete disaster for corporate trainers, who must learn and then teach both versions of the software to their students. A company as big as Microsoft has the brainpower and the money to do much better.

As I wrote this, Word 2016 had just entered the market, with one design goal being to make the Mac and Windows versions more similar in their interfaces and behavior. The interface will be more similar, but the software is so buggy that I can't, in good conscience, recommend using it yet. Check the book's Web site periodically for updates on this situation.

Looking to the Future

The 3rd edition of *Effective Onscreen Editing* should remain viable for quite some time, since the thought processes involved in editing won't change much. Because the version-specific instructions for Word will change with each new release, I'll keep the book current by updating the Web pages for each chapter and adding new Web pages as new versions of Word emerge. I'll typically remain one version behind the most current version because my time is limited, new releases are buggy for months after their release, and new versions rarely add features that would motivate you to upgrade—or me to spend weeks documenting them.

Table of contents

(continued)

(continued)

Chapter 5 (concluded)

(continued)

(continued)

(continued)

(continued)

Chapter 18 (concluded)

Chapter 1. My Goal and Approach in This Book

Web: http://www.geoff-hart.com/books/eoe/eoe3/eoe3.html
Note: Word 2010 is for Windows; Word 2011 is for the Macintosh

In this book, I'll teach you how to apply your editing skills to perform onscreen editing (i.e., editing using a word processor). I'm not going to teach you how to edit; this book is *not* a course in editing or grammar. I've also assumed you already understand the basics of using the Windows or Macintosh operating system, so I won't explain their basic operations unless some feature provides support for editing in ways you might have missed. If you're not already proficient in using your computer, I recommend that you invest some time becoming proficient before you read this book.

There's little reason to learn onscreen editing if there's no benefit. In Chapter 2, I'll explain the benefits of editing on a computer. Although *I* no longer do much editing on paper, this doesn't mean that you must edit exclusively on the screen; some editors have good reasons to continue editing on paper, at least occasionally. Many of the techniques I'll teach in this book can also be used to improve the effectiveness of your on-paper editing—the trick is to learn how to use the computer for things that computers do better than humans (particularly the boring, repetitive stuff).

In each chapter, I discuss the key editing principles and how software can help you apply those principles more effectively. Though I've attempted to make these techniques applicable to any word processor, learning how they work is easier with concrete examples. For this reason, I've chosen Microsoft Word to demonstrate the principles. Word remains the word processor most often used by editors and provides powerful tools for onscreen editing; unlike other programs, such as WordPerfect, it's also available for the Macintosh. Because many editors, including me, work on a Macintosh, I've provided separate Web sites for the Mac and Windows versions of Word. Both are accessible from the address that I've listed at the start of each chapter.

Microsoft offers many useful free tutorials for Word via its support Web site. However, Microsoft is no longer the only or best option. Use your favorite Web search site for information on the tasks described in this book and its companion Web site. You'll find many helpful hints, including YouTube videos that may be more helpful than long lists of procedural steps.

In designing this edition of the book, I've included only the most important screenshots: there are far too many differences among versions of Word for me to document all possible interface variations. As I noted in the Preface, most of the Word-specific visual content is available via the book's Web page for each version of Word I've found time to cover. Watch the Web site for updates!

The methods I'll demonstrate using Word should be easy to implement in other software if you do a little research to learn how that software works. Where relevant, I've mentioned other useful software, such as using your Web browser to research issues of fact or style.

Don't be dismayed by the size of the book. If you only study chapters 4 (customizing your computer so it's not so uncomfortable) and 6 (using revision tracking), that's all you need to begin editing using a word processor. The rest of the book provides examples of additional techniques that will make you more productive as you gain confidence with your software. Don't begin using all these solutions immediately. The most productive approach is to practice one skill at a time until you master it, then use the time you save to solve a new problem. For example, if you repeatedly type the same comments, learn to use the automatic text features (Chapter 11).

Because editing is a human endeavor, I'll discuss author–editor relationships in Chapter 3, along with their consequences. That information forms the basis for effectively managing the editing process and your relationships with authors, including your initial negotiations with authors, setting rates, and the final follow-up once you've completed a job. Adapting these processes to meet your specific needs facilitates the implementation of onscreen editing.

The book's meat lies in the four sections that follow this introduction:

- **Mastering the tools:** A description of the software tools you'll use to apply your existing editing skills to onscreen editing.

- **Identifying and overcoming barriers:** Word processors are imperfect, and pose many small problems you must solve even after you master their basic features.

- **Coping with the human factor:** Editors and authors must work together to revise manuscripts. This section shows you how to lower or eliminate the barriers to success.

- **A four-step approach to implementing onscreen editing:** I conclude by describing how you can apply the tidy theory presented in this book to the messy real-world editing environment.

Chapter 2. Advantages of Onscreen Editing

Web: http://www.geoff-hart.com/books/eoe/eoe3/eoe3.html
Note: Word 2010 is for Windows; Word 2011 is for the Macintosh

Given that on-paper editing has worked perfectly well for centuries, why waste time "fixing what works" by moving editing onto the computer? Largely because on-paper editing doesn't work particularly well; like the dog that sings opera, it's amazing that it sings at all. Software greatly facilitates most traditional editorial tasks. Moreover, given that most manuscripts are now created on the computer, printing them out just so they can be edited is both inefficient and ecologically questionable. But the efficiency argument proves most persuasive to authors, editors, and managers who must produce superior manuscripts under tight deadlines and budgets. This increasingly includes everyone who earns a living working with words.

So if the main reason to adopt onscreen editing is efficiency, what efficiency advantages does it offer?

Minimize Errors Incorporating Edits

When someone must retype handwritten edits, they inevitably miss some. A rough, unscientific estimate based on personal experience suggests that even skilled secretaries miss or misinterpret up to 5% of handwritten corrections. Authors who aren't professional writers—the majority of some editors' clientele—are even less accurate. In addition, typists routinely introduce new errors into manuscripts when they misread an editor's poor handwriting (one of my particular sins) or mistype a correction.

Onscreen editing eliminates many of these problems: the edits are already in the file, and so long as we carefully review our work before sending it to the author, those edits should contain no typos. The automation provided by a word processor's revision tools also helps ensure that the person who incorporates the corrections into the final manuscript won't miss any edits.

Of course, we can still err by dealing incorrectly with a given edit; for example, I've seen authors skip a correction by accidentally clicking the Find Next button to find the next edit before approving or rejecting the current edit, accept edits that should be rejected by clicking the **Accept** button, or reject edits that should be accepted by clicking the **Reject** button.

Variants of these problems also occur with on-paper edits, so whether you edit on the screen or on paper, it's still necessary to perform quality control on the results.

Reduce Correction Time

With on-paper editing, the best-case scenario is that the person responsible for entering the corrections into the word processor file carefully reviews their own work to catch any corrections that they missed during the first pass and fix any errors they introduced while making those corrections. Unfortunately, busy workers often skip this step, since it can double the time required to incorporate all the corrections. Even if this extra step were not necessary, retyping handwritten corrections into the original word processor document increases turnaround time. In effect, the edits must be "written" twice (once on paper and again in the word processor) and checked at least once.

With onscreen editing, all corrections are already present in the manuscript, and this eliminates the time required to transfer them from paper to computer. Because this also eliminates transcription errors, there's no need to fix this category of error in a subsequent review stage. There's also a small but important benefit in terms of clarity: typed edits are easier to read and understand than handwritten ones, and less likely to be misinterpreted.

Because we generally type faster than we can write by hand, we can also provide longer and clearer comments in less time. It's also likely that we can type the edits (enter them into the manuscript) faster than the authors who would otherwise have to do this. (Dedicated typing pools staffed by experienced typists who do the corrections for authors are generally a thing of the past.)

Edit Faster and More Consistently

On-paper editing relies on slow, inefficient handwritten comments. Even for those rare but annoying editors who always get their edits right the first time, with no need for revision, it's frustrating and time-consuming to repeatedly write the same comment by hand, perhaps dozens of times even in a short manuscript. Moreover, even the best editors have difficulty finding every instance of a problematic word or phrase on paper; a problem that becomes apparent several hundred pages into an edit (e.g., a word that has been used incorrectly) requires us to re-read the entire manuscript seeking out all instances of that problem—a tedious, slow, and error-prone process. In onscreen editing, the word processor's search function can quickly find each of these instances.

Onscreen editing solves these problems in several ways. For example, as I noted earlier, most of us learn to type edits faster with the keyboard than we could write them with pen or pencil. This is particularly true for edits that involve extensive rewriting, which require considerable juggling of words and phrases before attaining a satisfactory result; on a computer, an entire chunk of problematic text can be copied and pasted in a few keystrokes, then revised quickly by inserting new words, deleting old ones, and shuffling around the rest of the words until we're satisfied. The results are also easier for authors to read, understand, and review, since there's no sticky correction fluid or pools of glistening red ink covering the errors made *en route* to finding a solution.

Word processors also let us automate repetitive, tedious work. For example, we can now insert a standard comment such as "this reference is missing from your bibliography" with a few keystrokes rather than manually typing the same comment dozens of times per manuscript. (My personal record is close to twenty repetitions of a single comment in a short manuscript.) Similarly, it's far faster to replace all instances of an incorrectly used term with the correct term in a single step, using a global search and replace operation, than it is to hunt down each occurrence of the term and make the change manually. If only some occurrences of the term are likely to be incorrect, you can't perform a global search and replace, but you can still use the search tool to quickly and easily find all occurrences of the problematic wording.

But Some Things Remain the Same

None of these advantages minimizes the editor's role in the editing process: providing human insight into communication problems and applying human experience to solve those problems. Onscreen editing is one of the surprisingly few areas in which the promise of the computer revolution (freeing humans to perform creative work) has actually been fulfilled. Once we understand how to edit on the screen, we can combine the advantages offered by computerization (potentially flawless execution of simple, repetitive tasks) with the unparalleled strengths of the human mind (performing complex semantic analyses and determining how to solve problems). Learning to edit on the screen can potentially make us better editors, free us from the drudgery of many traditional editorial tasks, and let us concentrate on the best way to clarify and communicate the author's message.

None of these benefits *force* us to work exclusively on the screen. For example, it's possible to use the search tools to find each occurrence of a word in the word processor file, then manually indicate the problems on a printed copy if that works better for you. The key is to use the computer for what it does well: *supporting* our work. Each of us will find different ways to do that, using the tools and techniques described in this book.

Chapter 3. Writing and Editing are *Human* Endeavors

Web: http://www.geoff-hart.com/books/eoe/eoe3/eoe3.html
Note: Word 2010 is for Windows; Word 2011 is for the Macintosh

If you believed that editing involves nothing more profound than correcting typographical errors and changing words or phrases to suit your personal taste or the dictates of someone's style guide, you wouldn't be reading this book. (Also, your editorial career would be short and inglorious.) In reality, editing is about helping our authors to communicate clearly with their audience in a manner that makes the author (and their employer, if they're publishing on behalf of someone else) look good and that satisfies the audience that they've understood the author.

We've succeeded if the audience understands the intended message with as little mental effort as possible; important messages may be challenging, but their *presentation* must never be. To achieve this goal, we must also communicate effectively with authors, because writing is a *human* endeavor, and most authors are both proud of their accomplishment and insecure about its quality. When we take on the editor's role, our work is easily seen as criticism, since our role is to find errors, and each error demonstrates the author's fallibility. Sometimes we must alter their writing dramatically to communicate successfully with readers. How can such an activity *not* damage the author's self-confidence, bruise their pride, and possibly even anger them?

The answer is for us to change editing from an adversarial activity, in which we become the author's nemesis and unflagging critic, into a partnership in which the author sees us as their ally in the struggle to communicate. Editors and authors working together achieve synergies that neither could achieve alone. Even if we're unable to write an original word, we're well equipped to detect problems that authors can't detect because they lack the necessary distance from their manuscript; as experts in the concepts they want to communicate, authors have difficulty understanding what it's like not to share that expertise. As editors, we provide that essential distance. We also learn to detect and correct flawed writing, but must learn to put those skills to work in the service of our authors. The author–editor relationship is clearly a human relationship, and editing is clearly a human interaction. To become truly effective editors, we must engage in mutually respectful dialogues with our authors.

In this book, I define *onscreen* editing as any editing done using a word processor. It doesn't matter whether the edited text will eventually be printed or will remain forever on the computer screen. But successful onscreen editing requires more than altering text in a word processor. Rather, the approach must preserve or enhance the author–editor dialogue by using technology to facilitate communication, not as an end in itself. In using this technology, we must go beyond facilitating editorial tasks; we must also make it easier for authors to respond to our suggestions.

As you begin to develop a workflow for onscreen editing and refine your editing style, remember that you're part of a larger process. Find ways to account for the needs of those who are upstream from you (authors and peer reviewers) and those who are downstream from you (colleagues who will review your edits, desktop publishers, readers). Chapters 17 and 18 will help you to keep their needs in mind.

An evolving situation: The available options and underlying technologies are changing rapidly. Thus, some specific details in this chapter will be outdated or even obsolete by the time you read this. As in the rest of this book, I'll focus on general principles that will work in all contexts. You'll undoubtedly need to modify the details to account for new technological options. I'll provide updates on the book's Web site as time and opportunity permit.

Encouraging Dialogue

Word processors don't inherently encourage or discourage dialogue. However, the software provides relatively weak support for simultaneous revision of manuscripts by several people or even just by an author–editor pair. When I was the in-house editor at two large research institutes, I could sit in front of an author's computer and discuss my edits until we reached consensus on a solution. Nowadays, I'm a freelancer and work with authors in other countries and other time zones, which makes real-time interaction difficult. This can turn what should be an engaging dialogue into an exchange of messages, often separated by considerable time—the modern equivalent of collaborating on a manuscript using handwritten letters sent by surface mail. Although this approach still *permits* the give and take that is part of any dialogue, it doesn't *encourage* this dialogue and can't replace true discussion; in a discussion, the author and editor can immediately respond to each other's concerns and reach acceptable compromises.

In the time since I published the second edition of this book, the situation has improved for authors and editors who work at different locations and have no option to meet in person. Both Microsoft Office and Google Docs now offer Internet-based collaboration environments that let multiple people work separately or simultaneously on the same document.

Real-time, long-distance collaborations

A note before I begin: it would be horribly inefficient to use online collaboration tools for types of editing that don't require discussion, such as applying a publisher's paragraph formats and capitalization preferences, implementing style guidelines such as lists of words to be italicized, and other basic copyediting changes such as correcting the verb accord. These may require the author's *review*, but not any actual discussion.

The collaboration tools that I'll discuss in this section are most efficient for tasks such as substantive and developmental editing, in which the changes require discussion, brainstorming, comparison of alternatives, and consensus. In that context, you need a solution that lets you work on a manuscript file simultaneously with an author, using the same version of the file, while discussing what you propose to do and then doing it so that you and the author can immediately see the results. This might be the best way, for example, to develop the outline for a complex document before the author starts writing (i.e., developmental editing) or to discuss alternative ways to explain a complex concept (i.e., substantive editing). To collaborate in this way, you'll need to accomplish the following:

- Appoint someone to guide and focus the conversation.
- Display the document so both the author and the editor can see it.
- Discuss and implement changes while you view the document.
- Display the results of these changes.
- Repeat these steps, as necessary, until all substantive issues have been resolved.

In the rest of this section, I'll discuss how you can accomplish each of these tasks. I'll also assume that you're establishing the system on your own, possibly with some assistance from a suitably geeky friend. If you're working for or with a corporation that has its own dedicated system, such as Microsoft SharePoint, you'll need to discuss how to use that system with your client or their technical staff.

Guiding the discussion

As is the case in any meeting, someone should guide and facilitate (*chair*) the discussion. The chair will be responsible for ensuring that participants take turns rather than talking over each other, for keeping the review process moving forward, and (in many cases) for incorporating changes into the manuscript that's under review. This coordination role is just as important as it would be during in-person meetings, with the additional difficulty that online meetings can remove most of the social cues that guide conversations in an in-person meeting. Even when the meeting includes a video component so that participants can see each other, the interaction tends to be less fluid than in an in-person interaction due to limitations of the technology.

The chair or someone they designate starts the process by uploading the document to a central repository such as cloud storage (e.g., DropBox) or a Web site. They then send all participants an invitation to participate that includes a link to the document (e.g., its Web address) and instructions on how to become part of the communication channel or channels that everyone will use to discuss the document. To avoid software incompatibilities, all participants should use the same Web browser (e.g., Firefox), the same discussion software (e.g., Google Hangouts), and the same versions of each program. This will reduce the risk that participants will be distracted from the task at hand (reviewing the manuscript) by disagreements about what they see on the screen or will be prevented from participating fully in the discussion by software incompatibilities. However, in many cases these problems will be sufficiently minor to allow everyone at least some flexibility in software choices.

Controlling access to a document: It's best to avoid letting multiple individuals modify a document simultaneously. Anyone who wants to modify the document should obtain the chair's permission to proceed. This lets everyone participate effectively, without the chaos of everyone heading in a different direction or creating conflicting edits of the same text. I'll discuss this and related issues in more detail throughout this section.

Displaying the manuscript

During the review, the manuscript will be displayed in a Web browser window (e.g., Google Docs) or in a word processor window (e.g., the most recent versions of Microsoft Word, including Word 365). If you're discussing the manuscript by exchanging text messages addressed to all meeting participants, the software that supports this typed discussion will be open in a second window beside the manuscript window. This lets participants simultaneously see the document and monitor the discussion. Each time a change is implemented, the implementer then updates the file and asks everyone to refresh their browser or word processor window (if the software does not do this automatically) so they can see the results of the revision.

For a crude but effective approach that will be usable in just about any situation, and that does not require any special software, the easiest solution is to simply display the manuscript as a Web page during the discussion and revision. For example, it takes about 10 minutes to set up a blog site such as WordPress.com to display all or part of a manuscript that has not yet been heavily formatted. For more complex manuscripts that require you to rigorously maintain the format, you can export the file from your word processor in HTML or XHTML format (hereafter, *Web format*) and save the resulting file online. If you don't already have a Web site established for this purpose, a cloud service such as DropBox provides an easy place to store the document.

All modern word processors let you save (export) a file in Web format. This process translates formatting information such as paragraph styles (e.g., headings) and character styles (e.g., boldfaced words) into their Web page equivalents. In many cases, the translation process is sufficiently thorough that you can reopen the Web page in your word processor, and then resave the file in that word processor's native format to restore the original document with little or no loss of formatting. For complex documents, you'll want to test this to be sure it works well, and develop workarounds for any problems.

Once everyone receives a link to the Web file, they can view it during the discussion, but if they're viewing it in their Web browser, they may not be able to change the file. Allowing only one person to change the file solves several problems. First, it eliminates a common problem if you are working with a file saved in Word's .docx format: if two or more people open the same file in software that doesn't support simultaneous access (such as DropBox), the software creates a new copy of the file for each person. As a result, everyone will be looking at different versions of the file.

Second, allowing only one person to modify the file maintains all the edits in a single final file. This approach requires discussion of changes and leaves the chair free to implement them. The chair then re-saves the edited file or exports it again in Web format, everyone refreshes the display (i.e., reloads the Web page), and then the chair confirms that the result is acceptable (or responds to additional requests for changes), and the discussion continues.

A more efficient way to implement this approach would use software such as Adobe's Contribute or Dreamweaver to update the Web-format document, since both programs maintain the file in Web format and this eliminates the need to repeatedly re-save or re-export the edited document. In addition, such software lets meeting participants "check out" the document; only the person who has checked out the document can modify it. When they have finished their modification, they "check in" the document again, thereby making it available once more for editing by the next person who receives permission to check out the document. Depending on the software and how it's configured, it may be necessary to re-upload or re-display the file after it has been checked in.

Confirming consensus: When everyone appears to have reached consensus, the chair should ensure that everyone has achieved the same understanding. That's not different from in-person meetings, but it's such an important point that it's worth repeating.

Such an approach will remain valid for the foreseeable future because of its simplicity: the tools you use will undoubtedly change, but the overall procedure won't. The obvious disadvantage of this approach arises from its simplicity: it requires some degree of manual intervention at each step, and thus is less efficient than dedicated approaches that do the work for you. It also places control of the manuscript in the hands of one person, so even though the other participants can propose changes, only that one person can implement the changes. The delays that result from the lack of automation also cause a certain punctuated rhythm to the editing process, and the delays can be annoying. Finally, the approach may prevent the use of some features of your word processor that aren't supported in a Web browser, such as revision tracking and the ability to display comment balloons. Chapter 12 presents several suggestions on how to cope when revision tracking isn't available.

The most efficient approach is to display the manuscript in a word processor's document window, as if everyone were sitting around the same computer, sharing the same display, and taking turns using the same keyboard to make changes. This is the model adopted by the most recent versions of Microsoft Word and Google Docs. In contrast with the homemade approach that I described first, this approach is seamless: it's little different from working in a word processor, even though the file is being viewed and possibly edited simultaneously by the author, the editor, and other participants in the writing and revision process. This approach also provides revision tracking and commenting features that are integrated with the document, though the features aren't always sophisticated.

Note that in this description, I have implicitly assumed that changes will be made during the meeting and discussed before and after they have been made. It's also possible for participants to edit the manuscript independently or sequentially, and then discuss only the changes during the meeting. Provided that the chair sets guidelines for how to revise another person's changes (e.g., to insert a comment that suggests rejection of a change rather than just rejecting the change without consultation), this approach can also work well.

To see examples of how these processes work, visit the Web page for this chapter.

Efficient meetings: As in any meeting, preparation is the key. All participants should review the manuscript before the meeting and summarize their thoughts in writing. For any comments that will require much typing, the typing should be done before the meeting so as to avoid wasting the other participants' time. The results can then be copied and pasted into a chat window or the document.

Discussing, implementing, and displaying changes

If several people are working on a file simultaneously, there's a significant risk of overlapping and contradictory edits if they are using software that doesn't lock files at a sentence or paragraph level to prevent simultaneous changes or software that doesn't provide real-time screen updates. Since the whole point of collaborating is to discuss the changes, someone should guide the discussion. As I noted earlier, it's wise to appoint a chair for the meeting and agree on a revision protocol that defines who has permission to make changes at any given point. Taking turns works best, since that focuses the attention of all participants on a single change. In the context of this book, the editor is most often the person who proposed the changes that require discussion, and will generally have the most experience (thus, competence) with the collaboration tools. Thus, it's logical for the editor to serve as the chair. However, an author who is skilled at using the tools could also lead the discussion and implement the changes. It is, after all, their manuscript.

In terms of how to discuss the changes, there are three broad categories of options: onscreen text, voice (perhaps supplemented by video), and a hybrid approach that combines the two. In each case, the biggest problem you'll face is the same one that arises at in-person meetings: multiple participants may try to communicate simultaneously, creating babble. The problem is worse in an online collaboration because some or all participants may lack the visual and other social cues that help groups of people converse in person. (This is less serious in chat-based solutions because it's easier to *read* what people are saying than it is to pick one voice out of a crowd.) The meeting's chair should use the aforementioned revision protocol to guide the discussion in such a way that everyone has a chance to comment, uninterrupted by others. For groups that aren't accustomed to working together in this way, a "don't speak until it's your turn" rule may be appropriate, with the chair dictating the order of participation. This rule is not absolute, and can be relaxed once participants learn to participate effectively by "sharing the microphone".

Methods based on onscreen text use some form of chat (instant messaging) software. This may be integrated with the editing software you're using, or it may run separately in a second program window that sits beside the manuscript window. The choice between these methods depends largely on the editing software you've chosen and whether you're working in a corporate environment that requires the use of a specific tool. If you have the option of choosing your own chat tool, this offers the advantage of providing a wide range of options, many of which are free. You can evaluate them all until you find a tool that works well for you and the author. (See the software list on the book's Web site for some suggestions.) Built-in tools often have significant limitations compared with more mature third-party tools, but compensate by offering integration with the revision software (i.e., you only have one program to manage).

Voice discussions potentially strengthen the relationships among participants because the interaction feels less technological and more human. Voice also provides many cues and feedbacks that are unavailable in chat, particularly if you have access to some form of videoconferencing that lets participants see each other's face. This approach used to require expensive corporate teleconferencing systems (which you may still find yourself using occasionally), but most standard computers and even smartphones now offer versions of this technology (e.g., Apple's Facetime, the Skype software). There are unfortunate distractions inherent in a video-based approach that make it less than ideal. For example, participants who are looking at the screen while talking appear to be avoiding the eyes of listeners, whereas looking into the camera (usually mounted on the top of the monitor or on the desk below the monitor) means that you cannot simultaneously read or modify the document. Nonetheless, the technology works well once you get used to these quirks.

Chat offers several significant advantages over a voice plus video discussion:

- You can copy and paste text from the chat window. Thus, if a suggested revision is particularly good, the chair can simply copy the text into the document. If participants have written up text (e.g., suggested revisions) ahead of time, they can paste that information into the chat window at an appropriate moment, thereby eliminating the inefficiency that results from typing long texts and making everyone else wait for you to finish.

- Complex sentences or concepts are easier to examine and understand in writing. In a spoken conversation, it would be necessary to break them into smaller, more digestible chunks, which is slow.

- Chat software allows *side channels* that let participants brainstorm or request clarification privately without disrupting the primary discussion.

- Most chat software lets you save the contents of the chat window to preserve a record of the conversation. This is very useful if it becomes necessary to review the rationale for a decision days or weeks later. The record will refresh your memory of a participant's priorities or concerns. In some contexts, this record can be essential for legal reasons.

- Participants who are shy or reluctant to participate in person may take advantage of the partial anonymity provided by not having to look their colleagues in the eyes and may participate more.

- In our increasingly international and multilingual work environment, chat improves participation by those who have difficulty managing the spoken language used during the meeting.

- Chat may be the only option for deaf or hearing-impaired participants.

However, chat also has some significant drawbacks:

- With participants who don't type rapidly or accurately, and participants who have not typed up their comments in advance, the discussion can take a long time.
- Chat sacrifices the social cues you can obtain from a participant's voice or face and the human contact that voice and video provide.
- As anyone who's been misunderstood in e-mail or while texting on their smartphone knows, the lack of these cues increases the frequency of misunderstandings, particularly in an adversarial situation.

Voice has several advantages over chat:

- The interaction feels more natural, and therefore reinforces collaboration and a sense of partnership.
- In high-context cultures such as Asia, Africa, and many Spanish countries, the connection established by voice conversation can be an important part of the author–editor relationship.
- Discussions move faster because they are not limited by typing speed, particularly when a skilled chair enforces the revision protocol to guide the conversation.

Voice also has several disadvantages:

- Complex concepts can be hard to hold in one's head. Written communication provides more time to read, understand (or look things up in a dictionary or online), and respond appropriately to a statement.
- There's no text to copy and paste, so someone (ideally a fast and accurate typist) must be responsible for recording the consensus and implementing the changes.
- Unless you record the conversation, there is no permanent record of what was discussed.
- Even if the software you're using can record the conversation for subsequent review, recordings can't be skimmed or searched as efficiently as text.
- In a multinational, multilinguistic, or multicultural context, participation may be difficult for those with weak skills in the spoken language. Misunderstandings are likely, and there's a significant risk that some participants will fall behind in the discussion and become completely lost. The chair must remind speakers to slow their speech, enunciate more clearly than usual, and repeat or summarize key points.
- Dealing with these drawbacks becomes easier with practice, but particularly in the early stages of a collaboration, care and concern for the needs of one's colleagues are important.

To compensate for the limitations of both text and voice, a hybrid approach is typically most effective. Using a voice channel or a voice plus video channel lets you take advantage of all the benefits of this familiar form of human communication, such as picking up on social cues (tone of voice, body language), and this makes it easier to strengthen the collaboration. Simultaneously, someone who has been appointed to keep the minutes can type them directly into a chat window for everyone to see, thereby creating a record of the discussion and providing text that can be copied and pasted into the manuscript. For example, the Zoom Web-based conferencing system can bring together participants who only have a phone or computer microphone and participants who have computers with or without a camera, so they can see and hear each other if they have the appropriate hardware. The software associates each participant's name with their face or a cartoon avatar if they don't have a camera. The software provides screen-sharing so that all participants can see what's on your screen, and access control so only one person at a time can change the document that's being discussed. One cool feature is that the software automatically moves the image of whoever is currently speaking to the center of the screen; thus, if you're participating using a computer, you can tell who's speaking even if you don't recognize their voice.

Software options

Collaborative editing is increasingly being integrated with word processors and other authoring software. Unfortunately, the conceptual model that guided word processor design was derived from solitary writing, not group collaboration, so collaborative editing tools remain somewhat primitive and many feel like they've been duck-taped to the software. However, the integration of collaboration features is becoming more effective as the products evolve. In addition to Microsoft Word and Google Docs, there's a growing number of products that facilitate collaboration. To avoid cluttering the book with information that will become rapidly obsolete, I've moved this information onto the book's Web page. Please feel free to contribute your own suggestions.

If you don't have access to such online collaboration tools, or find that they are too clumsy to be efficient, then you'll have to rely on some of the communication tools that I've discussed in this chapter and later in the book. The lack of explicit support for give and take makes your work more difficult, because discussions reinforce the feeling of partnership and help authors and editors to see each other as allies rather than adversaries. For this reason, try to develop an approach in which you encourage authors to discuss any proposed changes they don't understand or with which they disagree. In this manner, you can explain your concerns (i.e., why you originally proposed a change), emphasize that other readers are likely to encounter the same problem, and propose one or more solutions; in turn, the author can explain what they were trying to say, and you can adapt your suggestions to help them accomplish that goal.

This emphasis on collaboration supported by software is fine in theory, but authors and editors are human, and vulnerable to all the flaws that afflict human communication. We all have annoyances, prejudices, fears, and a measure of unfamiliarity or discomfort with the unique aspects of each author–editor relationship. Ignoring these problems ensures that we'll fail as editors. An author may never learn to like us, or we may dislike an author's stylistic and other choices, and this friction will inevitably raise the level of tension. This tension makes communication more difficult, but should never prevent communication.

We must always remember our role: first and foremost, to help authors communicate with their audience. We do so by helping authors make effective choices, but in the end, the author has the final say. (Only a few workplaces give editors the authority to overrule authors, and even then, we must use this power judiciously.) Our editing must be sensitive to the author's feelings, must tactfully point out and explain problems, and must suggest solutions that let the author feel their voice is appreciated and preserved. This approach helps authors to recognize the value of editing, and encourages them to work with us in a friendly, or at least professional, way. Chapter 7 discusses how to craft effective comments and questions, and this advice also works well for real-time discussion.

For a comprehensive discussion of this form of cooperative review, including a much broader discussion of project management tools and human management issues, read *Managing Virtual Teams: Getting the Most from Wikis, Blogs, and Other Collaborative Tools* by Brenda Huettner, Kit Brown, and Char James-Tanny. They wrote and reviewed their book collaboratively, over the Web, so they know what they're talking about.

A Standard Process

The overall onscreen editing process is similar to the on-paper editing process, but with a few quirks related to the computer medium. In this section, I've summarized a process used by many editors that has worked well for me for nearly 30 years, and that should work equally well for you after modification to suit your personal tastes and unique circumstances. Most steps in this process should be familiar to experienced editors, but if you've been skipping a step, I recommend that you reconsider that choice. Each step solves an important problem, and skipping any step may someday cause you considerable grief. The goal of the process is to ensure that you understand what is required of you and how that differs from the author's responsibility, that the author shares that understanding, and that you'll be paid fairly for the work you do.

Determining your pay rate

If you're working for the same employer as your authors, you probably won't be charging them for your time. Thus, most of this section on setting fair pay rates won't be relevant. However, some workplaces treat editing as a cost center and charge editing expenses to the author's budget. Since the accounting methods used to determine this chargeback vary widely, talk to the appropriate manager at your workplace to learn the details. You may not be able to change this system, but you may gain some insights into pricing that will inform your relationship with that manager.

Editing should bring us pleasure and intellectual satisfaction, but it must also earn us a living and should never be our sole source of joy and satisfaction. Each of our lives offers a strictly limited number of hours, and that number decreases steadily, day by day. The rate we charge for our work must compensate us adequately for spending an hour of our time on someone else's priorities rather than doing something we'd rather be doing: spending time with a loved one, reading a good book, or traveling to distant lands. As Henry David Thoreau observed, "The cost of a thing is the amount of what I will call life which is required to be exchanged for it, immediately or in the long run."

On this basis, I set a standard rate for my time that's unaffected by the nature of the work: whether an author wants me to check the page numbers in a layout or rack my brain rewriting a document from scratch, an hour of my life will cost them the same amount. Other editors set different rates for proofreading, copyediting, and substantive editing. Except in cases where you have no bargaining power to negotiate rates, I don't recommend their approach.

There are other exceptions. The most important is when we really need the work, or must compete with editors who are willing to work for less money. Then, we must choose a rate we can justify to the client; if we fail, they'll take their work elsewhere, particularly if they don't understand the value of our work and award contracts based solely on price. The only good solution to this predicament involves learning what clients are willing to pay in our part of the world or in our field and learning about the competition we face (i.e., what rates we'll be competing against). Organizations such as the Society for Technical Communication and local groups of editors such as the Editorial Freelancers Association in the U.S., the Editors' Association of Canada, and the Society for Editors and Proofreaders in the U.K. are good places to learn this information.

If you're willing and able to do *pro bono* work, then you can award some clients a lower rate than you'd ordinarily accept. For example, when I began working with many authors in China, Chinese budgets were far below those in North America, particularly for graduate students. Because I wanted to work with these authors, I accepted less money for my work in exchange for the pleasure of establishing an ongoing relationship with them. Similarly, you may want to offer lower rates for work that you particularly enjoy and could never obtain if you charged your standard rate; literary editing is a good example, as this work generally pays far less than technical editing, but offers other compensations, such as the satisfaction of helping authors tell a memorable story.

How do you set a rate? The number of questions I've received on this issue suggest the calculation is sufficiently unobvious that it requires some discussion. The most common approach involves the following steps (illustrated with some basic numbers to make the math easy):

1. Define the gross amount you want or need to earn per year. Include the cost of your taxes, medical and other insurance, vacation pay, and a pension fund. (These expenses can amount to 30 to 50% of your base salary.) Example: $48 000
2. Decide how many weeks you want to work per year. Example: 48 weeks
3. Divide your salary by this time to estimate the income you must generate each week. Example: $48 000/48 weeks = $1000/week
4. Decide how many hours you want to work per week. Example: 20 hours. (Unrealistic, but let's have fun with this!)
5. Divide your weekly wage by this time to estimate your required hourly income. Example: $1000/20 hours = $50/hour

The result becomes the basic, non-negotiable hourly rate you require to earn your desired income. You can charge less for some clients if you can charge other clients more or work more hours to make up the difference.

To this rate, add enough to cover any expenses you'll incur over the course of a year: travel, postage, telephone calls, library research, money to pay for your next computer or software upgrade—whatever! If you have ongoing expenses such as office rent or Internet fees, divide those expenses by the number of hours you expect to work annually and add that to your hourly cost.

The calculation is simple in principle, but more complex in reality. For example, the numbers I chose were simplistic to facilitate the calculations. The notion of 20 hours of work per week assumes you can realistically generate this much paid work, and ignores the paperwork and other activities (such as marketing your services) that don't directly earn any money. Moreover, the resulting rate may be well above what local clients are willing or able to pay. The important thing about this calculation process is not that the numbers are precise, but rather that it gives you an objective starting point for estimating your rate. You'll still have to subject that rate to a reality check to determine whether it's feasible.

Now let's apply a similar process to the task of bidding on a job. If we're fortunate, our client trusts us enough to simply pay an hourly rate on the assumption we won't abuse this privilege. I work with many of my clients on this basis, but some prefer a fixed-price bid both so they can budget for my services and so they can cap the amount they'll have to pay. To provide a fixed estimate that will earn the desired hourly rate, we must learn to estimate how long jobs will take and thus, how much to charge for the work. This means we must be able to estimate both our productivity and the amount of work we'll be required to do. Once you know (for example) how many words you can edit per hour, and the number of words in the job, it's easy to calculate the time required and thus, the cost of the job.

For example, let's assume that we can charge the $50/hour we just calculated, can edit 1000 words per hour (including all time spent in hand-holding and record-keeping), and have been offered a 10 000-word job. The calculation becomes the following:
- 10 000 words divided by 1000 words/hour = 10 hours
- 10 hours @ $50/hour = $500

The most difficult part of this calculation is determining our productivity. Although many rules of thumb exist, these rules are too general to be useful because they cover a wide range of editors and a wide range of projects. As a result, these numbers are at best misleading because they reflect neither our personal productivity nor how that productivity changes for the different types of work that we do. The only way to usefully estimate our productivity is to track that productivity for long enough to obtain a good feel for our ability to handle a range of jobs. For example, I've been tracking my productivities (total number of words in a document, total number of hours required to edit the document, and thus, my rate in words per hour) for years, for a wide variety of clients and types of work. As a result, I have a good idea of the range of productivities I've been able to achieve for work ranging from near-total rewrites to quick and easy copyedits. This lets me bid on a range of projects with a reasonable probability of earning my desired hourly rate. There's *no* substitute for this kind of self-knowledge.

If you're just getting started, and have no productivity data on which to estimate editing times, ignore the rules of thumb related to pages per hour that you'll often hear discussed. Instead, ask to see a copy of what you must edit before you commit to a price. (This is wise even if you do have decades of productivity statistics. Even good authors have occasional bad days!) Skim through the manuscript sufficiently thoroughly that you can identify both the good and the bad parts, then edit a few pages of the worst parts to estimate how long this work will take. From this information, you can calculate your worst-case productivity and predict with some confidence that the rest of the manuscript should be easier.

Applying the worst-case estimates increases the likelihood that you'll earn your desired hourly rate even if the rest of the manuscript proves unexpectedly difficult. Unless you're intimately familiar with a particular client's style, and can thus predict the difficulty, it's best to expect the worst and charge accordingly.

Simple tracking: I track my productivity simply, using Microsoft Excel. When I start and stop work, I jot down the times and use that information to calculate how long I've worked. If you need something more formal, there are many programs available to automate the process. Check the list of utility programs on the book's Web page for a list of time-tracking programs.

Although we can offer discounts for work that ends up being easier than expected, I don't recommend this. If the client wants to pay us a fair rate for the job, they should agree to pay based on how long the work actually takes (i.e., based on an hourly rate). If they want a fixed price, and are thus trying to place the entire risk of a cost overrun upon us, they shouldn't expect a discount. In the long run, even with careful estimating, we'll inevitably encounter some manuscripts that take longer than expected, and earning a slight bonus for jobs that are easier than expected compensates us for the unexpectedly difficult jobs.

One useful compromise I've adopted for first-time clients is a hybrid approach: I offer to work on an hourly basis, but with a maximum price established based on my worst-case productivity for a particular type of edit. If I can beat that worst-case price, I pass along the savings to the client and thereby encourage them to work with me on an hourly basis in the future. Insisting on a fixed price would earn me more money in the long run, but my clients prefer this flexibility and it satisfies my sense of fairness.

Initial negotiations

Getting started: Although I provide some good tips on how to manage your relationships with authors, this is not a book on how to run a business as an editor. *Getting Started as a Freelance Copyeditor*, by Katharine O'Moore-Klopf, may be just what you need. Ruth Thaler-Carter has also entered the fray with her book *Freelancing 101: Launching Your Editorial Business*.

When we first begin working with an author, we must start with a clear understanding of what the author expects. Based on this requirement, we can describe the work we propose to perform to meet those expectations. Never rely on nominally standard terms such as *copyediting*, since it's only a slight exaggeration to state that every client has a different definition of what such editing involves; naïve authors often specify something as uninformative as *a light edit*, whereas seasoned pros may use an idiosyncratic definition qualified by dozens of specifications and clauses. A clear and detailed description of our work is far more effective. Consider, for example, the details of and differences between the following descriptions:

- *Substantive editing* ensure that the manuscript's content and structure are logical, clear, and effective. In addition to rewriting to improve clarity, this editing ensures that the organization and flow of the text effectively communicate the intended message, and that the text and any graphics work effectively together. This also ensures that the manuscript contains no internal contradictions and is consistent with the body of knowledge in a field. Although this editing may require heavy revision, the editor will provide no entirely new material; omissions will be identified and left to the author to resolve.
- *Copyediting* focuses on issues related to grammar, usage, spelling, punctuation, and any other aspects defined in a specified style guide. It also

involves checking the *internal* consistency of these aspects and of facts *within* the manuscript, but does not include external confirmation of facts, quotations, or references.

Whether or not you agree with these specific definitions, the important point is the level of detail they provide. Each definition clearly explains exactly what you will and will not do rather than leaving it to the author's imagination.

Initial negotiations with an author should define these and other details, such as the style guide the author expects us to use and what kinds of things (e.g., formatting) we can correct without querying the author. In addition, because we'll be working on a computer, we must specify what word processor we'll use and acceptable file formats. Ideally, we'll use the same word processor as the author, thereby eliminating potential incompatibilities, but if not, we should propose a method for identifying and solving any problems. Graphics formats are particularly problematic, since graphics embedded in a word processor file occasionally display incorrectly; requesting graphics in PDF format can avoid these problems. If we don't receive graphics in the native format of the program used to create them, describing any changes can take a long time. It's often more effective if the author copies the text from their figures into a word processor document that we can then edit using revision tracking.

These issues provide examples of the kinds of negotiation that may be necessary: Can we edit graphics directly in the software used to create them, or does the author want to make corrections based on written feedback? Can we review graphics in Adobe's PDF (Acrobat) format? PDF eliminates most display problems, but PDF files are difficult to edit if more than basic corrections are required; they let us add annotations and comments, but prevent really thorough substantive editing. Chapter 13 provides detailed advice on editing graphics. Chapter 16 provides some suggestions for editing PDF files.

Initial negotiations should also address a key brass-tacks issue: how you'll communicate with and exchange your work with the author. I'll discuss this in more detail towards the end of this chapter.

Contracts are *not* optional

Occasionally, it's safe to work without a contract, such as when you're working for a long-term client who understands how you work, who pays promptly and with no fuss, and whose financial stability (which we should verify periodically) is excellent. For example, I've been working with a former employer for years, and have full confidence that I understand their needs and that they'll pay me on time and in full. Those rare times when there's been a misunderstanding, we've worked together to resolve the problem with minor fuss and bother and no hard feelings on either side. As a result, I've never required this client to sign a binding contract. What I have done instead is clearly specify in writing or e-mail any unusual details that don't fall under our existing understanding of the nature of my work.

This is about the only situation in which you should consider working without a contract, and the archives of the Copyediting-L and Techwhirl discussion groups are full of tales of woe that could have been eliminated by means of a simple contract.

At a minimum, a contract represents a straightforward description of the entire nature of the work we will do and represents the results of our effort make at least some effort to discuss that work. The contract thus summarizes and formalizes the results of the preliminary negotiations before the start of a job, and explicitly states the basis for calculating the cost and for payment of the invoice. If human communication were always clear and precise, and free of subjective considerations and assumptions, such a statement might never be necessary. But given the fallibility of such communication, a written statement of intent is essential to minimize the risk of misunderstandings. The goal of creating a contract is to eliminate misunderstandings so you can work productively together, not to club a recalcitrant author into submission through deft blows with a lawyer. The fact that swarms of lawyers earn a lucrative living resolving contract disputes should be a clue that we cannot entirely eliminate this risk, but that doesn't mean we shouldn't try.

Do you need a lawyer? For large and expensive jobs, or for any situation that seems likely to become adversarial, you're wise to invest in a lawyer's services to draft a formal contract. If you do mainly smaller jobs, the expense may far outweigh the income you can expect to earn. In that case, asking a lawyer to draft a standard contract you can use for most of your work is a reasonable compromise.

That being said, when worse comes to worst, a contract becomes our only tool for ensuring that a difficult client treats us with respect and pays for our work. It also ensures that if the scope of the work changes, we can insist on compensation for any new work, and can specify our understanding of the expanded scope in an amendment to the contract. Most clients are neither evil nor incompetent, but some are, and they're the ones we need protection against. Many more clients are overworked, exhausted, stressed, or unfamiliar with the nature of our work. A contract educates them and thereby protects us against misunderstandings and ensures that we can meet their needs—something we can't do unless we first understand those needs.

Never begin work on a project, no matter how lucrative or how tight the deadline, until you have at least a firm statement of intent signed in writing. Verbal discussions can constitute proof of an intended contract, but proving what someone said isn't easy. E-mail messages also constitute proof, but because e-mail messages are relatively easy to forge, the jurisprudence in this area is likely to be evolving. A printed, signed, and witnessed contract is still your best bet for any large or expensive job. Even if you haven't hired a lawyer to review the contract (a wise idea for large, expensive, or potentially risky or contentious work), a written and signed statement counts as a legally binding contract in most jurisdictions. Unfortunately, legal English is not the English spoken by editors, and what seems to us to be clear wording may conflict with the legal definitions of certain terms or may violate local regulations designed to protect both parties. In a perfect world, we wouldn't need lawyers to deal with such issues. Sadly, it's not a perfect world.

In an emergency (e.g., you've worked without a contract and the author refuses to pay you), you have one final protection: copyright law. Under copyright law, any rewriting of the text that you have done for an author is copyrighted in your name until you receive payment for that work and transfer the copyright for your work to the author. (The original, unedited text that surrounds your edits remains copyrighted in the author's name.) If an author refuses to pay, you have a legal right to insist that they not use your writing. In some cases, sending a copy of the edited manuscript to the author's publisher with a note that you have not been paid and that use of any of your edits represents a violation of your copyright will encourage an author to pay; publishers fear the costs of a lawsuit resulting from their publication of *your* work without your permission.

If an author is publishing their own work, as is often the case with corporate clients, a good lawyer can obtain a court judgment that forces the client to withdraw any copies of your work from circulation, often at great expense to the publisher, and may even be able to obtain punitive damages from a sympathetic court. The downside of such a strategy is that it can earn you an undesirable reputation among potential clients, it can be expensive to pursue such legal action, and the outcome is not guaranteed. But if all else fails, don't neglect this strategy.

Initial and subsequent edits

Having agreed upon the nature of the job, we can move on to our initial editing. In on-paper editing, most editors insist on performing at least two passes through a document: once to correct the major problems, and a second time to correct anything we missed the first time, as well as any errors we introduced through our editing. In more demanding jobs, we may need three or more passes to ensure that we're satisfied with the quality of the work. This doesn't change when we move to onscreen editing, so budget enough time for at least two passes. Where possible, let some time elapse before the second pass. For example, I arrange my schedule so I can do my final edit at least one day after the initial edit, since experience has shown that this gives me the necessary critical distance to approach the manuscript with fresh eyes and lets me spot errors I would otherwise have missed. In addition, the delay gives me time to ponder what I've read and develop a fuller understanding of the manuscript that helps me focus more intensely on communicating the right meaning.

When we've completed both edits, we return the manuscript to the author and cross our fingers. We may never see the document again, and once it's in the author's eager hands, we have no control over what will happen to our edits. If we're lucky, the author will offer us a chance for a second or even third edit (see *The final edit*, later in this chapter) to correct any errors the author introduced in response to our edits, but that's a luxury freelancers must often forgo.

One key point to remember at this stage: Authors will not agree with all of our edits. Sometimes this is because they simply don't understand the problem. At other times, it's because we guessed wrong and made a change that altered the meaning or that made no sense to the author. In both cases, it's important to emphasize our willingness to work with the author to explain why a seemingly unnecessary change was necessary, or why we misunderstood the original wording badly enough to introduce an error through our edits. If *we* misunderstood something, it's clear that other readers will make the same mistake, and that's why the problem needs to be fixed rather than ignored. When you return an edited manuscript to the author, explain that they should never reject an edit without clearly understanding why we proposed that change, and that they should feel free to discuss and resolve the problem. Don't forget to budget for that discussion time when you estimate the cost of a job.

Saved work and backups

Computers and the software that infests them remain unreliable tools. Both the operating systems and the word processors we use as our primary tools crash occasionally, and the only solution is to save our work frequently. (For details on how to configure software to automatically save your work and create backup files, see *General behavior of your word processor* in Chapter 4. If your software doesn't provide a comparable feature, teach yourself to manually save the document every 10 to 15 minutes, or whenever you've completed a particularly difficult part of the edit.) A good rule of thumb is that you should save a document sufficiently frequently that if your system crashes, you won't mind redoing all the work you performed since the last time you saved the document.

Most important, whenever you finish your editing for the day, make a safe, reliable backup. This seems self-evident, but many of my colleagues have lost large amounts of work (and potentially lost a client due to missed deadlines) because they failed to make such backups. What with viruses and other malware, robberies, floods, inattention due to fatigue, and other misfortunes, you'll eventually lose a file, and sometimes even the whole computer. The only way to prevent such disasters is to make ongoing backups of the files that you're editing. Appendix I details what you need to know to develop a successful backup strategy.

> ***Ad hoc* backups:** Until you develop a full-fledged backup strategy, protect your files by creating an e-mail account (e.g., with Google) that offers a large amount of storage space. You can now e-mail yourself a copy of each file whenever you feel the need to create a backup, whether after a couple hours of work or at the end of the day.

Particularly in the middle of the editing cycle, you may exchange a file with authors several times before finalizing the manuscript. Retain copies of the following files:

- **The original manuscript the author submitted:** It's easy to modify a manuscript in ways that are difficult or impossible to undo. In that case, it's very helpful to have the original available as a reference. Thus, never work in that original file. Instead, duplicate the file before you start working and add "–original version" to its name.

- **The first version you will work on:** It's helpful to come up with a simple system for naming the files you work with. For example, for one client, I add "-e" (for "edited") to the name of the file I'll be working in. If the original is named *Geoff–original.docx*, the edited version becomes *Geoff-e.docx*.

- **A copy at the end of each work session:** For long and complicated edits or when it may become necessary to return to a previous version and start over from that point, it's helpful to create dated or numbered versions. Your operating system can do this for you. For example, I can duplicate a file on my Macintosh, and the name automatically becomes *Geoff-e copy.docx*. Subsequent duplicates are automatically numbered *copy2* and so on.

- **A copy before beginning complex work:** Before I begin any series of complex corrections, particularly if I'll be doing them early in the morning before the coffee has taken effect or late at night when I'm tired, I make a numbered copy. If I wasn't thinking clearly, this backup lets me start over again without having to undo all those changes.

- **Any revised manuscript received from the author:** Once again, I create a copy of the revised file received from the author, but this time I add "-r" (for "revised") or "–revised" to the name.

Recovering lost files: Word processor files sometimes disappear. For example, if you're tired, you might delete the wrong file or save a file in the wrong place. If you *deleted* the file, look in the Recycle Bin (Windows) or the Trash (Macintosh). If you saved the file in the wrong location, check the File menu; there's usually a Recent Files option (including one in the Windows menu or the Apple menu); this will let you reopen the misplaced file and save it in the correct location. Using the Save As option should also display the last directory you worked in, and the file may be there. You can also use your computer's "find file" utility to search for the file's name; you can also search by modification date to find all files that were changed since a given date. Microsoft has also provided a "How to recover a lost Word Document" article in their knowledgebase.

Final edits

Ideally, we'll arrange to see the edited manuscript after the author has finished incorporated our edits. This is our last chance to catch anything we missed the first time—and it can be distressing how many things we miss, particularly when we're in a hurry. It's also our chance to fix any problems the author introduced while reviewing our edits. Thus, I try to persuade my authors to send me what they consider to be the final version of the manuscript for a last review. Needless to say, if you want to do this, include the time in your estimated cost.

When we're confident the author will contact us to resolve any unclear comments or to negotiate alternatives to our suggested changes, we can assume that the author accepted all our edits or inserted comments to explain why they rejected a change. In that case, we can simply read through the final version of the manuscript looking for any final errors. However, if we suspect that the author will disregard some changes without understanding why we proposed them or asking us to explain the problem, it's fruitful to compare the final version of the manuscript with our edited version to see what they missed or chose not to change. This comparison is particularly important for manuscripts with implications for human health and safety or with legal implications. You can use a copy of your final edited version of the manuscript in this comparison. Most word processors offer a document-comparison feature that provides a quick reality check. Chapter 6 provides details of how to do this in Word. This has an additional advantage: it lets us identify where an author *thinks* they've responded appropriately to a comment, but they really haven't.

Checking on the author: In general, it's safer if *we* implement the corrections, since it's our job to be obsessive about doing everything right and we obsess better than most authors. However, then someone should confirm that we haven't missed anything.

Follow-up

Once we've returned a manuscript to the author and submitted our invoice, the hard part is over. But that doesn't mean our work is finished. Part of making editing a human endeavor involves keeping in touch with the author to maintain a friendly, ongoing working relationship. The goal is to help the author understand that they're more than just an invoice to us and that we're still willing to work with them to resolve any of the myriad small details that somehow never seem to be resolved the first several times we pass through a document. We should expect to be compensated for significant, ongoing work after we submit our invoice, but it's a kindness to the author and a wise investment in an ongoing relationship to answer a few follow-up questions, free of charge, while the author puts the finishing touches on their manuscript. In my experience, the willingness to treat an author as something more than a supply of cash repays itself ten-fold in customer loyalty and free word-of-mouth advertising.

Archiving

It's wise to retain copies of edited files for some time after submitting your invoice, since it becomes necessary to return to an old manuscript surprisingly often. Roughly once per year, I've had to supply an author with an old copy of a file when they lost their only copy to a virus or the naïve belief that they'll never need the file again after their manuscript has been published. In addition, we may want to see how we handled a specific editing problem or style issue for a past client, read an old manuscript that explains a difficult concept that we must understand before we can tackle a new job, or simply review our own work to see the kinds of edits we do sufficiently often to justify creating shortcuts. (See Chapter 11 for details on automation.) When I became a freelancer, my archives of old manuscripts also provided a valuable source of contact information for past clients, a useful source of references, and (with the author's permission, of course) a portfolio of my work.

Archival information should include all correspondence with an author during the course of our work, as well as copies of any correspondence, contracts, invoices, and other relevant information. This is useful for legal reasons, but it also preserves knowledge that may prove useful in future dealings with a client. Such records may alert us to payment difficulties, idiosyncrasies in how clients prefer to work with us, and other useful tidbits. Keep copies of important e-mail in your e-mail software, or copy the messages into a word processor document for ease of reference. Include both types of copy in your backups.

Of course, there's an important exception to any rule, and that exception has important consequences for archiving. Clients sometimes ask us to either destroy all copies of our work or to protect that work so that only we will be able to see it. For example, I once worked for a client whose manuscript involved confidential material related to law enforcement and pending court cases. He therefore asked me to exclude his manuscript from my archives and delete all copies once the work was complete. (I did, but did not erase my final copies for several months, just in case; as it happens, he required a second copy of the manuscript a few months after I sent him the final edits.) If you work with confidential or classified material, you may need to use passwords to protect the edited files or perhaps even purchase special-purpose encryption software such as AES Crypt to protect the information from prying eyes. If the consequences of these files falling into the wrong hands are serious, we must take correspondingly serious measures to protect ourselves and our clients.

Communication and File-exchange Issues

Even if we do most of our work on the computer, there are certain practical matters that can't be fully computerized. The biggest one involves communication with our authors, which can be trickier than you might expect. In this section, I'll discuss how to handle the main issues effectively. The next-biggest problem involves how to transfer manuscripts between author and editor. If we'll be editing manuscripts on the screen, it doesn't seem to make much sense to exchange them with our authors on paper, but there are reasons why this might sometimes be necessary. In this section, I'll also discuss several of the considerations you'll need to take into account when you exchange files with authors over the Internet.

Communication

The author–editor relationship should be a dialogue, not a one-way transfer of information. The purpose of dialogue is to develop a means of working effectively together—ideally in a friendly manner, but at a minimum, in a professional and mutually respectful manner. There are several key goals that define the different types of communication that must take place during this dialogue:

Getting to know each other

During this phase, we begin the dialogue that initiates a relationship with the author. This is particularly important for high-context cultures such as many of those in Asia, Africa, and Spanish countries. In addition to all the formalities (introductions and other pleasantries) that accompany any first-time conversation with someone we've never met, this initial dialogue provides an opportunity to reassure the author that they're in good hands and to build their confidence in us. It's also our chance to get a feel for whether we should be equally confident in the author. An author who seems disorganized or evasive sends a strong message that we should take extra care to define schedules, confirm understandings about the work, and protect ourselves (by, for example, signing a contract before beginning our work).

Reaching a mutual understanding

The next step is to identify the nature of the work that will be required and explain to the author what this involves. *Never* assume that you and the author understand each other based solely on an initial discussion. *Always* summarize this discussion so the author has a chance to confirm that you've understood their needs correctly, and offer them a chance to provide their own summary to confirm whether they've understood our needs.

Resolving differences of opinion

It's rare for us to agree with an author about everything. There's an old saying that "the client is always right—even when they're wrong", and it's important to keep that in mind. We are experts in our profession, but most of the authors we work with are experts in *their* profession, and if we're unable to persuade them that we're right by means of logic, appeals to authority (e.g., a respected style guide), or examples, it's necessary to take a long step back and recognize that it's the author's manuscript, not ours. In the end, the author has final authority, and all we can do if we disagree strongly with their choices is to insist politely but firmly that they not acknowledge our work in the manuscript.

Who's responsible? It's important to ensure that authors understand their role in the editorial process. Although we make a good-faith effort to introduce no errors, the author is the expert, not us, and must confirm that our work is correct. (Only rarely do we have the same level of expertise as the author.) When in doubt, they must learn to ask for clarification rather than simply accepting a questionable edit and thereby introducing a preventable error into the manuscript.

Solving problems

Most often, editing a manuscript is straightforward, but every now and then, problems arise. These may result from an error on our part, an unusually critical reviewer of the author's work, or a problem with a word processor file. The hardest thing for many editors to learn is to take responsibility for our errors and make things right for the author—without trying too hard to absolve ourselves of blame. But when we did do everything right, and the author still blames us for a problem, we need to try to make things better without defending ourselves so strongly that we alienate a client. Often, the best approach is to steer the conversation to a discussion of how we can make things better rather than focusing on who to blame. (Of course, some clients should be fired when they become more trouble than they're worth. But that should generally be a last resort.) Some authors simply need to vent steam and get over their stress, and providing a quiet and sympathetic sounding board is sometimes all that's necessary to get past the problem.

Arranging payment

When we first negotiate a contract, one of the terms should always be the payment date and the penalties for late payment (typically, interest charges or other fees). To avoid being forced to invoke those penalties, it's helpful to remind clients of your payment deadlines in your invoice, and send a polite reminder if they haven't paid before the deadline. If the deadline passes, we're within our legal rights to insist on payment of any penalty fees, and I've done this with government departments that had no excuse other than incompetence for late payment. For other clients, it's wiser to accept a slightly late payment without insisting on our rights; the penalty fee may not be large, and is unlikely to be large enough to make it worth the risk of alienating the client and losing their future business. Try to get what is owed to you and to avoid letting clients take advantage of you, but think carefully about how hard you can insist without endangering your relationship.

Relationship management

Because some clients only need our services infrequently (e.g., when we only edit a client's annual report), it's important to keep in touch periodically so they know we still exist. At a minimum, send out season's greetings and New Year's wishes in late December, and never use specific greetings such as "Merry Christmas" unless you know the client's religion. If you know of any other important holidays your client may observe, such as the Chinese New Year or the Indian Diwali festival, send out appropriate greetings for that holiday too—ideally in the client's native language if you can learn the correct protocol. (I've researched and stored copies of Chinese, Finnish, French, Greek, Japanese, Italian, and Spanish greetings, and I'm working on expanding my repertoire.)

How often should you communicate with authors? Any of the difficulties I mentioned earlier in this section may indicate a need for immediate communication. But don't stop with the bare minimum. Always confirm that you've received any material they sent you, and contact them within a day or two if they haven't confirmed that they received something you sent them. With e-mail, there are no guarantees your message made it past misconfigured spam filters, antivirus software, and network-based e-mail filters. Without being annoying, keep clients advised of your progress towards a deadline (provide appropriate status updates), and warn of any potential delays as far in advance as possible so you won't have to surprise them with a missed deadline; it's always better to negotiate an extension in advance than to simply return work late, with no explanation.

Think ahead, and alert your most important clients to any impending absences or busy periods. For example, I warn all my key clients of my annual vacation one to two months in advance—and that my availability will decrease sharply in the weeks before I leave (as clients compete for the few remaining days) and after I return (when I must deal with work that accumulated while I was away). I've also learned to tell them that I'm leaving a week earlier than my actual departure date. That way, if any work arrives at the last minute—and it always does—I have an extra week in which to handle it. Please note that I'm not advocating that you lie to clients; in an ideal world, I won't work right up to my departure because I'll need a few days to pack, take care of the pets, clean house, pay bills, stock the fridge for my return, and so on.

Similarly, if I receive enough advance warning to know that I'll be buried with work at a particular time, I'll warn my clients that I'm unlikely to be available. This lets them adjust their schedules to send me work before or after that busy period with the minimum possible disruption. It may also have the salutary effect of reminding clients that I exist; fairly often, I find that they send me more work shortly after I contact them.

Obtain at least two e-mail addresses: Because your main service provider may occasionally be unavailable, or may be blocked by a client's network administrator or even their country (e.g., China), it's wise to have a backup e-mail address in addition to the one you obtained from your service provider. Google and Yahoo are popular, reliable choices. Include both addresses in your e-mail signature lines, and remind clients to use your second address if they tried contacting you from the primary address and received no reply.

How to communicate with authors is a bit of a judgment call, and each individual has their own preferences. Busy people often prefer e-mail because they can answer at their leisure; nervous people often prefer a phone call because they can interact with you in real-time until you've soothed their nerves, and legalistically inclined people may prefer a fax or registered letter so they have a printed record. My daughter's generation seems to prefer text messages on their smartphones. No one method is inherently superior, so it's more a question of paying attention to the other person's needs and learning what kind of communication they prefer. When in doubt, ask them! It constantly amazes me how many people prefer to assume they know what a client wants so they can avoid asking; many end up with an unpleasant surprise when it turns out they guessed wrong.

One final issue related to communication concerns the fact that our clients may be scattered around the world; I currently have clients and colleagues on every continent except Antarctica and in most time zones. For me, e-mail works best because my correspondents can receive their e-mail and respond at their convenience; there's never any risk of accidentally waking them with a phone call (or of being awoken myself, as has happened once or twice) in the middle of the night. However, a phone call has sometimes been necessary, and in that case, it helps to know when it's appropriate to call. An atlas lets you calculate time zones, either directly (from times marked on the map) or indirectly (each 15° of longitude is roughly equivalent to a time difference of 1 hour later if your client is east of you, and 1 hour earlier if they live to the west). The easiest way, though, is to use a resource such as the World Time Server that lets you enter your current date and time and learn the corresponding date and time anywhere in the world.

> **Pay attention to time zones!** When you negotiate deadlines with a distant client, it's easy to forget they may be in a different time zone. Always learn their deadlines in their own time zone and carefully translate that into your own time zone.

Security and confidentiality

At the start of this section, I noted that there are reasons why we might not exchange files with our authors by e-mail, even if we'll be working entirely on the screen to edit and revise a manuscript. The biggest reason is security, which becomes important when the material we're editing is confidential and must be protected. Unfortunately, although e-mail is highly convenient, it provides little security in its basic form. There are several other issues we need to be aware of so we can protect ourselves.

If security is important, take appropriate precautions to protect yourself against viruses and other nasty programs (*malware*) that can damage the software components of your computer, harvest e-mail addresses, record your keystrokes, and sometimes even steal documents. These precautions are doubly important for editors because the worst-case scenario is that we might inadvertently transmit such malware to a client after it has damaged our computer. At a minimum, every computer connected to the Internet needs at least the following basic protections:

- **Antivirus and antimalware software:** For both Windows and Macintosh, consider Symantec's Norton Antivirus, AVG, and Bitdefender. Macintosh users are no longer as safe as we used to be, so don't neglect to install antivirus software on your Mac.

- **A software firewall to keep out intruders:** The Zonealarm software for Windows is well respected, but the Comodo software has become another good choice. Intego offers NetBarrier for Macintosh users. Both Windows and Macintosh OS X offer free built-in firewalls, but the software is less sophisticated than commercial software and is more likely to have been targeted by malefactors.

- **A hardware firewall:** If you have a high-speed connection, it's worthwhile activating a hardware firewall for extra protection. This is commonly included in the *router* or *cable modem* that lies between your computer and its connection to the Internet.

Unfortunately, we're currently in the middle of an arms race between the developers of ways to break into computers and those who try to defend us against such intrusions. Be vigilant!

Security for travelers: Customs and security officers at airports and border crossings have the right to impound and inspect your computer and any data storage media (e.g., flash drives, external hard drives) you're carrying. For some countries, such as China, this is a particular risk, but it can also happen in the United States. If your computer contains anything confidential, learn how to protect it against their eyes; better still, don't bring it with you in the first place.

E-mail problems

Apart from conscious attempts to cause us harm, the most common security problem we'll encounter involves misdirected e-mail. For example, I have two regular correspondents with very similar e-mail addresses, and because my e-mail software tries to automatically complete addresses as I type, I occasionally send a letter to the wrong person. There's no foolproof way to prevent such errors, but we can reduce their frequency. The most obvious and effective act is to simply pause and carefully check the e-mail address we've just typed before sending the message; if the address is at all cryptic, as many are, it's worthwhile looking up the client in our address book rather than simply assuming that we've guessed right. If your e-mail software helpfully completes addresses as you type, consider creating distinctive aliases (nicknames that take the place of a full address) for easily confused addresses. Another trick I use is to keep a copy of an author's original message (containing the file they want me to edit) in my e-mail software's inbox. That way, I can simply select that message and reply to it, thereby eliminating the need to type the address.

Another problem relates to the ongoing backups of data performed by the computer staff of our Internet service provider (ISP), as well as backups performed by staff at a client's organization. These backups are generally a good thing, because they're our main protection against the occasional disasters that strike computers before messages are delivered. But if we're transmitting a confidential document that absolutely must not be read by anyone other than us and our client, those backups are a bad thing: the staff at the ISP should not have a chance to read the manuscript if they happen to be bored, unethical, or corrupt. Although it's possible for someone to intercept e-mail and files as they travel over the Internet between our ISP and that of our client, that's a low risk. We're not an attractive target unless we're engaged in military research, investment banking, or other high-security fields. But if we are working in those areas, our clients will recommend or provide an appropriately secure solution.

If the client does not provide or propose a solution, it may be worthwhile learning how to encrypt our documents—that is, to use utility software such as AES Crypt to encode the document in such a way that only someone with the correct password can decrypt the document and read its contents. If that level of industrial-strength security strikes you as unnecessary, you can often achieve an adequate level of protection with nothing more complicated than a judiciously chosen password. Most word processors provide some form of password protection (in Word, for example, you can use the Protect Document feature). However, many free or inexpensive utilities exist for cracking these passwords. A nice compromise between that weak protection and a full-blown security system is to use a file compression utility such as StuffIt for Windows and the Macintosh; these programs allow you to protect the compressed files with a password. One particularly nice feature of this software is that the developer provides free decompression utilities you can ask your client to install.

In addition to the security problems associated with e-mail, you may encounter several limitations that require alternative strategies:

- **File size:** Some service providers limit e-mail attachments to 5 or 10 megabytes. You may be able to compress larger files using software such as StuffIt. Alternatively, use a secure service such as DropBox to store the file, and send the author a link to that file.

- **Attachment formats:** Because some viruses can be transmitted in Word's .docx files and in compressed *archive* formats (particularly the .zip format used by both Windows and Macintosh computers), some antivirus programs and corporate e-mail servers block these files. Thus, you may occasionally need to rename files to use innocent extensions such as .txt (shorthand for the *text* file format) to get past these guardians. However, you must then teach your client to rename the file with the correct filename extension (such as .zip) so that their software will be able to open it.

- **Confirmation of receipt:** Although we can request automatic confirmation that our message arrived when we and the author both use software that supports this option, more often we must rely on the author to confirm that they received the file. I always ask my clients to confirm they received my message, and resend the file from a different e-mail address if I don't receive confirmation within a day or two.

> **Files received by e-mail:** Although it's tempting to double-click a file that you received in e-mail to open it, resist that temptation. E-mail programs differ in where they store their attachment files and handle changes to those files differently. Thus, when you edit and save files opened directly from your e-mail software, the changes may be saved somewhere obscure—possibly somewhere you can't easily find if you need to recover the file that contains your changes. To be safe, always save files yourself, in a location you can remember, and work with the files in that location.

If you can't resolve these kinds of problems or the security issues I discussed in the previous section, you may need to investigate alternatives to e-mail. The first and most obvious option is to use a courier service to hand-deliver the file on a CD or DVD (protected by a hard plastic case and a padded envelope). If you work near your client, you can also hand-deliver the CD or DVD. *Thumb drives* (also called *flash drives*) are an increasingly popular choice, though they may be too expensive to use on an ongoing basis if the client will not return them. Diskettes (floppy disks) are generally a poor choice because they are fragile, many computers no longer include diskette drives, and it's easy to inadvertently overwrite the files they contain—something that can't happen with a CD. There are also persistent anecdotal reports (some more credible than others) that diskettes are vulnerable to the electromagnetic fields generated by older or poorly maintained X-ray scanners and other security devices—and particularly vulnerable to the metal-detector wands used at the airport.

Secure transmission of passwords

If the goal of using a password is to protect an e-mailed file from snoops while the e-mail is in transit, it makes no sense to include the password in the same e-mail message—yet surprising numbers of people, and many Web sites I've used, use that approach. If you have two e-mail accounts (as I recommended earlier) offered by different service providers, you can then send the file from one address and the password from the second address. If you don't want to send the password by e-mail at all, telephone your client and communicate the password orally or send it by fax.

Passwords everywhere: If you install a router or other hardware firewall, change the factory-installed administrator password. If you don't, anyone who purchased the same model can use that password to access to your network. Any password can be cracked with enough effort, but there's no sense making this easy. A strong password is at least eight characters long, and preferably a mixture of letters, numbers, and characters found above the number keys. Avoid words found in a dictionary or in publicly available information about you, such as your birth date. Of course, the password must also be something you'll remember. If, like me, you have trouble remembering the dozens of passwords modern life requires, record your password somewhere safe: far from your computer, where a thief cannot easily find it, or store it in software such as 1Password.

E-mail alternatives

To avoid the abovementioned problems with e-mail, some clients provide Internet-accessible directories that let you transfer files directly to them, without being stored on your ISP's computers. A common method is to establish a *file transfer protocol* (FTP) directory. Depending on how this directory is configured, it may be possible to type its Web address (URL) into your Web browser to open the directory, and then drag and drop the file into the browser window; in other cases, you may need to download FTP software to perform the transfer. FTP is inherently more secure than e-mail, particularly if you use a variant called *secure* FTP, because the full file never comes to rest on anyone else's computer during transit. (Bits and pieces of the file travel different routes through the Internet, so only a professional spy would be able to intercept and reassemble these packets.)

Virtually private: Because FTP transfers pass through your ISP's computers, they can (at least in theory) be intercepted. To prevent interception, you can create a *virtual private network* connection—a secure tunnel between your computer and another computer. This makes it difficult or impossible to intercept information as it is being transferred between the two computers.

If you only occasionally need to take advantage of this technology, a range of free FTP sites is available. These let you upload files to a private, secure server on the company's Web site, from which your client can download it. For example:

- Use free software (with paid options for greater storage needs) such as Apple's iCloud or Microsoft's OneDrive. Both are available for Mac and Windows users, and both provide ample space for file transfers.
- Mediafire provides 10 gigabytes of storage for free and up to 20 gigabytes per file with paid plans. Files remain until you delete them.
- SendThisFile offers a free service with no maximum file size, or a paid service with high security and various business options.

Storage durations: If you use such services to transfer files, confirm how long the service stores files on their server. If they don't automatically delete the files, add a note on your calendar to delete the file after the client receives it. You have to trust the integrity of the people who operate these services, but given that their business depends on their integrity, such services are generally a safe bet.

II. Mastering the Tools

"One of the universal rules of happiness is: always be wary of any helpful item that weighs less than its operating manual."—Terry Pratchett, *Jingo*

Although personal computers have been around for nearly 25 years, they're still primitive things compared with what they'll eventually become. A particular problem is that computer software is still designed by programmers who are unfamiliar with the modern science of user-centered design. As a result, the software we use for onscreen editing is initially uncomfortable and awkward to most editors. Many never try to overcome that bad first impression; instead, they feel too intimidated to use the software, or simply tolerate its many annoyances. Over the years, my informal observations of many computer users suggests that the fear of screwing something up or the fear of demonstrating one's incompetence is the single greatest barrier to overcoming these problems and learning to use a computer efficiently. It helps to remember, as I've often noted to the occasional petrified victim of their computer, that even if these infernal machines are smarter than we are, we can still turn them off whenever they annoy us.

Once you get past the initial intimidation factor, you quickly begin discovering how to make the computer your tool rather than your nemesis. Time invested in learning how software works will repay itself a hundredfold in subsequent time savings. Moreover, most software can be simply but extensively customized until you find a combination of settings that works well (comfortably and efficiently) for you. In this section, I'll teach you how to personalize your editing environment so that it becomes a comfortable place to work, with the additional benefit that doing so will improve your editing speed and accuracy. I'll also teach you to pay close attention to how you work so you can recognize editorial tasks that are particularly suitable for automation: these are tasks that take up lots of time, whether because we do them so often or because they're so cumbersome that they devour our time whenever we must do them.

Section II: Mastering the tools

Most computer users master a core set of perhaps two dozen tasks, and never bother learning anything more about their software. That's a shame, since modern software such as Microsoft Word offers an incredible depth and breadth of features that could make your editing life much easier. If you don't have the time to purchase and memorize a detailed book on your software, I've found an alternative that works well for most people: Every day, spend a mere five minutes exploring a single menu choice you've never used before until you figure out what it does. (If the menu choice introduces another dozen options, concentrate on each one in turn, one feature per day.) Spend a moment thinking about whether that feature of the software could help you work faster or better. By the time a year of exploration has gone by, you'll have explored most of the software's nooks and crannies. Of course, if you don't want to spend the time, read this section of the book instead; I've already done most of that work for you.

Chapter 4. Personalizing How Your Software Works

Web: http://www.geoff-hart.com/books/eoe/eoe3/eoe3.html
Note: Word 2010 is for Windows; Word 2011 is for the Macintosh

Among the most productive places to start your explorations of how software works are the *control panels* that each operating system uses to control (i.e., personalize or customize) how we interact with our computers. Control panels affect how we interact with the computer's operating system and (in general terms) with programs, but each program also offers ways to control its own behavior.

Details provided on the Web: Because there's so much variation in how the Windows and Macintosh operating systems and versions of Microsoft Word implement the features described in this chapter, it's not possible to illustrate them all here. Instead, visit this chapter's Web page for images and instructions.

In this chapter, I'll discuss personalization options at both the level of the operating system and at the level of your word processor. (For details, see *Overall Behavior of Your Computer* and *Behavior of Your Word Processor* later in this chapter.) In the first section, I'll provide details for both Windows 7 and the Macintosh's OS X (Mavericks); more recent versions of both operating systems function similarly. In the second section, I'll describe the general features available in most word processing software and show how Microsoft Word for Windows and for the Macintosh have implemented those features. If you're using another word processor, such as WordPerfect, OpenOffice, or LibreOffice, these descriptions provide an idea of what settings you should look for. The first and second editions of *Effective Onscreen Editing* cover older versions of Word, and both books are still available, on request.

Why not Linux? Though I recognize the growing popularity of Linux, it wasn't possible for me to cover it here. Most features described in this chapter should have obvious equivalents in Linux.

So many settings can be changed that many editors are paralyzed by the fear they'll screw something up, and this stops them from experimenting. Don't let this stop *you*! You can always change things back to the original setting if you remember two simple tricks:

- First, change only one thing at a time. Don't change anything else until you've observed the consequences of that initial change long enough to decide whether or not you like it.

- Second, record how you reached that setting and its original value on a notepad or in a word processor file as a record of what you've done. If you don't like the results of that change, follow the same path and restore that setting to its original value. Add a note about why you feel the change didn't work; you may want to revisit that change later.

The advantage of changing only one thing at a time is that if you don't like the way your computer is behaving, you won't have to guess which of several changes might have caused the problem. Note that you may need to work with a changed setting for 15 minutes or even an hour to ensure that you give it a fair chance: often what seems to be an incorrect choice is a symptom of the normal human discomfort with a change from what we've previously done. Spending a little time getting used to the change may reveal the change to be an improvement.

Overall Behavior of Your Computer

Control panels (Windows) and Preference Panes (Macintosh) are small programs that let us change many of the ways that we interact with our computer, including both the hardware and the operating system. The three most important groups of settings for editors are those for the keyboard, those for the mouse or other pointing device (hereafter, I'll use the term *mouse* for all such devices), and those for the screen display. To display the control panels and access these groups of settings:

- **Windows 7:** Start menu > Control Panels
- **Macintosh OS X:** Apple menu > System Preferences

Terminology note: For the sake of simplicity, I'll henceforth refer to all tools for reining in the computer as *control panels*.

Keyboard and mouse settings

The three main keyboard settings that affect our interactions with the computer are how long it takes for the computer to recognize that we're holding down a key, how fast the computer then repeats the specified action for that key (e.g., types a letter or scrolls the screen), and the language settings (layout) for the keyboard. Windows and Macintosh computers both offer separate keyboard and mouse control panels.

Keyboard controls

Finding the correct balance between delaying and accelerating the keyboard response requires some trial and error. To achieve the optimal balance, spend a few minutes paying attention to whether you're most annoyed by occasional repeated characters or by the delay before scrolling begins, and adjust the keyboard response rate accordingly.

- **Delay before repeating:** This setting defines how long the computer waits before it realizes that you're intentionally holding down a key and begins repeating the associated action. Set this value long enough that accidentally pressing a key doesn't trigger its action, but short enough that you don't waste time waiting for a response.

- **Repeat rate:** This setting defines how fast the computer responds once it recognizes that you're holding down a key. Set this slow enough that you don't insert repeated characters each time you touch the keyboard, but fast enough you're not always waiting for the computer.

Keyboard power tools: Many keyboards come with software that lets you program special buttons on the keyboard to perform additional tasks, such as launching your Web browser. Skim the keyboard's manual to see whether any of those features are useful.

Keyboard language settings (layout)

Many languages have special characters and accents that you will use repeatedly while you edit in that language. The easiest way to access these characters is directly from the keyboard; that way, you aren't forced to remember a series of keystrokes or codes. In Canada, for example, you may want to use the Canadian French keyboard layout. Since French keyboards come with accented characters and other special French characters clearly labeled on the keys, selecting that keyboard layout gives you immediate access to those characters. If you choose Canadian English instead, pressing the same keys will not produce the accented vowels and other special characters shown on the French keyboard. Using the control panels, you can make two or more keyboard layouts available, and can change among the available layouts via a menu item or keyboard shortcut.

If you can't find the control panel that lets you define these settings in the version of the operating system you're using, search the Web for the name and version of your operating system plus the terms "keyboard lay-out" or "switch languages or keyboards" to find appropriate instructions.

Mouse controls

Most of us quickly discover that the default settings for the mouse make its cursor move faster or slower than we like, and that we have to click the main button faster or slower than we prefer when it's necessary to double-click (for example, to launch a program or select a word). To mod-ify these settings, open the mouse control panel, then experiment until you strike the right balance between two settings:

- **Tracking speed:** This determines how fast the mouse pointer moves across the screen, which should be fast enough to get you to the desired location quickly without frequently overshooting the target.

- **Double-click speed:** This determines how fast you must click for the computer to recognize this action as a double-click. Set this interval long enough that you can easily launch programs or select words with a double-click.

Mouse power tools: As is the case for keyboards, many mice come with special *driver* software that lets you program their buttons to pro-vide additional features. Consult your mouse's manual to see whether any of those features will facilitate your work.

Display settings

Modifying three aspects of your display settings can prevent computer use from turning into a visual nightmare: the screen resolution, the refresh rate, and whether or not *anti-aliasing* is used. Each can be changed via the Display (Windows) or Displays (Macintosh) control panel.

Screen resolution

Screen resolution determines how many dots (*pixels*) are displayed on the screen. Most computer users now use a large display with a resolution of at least 1270×800 to provide a good compromise between sharpness and size, but many other resolutions are available. Unlike the older CRT monitors, LCD monitors have a fixed number of pixels; they can nonetheless fake different resolutions, although the image sharpness may suffer. Experiment with resolutions until you find one that lets you show the desired amount of text on the screen, thereby reducing the amount of scrolling you must do and providing a better view of page layouts.

At higher resolutions (more pixels), screen images will be sharper and potentially less fatiguing to view, but text and icons will be smaller than they would be at a lower resolution. The Display (Displays) control panel solves this problem by offering a range of icon and text sizes for each resolution.

Screen refresh rate

Most editors now use an LCD monitor, which provides a sharp, higher-resolution image. Because each pixel remains fully illuminated until the image changes, you generally won't notice any flickering. Videos and animations may display some blurring, but for the most part that won't be relevant for editors. Some LCD monitors may allow you to adjust the refresh rate, but as a general rule, this is not an option and should not be necessary.

CRT displays have largely disappeared, having been replaced by LCD monitors. Nonetheless, since some editors still use a CRT, a few words on how to use one with less pain: With CRT displays, the image is painted by a beam of electrons sweeping across the screen, and by the time the beam reaches the end of the screen, the first-illuminated pixels have begun to fade. This leads to flickering as the fading pixels are suddenly "refreshed" and replaced by brighter, freshly illuminated pixels. Many computer users find that the baseline refresh rate of 60 Hz (sixty times per second) is insufficient; the flickering is distracting and visually fatiguing. Flickering is particularly obvious in peripheral vision, so if you don't see flickering when you look directly at the screen, try turning your head or focusing your gaze to one side of the screen.

If you do notice flickering, increasing the refresh rate to 75 Hz or greater will solve the problem for most people. However, a low-cost computer using a large CRT at high resolution to display the maximum number of colors possible may not permit sufficiently high refresh rates. In that case, you may need to decrease the screen resolution or number of colors being displayed.

Anti-aliasing

Modern CRT displays provide sufficiently high resolution that it's difficult to see the individual dots that make up lines and characters on the screen. You can therefore select a wide range of display resolutions with little difficulty. However, the physical resolution of an LCD monitor is fixed when the display is manufactured, and even though you can choose other resolutions, doing so can result in fuzzy images. When you ask your LCD monitor to display more pixels than it actually possesses, it has to simulate those extra pixels somehow. This is done through *antialiasing*. Microsoft's solution is called ClearType; Apple calls this "LCD font smoothing". If you don't like the effect of this trick because you find the text blurry, turn off this feature.

> **Why "hardware"?** I joke that it's called *hardware* because computers are hard on your body—your personal editing equipment. The greatest danger results from overuse injuries (*repetitive stress injuries*) that result from spending sedentary hours at the keyboard without interruption. Appendix II (*Protecting Yourself From Injury While Using a Computer*) explains how to set up a safer, more comfortable work environment that will minimize the risk of such injuries.

Behavior of Your Word Processor

Most software, fresh out of the box, fits us about as well as a new pair of shoes that haven't yet been broken in accommodate the unique shapes of our feet. The blisters caused by new software may be metaphorical, but they're no less painful. Working comfortably on the computer will only become possible if you learn how to break-in the software—that is, learn how to personalize it so it works the way you want it to work.

The good news is that word processors provide many options for configuring their behavior. That's also the bad news, since discovering which of a bewildering array of options work best for you will take time. Because I've played with most of these settings at one time or another, I've created this section to describe the groups of settings most likely to make your editing life easier. There are many other options I don't have room to describe, so don't limit yourself to my suggestions; spend some time exploring to see whether some obscure setting might be highly relevant to your specific needs. To modify Microsoft Word's configuration options:

- **Word 2010:** Ribbon > File menu > Options
- **Word 2011:** Word menu > Preferences

> **Where did the Options (Preferences) go?** In many versions of Word, you can't access the Options or Preferences dialog box if no document is open. If Word won't let you open this dialog box, create a new blank document or open an existing document and try again.

Unless otherwise noted, all settings that I discuss in this section can be reached through these dialog boxes.

Personal **settings:** Most settings only affect how Word behaves on *your* computer. Thus, authors won't always see documents the same way you do. Remember this when you tell an author what to look for on their screen; you may need to describe this in general terms, or teach them how to configure Word to show what you're seeing.

Summary of Word's main settings

In this section, I've started by organizing the most useful settings into broad categories to help you find groups of useful options to explore. In the following section, I provide an alphabetical list of all these settings so you can quickly find each setting and learn its function. Because the names of the settings differ between Windows and Macintosh versions of Word, I've provided words that differ between versions in brackets.

- **Compatibility settings:** compatibility options, grid-based formatting in Asian versions of Word, missing fonts
- **File location settings:** autorecover, documents, templates
- **General settings:** confirm (file format) conversion at open, confirm launching applications in Open and New, (enable) background repagination, measurement units (Show measurements in units of), recently used files, update automatic links at open
- **Print settings:** print comments, print field codes (instead of their values), update fields and links
- **Save settings:** allow fast saves, always create backup copy, prompt to save changes to Normal template, save autorecovery information, save files in this format (save Word files as)
- **Screen display settings:** bookmarks, comments on rollover, hidden text, highlight, non-printing characters, paragraph markers, picture or image placeholders, screen tips, show field codes instead of their values (show field codes), tabs, wrap to window (text wrap)
- **Spelling and grammar settings:** check grammar as you type, check spelling as you type, Dictionaries button, (re)check document button, Settings button, suggest from main dictionary only
- **Track changes settings:** change bars, color, formatting, mark (style of insertion, deletion, or change), moved text and changed tables
- **Typing settings:** allow text to be dragged and dropped (drag-and-drop editing), Insert key behavior, overtype mode, show paste options button, typing replaces selection (or selected text), use smart cut and paste, when selecting automatically replace entire word

Word changes things you type without being asked: Word provides two features (AutoCorrect and AutoFormat) that make certain changes for you, without being explicitly asked to do so. If Word changes something on the screen and you didn't ask it to make that change, you've probably encountered these features being too helpful. I'll discuss how to tame these settings in Chapter 11.

- **User information settings:** conducting anonymous reviews
- **Window settings:** horizontal and vertical rulers, horizontal and vertical scroll bars, style area width, zoom (magnify) tool

Because Word's settings move around and change names almost every time Microsoft updates Word, it's hard to know exactly where to look for a given setting. I've added details (in brackets) of the locations that were correct as of Word 2010 and 2011, but in later versions of the software, you may need to do a bit of digging to find them. For simplicity, I'll use the term *tab* to describe their location, even though the Macintosh interface doesn't always use true tabs.

Details of Word's main settings

- **Allow fast saves** (Save tab)**:** No longer present in current versions of Word, but if you're using an older version, deselect this option. Files saved in this format are highly vulnerable to damage and can be difficult or impossible for other software to open. If you receive a file saved using this feature, save the file under a new name, in the current .docx file format. If this doesn't prevent subsequent problems, see Appendix III for various potential solutions.

- **Allow text to be dragged and dropped** (Word 2010 Advanced tab > Editing options) **or Drag-and-drop editing** (Word 2011 Edit tab)**:** This feature lets you select text, hold down the mouse button, and then drag that text to a new position. This is very useful for moving sentences and for juggling word order within a sentence without having to cut and paste the text.

- **Always create backup copy** (Word 2010 Advanced tab > Save, Word 2011 Save tab)**:** With this option selected, opening a new file causes Word to create a new copy named "Backup of...", followed by the document's name. Older versions of Word used the .wbk filename extension; current versions will use the same format as the original document. The file will be saved in the same directory as the original file. If you damage a file badly enough that you want to start over again from the version that existed when you first opened the document that day, rename and open this backup file. Note that this option does not, by itself, represent an adequate backup strategy. Appendix I explains how to create such a strategy.

- **Autorecover(y) file location:** See *File locations* later in this section.
- **Bookmarks** (Word 2010 Advanced tab > Show Document Content, Word 2011 View tab)**:** If you're responsible for inserting cross-references or checking their validity, or if you want to see how these special features have been inserted so you can make the formatting consistent, select this checkbox. Bookmarks resemble {field code} on the screen. (Note the curly brackets.)
- **Change bars** (Word 2010 Ribbon > Review tab > menu below the Track Changes icon; Word 2011 Track Changes tab)**:** This option displays a vertical line (a *change bar*) in the margin beside any line that contains a tracked edit. For heavy edits, this option isn't useful because most lines contain at least one change and the resulting change bar stretches from the first to the last line of the document. For light edits, these lines let you scan quickly down the screen or printed page to find changes. (However, it's more reliable to use the revision tools described in Chapter 6 to find changes, since unlike us mortals, Word won't miss any changes.)
- **Check (mark) grammar as you type** (Word 2010 Proofing tab, Word 2011 Spelling and Grammar tab)**:** This option highlights supposed grammatical problems as you work. Modern grammar checkers are wrong too often to be reliable guides, and this display clutters the screen, so I don't recommend using it. Chapter 10 provides details on how to use this feature productively despite its limitations.
- **Check spelling as you type** (Word 2010 Proofing tab, Word 2011 Spelling and Grammar tab)**:** This option sets Word to review each word as you finish typing it, and underlines the word if it can't find it in the selected dictionary. This option is of questionable value. In addition to cluttering the display, it encourages you to fix each typo as it occurs; it's generally far more effective to write or edit text first and worry about spelling later. More seriously, this option provides a false sense of security; Word sometimes forgets to underline words it has already checked, even if they contain errors.
- **Color (of tracked changes)** (Word 2010 Ribbon > Review tab > menu below the Track Changes icon; Word 2011 Track Changes tab)**:** This option defines the color used to display tracked changes; these

colors are limited to the choices provided by Word. If multiple reviewers revise a document, the By author option displays each reviewer's changes in a different color. Unfortunately, you can't choose the color for each reviewer. Although primarily intended for onscreen use, the selected colors also govern how the document will print if you review the edits on paper. Selecting a color for each type of tracked change will not display your changes in that color if the Mark style (discussed later in this section) is set to None. To display the desired color, select Color only or combine this with an option such as Double underline if you want both a color and that format.

- **Comments on rollover** (Word 2011 View tab): When you insert comments using Word's comment feature, as described in Chapter 6, this option lets you see the comments by moving the mouse cursor above the text that contains the comment. Word also displays the name of the editor, the date and time of the edit, and the nature of the edit (e.g., "inserted" to identify new text added by the editor). In Windows, Word does this automatically without requiring a special setting.

- **Compatibility options** (Word 2010 Advanced tab, Word 2011 Compatibility tab): Because Word's behavior has evolved over the years and many older versions of Word are still being widely used, it's helpful to maximize the compatibility when you and your author are using different versions. This group of settings lets you specify which version of Word your software should emulate, and provides fine-grained control over the document's page layout. This setting will be most important if you're working with clients who are publishing their information from Word and you want to see the layout the same way they do.

- **Conducting anonymous reviews** (Word 2010 Trust Center tab > Trust Center settings button > Privacy Options tab; Word 2011 Security tab): If you're asked to review a document without identifying who you are (e.g., for peer reviews of journal articles), you have two options: First, you can set Word to eliminate all personal information stored in the document using the Remove personal information from file properties on save option. Second, you can modify the user information settings (described later in this section) and change your name to "Anonymous reviewer" and your initials to "AR" (or similar pseudonyms) before you open the file and begin your work. After you've completed your review and closed the file, restore the original settings. If you do this often, record a macro that makes these changes for you. (See Chapter 11 for details on creating macros.)

- **Confirm (file format) conversion at open** (Word 2010 Advanced tab > General tab, Word 2011 General tab): Word can work with files in a wide range of formats. With this option selected, Word will ask you whether to leave a file in its original format or to convert it into Word's own document format (.docx). As a general rule, you should select this option so that *you* choose the format, not Word.

- **Confirm launching applications in Open and New** (Word 2011 General tab): If you inadvertently select a program instead of a Word file to open, this option gives you a chance to not launch (run) the program. This option does not appear to exist in Windows.

- **Dictionaries button** (Word 2010 Proofing tab, Word 2011 Spelling and Grammar tab): This button lets you specify which custom dictionaries Word should use with the current file. (See Chapter 10 for details of how to use custom dictionaries.) This function lets you use a specialized list of words (such as medical or legal terminology) to check spelling.

- **Document file location:** See *File locations* later in this section.

- **(Enable) background repagination** (Word 2010 Advanced tab > General, Word 2011 General tab): When you select this option, Word continuously recalculates the length of the document and your position within the document as you work, which is useful if you must edit a manuscript to fit within a certain space. This setting is automatic in the page layout (printing) view.

- **File locations** (Word 2010 Advanced tab > General, Word 2011 File Locations tab): By default, Word saves its files in predefined locations that can be difficult to find. Using the File Locations button (Windows) or tab (Macintosh), you can define the location of your documents, templates, and autorecover(y) files. For example, I changed the Documents setting to store my work files in the *Freelance Work* folder at the top of my hard disk hierarchy, and changed the Autorecover files setting to a directory on my desktop.

- **Formatting (tracking changes)** (Word 2010 Ribbon > Review tab > menu below the Track Changes icon; Word 2011 Track Changes tab): Word also lets you track format changes such as manually applied or removed boldface or italics, changed paragraph or character styles, or modified paragraph formats such as indents or line spacing and define how this group of changes (but not each individual type of change) will be displayed.

- **Grid-based formatting in Asian versions of Word:** Asian authors often use a grid to align characters so that each occupies the same amount of horizontal and vertical space. (This is analogous to the use of monospaced fonts such as Courier.) Unfortunately, this can render a manuscript unreadable on some Western computers, even when the text uses an English font, and can make it prohibitively difficult to select characters, words, and phrases. If you are willing to install Asian language support on your computer (search the online help for "Asian language support" to learn how), you can turn off this feature: for Windows, Ribbon > Page Setup tab > Document Grid icon; for the Macintosh, File menu > Page Setup.

> **Asian language support for the Macintosh:** Although Asian language support mostly works for the Macintosh, it can create several annoying problems due to unsquashed bugs. If you're not willing to risk mucking up a Word installation that has been working well, I've provided the code for a macro that will (when Word cooperates) turn off the Asian grid setting; see this chapter's Web page to obtain the macro, and see Chapter 11 for information on how to use it. You can also try saving the file in a format that doesn't support document grids; HTML format sometimes works, and you can then open this copy of the document and re-save it in Word's .docx format.

- **Hidden text** (Word 2010 Display tab, Word 2011 View tab): Text that has been formatted as *hidden* is only visible when this option is selected; it appears underlined by dots. Such text sometimes results from an error when moving files between old and new versions of Word, or when the author inserts notes using this format. Selecting this option lets you see this text so that you can apply the correct format or find and delete the notes if they're no longer relevant.
- **Highlight or Show highlighter marks** (Word 2010 Display tab, Word 2011 View tab): This option must be selected for Word to display highlighting applied using the highlighter marker, which I discuss in Chapter 6.
- **Horizontal and vertical rulers** (Word 2010 Advanced tab > Display, Word 2011 View tab): If it's necessary to measure horizontal positions, you can display a horizontal ruler at the top of any document, in any view mode. In Print Layout view mode, you can also choose to display a vertical ruler.

- **Horizontal and vertical scroll bars** (Word 2010 Advanced tab > Display, Word 2011 View tab): These settings define whether to display scroll bars at the bottom and right sides (respectively) of the document window. If space is limited on your screen or if you frequently click the mouse in the scroll bars by mistake, deselect these options until you need them.

- **Insert key behavior and overtype mode** (Word 2010 Advanced tab > Editing options, Word 2011 Edit tab > Overtype mode): Windows Word allows you to change the Insert key's function to pasting text from the clipboard; to enable this option, select the Advanced tab, scroll down to Cut, copy, and paste, and then select Use Insert key to paste. Because the Insert key sits above the forward Delete key on most keyboards, it's easy to hit by mistake, so this may not be a great choice. In older versions of Word, the Insert key switches Word between the familiar text insertion mode (in which typing pushes all characters to the right to make room for the new text) and overtype mode (in which each new character that you type replaces the character to the right of the cursor position). This can be annoying if you're typing without watching the screen, as many of us do while copying text from a printout or Web page; it's easy to erase much text before you look up and notice the problem. Current versions of Word appear to have eliminated this feature, but you'll see the following warning in older versions:

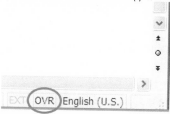

- **Mark (style of an insertion, deletion, or change)** (Word 2010 Ribbon > Review tab > menu below the Track Changes icon; Word 2011 Track Changes tab): This set of options lets you define the characteristics of each type of edit if you want them to be visually distinct. For example, you can set insertions to appear as boldfaced red text and deletions to appear as strikethrough black text. These formats only affect the display until a change is accepted or rejected, and don't permanently affect the underlying font characteristics. Because this formatting is only used by the track changes feature, you cannot remove or change the formatting as you would for other text; for example, if you set Word to use underlining to display inserted text, you can't remove this underlining by pressing Control+U (Windows) or Command+U (Macintosh), nor can you find this underlining by searching for underlined text (as described in Chapter 8).

- **Measurement units or Show measurements in units of** (Word 2010 Advanced tab > Display, Word 2011 General tab): This setting lets you specify the units that will appear in the horizontal and vertical rulers. It also lets you specify the units that will be used when you define indents, tab positions, and other layout settings in formatting dialog boxes.

- **Missing fonts** (Word 2010 Advanced tab > Show document content, Word 2011 Compatibility tab): Word provides compatible core fonts in all operating systems, and does a good job of replacing missing fonts with a suitable alternatives in most cases. If not, the Font Substitution button lets you choose which font to use to display the missing font. Because the underlying font is untouched, the author won't have to reapply that font when they receive the edited file.

- **Moved text and changed tables (revision tracking)** (Word 2010 Ribbon > Review tab > menu below the Track Changes icon; Word 2011 Track Changes tab): These options let you specify how moved text should be displayed and how changes to tables (inserted, deleted, merged, and split table cells) will be displayed.

- **Nonprinting characters or Always display these formatting marks on the screen** (Word 2010 Display tab, Word 2011 View tab): This group of settings determines whether to display visual cues for hidden characters such as paragraph markers (¶) and tab stops (→).

- **Overtype mode:** See *Insert key behavior* earlier in this section.

- **Paragraph markers:** See *Nonprinting characters* earlier in this section.

- **Picture (or Image) placeholders** (Word 2010 Advanced tab > Show document content, Word 2011 View tab): If a graphics-heavy document is scrolling slowly enough to reduce your productivity, select this option to replace the graphics with empty boxes (the *placeholders*); deselect this option when you need to see the images again.

- **Print comments:** In older versions of Word, it was necessary to specify that comments should be printed in the Print What? menu of the Print dialog box. In current versions, Word will automatically print any markup that is displayed on the screen, including comment balloons. To control that display, see Chapter 6 for details.

- **Print field codes (instead of their values)** (Word 2010 Advanced tab > Print, Word 2011 Print tab): This option lets you show (in brace brackets) the equations and other controls used to define the field instead of presenting the results of those equations or controls.

- **Prompt to save Normal template** (Word 2010 Advanced tab > Save, Word 2011 Save tab)**:** Because the Normal.dotm template stores many custom settings, it's important to protect the file. This option warns you if you have modified this template so that you have a chance to change your mind. If you have customized Word, save the changes when Word notifies you that the template has changed.

- **Recently used files** (Word 2010 Advanced tab > Display, Word 2011 General tab)**:** This option has been renamed Show this number of Recent Documents (Windows) or Track recently opened documents (Macintosh). It defines the number of files you have worked on most recently that should be displayed under the File menu. This provides fast access to these files, without having to navigate through your hard disk. Select a number large enough to show all or most of the files in the project you're currently working on.

- **(Re)check document button** (Word 2010 Proofing tab, Word 2011 Spelling and Grammar tab)**:** Word occasionally decides to save you time by not checking text that it thinks hasn't changed since the last spellcheck. To warn you that it's made this choice, it changes this button (concealed deep in the settings) to Recheck document; too bad if you didn't notice. If you find Word skipping entire sections of a document, missing obvious typos, or refusing to even begin a spellcheck, click this button to force Word to recheck the whole document. However, Word doesn't always cooperate; see Chapter 10 for suggestions on how to ensure that this recheck actually happens.

- **Save autorecover(y) information every** (Save tab)**:** When you select this option, Word automatically saves a temporary copy of any open file at the specified time interval. The file is named "Autorecovery save of...", followed by the original file's name. If Word crashes, you can reopen these files and recover all work that you completed up to the last time this file was saved. (See *File location settings* earlier in this section for details.) A good rule of thumb is to set a sufficiently short interval between saves that you're willing to redo all the work since the last time you saved the file if Word crashes. Unless you're using a computer that crashes frequently, Word is now stable enough that there's little reason to set the interval below 15 minutes. Indeed, too-high intervals may create too many temporary files, leading to instability.

- **Save files in this format** (Word 2010 Save tab) or Save Word files as (Word 2011 Save tab): By default, Word now saves files in the .docx format. Although this format is superior to the old .doc format in several ways, including increased stability, it includes features that are not supported by the older .doc format. If you will be exchanging files with authors who are using older versions of Word or are helping an author to prepare files for a publisher that does not yet accept the .docx format, you can set Word to use the older .doc format until you change this setting again. (Word will not change the existing format of a document unless you use Save As to save the file in a new format.)

- **ScreenTips or Tooltips** (Word 2010 Display tab): For Windows, the setting Show document tooltips on hover causes Word to display a yellow balloon that explains an icon's function when you hold the mouse cursor over the icon. For the Macintosh, there appears to be no way to turn off this option.

Learn keyboard shortcuts: For Windows, Word's ScreenTips feature can reveal the keyboard shortcut for a command. In the Advanced tab of the Options dialog box, scroll down to the Display section, and then select Show shortcut keys in ScreenTips. Macintosh Word no longer offers this option.

- **Settings button for Grammar checks** (Word 2010 Proofing tab, Word 2011 Spelling and Grammar tab): This button displays a dialog box that lets you define which rules Word's grammar checker should enforce. By judiciously selecting the options that are both reliable and most likely to help you, you can make Word's grammar checker into a semi-useful tool. See Chapter 10 for details.

- **Show field codes instead of their values** (Word 2010 Advanced tab > Show document content) or Field codes (Word 2011 View tab): Word uses field codes to perform calculations (e.g., determine the date) and insert the results in a document, or to perform certain functions (e.g., create cross-references and index entries). Selecting this option displays these codes so you see them and edit their contents; they appear in brace brackets {like this}; deselecting this option will show only the value of the field.

- **Show Paste Options button** (Word 2010 Advanced tab > Cut, copy, and paste section; Word 2011 Edit tab): This option displays a small clipboard icon each time you paste copied text: The icon provides access to a menu of options such as whether to retain the original formatting or adopt the formatting of the surrounding text. If the clipboard icon annoys you, deselect this option.

- **Spelling options:** See Chapter 10 for a thorough discussion.
- **Style area width** (Word 2010 Advanced tab > Display, Word 2011 View tab): If you're responsible for ensuring that paragraph styles have been applied consistently, in conformity with a publisher's style guide, you can display the styles used for each paragraph in the left margin in Draft and Outline views (discussed later in this chapter). Enter a sufficiently large number in this field that the style name will fit within this area. To eliminate this area, set the style area width to zero.

What's a *style*? Uncomfortable with paragraph and character styles? Never even heard of them? See *A Primer on Styles and Templates* later in this chapter to learn what you need to know.

- **Suggest from main dictionary only** (Word 2010 Proofing tab, Word 2011 Spelling and Grammar tab): With this option selected, Word uses only the main spelling dictionary and ignores any words you have added to your custom dictionaries.
- **Tabs (displaying):** see *Nonprinting characters* earlier in this section.
- **Templates:** Templates store information such as style definitions and any customizations you have performed following the advice in this chapter and later chapters. See *File locations* earlier in this section to learn where these files are stored so you can include them in your backups or modify them.
- **Typing replaces selection (or selected text):** see *Insert key behavior* earlier in this section.
- **Update automatic links at open** (Word 2010 Advanced tab > General, Word 2011 General tab): If a document contains links to graphics files, spreadsheets, and other objects that exist outside the document, selecting this option ensures that you'll see the most recent versions of those objects that are available. This is important if you'll be editing manuscripts that contain external components such as graphics that may be undergoing revision by someone else while you edit. This setting is particularly important if you're responsible for commenting on the contents of these components or comparing them with the text to ensure that the descriptions match.

- **Update fields and links** (Word 2010 Display tab, Word 2011 Print tab): This option updates any fields, such as page numbers and cross-references, before it prints the document.
- **User information settings** (Word 2010 General tab, Word 2011 User Information tab): These settings control how Word identifies you and distinguishes you from other reviewers of a manuscript. You can specify both your full name and your initials; when you hover the mouse cursor over an edit, Word will display your identifying information. (If Word doesn't display this information, select the Comments on rollover setting described earlier in this section.) In addition, this lets you edit your own revisions without tracking these modifications as additional changes. These settings also let you conceal your identity if you need to perform anonymous (*blind*) reviews. Finally, these settings define the creator information when you create a new document.

Word forgets who you are: Older versions of Word sometimes forget who you are, even though the User Information settings appear correct and you haven't changed them. If this bug bites, revising your own edits causes Word to track these changes as if someone else did the work rather than simply making the desired changes. To solve the problem, close all open files, retype your User Information settings *exactly* the way they originally appeared, and then close and restart Word. If that doesn't work, you can use the Compare Documents feature described in Chapter 6 to create a fresh copy of the file that contains all your edits.

- **Use smart cut and paste** (Word 2010 Advanced tab > Cut, copy, and paste section; Word 2011 Edit tab): Selecting this option then clicking the Settings button lets you customize how Word handles pasted text. For example, the Merge formatting option causes Word to apply the format of the surrounding text to the pasted text; another option automatically inserts a space between the original text and the pasted text.
- **When selecting, automatically select entire word** (Windows Advanced tab > Editing tab, Word 2011 Edit tab): When selected, this option causes Word to automatically select an entire word rather than individual letters. If you prefer to select and modify only parts of words, deselect this option.

- **Wrap to window (text wrap)** (Windows Advanced tab > Show document content, Word 2011 View tab): In Normal, Web, and Outline views, this option forces the text to reflow onto a new line as you resize the document window; as a result, the text remains constantly visible rather than disappearing beyond the right edge of the window. This option isn't available in Page Layout mode, where you must be able to see the actual line breaks.

Predefined display (view) modes

Most software offers at least a *page layout* view that simulates what the printed page will look like, plus a *normal* or *draft* view that focuses on the content rather than its layout. Word offers several display modes to meet your needs. (I won't discuss Notebook view, as this will rarely be used in onscreen editing.) Try each mode on your computer to find the ones that work best for you in different editing situations. To switch among these view modes, select the Ribbon's View tab (Windows) or open the View menu (Macintosh):

Draft (formerly, "Normal") view

In this mode, Word displays the text using only the basic formatting that applies to words (e.g., boldface), sentences (e.g., indents), and paragraphs (e.g., spaces before and after paragraphs), but not formatting that applies to the page as a whole (e.g., headers and footers, margins). Although this mode gives only a basic impression of what the actual page or screen will look like, it's flexible and easy to use for editing.

Print Layout view

In this mode, Word provides a good simulation of what the document will look like when you print it: all headers and footers, margins, line and page breaks, and other layout characteristics will be clearly visible and should be nearly identical to what you see on paper. If you need to edit the document's layout as well as its content, such as when you're shortening a manuscript to fit within a specified amount of space, choose this mode.

Web Layout (formerly, "Online") view

In this mode, Word simulates what the file will look like if you save it in HTML format, as if you were using Word to create a Web page. Word is *not* a good HTML editor or Web-authoring tool, so it doesn't do a great job; if you need to create Web pages and see what the pages will really look like, you're better off using a dedicated tool such as Dreamweaver and opening the pages in a Web browser. But if you don't want to constantly switch back and forth between Word, Web authoring software, and a browser while editing, this mode offers a reasonable compromise. Because this view does not include headers and footers and wraps the text to fit as you resize the document window, it provides a clean and uncluttered display that is highly suitable for editing.

Editing Web pages in Word: If you need to edit Web pages using revision tracking, you can (generally) accomplish this in Word. See Chapter 12 for details.

Outline view

Outline view mode is one of Word's hidden gems. A common criticism of onscreen editing is that it prevents you from seeing the structure of a document, but in Outline view, Word displays only the heading levels that you tell it to display. This screen provides access to a powerful toolbar; for details on how to use it to display and revise a document's structure, see this chapter's Web page. In summary, you can expand the outline to show more levels of heading, right down to the level of body text; you can collapse the outline to show fewer levels; or you can choose to show only specific levels (e.g., just the level 1 headings). If a section's level in the hierarchy must be changed, you can promote that section (e.g., change a level 2 heading to level 1) or demote that section (e.g., change a level 3 heading to body text). You can also expand or collapse the view of the sections beneath a specific heading by clicking the [+] and [–] icons, respectively, that appear to the left of the headings. This provides a clear and customizable view of a document's structure. In addition, it's very helpful if you're responsible for ensuring that each heading has been formatted using the correct style, verifying the consistency of capitalization, and so on.

For these features to work, the author must have created the heading structure using paragraph styles (e.g., with Heading 2 subordinate to Heading 1); the toolbar features won't work if the author created headings by (for example) manually boldfacing and centering the heading text because Word will not recognize these formats as a heading structure. For more information on styles, see *A Primer on Styles and Templates* later in this chapter.

Positions of styles in the hierarchy: To define where a paragraph style will appear within the outline view, edit the corresponding style definition. (See *A Primer on Styles and Templates* later in this chapter for details on how to edit styles.) The specific style characteristic to change is the Outline level.

If you decide a different order would be more effective, outline view lets you rearrange the text to produce a more logical and effective sequence by moving entire sections into new positions using the toolbar's up and down arrows. Before doing so, turn off revision tracking (see Chapter 6 for details) so that the movements won't be tracked as a single large change; when you're done, turn on revision tracking again and insert a comment to explain what you've done and why.

To move the entire section below a heading along with the heading, collapse the hierarchy (using the Collapse button in the toolbar or clicking the [-] that appears beside the heading) so that only that section's heading is visible; when you move the heading, all its subordinate sections will then move with it. This is far easier and less error-prone than trying to cut out a long section without missing anything and then pasting it into the desired new location.

If you move something and don't like the result, you can undo the move (Control+Z for Windows; Command+Z for the Macintosh). Alternatively, use the toolbar icon that performs the opposite action to the move you just performed. For example, the up arrow undoes moves performed using the down arrow, and vice versa.

Document Map view

This view resembles the Outline view, but displays the heading structure on the left and the document itself in a pane to the right side of that structure. The document map can be combined with any of the other view modes, including Outline mode. The headings at the left represent the map, and clicking any heading takes you to that part of the document. You can collapse and expand parts of the map by clicking the arrows beside the headings—without affecting the display of the full document on the right side of the screen. To turn the document map on or off:

- **Word 2010:** Ribbon > View tab > Navigation pane checkbox. Then click the leftmost icon, which has the tooltip Browse the headings in your document
- **Word 2011:** View menu> Sidebar submenu > Document Map pane

Master Document view

Word provides a Master Document feature that's intended to let you use a single "master" document to control formatting and other aspects of a series of subordinate documents, such as the chapters of a book. Unfortunately, this feature has a reputation for being unreliable and having a high risk of damaging documents beyond the possibility of recovery. Few people seem able to use Master Documents successfully (i.e., without damaging files and losing hours or weeks of work), and those who do can't explain why everyone else is having so much trouble. To be safe, I recommend that you avoid using this feature—in which case, you won't need this view mode.

Full Screen view

The Full Screen Reading option (Windows View tab) and Enter full screen view option (under the Macintosh View menu) greatly simplify the screen display, thereby offering more space and less visual distraction while editing. (It would be particularly useful on a laptop computer.) For Windows (but not the Macintosh), this option hides the Ribbon and leaves only the menu bar and window title visible at the top of the screen, with the text immediately below it. (To return to the previous view mode that you were using, simply press the Esc key.)

Working With Document Windows

Editors tend to work with several programs simultaneously, often with several windows or documents open in each program. As a result, it's important to learn how to work within, arrange, and move between multiple windows and how to move between programs on your computer. The most useful things to know are how to:

- Make text more legible by increasing its size without changing the font.
- Juggle windows to keep two or more windows open and visible simultaneously.
- Resize and reposition windows manually or automatically to fit your changing needs (e.g., to focus on a single document or to compare two documents).
- Switch quickly between programs and between the windows that are open within a given program.
- Split a document window or open a new window into a document to display different parts of that document simultaneously.

Making text more legible

Authors often use a monitor size or resolution that differs from those we're using, or have unusual text preferences that make their text an uncomfortable size or difficult to read on our computer. Fortunately, there are many things we can do to make the text more readable without creating any problems or additional work for the authors. It may also be helpful to fit more or less information on the screen simultaneously, particularly when we're trying to reduce the text length to fit within a given area and would benefit from ongoing visual feedback on our progress as we edit.

Zoom in

First, and easiest, we can change the magnification of the text. Most word processors offer a zoom (magnifier) tool, under the View menu or in the Ribbon's View tab. In addition to predefined magnification levels such as 50%, 100%, and 200%, some software (including Word) lets you enter a numerical value for the amount of enlargement or reduction. This change has no effect on the text properties (i.e., it does not change the actual font size), so it's a particularly good choice if the manuscript has already been partially or fully formatted before publication.

Not sure how much to zoom? If you have a mouse or other pointing device with a scroll wheel, hold down the Control key and rotate the scroll wheel to zoom in or out. This won't work in every program, but works in all current versions of Word. On a Macintosh, you can add this feature to most programs via the Accessibility control panel. Select the Zoom group of settings, then select the checkbox for Use scroll gesture with modifier keys to zoom. You can also define which keyboard shortcuts should be used to zoom.

Change the font characteristics

Your second option is to override the author's choice of font and type size. You can change both attributes temporarily, for the duration of the edit, or permanently if you're responsible for reformatting the document to meet a publisher's requirements. Where appropriate, ask the author for permission to permanently use a more suitable font; for example, many of my Asian authors use fonts that are only available to Asian readers, so (with permission) I change their text to one of the Windows and Macintosh core fonts, such as Times New Roman. Since many publishers formally require a specific font during the review process, you can generally persuade authors to accept such changes.

Beware special characters: If a manuscript contains special characters, such as non-English letters or math symbols, don't change the fonts without looking for potential problems. Correctly entered characters will remain correct if the new font includes them, but authors often insert special characters in ways that cause them to change when the font changes. Re-insert those characters correctly before you change the font. See Chapter 8 for tips on how to do this easily.

If you need to change the font and text size, you have two alternatives:

- Turn off revision tracking, record the font characteristics used in each paragraph and character style, then edit these definitions to use a more legible font and type size. When you finish editing, turn off revision tracking and restore the original font and font size for each style.
- Leave revision tracking on, then select the text in each section and manually change the font and size from the Ribbon's **Format** tab (Word 2010) or the **Format** menu (Word 2011). When you finish editing, restore the original characteristics by rejecting these format changes. (See Chapter 6 for details.)

The second option is easier, particularly if you set revision tracking to show only format changes (see Chapter 6 for details). If the only problem is the size of the text, not the typeface, Word offers an efficient alternative:

- Select the text you want to enlarge or reduce. (See Chapter 5 for a discussion of various ways to select text. To select the entire document, press Control+A for Windows or Command+A for the Macintosh.)
- Turn off track changes, then repeatedly press the keyboard shortcut that increases the font size (Control+Shift+> for Windows and Command+Shift+> for the Macintosh) until the text is easy to read.
- Turn on track changes and edit the document.
- When you're finished, turn off revision tracking and restore the original font sizes: select the text that you changed, and repeatedly press the keyboard shortcut to reduce the font size (Control+Shift+< for Windows and Command+Shift+< for the Macintosh) until you have restored the original size.

Juggling windows

For many editing tasks, it's helpful to keep multiple windows open simultaneously; for example, one window may contain the manuscript, a second may contain the style sheet you're using as a reference to impose consistency on that manuscript, and a third may contain a checklist of editorial tasks or client instructions. Resize these windows by moving the mouse cursor over one of the window's edges until it turns into a two-headed arrow, then hold down the mouse button and drag that border into a new position. To change the height and width simultaneously, click on and drag the resize tab at the bottom right of the window to create a diagonal double-headed cursor. To reposition a window, drag it by its title bar (the area at the top of the window that contains the document's name).

The more monitors, the better: Many editors find it helpful to add a second or even third monitor to their system to obtain more screen space. This lets you display different programs or different windows belonging to the same program on different monitors, saving many keystrokes per day by reducing the need to switch between programs or windows just to view their contents. The online help for your operating system will explain how to set up the monitors. Note that some CRT monitors must be widely separated because the magnetic fields they generate interfere with images on the adjacent monitor. (This is unlikely to be a problem with LCD monitors.)

If you have several documents open, you can ask Word to display all of them simultaneously so you won't have to manually resize and reposition each window. To accomplish this:

* **Word 2010:** Ribbon > View tab > Arrange All icon (formerly known as Tile documents) or View Side by Side icon
* **Word 2011:** Window menu > Arrange All

Arrange All resizes and rearranges the windows vertically into a series of non-overlapping windows. The Side by Side option (not available for the Macintosh) works better on the large, wide-screen monitors used by most editors. In either case, if you have many windows open, you'll have to resize them manually to accommodate the way you want to work. For example, when I'm checking literature citations, I position a narrow window that contains the reference list to the right of the wide document window so I can see at a glance (or with a little scrolling) whether a citation is correct. If you find that the text in one or more windows is too small for easy viewing at the window's new size, simply change the zoom (magnification) setting for that window, as described earlier in this section.

Displaying many pages simultaneously: Word's zoom feature lets you display multiple pages simultaneously if you need to examine facing pages or overall layouts. To do so, switch to Print Layout view, and choose a zoom percentage (e.g., 30%) small enough to fit the desired number of pages on the screen. To return to displaying only a single page, choose a zoom percentage of 100% or more.

In both Windows and the Macintosh, you can switch between open windows without using the mouse. In Word, for example, you can use the software's built-in window-switcher:

- **Windows:** Alt+Tab or Ribbon > View tab > Switch Windows icon
- **Macintosh:** Command+F6 or Command+` (the latter symbol is the accent on the key below the Esc key, beside the ~ character).

These keystrokes let you switch consecutively between windows without taking your hands off the keyboard, which is faster. However, you can also do this with the mouse; for Windows, click the Switch Windows icon and choose the desired window; for the Macintosh, choose the desired window under the Window menu.

Sometimes you may want to examine two parts of a single file simultaneously, such as when you're checking literature citations against the bibliography or confirming that certain jargon words have been defined in a glossary at the end of the document. A simple solution is to create a temporary working copy of that part of the file so you can position it beside the main document window. For example, I use this approach when I check literature citations.

If you don't want to open a new document, Word offers a neat trick: it can split the current document window into two *panes*, one above the other:

- **Word 2010:** Ribbon > View tab > click the Split icon. From the keyboard, press Control+Alt+S.
- **Word 2011:** Window menu > Split. From the keyboard, press Command+Option+S.

Once the window has been split into two panes, you can scroll each pane independently to display different parts of the document, and you can magnify each pane independently. Move the cursor between panes with the click of a mouse; the F6 keyboard shortcut may also work if it has not been reassigned to a different function by your operating system. To resize the panes, simply drag the bar that marks the split.

To restore the window to a single pane, repeat the keyboard shortcut, drag the split bar all the way to the top or bottom of one pane, or click the Remove split icon in the Ribbon's View tab (Word 2010) or open the Window menu and select Remove Split (Word 2011).

What a pane! Word can only display two panes simultaneously for any window. Thus, if you open the Reviewing pane (see Chapter 6 for details) in a window that's already split into panes, the pane that does not currently contain the cursor will close, and when you close the Reviewing pane you'll return to a standard, single-pane window.

Switching between programs

It's often useful to switch between programs while you're editing. For example, while I was revising this book, I opened the book file in InDesign and switched back and forth repeatedly between the book and the Windows and Macintosh versions of Word so that I could update my description of how feature names and locations changed; I also switched to my Web browser repeatedly when I couldn't figure out where Microsoft had moved a feature and I needed to consult the Web.

Both Windows and the Macintosh display icons for all open programs so that you can switch between them using the mouse; for Windows, they appear in the status bar at the bottom of the screen; for the Macintosh, they appear in the Dock. However, it's faster to switch without taking your hands off the keyboard:

- **Windows:** Press Alt+Tab.
- **Macintosh:** Press Command+Tab.

Press these keys repeatedly until you reach the desired program or window. Simultaneously holding down the Shift key reverses the direction of travel through the list of programs or windows. Release all of these keys when you reach the desired program.

Toolbars and the Ribbon

In previous versions of Word, Microsoft implemented a powerful option: the ability to create and display custom toolbars that you could populate with specific sets of functions to support specific writing or editing tasks. Better still, you could drag the toolbars to convenient locations around the screen, thereby transforming them into floating tool palettes. In the most recent versions of Word for Windows, Microsoft replaced these toolbars with a single Quick Access Toolbar. However, you can regain much of the functionality of the old toolbars and some new flexibility by adding new tabs to the Ribbon. Although you can't reposition these tabs to create free-floating palettes, the ability to create groups of commands within a tab compensates slightly for this loss of freedom.

Still using an older version of Windows Word? If you're still using an older version of Word that supports toolbars, you'll need to consult Chapter 4 in the second edition of this book. Contact me to request a copy.

In the rest of this section, I'll provide specific examples of how Word implements the Quick Access Toolbar for Windows, how it implements traditional toolbars for the Macintosh, how you can customize both types of toolbar, and how you can modify the Ribbon to achieve functionality similar to that of traditional toolbars.

Word 2010's Quick Access toolbar

The Quick Access toolbar is the row of icons visible above the Ribbon. If you have not yet modified it, it contains only three icons: one for saving documents, one for undoing changes, and one for repeating changes. To change its location, right-click or control-click in the toolbar, and select Show Quick Access Toolbar Below [or Above] the Ribbon. You cannot entirely eliminate this toolbar, but in its basic form, it doesn't take much space. Moreover, because you can use it to provide access to functions buried several levels deep in the software, it can greatly speed up access to these features.

Moving the Quick Access toolbar to a new computer: See the section on templates later in this chapter for instructions.

To customize the toolbar's contents, right-click or control-click on the toolbar and select Customize Quick Access Toolbar; you can also access these functions from the Options dialog box. Word displays a dialog box that provides access to all commands built into Word, plus any new commands (e.g., macros) you've created. You can now modify the toolbar's contents by selecting commands at the left side of the dialog box and clicking the Add button or commands on the right and clicking the Remove button to (respectively) add them to or remove them from the toolbar. Once commands have been added, you can select them and click the up or down arrows to change their positions within the toolbar.

Clarifying icons: Toolbar icons are cryptic and hard to recognize (particularly those for macros). To learn an icon's function, hold the mouse cursor above the icon to display a tooltip. You can change both the icon and the tooltip by right-clicking or control-clicking the toolbar and selecting Customize the Quick Access Toolbar. The right side of the dialog box lists the commands in the toolbar. Select the one you want to modify, click the Modify button below the list, then choose a more memorable icon or clearer text for the tooltip.

To find specific commands, open the menu labeled Choose commands from and select the appropriate category. Commands not in the Ribbon and Macros are two particularly useful categories. The All commands category provides access to the complete list of Word's built-in commands if your research reveals the name of a command but you can't figure out the category it belongs to.

At the top right of the dialog box, choose which files this toolbar should be associated with. The default is for all documents, but you can also create custom toolbars that are only available in specific documents or in all documents based on a specific template. (I'll discuss templates later in this chapter.) Toolbars created for a specific file are only available in that file, but toolbars created for a template are available for all files based on that template.

Customized destruction: Older versions of Word included the command ToolsCustomizeRemoveMenuShortcut, which was triggered if you pressed Control+Alt+Hyphen (Windows) or Command+Option+Hyphen (Macintosh). The cursor changed to an easy-to-miss thick − (minus sign) to warn you that you were about to "subtract" (delete) the next menu item or toolbar icon you clicked. Given the potential for mayhem, it's wise to disable this command. See the section *Keyboard shortcuts* later in this chapter for details of how to find and disable this command.

Word 2011's toolbars

Word's traditional toolbars are still available for the Macintosh. To manage them: View menu > Toolbars > Customize Toolbars and Menus. Select the Toolbars and Menus tab if it isn't already selected. From this dialog box, you can create new toolbars, decide which toolbars to display, and rename, modify, or delete previously defined toolbars. Word 2011's toolbars provide quick access to commands that might otherwise be difficult to access (e.g., commands buried deep in the software's interface). In addition, you can choose which of the available toolbars (if any) to display for support during a particular task. You can also change both their shape and their position; that is, you can transform them into tool palettes by dragging the bottom right corner of the toolbar (just like changing the size of a manuscript window) and can drag the resulting palette to any convenient position on the screen.

To create a new toolbar, start by deciding where you want it to be available. The default is Normal.dotm (i.e., the normal template, which I'll discuss later in this chapter), in which case the toolbar will be available in all Word files on your computer. Alternatively, open the Save in menu, which is at the bottom of the dialog box, and choose the currently open document; the toolbar will henceforth be available only in that document. To make a toolbar available to all documents based on a specific template, open that template before you create the new toolbar, and select the template's name from the Save in menu. Next, click the New button and give the toolbar a memorable name. Unfortunately, there's a small problem: the new toolbar is only one icon wide, and may appear at an obscure location on the screen; as a result, you need sharp eyes to find it.

Moving toolbars to a new computer: See the section on templates later in this chapter for instructions.

Once you've found the new toolbar, you can customize its contents by selecting the Commands tab of the dialog box, navigating to a desirable command, and then dragging it into the toolbar. As long as the dialog box is open, you can also drag a command within the toolbar to change its position or drag a command out of the toolbar if you no longer need it. To change how a command appears in the toolbar, right-click or control-click the command and select Properties from the popup menu. You can now edit the name that appears in the toolbar. Below that field, the menu labeled View lets you define whether the toolbar should display an icon, text, or both for the command. If the command is associated with an icon, that icon will be available for display; unfortunately, you can't choose new icons or add an icon if none was provided for that command.

Displaying or concealing toolbars: To display a toolbar or hide it once you no longer need it, open the Customize dialog box (as described above), then select or deselect the toolbar name, respectively.

Customizing the Ribbon

In Word 2011, it's not currently possible to customize the Ribbon's contents. To emulate this customization, you'll need to create and customize traditional toolbars, as I described in the previous section. However, in Word 2010, you can customize the Ribbon by choosing which tabs to display and by adding new tabs for specific purposes (e.g., editing versus proofreading). To customize the Ribbon, right-click or control-click the Ribbon and then select Customize Ribbon. From within the Customize the Ribbon dialog box, you can create custom tabs and custom groups within these tabs to provide collections of tools that meet your specific needs. You cannot remove the built-in tabs from the Ribbon, though you can remove groups from within these tabs to reduce the visual clutter and leave more room for the functions that are most important to you.

The Ribbon's hierarchy: Commands in the Ribbon are organized into groups that represent similar types of function (e.g., table formatting), and groups are organized into tabs (e.g., Tables) that represent collections of related groups.

To create a new tab, click the New tab button; to name or rename the tab, select it and click the Rename button. The tab name appears at the top of the tab. When you create a tab, Word adds a single command group and you can add more by clicking the New Group button; the group names appear at the bottom of the Ribbon, and describe the shared characteristics of the functions that belong to that group. (Note that a tab must contain at least one group before you can add commands to the tab.) You can rename a group by selecting it within the Customize the Ribbon dialog box and clicking the Rename button.

To add new commands to a group, start by selecting the group name at the right side of the dialog box. You can then scroll through the list of commands at the left side of the dialog box. When you find the desired command, select its name and then click the Add button. To change the order of tabs within the Ribbon, groups within a tab, and commands within a group, select the item that you want to move at the right side of the dialog box and then click the up or down arrows to move it (respectively) up or down in the list.

Damaged the Ribbon beyond repair? If you remove too many commands from the Ribbon and need to start over, you can restore the original commands by clicking the Reset button in this dialog box. You can reset individual tabs, or the whole Ribbon.

If you can't see the groups and commands stored in a tab or the commands stored with a group, click the [+] icon beside its name to show these details. To collapse the display and show only the highest levels of the hierarchy, click the [-] icons. To remove a custom tab, a group, or a function when you no longer need it, select its name at the right side of the dialog box and then click the Remove button.

> **Moving your Ribbon and Quick Access toolbar to another computer (Word 2010):** Ribbon > File menu > Options > Customize Ribbon tab. At the bottom right of the dialog box, click the Import/Export button and select Export all customizations to create a file that you can transfer to another computer; conversely, click Import customization file to replace your Ribbon and Quick Access toolbar with versions exported from another computer. If you want to preserve your settings, export them first and keep a copy of that file somewhere safe so you can import it again later.

Menus

In Word 2010, you can no longer customize the software's menus. There's a simple reason: the menus were removed from the software. However, in Word 2011, the software's menus are still present, so you can customize them. To do so: View menu > Toolbars > Customize Toolbars and Menus. Note that Word will display a small, easy-to-miss toolbar containing the menu names and contents below the standard menu bar at the top of the screen. All changes to your menus must be made by working within this small toolbar.

> **Damaged the menus beyond repair?** If you remove too many commands from the menus, you can restore the menus to their original condition by clicking the Reset button in this dialog box.

The Save in menu at the bottom of the dialog box lets you select which file or template should store your changes. Menu changes that are stored in a specific file will only affect that file; changes stored in a template become available to all files that are based on that template. Changing menus in Normal makes the changes available in all Word documents on your computer. If you want to affect all files based on a specific template, open that template before you open this dialog box. This makes the template itself available for modification.

Once you've chosen the file or template that will store your revised menus, you can begin modifying the menus:

- **To add a function:** Select the Commands tab in the dialog box, select the category of command under the heading Categories, and then navigate to the desired command under the heading Commands. Drag that command on top of the menu that will hold the new command; when the menu opens, drag the command to the desired position and release the mouse button.
- **To remove a function from a menu:** Open the menu in the toolbar, then hold down the left mouse button on the command, drag the command out of the menu, and then release the button.
- **To change the positions of functions within a menu:** Open the menu in the toolbar, hold down the left mouse button on the command, drag the command to its new position in the menu, and then release the button.
- **To rename a menu command or change how it is displayed:** Open the menu from the toolbar, then right-click on the command and choose Properties from the resulting menu.
- **To create your own custom menus:** Select the Commands tab in the dialog box, then under the heading Categories, scroll down until you see the option New Menu. Drag this option into the desired position in the toolbar that contains the menus, and then right-click on the menu name and rename it.
- **To add duplicate copies of existing menus:** Scroll down through the categories until you find Built-in Menus, then drag the menu into the toolbar that contains the menus.

Keyboard Shortcuts

Try the keyboard instead: Although you can use either the mouse or the keyboard for many Word functions, keyboard shortcuts are often most efficient, particularly when you're editing. Learning the existing shortcuts and creating new ones will make your editing more efficient. For example, Chapter 5 describes many efficient ways to move around a document and select text without using the mouse.

If you prefer to keep your fingers on the keyboard as much as possible, menus and toolbars pose a challenge. Fortunately, you can generally avoid the menus in all versions of Word by learning the existing keyboard shortcuts or creating new ones.

Navigating menus from the keyboard

The first and most broadly applicable set of keyboard shortcuts lets you use the keyboard to navigate between and within the menus and tabs of the Ribbon. This is easiest for Windows, where you can access any menu (including most menus in dialog boxes) or any tab in the Ribbon by pressing and releasing the Alt key. Doing so displays a letter beside the menu or tab name, and pressing that letter will move you to that menu or tab and display the names of its contents, with underlined letters for each item. (There are some exceptions, such as the Options dialog box; the keyboard shortcuts still work, but Word doesn't display the letters associated with them. Thus, you have to guess at what letters to use.) Pressing the underlined letter in a command name executes that command; pressing the letter for a menu opens the menu and displays new letters for all of its options. For example, Alt followed by F will select and open the File menu; pressing A will then open the Save As dialog box. Press the Esc key to cancel this function.

The Macintosh offers similar functionality; pressing Control+F2 will highlight the Apple menu, and you can use the left and right arrow keys to navigate between menus. Typing the first letter or letters of a menu name will move the highlight to that menu; you can then press the down arrow to open the menu and repeat this process or use the arrow keys to navigate among the commands. Unfortunately, the Macintosh does not display the letters you should type for each menu or command, so it's a bit of a guessing game if you want to reach the desired command without using the arrow keys.

> **Function keys stop working?** Many keyboards have a *function lock* (F Lock or FnLock) key at the end of the row of function keys (F1 to F12), at the top of the keyboard. If these keys stop working as expected, try pressing the function lock key; you may have pressed it accidentally, thereby disabling the function keys.

If Control+F2 doesn't strike you as particularly memorable: open System Preferences > Keyboard tab > Shortcuts tab > then select Keyboard in the list of categories at the left of the screen. In the list of commands, select the keyboard command to the right of Move focus to the menu bar, press the new shortcut, and then press Enter to complete the process. (I use F1, which I don't use for other functions, because this eliminates the need to hold down the Control key.) For example, F1 followed by F now selects the File menu. Press the same keyboard shortcut or the Esc key to cancel this function.

Learning, creating, and modifying keyboard shortcuts

Although navigating menus from the keyboard works well for infrequently used commands, it's less efficient than executing a command directly in a single keystroke. Word 2010 does not provide menus in most parts of its interface, but Word 2011 retains the old menus and displays keyboard shortcuts beside the command names. Thus, you can learn these shortcuts just by inspecting the menus. In both versions, you can learn the keyboard shortcut for any command, including obscure ones that are not present in the ribbon or menus, by taking advantage of a convenient feature provided by Word: the ability to assign keyboard shortcuts to any function the software can perform. (This is particularly useful when Microsoft's shortcut makes no sense to you or is hard to remember.) To access the dialog box that lets you modify existing keyboard shortcuts or create new ones:

- **Word 2010:** Ribbon > File menu > Options > Customize tab > click the Customize button beside Keyboard shortcuts.
- **Word 2011:** Tools menu > Customize Keyboard.

Displaying keyboard shortcuts for icons: Word offers the option Show shortcut keys in Screentips so that you can display the shortcuts when you hover the mouse cursor over an icon. To find this setting in Word 2010: Ribbon > File menu > Options > Advanced tab > scroll down to the Display group of options. In Word 2011: View menu > Toolbars > Customize Toolbars and Menus.

The rest of the procedure for learning, creating, and modifying keyboard shortcuts is the same for the Windows and Macintosh versions of Word. In the Customize Keyboard dialog box:

- **Choose where to store the shortcuts:** At the bottom of the dialog box, open the menu beside Save changes in: and select which template or which open document should store your changes. Select Normal if you want the changes to be available in all files on your computer.
- **Choose the category and command:** At the left side of this dialog box, under the heading Categories, Word lists all its Ribbon tabs, menus, and other useful categories such as Macros. When you select a

category, Word lists the commands in that category at the right side of the dialog box under the heading Commands. If you can't find a particular command, select the category All commands and scroll through the list of commands.

> **Finding Word commands:** Since you need to be able to discover the name of a command before you can customize it, the kind folks at Office Watch have provided a convenient reference: the "Word 2010 command finder". This should also be useful for previous and subsequent versions of Word, since the command names rarely change.

- **Modify the command's shortcut:** Select the command you want to modify. Under the heading Current keys, Word displays all keyboard shortcuts assigned to that command. To remove a shortcut (e.g., if you frequently trigger it accidentally), select the shortcut and click the Remove button. To add a shortcut, position the cursor in the field labeled Press new shortcut key (Word 2010) or Press new keyboard shortcut (Word 2011), then press the new keyboard shortcut. Shortcuts can combine the Shift, Control, and Alt keys (all versions of Word) or the Shift, Command, and Option keys (Macintosh), plus most other keys on the keyboard. Word won't let you use letters or numbers by themselves; after all, you might want to type those characters someday. It's generally unwise to use only Alt plus a letter, since many of these combinations are already used to access menu items. If your new shortcut has been assigned to another command, Word will display that command's name and give you a chance to change your mind; press the Backspace key to delete the shortcut. Click the Assign button if you want to save the new shortcut.

> **Learning what a keystroke does:** Open the Customize keyboard dialog box, select any command, and type the mysterious shortcut into the Press new shortcut key field. Word will tell you what command, if any, that shortcut executes. Delete the new shortcut from this field to avoid linking it to the command you selected.

- **Restoring the old shortcuts:** If you customize your keyboard to the point at which it becomes unusable, you can restore the original settings by clicking the Reset All button.

How can you remember shortcuts? Make them memorable using memory aids such as the notion that the Control key *controls* how the software functions, the Alt key *alters* how something behaves, the Option key specifies an *optional* behavior, and the Shift key *shifts* things around. Appendix IV summarizes the most commonly useful shortcuts. Even if you pick a memorable shortcut, it can be difficult remembering it until you've used the shortcut so often that your fingers remember the keystrokes for you. Although you can search the Customize Keyboard dialog box for the shortcuts each time you forget them, there are better alternatives. First, record a list of your customizations in a Word document; you can leave that document open as you work, print a copy and place it beside your computer, or read through the document periodically to refresh your memory. This approach lets you arrange the shortcuts in any order and format that makes sense to you, and you can use Word's search tools to find names in this list. Second, Word can create a list of all keyboard shortcuts for you. To do so:

- **Word 2010:** Ribbon > View tab > Macros icon > View Macros
- **Word 2011:** Tools menu > Macros > Macro
- In both versions of Word, open the menu labeled Macros in, select Word commands, and then scroll down to and select the macro List-Commands. Click the Run button to generate the list. Word offers the option of saving this as a file. That's the best bet because the list is long and it's very helpful to be able to search through the list. Save this file somewhere logical and modify it in a way that helps you find commands, or rely on the search function to find them.

Customizations disappeared? Unless you specify a different file, Word stores customizations in your Normal.dotm template. If you set Word to ask you to confirm changes to this template, it's easy to forget to accept changes to the template when you quit Word. For templates shared over a network, network administrators sometimes block changes to group templates to prevent conflicting changes. The easiest solution is to create a new template to store your customizations and use that template to create new documents. If you don't share templates, *open* Normal.dotm (instead of creating a new file based on that template), make the necessary setting changes, then save the file as a template (.dotm file), with the same name and location. Buggy add-ins (programs that enhance Word's functionality) can also interfere with Word's behavior. If the problem began after you installed a new add-in, contact the developer to request assistance.

A Primer on Styles and Templates

Mastering styles and templates: If you need to thoroughly understand this subject, consult Jack Lyon's *Microsoft Word for Publishing Professionals*. Details are provided in the Bibliography.

One editorial responsibility is to impose consistency on document formatting, whether by tagging text using special codes defined by a publisher or by applying the paragraph and character styles defined in a particular document template. (I'll discuss how style sheets can be used to support this process in Chapter 9.) Performing this aspect of onscreen editing requires a basic knowledge of how styles function in Word and how Word uses templates to organize and apply collections of styles. In this section, I'll summarize the aspects of styles and templates most directly related to editing. Other word processors work similarly.

Styles

In the parlance of word processors, a *style* represents a collection of predefined rules for how to format a chunk of text. By gathering all the necessary settings into a single style, the software lets you apply them all in a single step, rather than having to apply them individually to each word, line, or paragraph that requires those formats. Better still, when you revise the style's properties, the change is automatically applied to all text that was formatted using that style. When correctly used, styles are a powerful tool for imposing consistency on documents; for example, all headings can be formatted consistently using heading styles. Styles are most often managed by storing them in templates, which I'll describe in the next section. Word's styles let you define the following aspects of text:

- **Typography:** the typeface, font size, justification (e.g., ragged right), emphasis (e.g., boldface), spacing (within and between words, sentences, and paragraphs), and indentation (including tab settings).
- **Borders and shading:** ornamentation such as lines on any side of the text, or colors used to provide a backdrop for the text.
- **Language:** the primary dictionary that will be used for spellchecks. (See Chapter 10 for details of spellcheck languages.)
- **Numbering and bullets:** the symbol and style of the number or bullet that should be used for each level of heading or item in a list.

Word provides *paragraph* styles, which govern the appearance of entire paragraphs of text, and *character* styles, which govern individual characters, words, or sentences within a paragraph. In Word, a paragraph is defined as the text between two carriage returns (that is, a block of text that ends when you press the Enter or Return key), not in its grammatical sense. Thus, from Word's perspective, paragraphs can range from one-line sentence fragments to page-long collections of unstructured notes. Character styles apply exclusively to parts of a paragraph whose formatting with respect to the page has already been defined using a paragraph style, so character styles cannot override indents and other spatial characteristics of the surrounding paragraph. Instead, they can do useful things such as changing the font and language for a word or phrase; for example, you could create a character style called *Greek words* to format Greek words using a font that contains Greek letters and use a Greek spelling dictionary (rather than the English dictionary used for the surrounding paragraph).

During editing, our main style-related role will typically be to apply or reapply styles following client guidelines. For example, authors often create headings by manually increasing the font size and boldfacing the text instead of applying the correct heading paragraph style or they may apply the wrong heading style instead of the one specified by the publisher. As a result, formats vary widely throughout the document, making the document appear self-inconsistent or inconsistently different from other documents in a series (e.g., annual reports) or in a volume (e.g., the chapters in a book). As well, substantive editing often reveals that a document's organization is ineffective, and that it's necessary to add or remove headings or change the levels of certain headings to create a more effective structure. (See the discussion earlier in this chapter on the Outline and Document Map view modes for tips on how to display this structure and revise it more efficiently.)

If you're responsible for ensuring that the correct paragraph styles have been applied to each heading and paragraph, it's helpful to be able to control which style names Word displays. The easiest way to see which styles have been used is to set Word to display its style area, as described earlier in this chapter under the heading *Details of Word's main settings*. Alternatively, you can display the Styles palette:

- **Word 2010:** Ribbon > Home tab > click the icon below Change Styles (or press the shortcut Control+Alt+Shift+S). To control which styles should be displayed and in which order, click the Options button at the bottom of the palette.

- **Word 2011:** View menu > Toolbox heading > Styles. To determine which styles should be displayed, select one of the options in the List menu at the bottom of the dialog box.

As you scroll the cursor through the text, this palette (toolbox) highlights the style that has been applied to the text at the cursor position.

To apply a paragraph style in Word, position the text cursor in that paragraph, then select the desired style from the Style palette (toolbox). To apply a character style to part of a paragraph, select the text and then apply the new style. (See Chapter 5 for details on efficiently selecting text.)

> **More consistency:** For an overview of other forms of consistency, and the relevant word processor tools you can use to improve consistency, consult Chapters 8 and 9.

Preserving manually applied formatting

Word has a style-related quirk that's puzzling until you understand what's happening: applying a style to selected text may not change all of that text to use the new style. This is because Word correctly assumes that you want to preserve any manually applied formatting such as boldface that overrides the paragraph or character style originally applied to that text. (For example, it would be annoying and time-consuming if you had to reapply italics to all italicized words throughout a long manuscript each time you modified a paragraph style.) As a result, applying a new style won't remove this manual formatting. Unfortunately, this also means that applying new styles throughout a manuscript won't apply those styles to all parts of each paragraph, and will leave many inconsistencies. The easiest way to eliminate manually applied formatting and restore the underlying style properties is to select the text and press Control+Spacebar; alternatively, you can use Control+Shift+Z (Windows) or Command+Shift+Z (Macintosh) to remove the formatting. Note that in the Styles palette (toolbox), clicking Clear formatting and Clear all will remove all formatting and apply the Normal style if you don't select the formatted text first.

To edit the properties of any paragraph or character style in the Styles palette (toolbox), right-click the style name (Windows) or click the paragraph style (¶) or character style (**a**) indicator to the right of the style name (Macintosh), and select Modify from the menu that appears. Any changes will only affect the current document. Don't click the style name with the left mouse button; that will apply the style to the selected text.

Templates

In Word, the styles that are available for use in a given document can be found in three main places:

- Styles defined only within the current document are *local* styles.
- Styles gathered together for reuse in other documents are stored in a *template*. If the styles in that template are available for use in any document on your computer, the template is referred to as a *global* template.
- Templates can also be *attached* to specific documents, in which case only those documents can use the template's styles. *Attached* is a misleading term, because the template is not physically attached to the document. Thus, if you want to send a file and its attached template to a client, you must remember to send the template file too; it won't be sent automatically along with the file controlled by that template.
- Word templates only define the styles that are available when you create a new document using that template; the template file is no longer required once you start working on the new document. Thereafter, the file is largely independent of the template, so if you move it to another computer, the link to the original template is broken but the styles established when you created the document remain in the document.

Macintosh template problems: The OS X operating system uses a complex system of permissions to control the right to change files, and this system sometimes gets confused. If you can't save changes to Normal.dotm, select the file in the Finder and press Command+I. In the Sharing and Permissions section of the resulting dialog box, ensure that you have Read & Write permissions. A bug in Word sometimes causes it to ask whether you want to save changes to Normal. dotm when you quit the program; if you have not made any changes to the settings, click the Don't Save button.

Word's template files have the extension .dot (before Word 2007) or .dotm (Word 2007 and later) added to their names. (An older .dotx format was used for Word 2008 files, which could not include macros.) Normal.dotm is the most familiar global template; a version of this template is present on any computer that has Word installed, and if you delete this file, Word automatically recreates it. In addition to containing groups of styles, Word's templates define the layout (e.g., page size, orientation, and margins); they can also contain custom toolbars (Macintosh) or Quick Access toolbars (Windows), and can store shortcuts such as macros and automatic text. (See Chapter 11 for details on both types of tool.) This lets you create optimized sets of tools for specific document types (e.g., annual reports) or editing tasks (e.g., copyediting versus proofreading).

Templates can also hold *boilerplate* text, such as standard copyright statements, that should appear in every new document based on the template. This concept deserves more attention, because judicious use of boilerplate text supports two editorial goals: to help authors write faster (because they don't need to type the boilerplate text) and to reduce the amount of editing required (because the boilerplate text has already been edited). A template that includes (for example) a complete outline of a typical document in a specific report series, with all the main headings correctly formatted and followed by concise descriptions of what information should be typed under each heading, helps the author to remember what information they must provide, and in what order, in each document and in each section of the document. This can reduce the amount of substantive editing required: if the author follows these instructions, all the required information will be present and in the right location. Because the template also formats this information using the correct styles, the author can concentrate on writing rather than on remembering the style specifications for that document, thereby reducing their formatting burden.

Transferring templates between Macintosh and Windows: Don't simply copy a Macintosh template file to a Windows computer or vice versa. In my experience, there are enough incompatibilities that this is asking for trouble. Instead, copy the file to the other computer and then use the tools for organizing templates to transfer styles, toolbars (Macintosh), and macros. For Windows, open the Styles palette (Control+Alt+Shift+S), click the Manage Styles button (the third icon from the left), and then click the Import/Export button. For the Macintosh, open the Format menu, select Style, then click the Organizer button. In both systems, select the source file on the left and the destination on the right; you can then select items and click the Copy button to add them to the destination file.

Templates can also improve collaboration with authors. For example, we can store useful toolbars and shortcuts such as macros and automatic text in the template. (See Chapter 11 for details.) Rather than having to recreate these tools for each document, we can create them once in the template and distribute that template, thereby making those tools instantly available. Moreover, we can enhance the template as we learn new tricks or create new tools, and these changes automatically become available for future manuscripts created using the template. Templates can also be linked to custom or third-party dictionaries, as described in Chapter 10. By defining different dictionary settings for different types of project, spellchecks become more efficient. For example, if you edit manuscripts in a specific subject with its own jargon (e.g., history), and don't want to include that jargon in your main dictionary, you could attach a custom dictionary that contains only the jargon for that subject to the appropriate template.

Templates can also contain built-in links to writing and editing resources such as style guides and instructions on the company network and clickable links to relevant Web or intranet sites. For example, one template I helped create for a former employer contained links to planning documents produced jointly by the author, their supervisor, and me (as the editor); these included an approved outline for the document, and a list of key criteria for the writer and editor to keep in mind while writing and revising the document, such as the intended audience and the communication goals. A toolbar in the template also provided one-click access to an online style guide, thereby encouraging authors to consult the most recent version of our style guide. Some aspects of the style guide, such as a list of standard disclaimers, were included in the template so the author did not have to type them and the editor did not have to edit them; others could be easily copied from the style guide and pasted into the document. Making all these tools available via the template created what I call a *dynamic* style guide; rather than being a static book that gathers dust on the editor's bookshelf, the dynamic style guide integrates with the way authors and editors actually work. For more details, see my article on dynamic style guides (included in the bibliography).

In addition to using templates to collaborate with your authors before they start writing, you can apply the correct template to a document that was created based on an incorrect or outdated template:

- **Word 2010:** Ribbon > File menu > Options > Add-ins tab. At the bottom of the dialog box, open the menu beside the heading Manage, select Templates, then click the Go button. You can now attach and detach templates.
- **Word 2011:** Tools menu > Templates and Add-ins. From this dialog box, you can attach and detach templates.

Loading documents and templates automatically

Word provides a *startup* folder in which you can store documents. Each time you start Word, the software automatically opens any document or template in that folder. To find this folder:

- **Word 2010:** Ribbon > File menu > Options >Advanced tab > General heading > File Locations button
- **Word 2011:** Word menu > Preferences > File Locations tab

Select the Startup category, and then click the Modify button. You can now use the standard navigation tools for file dialog boxes to learn the location of the Startup folder or define your own location. If no location is specified, define a location yourself by clicking the New folder button and choosing a new directory name and path.

Because corrupted documents stored in this folder can stop Word from launching or running normally, you may need to prevent something in this folder from opening when you launch Word. To do this, close Word, open the folder, and either delete the offending item or temporarily move it to another folder.

Chapter 5. Moving Around Documents and Selecting Text

Web: http://www.geoff-hart.com/books/eoe/eoe3/eoe3.html
Note: Word 2010 is for Windows; Word 2011 is for the Macintosh

One nice thing about mouse-driven interfaces is how easy it is to move around: simply scroll to the right location using the mouse's scroll wheel, then click the mouse where you want to begin working. Unfortunately, repeatedly moving your hands between keyboard and mouse wastes considerable time; it may only cost you a second or three each time you grab the mouse and return your hands to the keyboard, but if you do that hundreds or thousands of times per day, the wasted time adds up. This is doubly true if you're using the awkward and unergonomic pointing devices found on most laptop computers. Since most editors are skilled typists, it's more productive to keep our hands on the keyboard even when we need to move around. Yet many editors never master this skill and remain ignorant of the powerful navigation shortcuts available in a modern word processor.

In this chapter, I'll present the most efficient keyboard-based tricks for moving around a document while editing, as well as a few non-keyboard or hybrid (keyboard plus mouse) tricks. Once you've mastered these techniques, the last part of the chapter will teach you how to use them to select text more efficiently. Because both Windows and the Macintosh have increasingly standardized their keyboard commands across programs, these tips will work in most software, albeit with occasional variations. If your software doesn't support a particular useful shortcut, check its documentation or search the Web to see if you can discover an equivalent command. Alternatively, record a macro that will achieve the same result. (See Chapter 11 for details of how to record macros.)

Same keystrokes—mostly: Rather than always presenting keystrokes for both the Macintosh and Windows, I've mostly presented the Windows commands. Macintosh users should substitute Command for Control and Option for Alt unless otherwise noted.

When all else (including your mouse) fails, you can access any menu command from the keyboard. Chapter 4 describes how to do this and how to create new shortcuts in the section *Keyboard Shortcuts*. In Word 2011, you can also move from tab to tab in most dialog boxes: press Control+Tab to move forward through the tabs and Control+Shift+Tab to move backwards. Word 2010 doesn't provide this shortcut because tabs are usually labeled with underlined letters, and pressing Alt plus those letters will move you to the specified tab. In both versions, pressing Tab and Shift+Tab will move between the fields in a dialog box.

> **Moving among directories in the Open File dialog box:** To move among the fields in the Open File dialog box, press the Tab key (or Shift+Tab to move in the opposite direction). To move upwards one level, press Alt+↑; for the Macintosh, press Command+↑.

Small Jumps

Most cursor movements during editing are between words, sentences, or paragraphs. You'll make these jumps so often that it makes no sense to be constantly interrupting your work to grab the mouse. Learn the following keystrokes instead:

- **Next or previous word:** Control+→ and Control+←, respectively.
- **Beginning or end of line:** Home and End keys, respectively.
- **Beginning or end of sentence:** There's no universal keyboard shortcut for doing this, so you'll have to research the shortcut for each program you use. (How to create such a shortcut in Word is described later in this section.)
- **Beginning or end of paragraph:** Control+↑ and Control+↓, respectively.

Word includes functions that jump between sentences, but to use them from the keyboard, you must define new keyboard shortcuts:

- Open the Customize Keyboard dialog box, as described in Chapter 4.
- Choose the template or file that should store these customizations. (Choose Normal.dotm to make the change available in all documents.)
- Under Categories, select All Commands, then scroll through the command list until you reach SentLeft, the command for "move to the beginning of a sentence". You can instead click inside the command list and start typing this name; Word will scroll automatically to that part of the command list as you type.
- In the field labeled Press new shortcut key, type the new key combination (e.g., Control+Alt+Home).
- Repeat this process for SentRight, the command for "move to the end of a sentence" (e.g., Control+Alt+Home).

- Both the SentLeft command and the SentRight command also work in right-to-left languages.

Moving Within Tables

With the text cursor inside a table, you can use variations of the Tab key to move within the table:

- **Move to the next or previous cell (all versions):** Press the Tab key and the Shift+Tab combination, respectively.
- **Move to the first and last cells of a column:** In Word 2010, press Alt+PageUp and Alt+PageDown, respectively. In Word 2011, use the Control key rather than the Alt key.
- **Move to the first and last cells of a row:** In Word 2010, press Alt+Home and Alt+End, respectively. In Word 2011, use the Control key rather than the Alt key.

Moving Around Documents That Contain Tracked Changes

I'll discuss details of using the Track Changes feature in Chapter 6. Here, I'll describe a few useful tricks for moving efficiently around documents that contain tracked changes. These movement shortcuts rely on two tricks: first, Word can move directly to tracked changes, and second, Word can selectively display or conceal certain types of tracked changes.

For a lightly edited document, you can move rapidly to the next or previous changes by clicking the Move to next change or Move to previous change icons in the Ribbon's Review tab. These commands skip all intervening text between the cursor position and the next or previous tracked change. You can move even faster if you create keyboard shortcuts for these commands:

- Open the Customize Keyboard dialog box, as described in Chapter 4.
- Under the Categories heading, select Review tab (Word 2010) or All Commands (Word 2011).
- Under the Commands heading, scroll down to NextChangeOrComment and PreviousChangeOrComment.
- Create keyboard shortcuts (e.g., Control+Alt+↓ and Control+Alt+↑).

In heavily edited documents, this is less efficient because there are too many changes. Instead, select the Ribbon's Review tab, open the Show

Markup menu, and deselect any categories of tracked changes that you don't want to show. For example, if you deselect all options except format changes, these keystrokes move you to the next or previous format change and ignore all insertions and deletions.

If you want to ignore all tracked changes while you move around (e.g., if you want to check the positions of graphics in a page layout), open the Display for Review menu in the Ribbon's Review tab and select Final view so that only the results of your edits appear on the screen. Move to your destination using any of the movement shortcuts described in this chapter, then display your tracked changes again by selecting Final Showing Markup from this menu. If you do this often, it's worthwhile recording this as a macro, and creating a keyboard shortcut that runs the macro. I use Control+Shift+D to "shift the display" between showing and concealing the tracked changes.

Moving Using the Search Tools

Many of the most useful movements you'll need to make while editing are not built into Word. The solution? Use the Find dialog box to do the hard work for you! The basic principle is simple: Word can move to any character or pattern that you can find using the Find dialog box (see Chapter 8 for details), so all you need to do is figure out what you're looking for and then record a macro to find it. (See Chapter 11 for instructions on how to record a macro.) Use the following steps:

- Open the Find dialog box (Control+F).
- Type the character or pattern you want to find.
- Click the Find Next button to move to that the character or pattern.
- Close the dialog box.
- Assign a keyboard shortcut to each macro. (See Chapter 4 for details.)

Using this approach, I created many remarkably useful ways to zip around a document at top speed based on things I frequently need to move to. Here are some examples to inspire you to create your own movement shortcuts, and the keyboard shortcuts I defined for each of them:

- **Next or previous punctuation:** I created macros to find periods (Control+.), commas (Control+,), semicolons (Control+;), and colons (Control+:).
- **Numbers:** Since I mostly do scientific editing, I deal with a lot of numbers. Word's code to search for a number is ^#, and the keyboard

shortcut I use is Control+3, since the number sign (#) is above the 3 on the keyboard.

- **Brackets:** My authors insert many parenthetical comments and equations, so I've created search functions for each bracket type; the keyboard shortcut is Control plus the specific bracket; for example, Control+[takes me to the next opening square bracket.

- **Years:** Since I need to check literature citations based on the author/date citation method, I use the search text ^#^#^#^# (Word's code for "find four numbers in a row"), and implement this search using the keyboard shortcut Control+Y. (Mnemonic: Y = year.)

I created matching shortcuts to perform most of these searches, but moving backwards through the document, using the Find Previous button. To take advantage of the keyboard shortcuts I've already memorized, I simply added the Shift key to each of these shortcuts. Depending on the type of editing you do, you'll likely have a whole series of things you need to be able to move to. Pay attention to the kinds of movements you're doing most frequently, and create search macros that help you perform those moves in a single keystroke.

Bigger Jumps

Sometimes you need to jump farther, such as between screens, pages, or sections. Learn the following keystrokes instead:

- **Next or previous screen:** PageUp or PageDown, respectively.

- **Section break or manual page break:** Open the Find dialog box (Control+F) and search for the code used to define the break. Word uses ^m or ^k (*m* for a *manual* page break; *k* for any kind of *breaK*) or ^b (for a section *break*).

- **Format codes and document content (such as graphics):** Word can search for formatting codes such as those used to indicate the presence of a graphic or a table. To do so, open the Find dialog box, then expand it to show more options: in Word 2010, click the More button or press Alt+M; in Word 2011, click the expand arrow or press Command+M. Then open the Special menu to display a list of the special characters you can search for. Although these characters are easily available from the menu, you'll find it more efficient if you memorize the ones you use frequently. This lets you type them instead of relying on the mouse to select them from the menu.

- **Beginning or end of a document:** Control+Home or Control+End, respectively.
- **A specific section:** Open the Find dialog box (Control+F) and type a word or phrase you know will appear for the first time in the section. For example, if you want to move to the next chapter and each chapter title begins with the word *Chapter*, type that word as the search term. Alternatively, type part of the title or heading text for the section.

> **Finding a section by its title:** Word lets you search for words that appear at the start of a new paragraph by typing *^p* (the code for a carriage return) before the word. Similarly, if you need to find a word that has been forced onto the next line using a soft return (i.e., by holding the Shift key and pressing Return or Enter), type *^l* (lower-case L) instead. If the word has been forced to the beginning of a new line by inserting a page or section break, type *^m* or *^b* instead.

Chapter 4 describes Word's Outline and Document Map view modes. Both let you move quickly around a document when you don't remember details of a title or heading. Because Outline view allows you to expand and collapse the display of the document's headings and their subordinate text, it also lets you eliminate the distance between consecutive headings by collapsing the outline to show only headings. You can then move from one heading to the next with a single keystroke (e.g., by pressing the down arrow key), and once you arrive, you can expand the outline again and resume your editing. In Document Map view, you can click anywhere in the map to move to that position in the file, and immediately begin editing from that point. Although this requires the mouse, the distance you're moving makes this approach acceptable.

Moving to a bookmark

Software that provides bookmarks lets you jump to any named bookmark using a *go to* or *jump to* function. In Word 2010, the keyboard shortcut is Control+G; in Word 2011, it is Command+Option+G. Both in Word and in software that doesn't provide bookmarks, you can accomplish the same result by using symbols or words as placeholders and searching for those targets. An ideal marker won't appear in the file, because you want to avoid having to skip repeatedly over normal uses of the marker in the text. Typing special characters around a marker makes it stand out and makes it easier to find; consider, for example, *[continue]* or *&check this&*. Such phrases are good choices because they clearly identify the bookmark's role. If you use such bookmarks, always add a reminder in your editing checklist to remove them during your final edit.

To use Word's built-in bookmark function, position the cursor at the desired location, then open the Insert menu, select Bookmark, and name the bookmark. To move to the bookmark, open the Find dialog box (Control+F), click the Go to tab, and type the bookmark name. The dialog box also lets you go to several other things, such as sections, lines, comments, and tables.

Moving to a specific page

Most *go to* functions also let you jump to a specific page; in Word 2010, pressing Control+G (or Control+F, then clicking the third tab of the dialog box) lets you specify the page number; in Word 2011, use Command+Option+G instead. If you're willing to use the mouse, many programs that provide a page number at the bottom of the screen let you open a popup menu beside the page number and select a page. Double-clicking the page number may also open a dialog box that lets you enter a new page number. This works in both versions of Word.

Returning to your previous position

If you need to temporarily stop editing so you can move elsewhere in the document (e.g., to confirm the wording of a chapter title so you can type the correct cross-reference), it's easy to leave a bookmark in the file and use the Find function to find and return to that bookmark. I've standardized on [ ])(two square brackets) or <> (two angle brackets) because this is short, easy to type, and unlikely to occur in anything that I edit.

Getting back to where you started: Word offers a nifty shortcut (Shift+F5) that steps backward, one jump at a time, to previous positions where you changed text. Clicking the double arrows at the bottom of the vertical scroll bar accomplishes the same purpose:

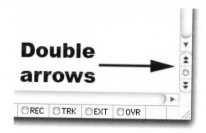

Unfortunately, Word frequently gets confused (particularly if you insert a comment) and loses track of these positions. This means that it's wise to use another strategy, such as manually inserting a bookmark, to ensure that you can easily return to your starting point.

Really **Big Jumps**

Sometimes you actually want to jump much farther than within a document—between files or programs, for example. Try the following:

Recently used files (across all programs)

Both the Macintosh and Windows let you display recently accessed documents for the operating system as a whole:

- **Windows:** Recently used documents or favorite documents are now displayed under the Start menu. For each program in that menu, click the arrow to the right of the program name to show the files. If you don't see these files: Right-click the task bar > Properties > Start Menu tab > Start Menu > Customize button. At the bottom of the dialog, select the number of recent items to display.

- **Macintosh:** Under the Apple (🍎) menu, the Recent Items option initially only shows recently used programs. To add recently used *documents*: Apple menu > System Preferences > General control panel > Recent items menu. Choose a number. Note that in OS X 10.9, there's a bug in this dialog box: you may have to select a number, close the dialog box, then repeat the process with a different number to display the correct number of items.

Recently used files (for the current program)

Most software now provides a Recent files or Recent items option under the File menu that provides access to the files you recently worked on:

- **Word 2010:** Ribbon > File menu > Options > Advanced tab> Display options. Choose a number from the menu beside Show this number of recent documents.

- **Word 2011:** Word menu > Preferences > General tab. Select a number for Display __ documents in Open Recent.

Frequently used files

It's helpful to place shortcuts to frequently used documents in convenient locations, such as on your desktop. To create shortcuts (Windows) or aliases (Macintosh) that point to a file:

- **Windows:** Right-click the file and select Create Shortcut. Drag the shortcut to a convenient location. To make it appear under the Start menu, drag the shortcut into the Start menu.

- **Macintosh:** Press Command+L to create an *alias*. Although you cannot add individual documents to the Apple (🍎) menu or the Dock, you can create a folder that holds these shortcuts and drag that folder into the right side of the Dock (beside the Trash icon) or into the Sidebar of a Finder window.

- **Libraries:** Some software (though not Word) also offers a "library" function that provides fast access to frequently used files.

Word used to offer a separate Work menu that you could add to your menu bar, beside the other menus, to provide access to documents that you use frequently. This menu is no longer available, but there's an alternative:

- **Word 2010:** In the list of recent documents under the File menu, you'll see a push-pin icon. Click that icon and the currently open file will remain in the menu until you click the push-pin again to unpin the document.

- **Word 2011:** Doing this is considerably more complicated. See the Web page at the start of this chapter to learn the steps.

Once you've added documents to the menu, you can open any document that you added to the menu without having to first find it on your computer.

Other open windows in an application

In most software, you can switch between two open documents via the Window(s) menu. For Windows, the standard keyboard shortcut for switching between documents is Alt+Tab; for the Macintosh, the keystroke is Command+` (the accent character below the Esc key on most keyboards).

Other open programs

If you're editing software documentation or researching something on the Web and must switch repeatedly between the software or Web browser and your word processor, it's particularly useful to be able to switch between programs using the keyboard. The shortcuts are Alt+Tab for

Windows and Command+Tab for the Macintosh; press that shortcut repeatedly until you reach the desired program.

Experiment!

Some of these shortcuts can be expanded or customized with a little creativity. For example, if you frequently have to move to the next instance of a particular heading style, record a macro that opens the Find dialog box and defines the search target as that heading style, then create a keyboard shortcut for that macro. (For details on finding text properties such as heading styles, see Chapter 8. For details on recording macros, see Chapter 11.) Pay enough attention to how you work so that you can identify the kinds of jumps that you need to do repeatedly, then find or develop a keyboard shortcut that lets you make those jumps quickly and easily. The time savings can be enormous. Plus, as a bonus, you'll impress the heck out of your friends and colleagues when they see you doing this.

Selecting Text

The tasks we perform during editing often involve selecting blocks of text, whether to change its format or to delete, copy, or move the text. Understanding how to efficiently select text prior to taking any of these actions is particularly important when we're reorganizing a document to improve the effectiveness of its structure, which is a common task for developmental editors who must help authors to organize their thoughts before they actually begin writing and for substantive editors who must fix the problems that result when authors skip the developmental edit.

Most computer users know at least one way to select text, but it may not be the most effective way for certain tasks. In this section, I'll present a range of alternatives you should experiment with until you find the one that works best for you in each situation. I'll start with keyboard-based methods, since most editors eventually find that using the keyboard is faster and more effective, then conclude with mouse-based methods because (my beliefs about the efficiency of the keyboard notwithstanding) the mouse may be more effective for some tasks and for some people.

Selecting with the keyboard

One of the most useful keyboard tricks involves extending the selection from the cursor's current position by holding down the Shift key and scrolling in the desired direction using the arrow keys. What's less well known is that you can combine many other keys with the Shift key to select text more quickly. For example, to select from the cursor's current position to another position:

- **Beginning or end of the line:** Shift+Home or Shift+End, respectively.

- **Selecting to the start or end of a sentence:** To select from the current cursor position to the start or end of the sentence in a single keystroke, open the Customize Keyboard dialog box (see Chapter 4 for details), select the category All Commands, and scroll down to the commands SentLeftExtend (to select to the start of the sentence) and SentRightExtend (to select to the end of the sentence). For these commands, I use Control+Alt+Shift+Home and Control+Alt+Shift+End, respectively. Don't worry: they're easier to type than they look.

- **Start or end of the document:** Control+Shift+Home or Control+Shift+End, respectively.

- **Previous or next screen:** Shift+PageUp or Shift+PageDown, respectively.

Earlier in this chapter, I listed many keyboard shortcuts for moving around within a file, and many of them can be combined with the Shift key to quickly select large chunks of text. So long as you hold down the Shift key, you can use most of those keystrokes to continue extending the selection. For example, you could press Shift+PageDown to select a full screen of text, then continue holding down the Shift key, but press the down arrow key repeatedly to extend the selection for a few additional lines.

Extending selections from the keyboard: Holding down the Shift key can be awkward. Word lets you extend the selection more easily using a little-known feature. Position the cursor at the start of the text, then press and release F8. Press the right arrow to extend the selection to include the next character, the down arrow key to include the next line of text, or PageDown to include the next screen. Press any keyboard character to extend the selection to the next instance of that character. Repeatedly pressing F8 selects the next word, then the whole sentence, then the entire paragraph. If you err, press Shift+F8 to reduce the selection to the previously selected chunk of text. You can now do whatever you like with the selected text (e.g., delete it, copy it). Press Esc to cancel the selection. You can combine this with the Find function to extend the selection to distant locations.

Selecting with the mouse

Most computer users quickly learn the basics of selecting text with the mouse: simply hold down the left mouse button and drag the cursor across the text. You can drag the mouse cursor in any direction from your starting point. In most software, double-clicking will select a word, and in some software, triple-clicking will select a sentence or (as in Word) an entire paragraph. If your fingers aren't fast enough to double-click or triple-click easily, Chapter 4 explains how to customize the mouse-click speed.

Selecting text with the mouse works well if all the text you want to select lies within a single screen, but if the text spans multiple screens, continuing to drag past either the top or bottom edges of the window typically causes the document to scroll too fast, causing you to overshoot the desired endpoint and select more text than you intended. In some word processors, there's nothing you can do about this, but in others, scrolling moves faster the farther outside the window you drag the cursor; try dragging only as far as necessary to begin scrolling, then move the cursor farther until the text scrolls at a suitable speed. If your mouse has a scroll wheel, most software lets you control the speed based on how fast you spin the wheel.

Control the scrolling speed with your mouse (Windows only): If Word scrolls too slow or too fast, use the techniques described in Chapter 4 to add the AutoScroll function in your Quick Access toolbar. When you click this icon, the cursor changes to a thick arrow; the more you move the cursor towards the top or bottom of the document, the faster the text will scroll. To cancel this function, press the Esc key or click the mouse inside the document window.

If you can't control the scrolling speed to your satisfaction, either because your software won't cooperate or because your reflexes aren't fast enough, you can achieve similar effects by combining the mouse with the keyboard:

- Click the mouse once to position the text cursor at the start of the text that you want to select.
- Click the mouse in the vertical scroll bar (or click the scroll arrows in the scroll bar) to scroll through the document. Each click in the scroll bar moves the display one screen at a time without changing the position of the text cursor. Clicking the up or down arrows in the scroll bar and then holding down the mouse button will cause the document to scroll continuously at a manageable rate.

- When you reach the end of the text that you want to select, hold down the Shift key and click the mouse at that point.

Selecting sentences and paragraphs: In Word, you can select an entire sentence by holding down the Control key (Windows) or the Command key (Macintosh), then clicking the mouse in that sentence. Holding down the Shift key and clicking again anywhere in a subsequent sentence or paragraph (respectively) will extend the selection to include the intervening text.

If your software lets you display style names beside paragraphs of text (usually in a separate column to the left of the text), you can use this feature to select several paragraphs with a series of mouse clicks. (To use this feature in Word, you must first display the style area. See the description of defining the style area width in Chapter 4.) Clicking on a style name selects the associated paragraph; holding down the Shift key and clicking on a style name elsewhere in the list selects all paragraphs between the initial paragraph and the paragraph you selected with your final click. As described above, you can also click with the mouse in the scroll bar or hold down the mouse button on one of the scroll arrows to move to the desired point without losing the starting point for your selection.

Moving text between window panes: If you split a Word document's window into two *panes*, as described in Chapter 4, you can drag and drop text between the panes. Scroll the top and bottom panes so that they show the starting point and endpoint for the move, then select the text in one pane and drag it to its new position in the other pane. (This did not work reliably in Macintosh versions of Word, but it seems to be stable in the most recent version of Word 2011.)

Selecting in Outline view

If your software provides a full-featured outline view, you can achieve a similar effect to using style names in that view mode. For example, Word's Outline view (see Chapter 4) lets you expand the displayed text to include subheadings and paragraphs, or collapse the displayed text to show only higher levels of headings. You can then select individual components of the outline (e.g., all text from the current level 1 heading to the next level 1 heading) in exactly the same way as using the list of styles: click once to select the initial section, then shift-click on the final section that you want to include.

An advantage of using the outline view is that you can collapse the outline to show only the amount of the document that is appropriate for the amount of text that you want to select. For example, if you want to select an entire section (e.g., a heading and all of the text and subheadings between it and the next heading), collapse the outline until only the section name is visible. Selecting the section name then selects the entire section. This is an efficient tool for quickly reorganizing entire documents, particularly if (as in Word) your software lets you select a heading and drag it to a different position in the sequence, thereby moving the contents of that section to the new position.

Undoing a selection

If you select a large chunk of text and decide that this isn't what you wanted to do, you can easily undo the selection: simply release the Shift key (if you are pressing it) and then press any arrow key or click once with the mouse anywhere in the text. In most cases, you'll want to press the left or up arrow keys or click at the start of the selection, because this puts you back where you started so you can try again. You can also press the Esc key.

Because it's easy to inadvertently hit a key and delete all the selected text, particularly if you're working on a laptop, pay careful attention whenever you prepare to select text. One helpful strategy is to save the document immediately before you perform any potentially disastrous action; that way, if you cause a problem that you can't easily solve, simply close the document without saving it, then reopen it and try again

If you haven't saved the file, and you inadvertently delete a large selection, immediately press Control+Z (Windows) or Command+Z (Macintosh) to undo that deletion. If you've cut text and pasted it in a new position, pressing these undo commands twice will restore the text to its original condition: the first press undoes your insertion of text; the second press undoes the deletion.

Selecting noncontiguous text

Noncontiguous text means two or more chunks of text that are not touching, such as the first and last sentences of a long paragraph. Most software does not let you select noncontiguous text. In that case, your only option is to make each selection independently, perform the necessary work on that selection, including moving it to its new location, then repeat the procedure for the next chunk of text.

There are other useful workarounds, such as using Word's *spike* feature (for details, see the next section). If you're not using Word, your software may accomplish the same effect using multiple clipboards. Clipboard-replacement software is available for both the Macintosh and Windows to provide similar features; search your favorite download site using the keyword "clipboard" and you'll turn up a variety of options.

Word 2003 and later versions let you select noncontiguous text. In these versions, you select the first block of text using any of the abovementioned methods, then for the second and subsequent blocks, hold down the Control key (Windows) or Command key (Macintosh) and drag the mouse to make additional selections. When you finish selecting the noncontiguous text, you can do anything you want to it (e.g., copy the text, apply a format such as boldface or a style). When you're done with the selection, click anywhere outside the highlighted text or press the Esc key to deselect it, then continue working.

Most times, we want to select contiguous text by moving the cursor horizontally within a line, then moving it vertically to select text on additional lines. However, Word also lets us select vertical swaths of text while ignoring words to the left or right of the selection. This is only really useful when you're working with *delimited* text that has been imported into Word in columns, such as text extracted from a database or a spreadsheet that uses a character such as a tab or a comma to mark (i.e., to *delimit*) the start and end of each column of information. To select only that one column of text, hold down the Alt key (Windows) or the Option key (Macintosh), then hold down the left mouse button at the starting position and drag the mouse until you've selected the final character in the column of text. You can now do anything to this text that you could do to other selected text: copy it, delete it, or apply a format such as boldface.

If that approach doesn't work or if you find it difficult to use, try this alternative: use Word's *rectangular selection* tool. First, position the text cursor at the start of the area you want to select. Next, press the keystroke Control+Shift+F8 (Command+Shift+F8 for the Macintosh) to activate this feature, and use the arrow keys to expand the selection. If you make a mistake or change your mind, press the Esc key to cancel this feature. Once the text is selected, you can again do whatever you could do to any other selected text.

Spiking text in Word

Word 2003 and later versions let you select noncontiguous blocks of text and cut them out of the document and store them in a different form of the more familiar copy/paste clipboard. This variant is called *the spike*. Think of this feature as a large metal spike onto which you can impale pages of paper, face down, with each new page added at the top of the pile. When you remove the items from the spike, they come off in the same order in which you placed them there. (Here, the metaphor breaks down because you must remove all items from the spike simultaneously.) To use the spike:

- Select the first chunk of text using any of the methods described previously in this chapter.
- Hold down the Control (Windows) or Command (Macintosh) key and press the F3 key. The text disappears from the screen and is now stored on the spike.
- Repeat these steps (select more text, then spike it) for each additional selection that you want to place on the spike.
- When you're done, position the text cursor at the desired destination, hold down the Shift key plus the Control (Windows) or Command (Macintosh) key, then press F3 again. Word inserts all of the spiked text at that location.

Unlike regular copy and paste operations, which leave the copied text on the clipboard so you can reuse it, this approach empties the spike, so you can't paste the same spiked text repeatedly. However, you now have all the formerly noncontiguous text together in one place, and can easily reselect it and copy it to the clipboard for reuse.

The spike also lets you move text containing tracked changes without losing the tracked changes. Turn off Track Changes before you cut text to the spike, then turn it on again after pasting the text so you can continue editing.

Chapter 6. Using Revision Tracking

Web: http://www.geoff-hart.com/books/eoe/eoe3/eoe3.html
Note: Word 2010 is for Windows; Word 2011 is for the Macintosh

Thus far, I've focused on providing a firm grounding in the nuts-and-bolts tools that will let you efficiently use Windows and Macintosh software for onscreen editing. This is clearly important, since you can't edit productively if you don't know how to use the basic tools. In this chapter, I'll begin to discuss the actual meat of this book: editing.

The simplest approach relies on revision-tracking tools that let you communicate your edits (*revisions*) to the author so you can work together to revise your suggestions and (if necessary) implement the changes. I have not used the term "editing tools" in this book because the documentation for most word processors refers to changing a document in any way as *editing*, and searching through user manuals or online help for advice on editing inevitably turns up the wrong information. For better or worse, we're stuck with the term "revision tracking", or its cousin in Microsoft Word, "track changes". If you've skipped the previous chapters because they didn't seem to relate directly to onscreen editing, I urge you to at least skim those chapters before continuing. You'll be glad you did.

Because a discussion of these tools is necessarily specific to a given program, it's not possible to provide a completely generalized description of revision tracking. To fully understand how a feature works, you need to experiment with that feature *as it is implemented in your software* until you understand its logic—or at least until you reach a *modus vivendi* in which you don't really understand how the features work, but can at least use them to predictably accomplish the desired results. Again, I'll focus on Word's Track Changes feature. Based on my description, you should be able to figure out the tools provided by other software.

Effective revision-tracking systems clearly identify insertions, deletions, and comments or questions. This lets both the editor and the author easily locate the changes and queries and understand their rationale. In addition, most programs provide an automated way to find and review (accept, reject, or temporarily skip) each edit. Don't be intimidated by the revision tracking tools, since they closely mimic the act of using a pen to edit on paper: where you previously wrote insertions using a pen, you now type them using a keyboard; where you deleted words by drawing a line through them with a pen, you now delete them with the keyboard's Backspace or Delete keys. These two activities account for the majority of what you'll be doing when you edit on the screen; most of the remainder involves typing comments to explain what you've done or adding requests for clarification. Everything else you learn in this book is a tool that supports these activities.

> **Don't like editing in Word?** If you dislike Word's interface for revision tracking, but have to use this software for a client, try this compromise: Edit the file in your favorite word processor, without tracking the changes, then save the file in Word's .docx format. You can then use Word's Compare Documents feature (discussed later in this chapter) to display differences between your edited file and the original Word file. This works particularly well when there's only one editor, since there will be no overlapping or contradictory edits. Because the original file never left Word, there should be little risk of the kind of creeping corruption that results from repeated file format conversions. An additional bonus: Word will record the changes more cleanly than the confusing mess we sometimes create when we edit.

Although it's possible to simply go through a manuscript, make all the changes you feel are necessary without identifying them, and leave it to the author to figure out what you've done, this is unreliable and unwise. The *unreliability* comes from the fact that authors have generally seen their manuscript so many times before it reaches you that they are too familiar with it, and can no longer force themselves to concentrate on the details. In my experience, this is true of most authors—including me, when I was revising this book. This creates a risk that authors will miss small or subtle changes that perhaps we shouldn't have made. The solution is to ensure that they can see each change.

The *unwise* aspect arises from the fact that it's always more difficult to examine a fully revised manuscript that provides no evidence of what was done (think of this as forensic science) than it is to examine each individual change and ensure that it's correct. Authors naturally resent the extra work, and resent it even more if an editorial error escapes their review, makes it into print or is published on the Web, and causes them embarrassment. The solution? Again, make sure they can see each change. Tracking changes turns the review and revision from a hunt for unpleasant surprises into a collaborative dialogue, and that's a good thing indeed when it comes to working productively with authors.

In this chapter, I'll focus on the mechanics of using the revision tracking tools provided by Word. Chapter 7 provides some general principles on how to handle insertions, deletions, comments, and questions (whether you're working on paper or on the screen), but with an emphasis on the main quirks related to onscreen editing. I'll discuss Word's comment feature in that chapter to integrate the description with details of how to write effective comments. Chapter 12 describes how you can use your word processor's revision tracking feature for types of files you wouldn't ordinarily think you could edit in a word processor, including spreadsheets and Web pages. Last but not least, Chapter 13 describes some last-ditch methods for clearly communicating your changes when you don't have the luxury of using revision tracking. Think of that chapter as the "clay tablet plus stylus" approach to onscreen editing: it ain't pretty, but it works.

Enabling and Disabling Revision Tracking

There's no point in using a tool that makes our lives easier if it makes the author's life significantly more difficult. For onscreen editing to be truly effective, it must also make the author's life easier. The key feature that makes revision tracking so useful is that once we turn it on, any changes we make will be identified so the author can see exactly what we've done and can approve or reject our changes or suggest a compromise solution. (For details on customizing how revisions appear on the screen, see the section *Track changes settings* in Chapter 4.) Word offers several ways to turn revision tracking on and then off again:

- **From the Ribbon:** Select the Review tab. In Word 2010, open the menu beside the Track Changes icon and select Track Changes; in Word 2011, move the slider above Track Changes between On and Off.
- **From the keyboard:** In Word 2010, press Control+Shift+E; in Word 2011, press Command+Shift+E
- **From the menu (Word 2011):** Tools menu > Track Changes > Highlight Changes > checkbox for Track changes while editing

Note that when you enable revision tracking in Word, the software provides a clear visual indication that it is tracking changes. In Word 2010, the Track Changes icon in the Ribbon is highlighted in bright orange; in Word 2011, the On setting is highlighted in green. It's worthwhile keeping the Review tab visible while you edit so you can see at a glance whether Word is still tracking changes. This is most important when you're working with the changes concealed so that you can see the results of your edits instead of the individual edits. (It's easy to inadvertently turn off revision tracking if you use keyboard shortcuts and press the wrong key combination. For example, my keyboard shortcut Control+Shift+D to switch between concealing and displaying changes is close to Control+Shift+E.) I'll discuss editing with the changes concealed later in the chapter.

If you're using an older version of Word that doesn't support these methods, use the instructions in Chapter 4 to customize the keyboard and create a shortcut. Here's what to look for in the Customize dialog box:

- Under the Categories heading, select Review Tab. (This may be named Tools or All Commands in older versions of Word.)
- Under the Commands heading, scroll down until you find ToolsRevisionMarksToggle.
- Assign a keyboard shortcut to this command.

As a general rule, you should track all changes the author must review, but you can stop tracking changes whenever you must make changes the author shouldn't have to deal with (such as replacing all double spaces with single spaces) or doesn't have the authority to reject (such as applying the paragraph styles specified by a publisher). Use this power judiciously! Although authors generally appreciate not having to confirm trivial changes or review changes they can't reject, it's dangerous to create the impression that you're doing anything behind the author's back. Our goal should always be to build a trusting relationship, and the smallest hint that we're trying to sneak something past the author can completely undermine that trust.

This is one example of a large and important guiding principle: during your initial discussions with an author, ask for permission to make these types of changes without tracking them. If you receive such permission, remind the author about what you're doing in your cover letter when you return the document, or insert a comment directly in the manuscript to explain what you've done; authors often forget this kind of detail. (See Chapter 7 for details on crafting and inserting comments.) If the author spots a change that you haven't tracked, your explanation will help them understand why you made that change rather than wondering what other changes you might have made without their approval.

Most authors also learn that they can turn off change tracking, and this can be problematic if they use this knowledge to make changes behind *your* back. Ask them to offer you the same courtesy that you offered them: a commitment to not make any changes without tracking the change or discussing their decision beforehand. Remind them that if they rewrite any text without tracking those changes after you've already edited the manuscript, you'll have to work your way through the entire manuscript one more time to find the changes before you can review them. In contrast, remind them that if they track their changes, you can find the changes quickly, edit only the text that changed, and return the manuscript faster than would otherwise be possible. In my experience, many authors never understand this until I've explained it; after hearing the explanation, they realize they can save time and money by tracking their own changes.

In some cases, it may be necessary to prevent an author from making changes without tracking them or to prevent them from disregarding our changes. Some publishers, including one university press I'm familiar with, have experienced enough problems that they no longer return the edited files to their authors. Instead, they require authors to review printouts or a PDF file of the edited manuscript; the editor then transfers the author's responses from the printout into the edited file and accepts all the edits that remain after incorporating those responses. This is clearly effective, albeit inefficient, but may be too draconian a solution when we're working with professional writers and have established a trusting relationship.

A compromise solution may be to *protect* or *lock* the document so that authors cannot make any changes without tracking them and cannot accept or reject our changes (i.e., they can only comment on the changes). To protect a document in Word:

- **Word 2010:** Ribbon > File menu > Info > Protect Document icon > Restrict Editing. Choose the types of editing you will allow the author to do. For example, if you only allow comments, the author will be able to comment on any changes they disagree with, but they cannot modify your edits. You can also select parts of the document and specify who can modify those parts. Click the button Yes, Start Enforcing Protection to apply the protection.

- **Word 2011:** Word menu > Preferences > Security button > Protect Document button. Choose one of two options: Tracked Changes means that any modifications will be tracked (the author cannot override this setting); Comments means that the author can only comment on your changes.

- In both programs, create a password that will be used to disable the protection. Record it somewhere safe, since it will be difficult to restore full access to the document without the password. Although you can obtain software to crack Word's passwords, it's pricey, and you may not want to trust its developers with access to your computer.

Overview of the Screen Display

Before I describe what you'll see as you edit, it's helpful to understand how Word divides the screen. Word can divide each window into two smaller windows called *panes*. Think of *window panes* and you'll get the idea. I discussed this briefly in Chapter 4 when I described how to split a document into panes that show different parts of the same document and when I discussed the Document Map view. In the context of editing, Word also offers a Reviewing Pane (Word 2010) or Review Pane (Word 2011) that lists all your edits. For simplicity, I'll use the term *Review Pane* everywhere. I'll discuss this pane later in the chapter.

Second, Word can only display two panes at a time, so if you open a new pane, Word must close one of the old panes. Thus, you can't split a document into two panes that show different parts of the document and then open the Review Pane as a third pane. If you need additional views into a manuscript, you'll need to open a copy in a new window.

Displaying original versus final text

In addition to the various display modes described in Chapter 4, Word provides sophisticated—and correspondingly complicated—controls for managing what you see while you're editing. You access these controls through the Ribbon's Review tab. Because the Windows and Macintosh versions of Word are so different, please consult the Web page for this chapter, where I've provided a screenshot of the Review tab with all icons labeled.

There are two key display-related components in the Review tab that you must work with simultaneously to define what you see. First, the Show for Review menu lets you choose which version of the document you want to see:

- **Original:** the original file, with none of your editing displayed.
- **Final:** what the file will look like with all of your edits accepted.

Second, you can show Original Showing Markup or Final Showing Markup. These both display your tracked changes, and differ in only one significant aspect: in Print Layout mode in Word 2011, the former mode displays changes inline, whereas the latter shows changes tracked in balloons.

Note that if you have turned on track changes and have edited the manuscript, your changes will be present but invisible if you chose the Original or Final views: that's what those names mean. You must select one of the options with Showing Markup in their name to see your edits.

Choosing which markup to display

If you've chosen to work in either of the two view modes that includes Showing Markup in its name, you can then specify which edits should be visible. You do this via the Review tab's Show Markup menu, which lets you specify the following groups of changes for Word to display:

- **Comments:** This option lets you switch between showing and concealing comments inserted using Word's Comment feature. If the Review Pane is displayed (see below), this also controls whether your comments appear in that pane. It's best to leave this option selected to ensure that you don't miss any comments.

- **Ink (Word 2010):** Users of tablet computers or of graphics tablets can write on the screen (annotate the document) using a stylus, and these changes can be tracked. However, because Word cannot convert this handwriting into editable text, any edits made in this manner must be retyped manually into the document.

- **Insertions and Deletions:** This option lets you choose whether to display or conceal inserted (added) and deleted text. Unfortunately, it currently isn't possible to show or conceal only insertions or only deletions. If the Review Pane (see below) is displayed, this setting also controls whether your insertions and deletions appear in that pane.

- **Formatting:** This option lets you choose whether to display changes in formatting (e.g., manually boldfaced text, font changes, page layout changes), or just the results of these changes. If the Review Pane is displayed, this also controls whether your format changes are summarized in that pane.

- **Markup area highlight:** If you are not using the Review pane (see below), selecting this setting creates a light grey background in the right margin of the document window, which is the part of the screen that contains the markup (i.e., comments, indications of format changes). This highlight only appears in Print Layout and Web view modes.

- **Balloons:** In Word 2010, balloons let you display all your edits (messily) or only your comments (neatly) in the right margin when you are viewing the document in Print Layout and Web Layout views. Balloons are sufficiently important and useful to merit their own section later in this chapter. In Word 2011, the limited balloon settings are available via the Preferences dialog box (see below).

- **Reviewers:** This option lets you display the changes made by all reviewers or only the revisions made by specific reviewers. In the latter case, this is convenient if you want to focus on the edits of one or two reviewers at a time without being confused by everyone else's edits.

- **Highlight updates:** If you're working on a document stored in Microsoft SharePoint, Word will indicate updates made via this system so that you can see them more easily.
- **Other authors:** If you're working on a document stored in Microsoft SharePoint, this setting lets you see whether other authors have provided updates.
- **Options (Word 2010):** The options for how changes are displayed (e.g., their color) are available from a menu attached to the Track Changes icon. Details of these options are provided in Chapter 4 and illustrations are provided on the Web page for this chapter.
- **Preferences (Word 2011):** The options for how changes are displayed (e.g., their color) are available via Word menu > Preferences > Track Changes tab or by opening the menu beside Show Markup and selecting Preferences. Details of these options are provided in Chapter 4, and illustrations are provided on the Web page for this chapter.
- **Review Pane:** This option lets you switch between displaying and concealing the Review Pane. With this pane displayed, the other settings in the Show Markup menu define which types of changes will appear in the Review Pane. Word 2010 can display the review pane at the left side or bottom of the document window by selecting the desired position from the menu beside the Reviewing Pane icon. Word 2011 only lets you display the pane to the left of the document window.

Taking full advantage of the screen display

When combined, the Show for Review and Show Markup menus provide a high level of control over what you see as you work, and once you understand their relationship, using them judiciously can greatly improve your editing efficiency. In particular, they offer two main benefits:

The first benefit is that you can choose whether to display your actual edits or only the results of those edits. While you're editing a manuscript for the first time, it's often helpful to see all of the changes you've made so that (for example) you can confirm whether you made a certain type of change consistently throughout the manuscript. You can examine what you did and figure out how the text ended up in its current condition and you can tidy up any messy changes so they're easier for the author to understand. Alternatively, you can focus on the results of all your changes (i.e., the final manuscript). For example, I usually edit a manuscript for the first time with the changes displayed (Final Showing Markup view), then perform a second pass with these changes concealed (Final view) so that I can eliminate the visual clutter created by my abundant additions and deletions and see only the results of my edits. This lets me focus on finding errors that I missed and errors that I introduced myself, such as typos.

Always do at least two passes: Although I've met editors who claim that they can do a complete edit in a single pass, I don't believe them. At a minimum, you should do one pass to complete the majority of the work, then a second pass to catch your own errors.

The second benefit is that you can focus on a particular subset of your edits instead of being forced to see all changes simultaneously. For example, if one of your responsibilities is to format a document for a publisher, you can deselect all options under the Show Markup menu except Formatting. The resulting view lets you review only the format changes and ignore all others. You can then deselect every option but Comments under the Show Markup menu so you can ensure that all of your comments are clear and correct, then deselect every option but Insertions and Deletions and review only that group of edits. Minimizing the distractions in this way helps you focus better on each type of edit.

Useful Keyboard Shortcuts

Since most edits will be insertions and deletions, it's helpful to be able to quickly switch between showing and concealing these changes without taking your hands off the keyboard. The keyboard shortcut for this used to be Control+Shift+D (mnemonic: control the Display by shifting between displaying and not displaying changes), but around 2007, this shortcut was reassigned to apply a double underline. Unless you use double underlines a lot, I recommend that you use Word's Customize Keyboard feature (described in Chapter 4) to restore this older shortcut. In summary:

- Open the Customize Keyboard dialog box.
- Under the heading Category, choose All commands.
- Under the heading Commands, scroll down until you find ShowInsertionsAndDeletions.
- Type the desired keyboard shortcut (Control+Shift+D).

- Click the **Assign** button.

It's also useful to be able to open the **Show Markup** menu from the keyboard so you can simplify the display of tracked changes when necessary:

- **Word 2010:** Press Alt+R to switch to the **Review** tab, then press T and M to display the types of markup. You can then press the displayed letters to select or deselect a display option.
- **Word 2011:** There are no keyboard shortcuts for this menu. Instead, create custom keyboard shortcuts for each type of change that you want to display. Most of these are listed under the **All commands** category and have reasonably obvious names that begin with the word **Show** (e.g., **ShowComments** for comments, **ShowFormatChanges** for format-related edits).

Solving Display-Related Problems

Editor name changes to "Author"

If you've set the **User Information** settings to use your name and initials, but your edits are labeled as having been made by **Author**, the problem lies in Word's privacy settings:

- **Word 2010:** Ribbon > File menu > Info > Check for Issues button > Inspect Document option. Deselect the Document properties and personal information checkbox, then click the Inspect button. Close the dialog box when the inspection is done.
- **Word 2011:** Word menu > Preferences > Security > Privacy Options. Deselect the Remove personal information from this file on save checkbox. Click OK to close the dialog box.

> **Changing the user name for edits and comments:** If you've edited an entire document and belatedly realize that you need to make your comments anonymous, you can change your user name temporarily and create a new document following the instructions in the section *Comparing Documents in Word* later in this chapter. However, it's easier to set Word to remove personal information from a file when you save the file. Follow the instructions earlier in this section, but *select* the checkbox.

Inability to delete text

If you're editing a document and tracking your changes, but concealing the changes so you can focus on the results of your edits, the changes are still present in the file even though you can't see them. Even though you can't see the changes, Word can, and the software must account for this "ghost" text as you move through the document or make additional edits. This sometimes leads to surprises, such as when you press the Delete or Backspace key and nothing happens.

Here's what's happening: *You* see the cursor sitting next to the text that you want to delete, but *Word* sees the cursor next to concealed text that you have already deleted. If you keep pressing the deletion key, Word will eventually move through the deleted text, one character at a time, until it reaches the first undeleted character that you *can* see on the screen; only then will it delete the visible character. Unfortunately, you can't see this happening because you've chosen to conceal the deleted text. Displaying your tracked changes will reveal what is happening.

Invisible tracked changes

Authors sometimes need reassurance that the changes are really there while they're learning to use revision tracking. As a general rule, you should always send edited files to your authors with the markup visible so they can see what you've done. Starting with Word 2007, Microsoft chose to always open edited documents with the tracked changes clearly visible. If an author reports that they can't see your changes, they're probably using an older version of Word. Teach them how to change the display settings in the Reviewing toolbar (replaced by the Ribbon's Review tab in Word 2010 and 2011). To prevent the problem in the first place, authors can open the Options or Preferences dialog box, select the Security tab, and select the option Make hidden markup visible when opening or saving.

Problems with fields, automatic numbering, and notes

Word offers several related features that interact badly with revision tracking: field codes, automatic numbering, footnotes, and endnotes. Field codes are tools that tell Word to "do the following calculation" (e.g., calculate the current page number) or "insert the following information" (e.g., a cross-reference). Automatic numbering lets Word correctly number items in a list. The footnote and endnote features, beloved of academic writers, let you insert and automatically renumber these notes to the reader. If you change one field, Word will helpfully update all related fields. For example, if you add an item in the middle of a numbered list, Word must update all subsequent numbers.

If you're using revision tracking, each updated field value will be tracked as a separate change. For example, if you add an item at the start of a procedure with 20 numbered steps, Word will update the following 20 numbers and track each of these as a change. If many fields change, this requires a lot of additional work from the author, so it's best to avoid this problem. To do so, simply turn off revision tracking before you edit fields, but insert a note to tell the author what you've done. After you've made the necessary changes, turn on revision tracking again and continue your work.

Updating field codes: Word doesn't always remember to update all field codes. To remind it, select the whole document by pressing Control+A (Windows) or Command+A (Macintosh), and then press the F9 key.

If you have problems editing the text at the end of a file, field codes may be the explanation. Recently, while editing a manuscript's bibliography, I found I couldn't move references into alphabetical order or insert comments. The clue that let me solve this mystery was that the citations, though inserted in the author/date format, were numbered: that is, they'd been inserted as endnotes. Word's endnote feature generates the bibliography using a field code, and you can't revise the bibliography when it's present in this format. The solution? Convert the endnotes into editable text by selecting them and pressing Control (Command)+Shift F9, the keystroke to convert fields into editable text. The author can easily regenerate the bibliography after they make the changes you have requested. If you're not comfortable making such a change, you can instead insert comments that describe the required changes and let the author do the work.

Cursor position changes after switching between displaying and concealing changes

When you switch from concealing to showing tracked changes or back again, the cursor position may shift—potentially by many screens of text if you deleted several paragraphs. This makes it difficult to return the cursor to where you were when you changed the display setting. Though you can type a short bookmark such as <> before you switch views, and use the

Find tool to find and move to that bookmark, there's a simpler solution: Before you change the display, hold down the Shift key and use the right arrow key to select the first letter to the right of the cursor position. When you switch views, that character remains highlighted, and pressing the left arrow key moves the cursor to the left of the selected text—that is, to your original position. You can use any pair of opposing arrow keys (e.g., left versus right, up versus down) to select the text and then move to its start position.

If you forget to do this, and you lose your place, try pressing Word's shortcut to return the cursor to its most recent position: Shift+F5. This won't always work (Word sometimes forgets that position), but it works often enough that it's worth a try.

Using the Highlighter Marker

The highlighter marker tool (in the Ribbon's **Home** tab) works the same way as those thick yellow markers we've all used to highlight key points in a printout or textbook. To use this tool in Word, select the marker color from the menu beside the marker icon, select the text you want to highlight, and then click the icon to apply the highlight color. Alternatively, click the marker icon and drag the mouse cursor across the text you want to highlight. (In the second case, press the Esc key to *escape* from using the marker.) If revision tracking is enabled, Word will add the note **Highlight** in the right margin in Print Layout or Web views to track the change; thus, turn off revision tracking if you don't want to track this change.

You can use this tool to highlight any text that you want to remind yourself to check later or to remind yourself of the status of certain checks you must still perform. For example, you can use green highlighting ("Keep going: this point is okay!") to indicate that you've already checked a fact or applied a particular style, and red highlighting ("Stop! Check this!") to indicate that you have not yet performed some action. To remove the highlight color, open the menu beside the icon to reveal the available colors and select **No Color** (Word 2010) or **None** (Word 2011), then repeat the process you used to apply the highlight color in the first place.

The highlighter is also useful when you must ask an author to confirm whether a change is necessary in many places in a manuscript. Instead of inserting a comment for each instance, you can use the search tool (which I'll discuss in more detail in Chapter 8) to find each instance of the text that may need to be changed and apply the highlight color:

- First, turn off revision tracking if you don't want to track each change.
- Select the desired highlight color from the menu beside the icon.
- Open the Find and Replace dialog box, then expand it to show more options if it isn't already expanded.
- Type the text you want to highlight in the Find what: field.
- Press Tab or click the mouse to move the cursor to the Replace with: field, and delete any text that is present in that field. Then open the Format menu and select Highlight.
- Click the Replace All button. Turn on revision tracking again.

> **Highlighter color choice:** Many of the neon colors are distracting and bother the eyes. Use more subdued colors to avoid irritating the author. If you use green and red to highlight different types of change, remember that nearly 10% of all men suffer from red–green colorblindness and may be unable to distinguish between the colors. Ask the author to confirm that they can see the difference.

If you use this tool to communicate with authors, remember that many authors never learn where this tool is located or how to use it. Thus, they cannot figure out how to remove the formatting. I've seen authors moved to tears of frustration because they couldn't figure out how to remove the highlighting. Tracking the format change gives them an easy way to remove the format; they can simply reject the change after they've dealt with it. However, to be safe, insert a comment to tell the author where they can find the tool and how to use it. The easiest way to remove many highlights is to turn off revision tracking, select the whole document (Control+A in Word 2010, Command+A in Word 2011), then open the menu beside the icon and select No color or None. You can also repeat the search and replace process described earlier in this section, but in the Replace with: field, select Highlight *twice*: the second time you do this, the description below this field changes from Highlight to Not highlight (Word 2010) or Highlight not (Word 2011). Click the Replace all button to make the change.

Modifying Where You See Revisions

Earlier in this chapter, I described settings for *how* Word displays revisions (e.g., in color). In this section, I'll extend that discussion to explain *where* the changes appear. Word lets you display your tracked changes in three locations, according to your preference, and each has its own range of display settings:

- **Directly in the document window:** All changes appear within the lines of text, and are therefore directly associated with the affected text. You can modify or respond to each change in this window. This method is one of the two options available in Normal or Draft view mode; the other option is the Review Pane (see the next point).

- **In a Review Pane:** This pane, which is available in any view mode, can appear at the side or bottom (Word 2010) or side (Word 2011) of the document window. It presents a long, vertical list of changes, but they are only indirectly linked to the document text. Although you can directly modify many of the changes within this pane, it's more awkward than working within the document window. I'll discuss this pane in more detail in the next section.

- **In balloons:** Word's balloons, which resemble the speech balloons in comic strips, appear to the right of the document window. The balloons are linked by a dashed line to the changes they describe. I'll discuss how to manage balloons later in this section. Balloons are only available in Web and Print Layout view modes.

Play with each of these methods until you understand how they work. More importantly, pay attention to how they *feel*. You're likely to find some combination of these views that feels most comfortable as you edit or review someone else's edits. The tradeoff is that some effort is required to learn how to benefit from each mode's advantages and overcome its drawbacks.

Earlier in this chapter, I described how to work with your changes displayed in the document window. With some exceptions described later in this section, you'll still see all of your changes in the document window even if you use the Review Pane or balloons to display your edits. Moving the mouse cursor over changed text provides additional details. For example, if you select text before you insert a comment, the selected text will be highlighted to indicate which words the comment describes. Moving the cursor over the highlighted text will display the editor's initials and the comment number (e.g., mine look like [GH1]). In Draft view, Word adds a pair of nearly invisible brackets around the selected text:

(This text was selected before inserting a comment)

For comments displayed in balloons, you can click inside the balloon and edit the comment directly. If you can't see the balloons, right-click or control click on the comment marker and select Edit Comment, or open the Review Pane (see the next section for details).

Review Pane

To access the Review Pane, select the Ribbon's Review tab and click the Review Pane icon. Click the icon again to close this pane. To change the size of the pane, move the cursor over its edge until you see a double-headed arrow, then drag the edge of the pane: if the pane is at the bottom of the screen, drag it up or down; if it's at the side of the screen, drag it left or right. Dragging the edge all the way to the bottom or left side will close the pane. You can also open and close the pane and change its position from the keyboard:

- **Word 2010:** Press Alt+R to select the Ribbon's Review tab, then press T followed by P. From the resulting menu, choose whether to display the pane vertically, at the left side of the window, or horizontally, at the bottom. Repeating the same menu choice closes the pane.
- **Word 2011:** There's no default keyboard shortcut to open and close this pane, but you can create one using the Customize Keyboard feature, as described in Chapter 4. In the Customize dialog box, select the category All commands, then scroll to the command ReviewingPane and create a keyboard shortcut. The same keystroke closes the pane.

The default Review Pane contains so much information it's difficult to focus on specific changes amidst the clutter. To tame that mess, open the Ribbon's Show Markup menu (discussed earlier in this chapter), then select any types of edit you want to display and deselect any you want to conceal.

Word uses a separate zoom (magnification) level for the Review Pane, so if you find the text in the Review Pane too small to read easily, click the cursor inside the pane. Next:

- **Word 2010:** Ribbon > View tab > Zoom icon. Choose a value large enough for easy reading.
- **Word 2011:** View menu > Zoom. Choose a value large enough for easy reading.
- **Both versions:** If you have a mouse with a scroll wheel, hold down the Control key and rotate the wheel to change the zoom level.

There are two common problems associated with the Review Pane. First, the AutoCorrect and AutoText automatic text features (described in Chapter 11) don't work in this pane. Currently, the only solution is to either close the pane and work with comments displayed as balloons, or to type the comment in the text, then copy and paste it into the Review Pane.

See the section *Combining balloons with the Review Pane* later in this chapter for tips on how to take advantage of both views.

The second problem, which appears to have been solved in current versions, relates to excessive repagination: Word automatically repaginates the document as you add or delete text, and it usually does so without causing any problems. However, sometimes this happens so often it interferes with your typing. If you encounter this problem with the Review Pane open, close the pane and work directly in the document window.

Balloons

You'll either love or hate the balloons that were introduced with Word 2003; few people remain indifferent. In Print Layout or Web (Online) view modes, this feature displays your tracked changes and details about the changes (e.g., who made the change), including comments, in the margin to the right of the document window. As noted earlier, the balloons resemble the speech balloons in a comic strip and are linked by a dashed line to the text they describe. Balloons offer several advantages:

- The page layout (e.g., line breaks) is not affected by the presence of comment markers such as [GH1]. This can be particularly helpful in tables, where the comment markers can interfere with the text wrap and alignment within cells.

- Balloons remain constantly visible outside of the text you're editing, so they don't get in the way, you don't need to hold the mouse cursor over the highlighted areas to display them, and you don't need to open a separate window pane to see your comments.

- If you like working with a window split into two panes that show different parts of the document simultaneously (see Chapter 4 for details), you don't have to close the second pane just so you can see your comments. (Word can only open two panes per window, so you can't show both the split document and the Review Pane simultaneously.)

- If you want to print an edited document, the comment balloons will print beside the text. In older versions, comments appeared at the end of the printout, making it difficult to associate them with the text they described.

Escaping from comment balloons: If you hate to take your hands off the keyboard while editing, you can escape from a comment balloon and return the cursor to the main document window by pressing the Esc key. Thanks to Jack Lyon (Editorium) for this trick.

Unfortunately, the number of balloons that can appear in heavily edited documents makes it difficult to determine which balloon describes a given change. One solution is to change the line spacing to double-spaced or larger until you've finished editing or reviewing your edits. This mitigates the problem by increasing the space between lines and thus, between balloons. You can also make the lines connecting the balloons to the edited text easier to untangle by setting Word to only display comments in balloons.

Word 2011 balloon problem: Word 2011 implements balloons so badly (it shows every change in a balloon) that I find them unusable. The only solution is to open the Track Changes preferences and turn off the use of balloons, or work in Draft view. In both cases, all changes appear inline with the text. Unfortunately, to see comments in this view, you have to hold the mouse cursor over the comment or work with the Review Pane open.

There doesn't seem to be any way to reposition balloons in either version of Word, and Word 2011 makes balloons particularly hard to use. If you have many comments that apply to a small area of text, you may have insufficient room to display all of the comments even in triple-spaced text. Fortunately, you can change the width of the area in which the balloons appear to mitigate this problem:

- **Word 2010**: Ribbon > Review tab > menu beside the Track Changes icon > Change Tracking Options. Under the heading Balloons, choose a larger value for the Preferred width setting.
- **Word 2011:** There doesn't appear to be any way to increase the width of the area in which the balloons appear. The only option seems to be to work in Web Layout view and reduce the width of the document window enough that you simultaneously increase the space between the balloons.

If you find the clutter created by the balloons distracting, you can selectively enable and disable some aspects of the balloons:

- **Word 2010:** Ribbon > Review tab > menu beside the Track Changes icon. Under the heading Balloons, open the menu beside Use balloons (Print and Web layout) and choose Only for comments/formatting.
- **Word 2011:** There's no way to choose which changes to display in the balloons, though changing the display to Original Showing Markup or

changing the Show Markup menu to show only comments can make the display less horrible. But until Microsoft fixes the problem, your best bet may be to refrain from using the balloons.

Combining balloons with the Review Pane

It takes some experimentation to find a pleasing and efficient combination of settings under the Show Markup menu with a judicious mixture of balloons and the Review Pane, particularly in Macintosh versions of Word. Spend some time experimenting with combinations of these settings until you find a combination that uses each feature to maximum advantage while overcoming that feature's main annoyances. There's no one right solution; you'll need to find the combination that works for you.

Enlarging text in balloons

If you find that the text that appears in balloons is difficult to read, you can fix this by editing the properties of two paragraph styles: Comment Text and Balloon text . To do so, display the list of styles that can be used in the document:

- **Word 2010:** Press Alt+H to select the Ribbon's Home tab, then press F followed by Y to open the Styles palette. Alternatively, click the small icon below the Home tab's Change Style icon. Click the Manage styles button to choose which styles to display and how to display them.
- **Word 2011:** Format menu > Style. Open the List menu to specify which styles to display.

Both versions of Word let you specify which styles it should display, but the options differ between the versions. If you cannot see Comment Text and Balloon Text in the list of styles, select All styles and Alphabetical order (Word 2010) or All styles (Word 2011) and scroll through the list until you find them. To edit their properties (e.g., change the font size), select the style name, then click the Modify button.

There are several properties you can modify in this dialog box. First, change the typeface, font size, and other properties (such as line spacing) to make the text more readable. Next, set the style to be based on no style, which is the first entry at the top of the list of styles. This prevents changes in other styles from affecting the comment text style. If you'll be making this change frequently (e.g., in each manuscript you edit), you can save considerable time by recording a macro (as described in Chapter 11) to do this work for you.

Comparing Documents in Word

Sometimes, particularly after extensive revisions of a manuscript by multiple reviewers or really messy edits by a single editor, it's helpful to be able to see how the current version of a manuscript differs from the original version. Word's Compare Documents feature lets you do this. In summary, the software compares two versions of a document, then uses the revision tracking tools to produce a single document that shows what changed. The feature works quite well if you will only compare two versions of the manuscript and only one or two editors have modified the text without overlapping edits. A related option lets you copy changes from several versions of a manuscript into a single file:

- **Word 2010:** Ribbon > Review tab > menu under the Compare documents icon > Combine
- **Word 2011:** Tools menu > Merge

Trying to extend the approach to three or more heavily edited versions of a manuscript creates problems when there are overlapping and contradictory revisions that even a human editor would find difficult to reconcile, so it's not surprising that Word can't do this job perfectly. My guidelines for collaborative editing by multiple reviewers (see Chapter 3) can help you avoid the necessity for such difficult work.

The procedures to compare the original and edited versions of a document in Word differ between versions. In all versions, however, the results will be much cleaner and easier to interpret if you accept all changes in the edited manuscript to produce a final edited version that you will then compare with the original manuscript. (See *Accepting or Rejecting Changes* later in this chapter for details.) Give the files clear names, such as "Original MS.docx" and "Edited MS.docx". Once you have done so:

- **Word 2010:** Ribbon > Review tab > menu for the Compare icon > Compare. Specify the original and revised documents, then expand the dialog box (if it's not already expanded) so you can select which options (types of changes) you want Word to display. Word will then display three document windows: on the left, the comparison document; on the right, the original and final documents that you compared. Save the comparison document under a new name.
- **Word 2011:** Tools menu > Track Changes > Compare Documents. Specify the original and revised documents, then expand the dialog box (if it's not already expanded) so you can select which options (types

of changes) you want Word to display. In the field Label changes with, specify how you want to identify the person who made the changes that will appear in the comparison document; by default, this will be your name. Word will then create a new file containing all the changes. Save the comparison document under a new name.

This comparison is an excellent way to recover edits if a reviewer inadvertently reviews a document without using revision tracking or if an author accidentally accepts all tracked changes before reviewing them, and neither has access to the original document. (This happens more often than you might expect.) The comparison also provides a useful way to check whether an author has been careful in reviewing your edits by revealing which edits they rejected, which edits they implemented differently, and whether the author added any new text. If you're responsible for catching any errors that slipped past the author, this is an efficient way to accomplish this task.

Older versions of Word sometimes forgot our identity (i.e., lost track of the user information settings), preventing us from revising our own edits without tracking these as changes made by a different editor. This problem is now rare, but if it strikes you, try retyping your name in the User Information settings. (See Chapter 4 for details.) If that doesn't solve the problem, the document comparison feature provides an easy way to recreate all your changes in a new document.

Accepting or Rejecting Changes

Once someone receives an edited document, they must review all the tracked changes and accept or reject each change or insert a comment containing their response to a change. Prolific authors may perform this task more often than we do, but we may be called upon to review an author's responses to our edits, to teach an author how to use the revision tracking features, or even to implement all the changes for an author if we're the only one allowed to modify the document. Unfortunately, if you don't know the trick I'll reveal towards the end of this section, each change requires at least one action to review and implement. For example, a simple insertion takes only one action: accept or reject. In contrast, a deleted word correctly replaced by a new word requires two actions: one to accept the insertion and one to accept the deletion. More complicated changes require correspondingly greater numbers of actions to implement.

Table problems: Word occasionally won't let you accept or reject tracked changes in a table. To solve the problem, turn off track changes before you accept or reject the change. If the problem persists and relates to a format change, apply the same format change *two more times*: for example, if you boldfaced the heading row, select that row and apply boldface once (to remove the format), then again to reapply the format. If the problem relates to inserted text, copy and then paste the inserted text. If the problem relates to deleted text, simply retype the text. For large amounts of text, open the Review tab's Show for Review menu and select Original with no changes; you can then copy and paste this text. Turn on track changes and continue editing.

With a heavily edited manuscript, implementing all the changes can take an enormous amount of time, and the more times someone must click an icon in the Review tab, the greater the risk of error. Fortunately, Word provides a variety of ways to review changes. Moreover, there's a highly efficient way to implement all the changes in as few actions as possible. I'll start with the basics, which are adequate for lightly edited documents, then I'll describe an efficient way to deal with heavily edited documents. Finally, I'll describe how to deal with reviews by multiple reviewers.

One change at a time

If there aren't many changes, it makes sense to accept or reject each change individually. The process works similarly in any software that provides tools for reviewing changes:

- Use the software's tools (e.g., the Find next icon in the Ribbon's Review tab) to find the next change.
- Decide whether the change is correct, then click the appropriate icon (Accept or Reject) to accept or reject the change. If you're unsure how to deal with a change, insert a comment to remind yourself to return to that change, and then move on to the next change.
- Repeat this process until you reach the end of the document. You can use the Find next icon again to start over from the top of the document and confirm that you haven't missed any edits.

Use the Ribbon's Review tab

In the Review tab, Word offers Previous and Next icons that let you move (respectively) to the previous or next tracked change. Click these icons to move through the document one change at a time. Click the Accept or Reject icons to (respectively) implement or reject the change, or click the New Comment icon to insert a comment if you want to discuss the change with the reviewer.

Note the presence of popup menus beside the icons for accepting and rejecting changes. Open those menus to reveal additional options. For example, Accept All Changes in Document and Reject All Changes in Document let you quickly create versions of an edited manuscript with (respectively) all changes accepted (i.e., the final document if all the edits are correct) and all changes rejected (i.e., the original unedited document). This is useful when you need to compare documents, as I described earlier in this chapter.

Use the mouse

- Scroll through the document, with the changes displayed.
- When you encounter a tracked change, right-click or control-click the mouse cursor on the changed text.
- From the popup menu, select Accept Change or Reject Change.
- Repeat these steps until you reach the end of the document.

Use the keyboard

Word provides no default keyboard shortcuts to find, accept, and reject changes, but you can define your own keystrokes using the Customize Keyboard dialog box, as described in Chapter 4. Under the Categories heading, select All Commands. Under the Commands heading, scroll to the following commands:

- Find the next change: ToolsRevisionMarksNext
- Find the previous change: ToolsRevisionMarksPrev
- Accept the change: ToolsRevisionMarksAccept
- Reject the change: ToolsRevisionMarksReject

Choose a keyboard shortcut you can easily remember for each command. For example, I use Control+Alt combined with the following keys: → to find the next change, ← to find the previous change, and A to accept or R to reject a change.

Use a combined approach

With a little dexterity, you can combine the Review tab with the mouse and the keyboard. For example, use the icons in the Review tab to find the previous or next change, then use the mouse to right-click and accept, reject, or skip that change. But for maximum efficiency, use only the keyboard commands.

Implementing many changes efficiently

The more heavily a document has been edited, the greater the need to review and implement changes efficiently by minimizing the number of mouse clicks or keystrokes. If the editor did a good job, this is easy: most of the changes will be correct, so there will be few changes to reject. This lets the reviewer reject the few errors, insert any necessary explanations, then accept all the remaining edits in a single step. Here's how it works:

- Save the document under a new name before you begin (e.g., "Geoff-final.docx") in case you make a mistake and need to return to the original edited document. Set Word to display all tracked changes.

- Move through the document looking for comments. You can do this most efficiently if you set Word to display only the comments, as described earlier in this chapter. Respond to each comment. If you disagree with a comment, add your response (e.g., explanation) inside the original comment. If you agree with a comment, make the necessary changes, then delete the comment.

- Return to the start of the document, and scroll through the document so you can examine each change, one change at a time. (You can also use the icons in the Review tab to move to the previous or next change.)

- If a change is acceptable, move on to the next change.

- If a change is incorrect or imperfect, reject the change and (if necessary) fix the problem yourself. If you must justify your choices to the editor or discuss them with a reviewer, insert a comment to explain your reasoning. For example, copy the text that contains the suggested change, insert a comment, paste the copied text into the comment, then type your explanation: "You suggested [pasted text]. Unfortunately, this doesn't work because [explanation]. Could we do [alternative suggestion] instead?"

- Continue until you reach the end of the document.

- Since all the remaining changes should be correct, you can accept them in a single step: in the Review tab, open the menu beside the Accept Change icon and select Accept All Changes in Document.

- Save the file and return it to the next person who must review it.

Final quality control

Some authors learn to trust us so much that they accept all our changes without carefully reviewing or discussing them, then review only the final document that results. Try to discourage this approach. Even the most careful editor occasionally makes mistakes, and authors have usually revised their manuscript so many times that they're too familiar with its contents and can no longer pay careful attention to the details. Inevitably, authors who adopt this approach miss editing errors, leading to embarrassment for everyone—if we're lucky. In the worst-case scenario, someone may get hurt or even killed as a result of following instructions that contain a serious error. If the consequences of an error are severe, there's no substitute for having a third person (preferably an expert who is less familiar with the document) perform a final review.

Some authors prefer to read the entire document that results from our edits, then display our changes only when something looks wrong. This is easy to accomplish using the **Show for Review** menu (described earlier in this chapter): set the display to **Final** initially, then change to **Final Showing Markup** whenever something looks fishy so you can review the changes that created the problem. This works better than simply accepting all changes outright, but it doesn't eliminate the problem of over-familiarity with a document. Again, try to arrange a final review by an expert.

Whatever approach the author and editor choose to review the edits, the last step should always be to use the tools in the **Review** tab (or the keystrokes you created) to search for any tracked changes missed during the first pass. (It's surprisingly easy to accidentally click the **Find next** button twice, or press the keyboard equivalent twice, thereby skipping an edit.) Once again, someone who is not intimately familiar with the document should do a final read-through of the manuscript to provide a reality check.

Dealing With Multiple Reviewers

When a document must undergo several reviews, the most effective approach is to edit it heavily first to eliminate distractions created by grammatical problems or fuzzy wording. This will help subsequent reviewers focus on more important issues such as the completeness, correctness, logic, organization, and safety implications of the text.

Real-world results: Much of the description in this section is based on a highly successful process-improvement exercise conducted with my previous employer. Details are provided in two articles (Hart 2011, 2012) in the Bibliography.

This approach requires at least two review stages: a preliminary cleanup by the editor and a subsequent technical review. However, it is rare to see such a simple review process in the real world. Most traditional review and revision processes have evolved over time to require many review stages. For example, a particularly thorough review process might include the following stages:

- editorial review (by an editor)
- peer or technical review (by experts in the subject)
- external review (by colleagues or customers)
- management review (often by several levels of manager)
- sales reviews (by marketing and sales specialists)
- legal review (by one or more lawyers)
- safety review (by workplace safety experts)
- final editorial review

Some of these reviews can proceed simultaneously. For example, most publishers ask two or more peer reviewers to simultaneously perform a rigorous technical review on an early draft of a manuscript. Ideally, these reviewers can review the manuscript collaboratively, as I discussed in Chapter 3. This won't work when some reviewers can only review documents that have already incorporated edits that resulted from previous review stages. For example, managers, safety officers, and corporate lawyers all typically want to sign off on the final document after everyone else has provided their input. As a result, authors and their editors may receive a single file that contains edits by multiple reviewers, a separate file from each reviewer, or a combination of combined edits and separate edits.

Protecting files from certain modifications: Word lets you protect documents to prevent reviewers from making certain changes. In Word 2010, Ribbon > File menu > Info > Protect Document icon > Restrict Formatting and Editing. For format changes, select the checkbox for Limit formatting to a selection of styles, then click the Options button and deselect any styles that you want to protect. For text changes, select the checkbox for Editing restrictions, then select the types of revisions you will allow. In Word 2011, you can't protect styles, but you can restrict the types of editing allowed: Word menu > Preferences > Security tab > Protect Document button. Choose the edits you will allow. Both versions ask you to define a password that must be entered before you can unlock the document. Don't lose this password!

When a single file contains edits and comments from two or more reviewers, it's useful to be able to examine each reviewer's changes and comments while ignoring the changes and comments of other reviewers. To do this in Word: Ribbon > Review tab > menu beside the Track Changes icon > Reviewers. You can now choose to reveal or conceal edits made by any given reviewer.

When two or more reviewers perform simultaneous (parallel) reviews, each reviewer is likely to work on a different copy of the manuscript. The author or their editor must then compile these separate reviews into a single final document. For light edits, it's possible to do this manually. However, the section *Comparing Documents in Word* earlier in this chapter describes how you can automate this process using the "combine" or "merge" feature. Word can automatically extract the proposed changes from several documents and combine them into a single final document that contains all the changes.

In practice, merging proposed changes from several different copies of a document becomes difficult whenever there are multiple conflicting edits of the same text. Even for humans, it can be confusing trying to disentangle the results, particularly when the sequence of edits (which reviewer commented on or revised a previous reviewer's work) is not clear. Where this situation seems likely to occur, it would be wise to discuss alternatives such as the collaborative review process I described in Chapter 3.

Given the complexity of reconciling edits from multiple reviewers, it's wise to appoint someone who will carefully review the original edited documents to ensure that no important changes were missed. As I noted earlier in this chapter in the section *Final quality control*, someone (usually the editor, working closely with the author) should always take responsibility for ensuring that all appropriate suggestions have been implemented, that the author had a satisfactory reason for any changes they rejected, and that the final manuscript accomplishes the goals of the author and their employer.

Revision Tracking When You're Not Using Word

Word is both powerful and ubiquitous, but not everyone uses it. Other word processors, such as WordPerfect and OpenOffice Writer, have their own revision tracking tools, and most of the tools I've described for Word have equivalents in those programs. However, technical writers increasingly use more powerful and sophisticated tools, and many of these have their own versions of revision tracking:

- **Framemaker:** FrameMaker now includes revision tracking.
- **InDesign and InCopy:** InDesign now offers built-in revision tracking, but you can also use the tools provided by InCopy.
- **MadCap software:** MadCap's Contributor software offers powerful tools for collaborative editing.

If the software you're using doesn't provide revision tracking tools, search the Web to see whether a revision tracking plug-in or document comparison program has been developed by another company.

Chapter 7. Inserting Text, Deleting Text, and Commenting

Web: http://www.geoff-hart.com/books/eoe/eoe3/eoe3.html
Note: Word 2010 is for Windows; Word 2011 is for the Macintosh

As editors, we spend most of our time inserting missing punctuation, letters, words, phrases, and sentences, and deleting redundant or incorrect punctuation, letters, words, phrases, and sentences. In most cases, the reasons for these changes are sufficiently obvious they require no explanation. But sometimes our rationale isn't obvious, or we're not sure how to solve a problem. When that's the case, we must propose a solution, explain a tentative solution (what we've done and why), or ask the author questions designed to help them clarify their thinking so that they can propose their own solution. These suggestions, explanations, and questions are all *comments*, since we're commenting on what we've done or what needs to be done. Writing comments requires considerable tact to encourage the author to respond appropriately. In this chapter, I'll describe how to insert and delete text, and to explain why using comments, in ways that strengthen your relationships with the author while helping both of you work more efficiently.

There are two common philosophies about how best to modify a manuscript. The "teach them how to write" school believes we should enter each correction directly where it occurs, no matter how complicated the resulting changes. For example, if a single word contains three typos, this school's philosophers recommend correcting each typo rather than retyping the whole word. This approach follows the rationale that by seeing each correction, authors will learn from their mistakes and gradually begin to write cleaner manuscripts. Less charitably, this could be described as the "demonstrate our attention to detail and how good we are by emphasizing every correction, no matter how small" approach, since it makes the results of our edits seem more complicated and demanding than they might actually be.

This approach may be useful for students who are learning to write or for unusually picky authors who want to review every tiny change. But in practice, most authors are more interested in reviewing our edits quickly than in learning how to write, and even picky authors quickly lose patience with unnecessarily complex edits. That being the case, I recommend a second philosophy—the one taught by the school of "editing to maximize efficiency for both the editor and the author".

A Brief Digression About Efficiency

Editing can require a lot of work for both the editor and the author, so it's important to learn how to revise a manuscript efficiently; we rarely have the luxury of sufficient time to edit as thoroughly as we'd like. However, efficient editing *does not* mean that you should minimize the number of keystrokes required to make a given change, though it may have that salutary effect. Instead, it emphasizes techniques for quickly entering changes while making the revisions easy for the author to understand and assess. Because changes are clearer and easier to see, this also decreases the risk that authors will miss small corrections. Whenever possible, edits and comments should also be designed to minimize the risk of error when the author reviews and responds to our revisions.

This approach also reduces the risk that authors will lose patience with us and stop cooperating or paying attention. I can't emphasize the latter point strongly enough: If you edit in a way that makes it unnecessarily difficult to review your work, authors look for shortcuts to simplify their task, and these shortcuts lead to errors. Moreover, if you're a freelancer, it's sobering to remember that clients who dislike your approach to editing won't provide additional work or recommendations. In contrast, making it easy to review our edits is a good investment in a long-term relationship with an author. Moreover, if you're working in a corporate setting, it may be considerably more important to minimize the *total* time spent reviewing a document than it is to minimize *your* editing time. This is particularly true when the author works more slowly than we do, which is often the case when we work with occasional authors such as engineers and scientists rather than professional writers such as journalists or technical writers. We do much more onscreen editing than they do, and thus, can use the tools much faster than they do. From the employer's perspective, helping authors work faster produces a greater net benefit than focusing on our editorial needs, even if this costs us time.

Chapter 6 provides details of the most efficient way for authors and editors to review an edited manuscript. In the present chapter, I'll explain how to make the process as painless as possible for both you and your authors. Fortunately, the same techniques improve life for everyone. With a little practice, the skills you'll learn from this book will help you work so much faster and more effectively that you'll be able to afford to spend more time pampering your authors, whether through spending time cleaning up your edits before you return the manuscript or through explaining your decisions. Although encouraging authors to think is an inherently good thing (society benefits whenever we encourage someone to think better), that's not necessarily a goal we should try to achieve by forcing them to decipher our work.

Editing is an inherently adversarial relationship, since every edit says "your writing is poor and this edit proves that I'm a better writer". Increasing our own efficiency must never come at the cost of emphasizing this message, and forcing authors to repeatedly stop and figure out the subtle brilliance of our editorial reasoning can only exacerbate the problem.

Insertions and Deletions

There are two main things you must remember to insert or delete text efficiently. The first is that it's inefficient to move the text cursor painfully within a word to make multiple corrections, whether entering missing letters or deleting superfluous letters. In most cases, it's more efficient to retype the entire word; most editors type sufficiently fast that we can retype a word faster than we can correct multiple errors one keystroke at a time. After typing the corrected word, delete the word that follows it with a single keystroke: Control+Delete for Windows and Command+Delete for the Macintosh.

The second thing to remember is that a retyped word or phrase is easier to understand at a glance than a puzzle that contains several tiny corrections that force the author to reconstruct the final word by assembling and integrating those corrections, like assembling the pieces of a jigsaw puzzle.

There's no one right way to avoid creating puzzle words and puzzle sentences, but there's a good general rule of thumb: group your changes so that related changes can be accepted or rejected in a single step rather than requiring multiple steps. Thus, changes that should be accepted in a single action should be entered as a single uninterrupted change. For example, if you're replacing "considered" with "are considering", delete "considered" and type the two new words rather than changing "ed" to "ing" and then adding the word "are". Compare the results:

are consider~~ed~~**ing**
are considering ~~considered~~

The corollary to this rule is that you should enter multiple changes separately if they should be accepted or rejected separately. An example might be if you need to edit "considered", as described above, and then change the details that follow this word. Compare:

are considere~~d~~**ing gather**~~holding~~ **for** a ~~meeting~~ **discussion**

are considering ~~considered~~ **gathering for a discussion** ~~holding a meeting~~

Puzzle sentences that result from edits in every second or third word can also be difficult to untangle. As in the latter example, retyping (or copying and pasting) a sequence of several words produces a result that is much easier for the author to understand. The resulting changes are also simpler for the author to accept: one click to accept the insertion of the correct word or phrase, and one click to accept the deletion of the incorrect word or phrase, for a total of two actions rather than one action per correction.

This approach makes increasing sense for the author as the number of corrections increases, because each insertion or deletion requires another action to accept or reject. As soon as the number of insertions and deletions exceeds two, retyping makes reviewing faster for the author. It may seem that retyping long phrases or entire sentences greatly increases our difficulty. Fortunately, there's a shortcut that makes the process highly efficient:

- Select the text that requires multiple corrections using the techniques described in Chapter 5.
- Copy the text (Control+C for Windows, Command+C for the Macintosh).
- Without touching any other keys, paste the text (Control+V for Windows, Command+V for the Macintosh) to replace the original with the copied text. Because the original text is still selected (highlighted), this accomplishes both the insertion and the deletion in a single step.

You can now fix the individual problems in the pasted text. (Alternatively, make your changes first, then copy and paste the entire revised text. Both approaches work well.) This is particularly efficient when the corrections involve juggling word order, since most software lets you select words with the mouse and drag them around the sentence until they're in the right locations. In Word, this feature is referred to as *drag and drop editing*. (Chapter 4 describes how to enable this feature.)

I recommend that editors place inserted text *before* the deleted text that it replaces. This lets the author read the revision, which is often self-explanatory, rather than encountering an unexplained deletion and having to figure out whether the deleted text is simply gone or has been moved somewhere else. That eliminates one stumbling block in the process of understanding and approving our edits. Authors who are interested in figuring out what we did (most aren't) can still compare the inserted words and phrases with those we deleted; if they agree the edited text is correct, they can simply move on to the next edit. Some colleagues prefer to insert new text *after* the deleted text, in part because (in Word) selecting the text you want to delete and starting to type causes the new text to appear after the selected text. This is slightly more efficient for the editor.

I'm not convinced there's any significant difference between the two approaches, and authors will learn your editing style as they work with you. As long as you're consistent in how you insert and delete text, neither approach should pose a major obstacle to authors. Of course, if your author expresses a preference, it's wise to accommodate that preference as much as possible.

Moving Text to a New Location

When it's necessary to move text to a new location, I recommend that you move the text without recording the move as a tracked change. That is, instead of tracking both deletion of the text at the original location and insertion of the text at its new location, turn off revision tracking before you move the text. This approach offers an important advantage over tracking both changes: the farther apart the original and final positions, the greater the risk that the author will accept the insertion and reject the deletion, thereby leaving the same text in two places. They might also do the opposite, thereby eliminating important text from the manuscript.

Of course, some explanation is helpful whenever you feel that you need to move whole sentences or larger chunks of text to a new position, particularly if that position is far enough from the original that the author can't see where the text has gone. In that case, simply delete the text and insert a comment explaining that you've moved it elsewhere. For example, if you need to move the text to a position later in the manuscript: "I moved the description of this procedure into section 3.2 because it will be easier to understand after you've explained the procedure's context, which you do in that section." Conversely, if you move the text to an earlier position in the manuscript, add a comment at the new location to explain the sudden and otherwise mysterious appearance of the new text. For example: "I moved this paragraph here from the end of the instructions because warnings should always *precede* the procedures that require them."

In summary, add explanations both where the moved text originated to explain its absence and where it comes to rest to explain its appearance. The author might remember what you did without these notes, but in case they've forgotten, the notes decrease the likelihood that they'll reinsert the moved text.

Another option would be to leave the text in its original location, but insert a comment that tells the author where you believe they should move the text after reviewing your edits. This approach is best if you're not certain the move is essential, and your goal is to spare the author the need to undo the move (possibly introducing a new error) if they reject your suggestion. If you use this approach, it's helpful to insert another comment at that destination to reduce the risk that the author will move the text to the wrong location. For example, "See my note on page 5 about moving a paragraph of text into this section. If you agree, insert the moved text here."

Over-explain, at least initially: Remember that authors wrote something in a specific way because that way made sense to them. Thus, our changes are rarely as obvious as we might hope. Once an author begins to understand how we think and to trust our logic, less explanation will be necessary.

If you need to both edit text and move it somewhere new, it's most efficient to disable revision tracking, move the text to its new location, then turn on revision tracking again and make the necessary (tracked) changes. As I noted in Chapter 6, moving text that contains tracked changes can be tricky. If you leave revision tracking enabled and move text that contains edits to its new location, the final result of your editing will be tracked as a single insertion in which all of your changes have been implemented, making it difficult for the author to see what you did. Although this is efficient from the perspective of reducing the number of actions required to approve the edits, it forces the author to examine the moved text carefully to detect your changes, which can be difficult when you move whole sentences and paragraphs. Even if the author is meticulous, there's a high risk of missing subtle but potentially important changes.

If you belatedly discover that you'll have to move an extensively edited chunk of text to a new and more effective location, this can be tricky to do with revision tracking enabled. In Word, if you cut and paste edited text, the software will mark the original text as having been deleted, and will not preserve your edits; it will then insert only the results of your editing at the new location, so the author will not see your individual edits. Turning off revision tracking before you move the edited text will solve this problem: the author will see both the original text and your edits. You must also turn off revision tracking if you want to use *the spike* to cut out text and move it to a new location. See Chapter 5 for details on using the spike.

If your software won't let you move text containing tracked changes without losing details of the changes, try the following trick:

- Save the file to preserve your most recent changes.
- Save a temporary copy under a new name (e.g., "Temporary").
- In the temporary file, turn off revision tracking, then delete all the text except the chunk that you want to move. To do so, position the cursor before the text you want to retain and press Control+Shift+Home (Windows) or Command+Shift+Home (Macintosh) to select all the text before that point in the file, then press the Delete key. Next, move the cursor to the end of the chunk of text you want to move, and press Control+Shift+End (Windows) or Command+Shift+End (Macintosh) to select all subsequent text, then press the Delete key.
- Save and close the temporary file.
- In the original file, insert a comment to explain the proposed deletion, then turn off revision tracking and delete the text that you want to move.
- Move the cursor to the position where the edited text should appear.
- Insert the temporary file at that location. In Word 2010, Ribbon > Insert tab > Insert Object > Text from File. In Word 2011, Insert menu > File.
- Select the temporary file, then click OK.
- Turn on revision tracking and continue editing.

Comments and Questions

In an ideal world, editing becomes a dialogue between editor and author in which each learns from the other and we work together to produce the best possible result: a manuscript that communicates clearly with the reader, while retaining the author's unique voice. One problem with on-screen editing, particularly when you work at a distance and will rarely or never meet your authors, is that it can eliminate this dialogue. I've found that it's possible to mitigate the distance between author and editor that onscreen editing creates by recreating the dialogue in the form of comments. The dialogue never reaches the level of a post-work chat over beer, but it can at least approach the epistolary dialogue of traditional handwritten letters and modern e-mail conversations.

> **Real-time dialogue:** When it's necessary to discuss something with a distant author, a phone call is always an option. A visit to a nearby office may even be in order. But where neither is possible, there are alternatives. One is to use chat or instant messaging, possibly with the document displayed on a Web site (as described in Chapter 3).

In this section, I'll describe my best practices and learned wisdom relating to comments. A comment may be a simple statement that explains a change, a statement that indicates we don't understand something, a list of possible alternative wordings for the author to choose among, or a short essay that describes a problem and proposes a solution. Most comments involve explanations of some sort, even when that explanation takes the form of a question such as "Do you mean [proposed explanation]? If not, please reword this text to make the meaning clearer. If you e-mail me an explanation, I'll help you choose clearer wording."

Deciding when to explain what we've done rather than leaving the reason implicit is more of an art than a science. As a general rule, it's safer to insert too many comments than too few because being misunderstood has more serious consequences than over-explaining; if an author can't understand the problem that prompted us to make a change, they may arbitrarily reject the change and leave the problem to trip the next reader.

Explanations also remove a common obstacle in the author–editor relationship: the perception our edits are arbitrary and done primarily to impose our style on the author. (This attitude is widespread, particularly among authors who have had bad experiences with editors and haven't yet learned to trust *us*.) Good explanations persuade the author that we have a sound reason for everything we do, and over time, that perception establishes a belief in our expertise, a willingness to trust our judgment, and the understanding that our edits really do help them communicate their message. Similarly, demonstrating that we understood the author's message and tried to make that communication more effective establishes both our authority and the feeling that we're trying to help the author, not criticize them. This changes the relationship from criticism or confrontation to a more friendly collaboration.

Is a comment truly necessary?

The main risk of over-explanation is that the author, wearied by our solicitude and numbed by the consistent correctness of our changes, may come to trust our judgment so implicitly that they accept our edits without carefully reading each comment and without fully considering whether we might be wrong. You can do a few things to minimize this risk:

- Explain a given point once, the first time it arises in the manuscript, rather than repeating the explanation for each instance of the problem. Subsequently, highlight the problem with a simple comment such as "make the same change here that you did in response to my previous comment" or a comment that contains only the proposed correction, such as "delete this word?" If you're confident your suggested change is right, make the change without further explanation. So long as you track the change, the author can undo it if necessary.
- Write concisely to minimize the amount authors must read, but don't create sentence fragments; take the time to write clearly.
- Obtain the author's permission to make certain changes (e.g., applying the correct heading styles) without explanation. This eliminates the need for many comments.
- Only insert truly necessary comments.

The last suggestion seems to contradict my statement that it's better to over-explain, but I've retained it to remind you to never insert a comment without carefully considering whether it's truly necessary. Don't waste the author's time explaining obvious points of grammar such as subject–verb accord or the use of articles such as *the*, but do explain why the verb the author used was wrong or the implications of articles that communicate different meanings (*the* vs. *a* is a particular problem for authors whose native language doesn't use articles). That being said, there are several situations that suggest the need to insert a comment:

Introductions

If this is your first time working with an author, consider inserting a comment right at the start that *briefly* explains who you are and makes it clear you want to work with the author to come up with mutually satisfactory solutions. This is also an opportunity to remind the author not to reject an edit out of hand simply because *you* misunderstood the text; remind them that if you misunderstood, someone else may misunderstand too. Offer a chance to discuss alternatives if the author doesn't like your solution. This introduction can instead be part of your cover letter when you return a manuscript to the author, but placing it directly in the body of the manuscript makes it harder to miss or ignore.

Explanations

Sometimes the original wording appears reasonable, but ignores a problem you've encountered before, such as a particular phrase that a journal's peer reviewers object to. Other times, your edit represents a better solution—once the author understands why. In such cases, a brief explanation is the spoonful of sugar that makes the medicine go down more easily.

Confirmation requests

Sometimes we're only 90% confident we've correctly understood the author's mangled prose, and that our rewording is clearer and correct; this is often true when we attempt to fix unclear antecedents or pronouns. It's the 10% of the time when we're wrong that can destroy all the good will we've earned through our skillful edits up to that point. Specifically asking the author to confirm an edit—when no such request accompanies any of your other edits—emphasizes the need to pay particular attention to this change to ensure that we got it right. If you prefer, you can use the comment to remind the author that they can always contact you to discuss alternatives. (You don't need to make this offer more than once.)

Collaboration and options

Offering a choice of two alternative wordings demonstrates whether we have understood or misunderstood the author's meaning, and gives the author an opportunity to collaborate in choosing a solution that we both like, rather than imposing our choice on the author each time. Even if we guessed wrong, we've at least provided the author with a starting point for understanding why we might have misunderstood and hints on how they could improve the wording. Of course, if we guessed right, they can simply copy our solution and paste it into the text, and that's one less thing for us to edit during the next pass.

Only provide two alternatives: If you provide too many alternatives, authors are sometimes paralyzed by the number of choices. Provide your two best guesses, and offer the author an opportunity to explain their meaning if neither alternative is correct.

Sometimes a sentence has two or more possible interpretations, and we can't eliminate this confusion until we know which one the author means.

Since we can't propose all possible clarifications, it's helpful to instead insert a comment that explains the problem and offers solutions. For example: "The highlighted text could refer to either A or B. If you mean A, write [suggestion 1] but if you mean B, write [suggestion 2] instead". If we're confident one option is correct, we can replace the original wording with that option, then add a comment that presents an alternative in case we guessed wrong: "My revision means [explanation]. If you mean [alternative interpretation], write [suggestion] instead." If a third or fourth possibility exists, it may be appropriate add those possibilities as options C and D, with explanations of when each option would be correct. However, the more options you provide, the harder it becomes for the author to choose.

Questions

Sometimes we don't have the faintest notion of what the author is trying to say, or aren't sufficiently confident we're correct to make any changes. Then, the only option is to gently explain the problem and ask the author to propose a solution. Try something like the following wording: "I'm sorry, but I don't understand what you're trying to say here. Please e-mail me an explanation so I can help you choose clearer wording."

Explanation of a recurring problem

For recurring problems that are easy for authors to fix, you can simply report the problem once and leave it to the author to resolve. For example: "This author's name (*Smith*) is spelled *Schmidt* in the References section. I found both spellings in a Web search. Which is correct? Please make the necessary corrections everywhere in the manuscript." This type of question avoids the need to insert the same comment at each of many locations where the problem occurs. However, this approach relies on the author to find and fix all those problems, and that may not always be a wise choice. It's often more effective to repeat the comment concisely each time. For example, the previous comment might subsequently be condensed to "Schmidt?" where the text says *Smith*, or "Smith?" where the text says *Schmidt*. Though the comment is terse, its conciseness and clarity make that terseness acceptable.

Alternatively, you can use Word's highlighter marker tool (described in detail in Chapter 6) to highlight each place where a particular problem occurs, and insert a comment that tells the author what this highlighting means when they first encounter it. That's far more efficient than having to repeat the same comment *ad nauseam*, particularly since you can apply this format to all instances of a word or phrase in a single step using a global search and replace (as described in Chapter 6) to both apply and remove highlighting in a single step. If you choose this approach, remember that many authors never learn where this tool is hidden and thus have no way to remove the highlighting. When you first explain the meaning of the highlighting, explain where they can find the tool and how they can remove the highlighting. Though you can use different highlight colors for different purposes, this creates a potentially complex coding scheme. Use multiple highlight colors cautiously, and err on the side of simplicity.

Explanation of an error of omission

Sometimes authors omit necessary definitions or create logical *non sequiturs* by omitting a few key words. In that case, explain the problem and propose the solution. For example: "Because readers of this journal may not be experts in your field of study, I recommend adding a brief explanation of [a key concept readers must understand before they can understand the rest of the manuscript]." Sometimes the existing text is adequate, but would be clearer in another form. For example, "A photo or illustration would show this more clearly."

Explanation of an error of commission

When authors blunder, explain this tactfully. Error-prone authors grow progressively more frustrated as they deal with repeated reminders of their fallibility, so you must be particularly diplomatic. For example, the annoyed editor's "Can't you even add three numbers correctly? Try again, Einstein!" should become "I calculate an average of 4.55 (or 4.6 to one decimal place) for these three numbers, not 4.8. Please confirm that there are no typing errors and change whichever number is incorrect."

Explanation of ineffective organization

Authors sometimes gather all the necessary information and describe it clearly, but present it in seemingly random order. Explain the problem and provide a solution. For example: "Because readers must learn basic concepts before they can understand an advanced concept, I recommend that you move these definitions to the Introduction, before the procedural information. You could also create a glossary that defines these terms."

Explanation of mandatory changes related to the publisher's style guide

If some of your edits are mandated by a publisher's style, it helps to explain why you've made a change to text that superficially appears correct. For example: "this magazine places captions *below* figures" or "this journal only uses *metric* units". However, this kind of change is something you should obtain permission to make without an explanation.

Pointers to relocated text

As I noted earlier, you should alert authors about what you've done if you move sentences or paragraphs to more effective or appropriate locations. Explain your rationale for the move.

Effective comments and questions

As the sample comments that I've provided indicate, there's an art to creating an effective comment. Despite the facetious quotation from my former research director that appears on this chapter's Web page, comments should always be professional, tactful, and designed to encourage dialogue and collaboration. Tactless comments increase the natural resistance to being edited. Editors often joke that the real reason we make a second pass through manuscripts is to eliminate snarky quips and communicate in a manner that encourages the author to adopt our suggestion. An effective comment has the following characteristics:

It's polite

Most of us don't say *please* nearly often enough. This magic word turns a comment into a request rather than a demand and thereby changes the author's perception of the comment. A demand increases resistance; a request encourages the author to consider what we're asking.

It focuses on reader needs rather than attacking the author

Comments should focus on our difficulties rather than criticizing the author. Such comments explain why *we* are having difficulty understanding. The author clearly still failed to communicate successfully, and has thus failed as a writer, but we're not rubbing their nose in their failure.

It's tactful

We can't establish a collaborative working relationship with an author if we repeatedly criticize or demean them—even if they seem to deserve such criticism. (That *is* obvious, right?) Yet you'd be surprised how often editors slip and let their frustration show, particularly under deadline pressure. *Always* leave time to edit your comments to ensure that they focus on the problem and its solution, not on the author's deficiencies.

It explains the problem

By explaining a problem (e.g., "In my experience, *Editor* is more commonly used than *Mutilator of Text*"), we emphasize why we misunderstood something or felt obliged to correct it, and thereby suggest that other readers are likely to encounter the same problem. Understanding the problem also lets the author see how our proposed solution solves the problem, or leads them to think about how to solve the problem in another way, in their own words.

It offers an effective solution

Rather than just stating that you don't understand something, propose a solution to the problem you've described. Provide full replacement phrases or sentences rather than fragments so the author can adopt a solution, perhaps after modifying it slightly, rather than having to come up with one of their own. It's always easier to accept an editor's carefully crafted solution than it is to develop a wholly new solution.

It's clear and grammatically complete

Cryptic, telegraphic comments are difficult to understand; instead, write full sentences with easily understood explanations, even though these take longer to craft. (Chapter 11 explains how to automate the creation of often-repeated comments.) This is particularly important when you're working with an author for whom English is their second or third language. Such authors have more difficulty than native speakers of the language when it's necessary to decipher terse comments.

Example of an effective comment

The following example illustrates all the characteristics of an effective comment:

> "In this sentence, *them* refers grammatically to your colleagues, but I suspect you mean the lab equipment. If you mean *your colleagues*, reword the sentence to read 'unpleasant odors from my colleagues'; if not, say 'unpleasant odors generated by the lab equipment'. If neither interpretation is correct, please rewrite the sentence to clarify the meaning. Feel free to e-mail me an explanation so I can propose a better rewording."

This comment explains the problem in a tactful way, focuses on the problem (an unclear antecedent) rather than on the author, offers instantly usable solutions based on the two most likely interpretations, asks the author to choose one of these alternatives, and reminds the author of the opportunity to collaborate.

Reviewing a Previously Edited Document

You may occasionally find yourself editing the work of another editor or reviewer, and discover that they made a mistake. How can you correct the problem without making the other person look foolish? The simplest solution is to contact that person, explain the problem, and get their permission to fix it so that nobody else will see the error. Once you have permission, you can use the revision tracking tools to reject the changes that produced the error, thereby restoring the original text, and (if necessary) you can then make your own changes.

Unfortunately, this kind of dialogue often isn't possible. For example, you may be working across time zones, or deadlines and other factors may leave insufficient time to discuss the problem with the other editor. In that case, you have to solve the problem. If you're certain you're correct and the other editor is wrong, you can simply go ahead and fix the problem. That's risky, since you might not be correct. If the error resulted from a reasonable misunderstanding, insert a comment that provides a plausible justification for the incorrect change and a solution. For example, you can state that the first editor's change is correct based on a certain understanding of the sentence, and provide an alternative change if that interpretation is wrong. If there isn't any obvious way to sugarcoat the mistake, you can instead insert a comment that entirely ignores the other editor's change (to avoid drawing attention to the error), but that provides your own suggestion. Editors differ in their opinions, and authors learn to expect this, so contradictory recommendations should not embarrass either editor.

Working With Word's Comments

Thus far, I've discussed the *contents* of comments, but not how to actually use a word processor's tools to insert comments in a document. In this section, I'll describe how to use the comments feature effectively.

The first step is to learn where the comment feature is hidden. In Word, you can insert a comment by selecting the Ribbon's Review tab and clicking the New Comment icon. You can also insert comments directly from the keyboard:

- **Word 2010:** Press Alt+R to select the Ribbon's Review tab, then press C (New Comment).

- **Word 2011:** There's no default keyboard shortcut, but you can create one using the Customize Keyboard dialog box, as described in Chapter 4. Under the Categories heading, select Insert; under the Commands heading, select InsertAnnotation. Define a keyboard shortcut for this command.

What happens to the screen display when you insert a comment depends on how you've customized the screen display. Chapter 6 describes the display settings in detail. If you've chosen to work with the Review(ing) pane, Word will open the Review(ing) Pane at the side or bottom of the main document window, and you can type your comment in that pane. To escape this pane and return to editing, you'll need to click the close button at the top or side of the pane or click the icon for this pane in the Ribbon's Review(ing) tab. If you've chosen to work with comments displayed in balloons in the right margin, Word will create a new balloon at the right side of the document window, and you can type your comment in the balloon. To escape the balloon and return to your editing, press the Esc key.

Editing comments from the keyboard: There doesn't seem to be any built-in command to move the cursor into a comment balloon so you can edit comments and I wasn't able to record a macro to accomplish this. However, you can display the Review(ing) pane and use the arrow keys to scroll to the comment. If a comment is not attached to a tracked insertion or deletion, Word 2010 lets you press the Menu key (usually located two keys to the right of the space bar) to display a contextual menu; press E to select Edit comment and execute that command. (Sadly, this command is not available if the cursor lies inside inserted or deleted text.) Note that you must first position the cursor inside or to the left of the shaded area that indicates the comment's location before you use these shortcuts.

Describing which word or group of words a comment refers to is time-consuming and imprecise. Fortunately, there's a better way to communicate the word, phrase, or section a comment applies to. If you select the relevant chunk of text (e.g., a problematic phrase or even a full sentence) *before* you insert the comment, Word will highlight the selected text, thereby clarifying which words the comment applies to. This is efficient for you, because it eliminates the need to type explanations such as "in this sentence" or "in the third word of the second line of this paragraph". It's also efficient for the author, because they immediately see the comment's target. Here's what the comment highlighting typically looks like:

(This is a comment)[GHT1]

The brackets that mark the start and end of the comment and the text inside these brackets will be shaded in the color you specified in the Track Changes settings, which are described in detail in Chapter 4. Some color choices are difficult to see, so experiment until you find a suitable color. The [GHT1] at the end of the comment represents the initials (abbreviated name) that you specified in the User Information section of the Options or Preferences dialog box, followed by the comment number. It will only be visible if you are not displaying comments in balloons.

If you don't select any text before you insert a comment, Word will generally pick the word nearest to the text cursor and highlight that word to indicate that the comment applies to that word.

If the comment applies to a large chunk of text such as an entire paragraph or section, highlighting the entire block of text is ineffective because that context is too broad to be meaningful. Moreover, any additional comments you insert to describe smaller parts of the selected text will be obscured by the original comment's highlighting, making it difficult to see which part of the text they apply to. To avoid this problem, select only the first word in the block of text to associate the comment with that word, then add a brief description (e.g., "In this paragraph...") to clarify the comment's scope.

Holding the mouse cursor over the highlighted text will display a pop-up that contains the full text of the comment. (In some cases, an erratic bug in Word requires you to click first to position the text cursor inside the highlighted text. The bug may also cause the text of a long comment to disappear before you can finish reading it.)

To make the comment feature even more effective, teach authors how to cut and paste text from your comments into the main document window:

- With the Review(ing) Pane open, scroll to the correct comment and select the text. With balloons displayed, click to position the cursor inside the balloon that contains the comment text.
- Select the replacement text and copy it (Control+C for Windows; Command+C for the Macintosh).
- Click the mouse cursor at the correct location in the manuscript and paste the copied text (Control+V for Windows, Command+V for the Macintosh).
- Delete the comment, as described in the next section.

To define how the text will be formatted, in Word 2010: Ribbon > Home tab > menu below the Paste icon > Paste Special. In Word 2011: Edit menu > Paste Special. Word offers the options of having the pasted text take on the properties of the surrounding text or of preserving its formatting. To make the latter choice most efficient, edit the properties of the Comment Text paragraph style so that it resembles the body text. (See Chapter 4 for details of how to edit styles.) Authors most often paste the comment text into the body text, so using its characteristics is the best bet.

Inserting and removing comments

If you find yourself endlessly repeating the same comment, perhaps with minor variations, it's easy to type it once and then copy it so you can paste it into each new comment that you create. But there's a faster way: use your software's automatic text features to create abbreviations that will automatically expand into the full sentence. In Word, the most useful tool to accomplish this is called AutoCorrect. (See Chapter 11 for details on how to use this tool.)

If your software doesn't provide this feature, create a file that contains the comments you routinely type while editing, then keep this file open beside the manuscript while you work. You can switch between the manuscript window and these comments (see the section *Juggling Document Windows* in Chapter 4 for details), copy the comment, switch back into the manuscript, and paste the comment at the desired location. If you're a gadget geek and love adding programs to your computer, various clipboard-replacement utilities let you store multiple items on the clipboard to facilitate pasting them into a document. In addition, there are many text-expansion utilities that will let you emulate Word's AutoCorrect function. I've listed some possible programs in both categories on the Web page for this chapter.

To inspire you to create your own shortcuts, here are some examples of comments I found myself repeating so often that some kind of shortcut was clearly necessary:

- This reference is not cited in the text. Either insert a citation at the correct location or delete the reference from your bibliography.
- This reference is missing from your bibliography. Please add it there, or correct the current citation to match one of the references that is already present.
- This date does not match the date (i.e., [actual date]) in the bibliography. Please confirm the correct date, then make the necessary changes everywhere.
- If [interpretation] is not what you mean, please change the wording to make the meaning of [problem phrase] clearer.

- Do you mean [suggestion]? If not, please reword the highlighted text to make the meaning clearer. Feel free to e-mail me an explanation so we can discuss alternatives.

Pay careful attention to the kinds of errors that you must describe most frequently or that require the most typing when you encounter them. Some problems are so common in the work my authors do that I may insert dozens of the abovementioned comments in even a short manuscript.

Creating such shortcuts accomplishes two goals: First and most important, it lets me communicate concisely with the author, but in full sentences that both describe the problem and propose a solution. Second, it saves me from having to type these long explanations myself (Word does the work for me), so I have time to use longer, author-friendly explanations instead of cryptic sentence fragments. Last but not least, I carefully checked the comments when I first created them, so there are no typos to correct.

Removing a comment once you've responded to it is simple: right-click or control-click inside the comment and select Delete Comment. Older versions of Word sometimes marked a comment as deleted but didn't actually delete it; if this happens, simply click the Accept icon in the Ribbon's Review tab to accept the deletion. Alternatively, turn off revision tracking and try deleting it again. However, you may not want to teach authors the trick of disabling revision tracking until you're confident that they won't abuse this knowledge by making untracked changes behind your back.

Deleting comments from the keyboard: To create a keyboard shortcut in both versions of Word, open the Customize Keyboard dialog box (as described in Chapter 4), select the All Commands category, and then scroll down to the DeleteAnnotation command. Assign a memorable keystroke. Word 2010 lets you press the Menu key (usually located two keys to the right of the space bar) to display a contextual menu; press M twice to select Delete Comment, and then press Enter to execute that command. (The command is not available if the cursor lies inside inserted or deleted text.) Note that in both cases, you must first position the cursor inside or to the left of the shaded area that indicates the comment's location before you use these shortcuts.

If you really don't like using Word's comment features, an alternative would be to type *inline* comments. Such comments can be typed directly into the text and set off with [brackets] or <other special characters> to make them stand out from the text. Working with such comments is far more intuitive, and is a suitable choice if the author is willing to work in this manner. In Chapter 13, I provide several suggestions on how you can do this most efficiently.

Printing Comments

When editors or authors want to review a printed copy of a manuscript, they often print the comments separately so they can place the printout beside the manuscript as they work. The major motivation for this is that long comments may not fit within the comment balloons, causing much of their contents to disappear when you print the manuscript.

In older versions of Word, you could print only the comments from the Print dialog box by selecting Comments from the Print What? menu. This option is no longer available. Instead, there are two good alternatives: First, create a new macro manually (following the instructions in Chapter 11), and add the following line:

ActiveDocument.PrintOut Item:=wdPrintComments

Second, copy the comments into a new file from the comment balloons. To do this, start by creating a new file, then display the comments in the edited file as balloons (following the instructions in Chapter 6) if they are not already displayed this way. Before the next step, delete paragraph breaks in any multi-paragraph comments to that each comment contains a single paragraph. Next, place the cursor at the start of the first comment balloon, then select all the comments and copy them into a new document:

- **Word 2010:** Press Control+Shift+End to select the comments, Control+C to copy them, and then switch to the new document and press Control+V to paste them.
- **Word 2011:** Press Command+Shift+End to select all the comments, Command+C to copy them, and then switch to the new document and press Command+V to paste them.

To add numbers that match the comment numbers in the text, select all the comments (Control+A for Windows, Command+A for the Macintosh) and then use Word's autonumbering. In Word 2010: Ribbon > Home tab > Numbering icon. In Word 2011, Ribbon > Home tab > Numbered List icon.

There are two cautions to keep in mind about this approach. First, any comments with multiple paragraphs will be assigned two or more numbers, so the numbers won't match what the author sees in the document. Second, warn the author to not delete comments in Word as they work through the printout and resolve the problem described by each comment. If they do this, Word will automatically renumber the remaining comments, whose numbers will no longer match those in the printout. Delete the comments only after all changes have been made.

Cleaning Up

After heavy editing, a document will be littered with insertions, deletions, and comments. Even the most well-intentioned author is likely to grow weary dealing with the editorial carnage and miss an occasional edit. Less well-intentioned authors, and careless authors, are likely to miss many comments or even introduce errors while responding to our edits and comments. Even with relatively straightforward edits of short documents, human nature makes it likely some errors will still slip through. For this reason, keep two things in mind:

- Invest some time reviewing and revising your edits and comments to ensure that they're as clear as possible.
- Designate someone to take responsibility for reviewing the final manuscript. Ideally, this person will be you, since you (as editor) know what problems you asked the author to solve and are thus best suited to confirm that they actually solved the problems.

In corporate settings, it's quite common for the editor to be given a chance to review the document after the author incorporates all the edits and responds to all questions and comments. But in some cases, particularly for freelancers whose clients live halfway around the world, we may never see the document again. In that situation, it's important to remind the author that someone must read carefully through the final manuscript to ensure that nothing was missed and that no new errors were introduced while responding to questions or editing the edits. Offer to do this as a standard part of your work, but build this additional work into your cost estimate. Authors will be grateful for the additional quality control and you won't be doing hours of unpaid labor.

Chapter 8. Using the Search Tools (Find and Replace) to Improve Consistency

Web: http://www.geoff-hart.com/books/eoe/eoe3/eoe3.html
Note: Word 2010 is for Windows; Word 2011 is for the Macintosh

> **Word's Find and Replace dialog box:** If you're not already familiar with the basic elements of this feature, see the overview presented on this chapter's Web page. If you don't like the sidebar that opens when you press Control+F in Word 2010 or Command+F in Word 2011, you can restore the old dialog box using the Customize Keyboard dialog box. (See Chapter 4 for details.) In Word 2010, select Home tab under Categories, and EditFind under the list of commands. In Word 2011, select All Commands under Categories, and EditFind-Dialog under the list of commands. Define an appropriate keyboard shortcut.

At times, authors are bemusingly and amusingly inconsistent: they use several words to mean the same thing or the same word to mean several different things, make contradictory claims in different parts of the manuscript, or provide cross-references to the wrong section or to a section that no longer exists after previous revisions. The text contradicts the accompanying graphics and tables, or cites the wrong graphics and tables. Literature citations don't match their corresponding entries in the bibliography, or are missing from the bibliography. Careless application of paragraph styles, combined with manual formatting, produces headings at the same nominal level that differ so wildly in appearance that they obscure the document's structure. Really creative authors commit all these sins simultaneously, as well as inventing other clever types of inconsistency.

Henry Fowler used the term "elegant variation" sarcastically to criticize authors who did not understand the meaning of elegance: elegance requires judicious use of synonyms to communicate shades of meaning rather than to demonstrate that the author owns a thesaurus. Unfortunately, both elegant and inelegant variation challenge editors who must attempt to impose consistency on a manuscript. A few scattered problems aren't fatal, but as inconsistencies mount up, they undermine the reader's confidence in the author and sabotage the reader's ability to comprehend the author's message. As editors, we're responsible for restoring confidence in the author and clarifying their message by imposing consistency on the manuscript. When we edit on paper, we rely on a capacious memory for detail to remember a specific date or how a word was spelled many pages earlier. To support this work, we keep notes on the preferred way to say something—a style sheet—and consult those notes whenever we spot a possible discrepancy. (I'll discuss style sheets in more detail in Chapter 9.)

This is a particular concern in technical writing and nonfiction, where changing the word used to describe a concept forces readers who may already be struggling with impenetrable jargon or difficult concepts to decide whether that change conveys a special new meaning. For example, does the instruction to "click" a button somehow differ from the instruction to "select" a button, and is there any difference between "click" and "click on"? If there's no difference, this variation wastes the reader's time. Of course, it's also important to be consistent in fiction. Character names, for example, must be spelled consistently everywhere—and the same person must not have two different names or variable eye color unless they're spending part of the story in disguise.

Unfortunately, large manuscripts with many inconsistencies tend to overwhelm our memory, and it becomes increasingly easy to miss some of these problems as we grow fatigued. Worse still, discovering (say) on page 400 that the spelling of a name we'd been using consistently for the previous 399 pages was wrong used to mean that we faced a tedious rereading of those 399 pages to find and fix each instance of the problem. Similarly, on seeing the author say "white" on page 200, we might feel a sudden suspicion they said "black" earlier in the manuscript—so back we go, rereading the previous 199 pages and hoping we'll recognize related problems, such as saying "grey" somewhere in between. In hindsight, it's amazing we ever managed to make manuscripts self-consistent within the allotted time.

Fortunately, computers do a great job of performing such repetitive, memory-intensive tasks. In Chapter 4, I discussed how using styles and templates correctly can impose consistency on the visual appearance of the text. A more broadly useful advantage of onscreen editing is the ability to use the software's search tools to confirm previous statements or scrutinize all occurrences of a particular word or phrase, its synonyms and variant forms, and the preferred replacements. Each time we spot a suspicious statement, we can immediately check it against all previous and subsequent statements. After finishing our first pass through the manuscript, we can run through our style sheet, one line at a time, using the search tools to find inconsistencies we missed. This approach isn't foolproof, but it moves us considerably closer to perfection—once we know how to use the search tools to support our work. In this chapter, I'll show you how to use those tools effectively.

Consistency on steroids: Of course, manually running through a style sheet is so 20th century. Why not automate the process? Fortunately, you can! Check out Editor's Toolkit Plus, PerfectIt!, and Edit Tools. Sadly, only for Windows. Details on this chapter's Web page.

Searching for Variations on a Theme

In this chapter, I'll use the phrase *search term* to describe the thing we're searching for and that we'll type into the Find what field of the typical Find and Replace dialog box. Search terms can be a single letter or number, a complex pattern that must be matched, or even a long chunk of text such as a sentence. (The maximum length of the search term varies among programs.) In the Replace with field of the dialog box, we can type new text to replace the old, specify a new format (such as italics or a paragraph style) that we want to apply to the search term, or apply some other property to whatever the software finds.

Imposing consistency on long manuscripts can be one of our more tedious and error-prone tasks. In short manuscripts, it's easy to ensure that the author wrote "user manual" everywhere instead of an occasional "reference book", but long manuscripts pose a greater challenge. There may be tens or even hundreds of terms we must help the author to use consistently throughout a book that spans hundreds of pages, and we must keep that list in mind throughout our editing so we can use the preferred wording. As the number of terms to juggle grows, we're increasingly likely to miss important but sometimes subtle inconsistencies.

The search tools, combined with a style sheet that we build as we work, helps us meet this challenge. When we see the author using new terminology for a concept they've already described, consulting our style sheet lets us find the words they used previously and decide which alternative is best. What we cannot easily do with paper style sheets, we can easily do with an onscreen style sheet: rearrange it, whenever necessary, to suit our present needs. If the style sheet grows too long to scan at a glance, we can use the search tools to locate what we're seeking. Search tools also permit *ad hoc* consistency checks. For example, let's say that late in a manuscript, we see a date of 1067 for an event but remember the date being described as 1066 earlier in the manuscript—only we're not sure where the inconsistency occurred or whether that was the only inconsistency related to this date. In onscreen editing, we can use the search tool to find all references to 1066—or even to "106" if we're only confident we remember the first three digits correctly or if other years in that decade may also be wrong. If searching for the year doesn't find other references to that date, we can try related search terms, such as "Norman conquest" and "French invasion", to see what dates emerge.

Returning to where we started: Before departing on a wild Norman chase, it's helpful to be able to return quickly to our point of departure and continue editing. See the section *Distractions and Getting Lost* later in this chapter for tips on ensuring that you only *interrupt* your train of thought rather than derail it completely.

One of the unfortunate realities of editing is that we can't trust our authors to get anything right more than once; every statement must be checked to ensure that it's correct and is consistent with related statements throughout a manuscript. It's not that authors are stupid. Really! It's just that this kind of consistency is not their primary interest. Most learn to rely on us to obsess over such details.

So how can search tools help? Consider the example of checking the literature citations in a long manuscript. First, we need to confirm that every reference cited in the body of a manuscript appears in the bibliography with matching author and date information—and conversely, to ensure that every bibliographic reference has been cited somewhere in the text if that's required by the publisher. (You'd think this would be relatively easy, but in nearly 30 years of editing, I've seen no more than one in ten of my authors manage this feat, and usually fewer.)

Working on paper, we'd separate the reference list from the manuscript, set it aside, and then consult it each time we encountered a citation. This was time-consuming and disrupted the flow of our editing—a problem during substantive editing, when we were struggling to grasp a subtle argument's complexities and ensure that they were clear and without contradiction. But waiting until after we'd completed our editing to check the citations meant rereading the entire text to find the citations—and time for that read-through wasn't always available. Workarounds such as using highlighter markers or marginal notes were ineffective; it was easy to forget to label some references, and even when we remembered, it was a distraction to drop the red pen and grab a highlighter.

> **You *could* print the references:** Though I recommend that you *don't* print your references, this doesn't mean you shouldn't do so if working partially on the screen and partially on paper proves most efficient or comfortable. Onscreen editing is a tool for making editing easier, not a dogma you should embrace to the point of foolishness. For example, I usually print out figures both to confirm that they will print correctly and so that I can consult them as I work.

When we're working onscreen, the search tools let us ignore literature citations until we've completed our editing, then complete the reference check in a single efficient pass. The search tools let us reliably find each citation without having to scan through the document ourselves—a tedious, error-prone process. I'll describe the process in some depth because it's easy to generalize the approach to other types of consistency check.

If we want to work entirely on the screen, the first step is to copy all of the bibliography into a separate document so we won't have to scroll down to the bibliography each time we find a literature citation. Instead, we can switch between windows (using the keyboard shortcuts described in chapters 4 and 5), confirm the details of that reference, and add a checkmark to confirm that the reference has been cited somewhere.

> **More monitors merrier:** This kind of task is easier if you have a large monitor or two monitors. Keep the bibliography window open beside the document window, and only switch to the bibliography window when it's necessary to add a note or scroll in that window. This saves many keystrokes in long documents such as books.

The trick in searches is to identify the element that will be present in each of the things we're seeking. If the manuscript uses the author–date citation style, in which the citations resemble "Poe (1850)", that element is a four-digit year. Of course, a history textbook that cites older documents, might also include dates with one, two, three, or four digits. (For example, the author may be citing ancient manuscripts rather than more recent sources that quote the older manuscripts.) In that case, the things that remain constant in each citation are the "(" character that comes before the number that starts the year or a number followed by the ")" that follows the year. We can search for either or both of these patterns. (Unfortunately, if the author likes parenthetical comments as much as I do, that could become tedious. I'll discuss a more efficient approach when I discuss pattern matching later in this chapter.)

Another common citation style numbers the bibliographic references sequentially, and cites the number in square brackets: "[42]", for example, rather than "Hart (2010)". In this case, the search term could be either the opening square bracket followed by a number or the closing bracket preceded by a number.

To make this search process more concrete, let's consider the details involved in checking literature citations. Here's how this might work in the author/date system:

- Copy the bibliography into a new document and save the file.
- Move the cursor to the start of the manuscript, and search for the first reference. For example, if we know that all references are in the first decade of the 21st century, we would specify "20" as the search term. (I'll describe a more sophisticated search strategy later; for now, let's stick with simple patterns.)
- When you find a match, close the search tool and switch to the window that contains the bibliography. Confirm that the citation matches the bibliographic entry: the author name and year must match those in the citation, and the title must seem plausible. For example, if the citation states that "*The Raven* (Poe 1846) is a touching tale of found love", yet the Poe (1846) reference is for *The Cask of Amontillado*, the author has cited the wrong reference. (You can't always perform this check, since many citations refer to details that aren't evident from the title.)
- Perform any necessary edits. For example, if there's an error, insert a comment that describes the problem and proposes a solution: "Should the date be 1845? The 1846 reference is *The Cask of Amontillado*, not *The Raven*. Also, please confirm your description; "a touching tale of new-found love" is not accurate for either work."
- If the publisher's guidelines require that each item in the bibliography be cited in the text, add a checkmark in the bibliography beside the reference to indicate that it was cited. Any character will do; I use * because it's easy to type and is visually different from the author names.
- Continue by searching for the next instance of the search term, using the appropriate keyboard shortcut. In most software, you won't need to repeatedly open and close the search tool. In Word, you can click the

double-up or double-down arrows at the bottom of the vertical scroll bar to (respectively) find the previous or next instance of the search term.

- Continue this process until you reach the end of the manuscript.

Search with the dialog box closed: Most software offers a "find again" or "find next" function under the Edit menu so you can close the search dialog box and use a keyboard shortcut to find the next instance. In Word 2010, the keystroke is Control+PageUp or Control+PageDown to find (respectively) the previous and next instances. Word 2011 uses Command instead of Control.

- Scroll through the bibliography to find any references that lack a checkmark. For each one, search for the author's name or the year of publication to confirm that the item wasn't cited; it's easy to skip an instance of the search term if we press a keyboard shortcut twice or click twice with the mouse, and sometimes we forget to add a checkmark. If the reference really hasn't been cited, ask the author to add a citation at an appropriate location or delete the item from the bibliography.

You can use the search tool in this manner to find anything that has a predictable pattern. I'll discuss more sophisticated ways to find specific patterns of characters in the section *Advanced Find and Replace* later in this chapter. Here are some examples of the kinds of things you can search for as part of your efforts to make a manuscript self-consistent:

- You can confirm the correctness of any sequence, such as the numbers assigned to sections, figures, and tables. For example, search for each occurrence of the word *Figure* (or its abbreviation, *Fig.*) to ensure that the author has cited each figure, with no gaps or duplications in the numbering.

Don't trust Word's automatic numbering: There's a long-standing bug in which Word restarts numbering when it shouldn't or forgets to restart numbering when it should. Searching for the paragraph style that uses the automatic numbering lets you quickly spot these problems. Appendix III provides suggestions on how to fix the numbering problem.

- You can confirm that every term in a list such as a style sheet (see Chapter 9) has been used correctly throughout the manuscript.

- You can check for minor variations in spelling, such as whether a compound word is set solid, hyphenated, or left open (e.g., *onscreen*, *on-screen*, and *on the screen*).
- You can search for all headings formatted using a specific paragraph style (see the section *Advanced Find and Replace*, later in this chapter, for details) to confirm that the style has been implemented correctly. For example, authors often seem to capitalize headings randomly, and searching through the document one heading at a time quickly reveals such inconsistencies.
- In a statistics or mathematics manuscript, variables and parameters are usually italicized and vectors and matrices are usually boldfaced. When you encounter any variable, you can search for all occurrences of the variable's name and italicize any that are not already italicized. Similarly, you can ensure that all vectors and matrices are boldfaced.
- If your style guide requires the use of serial commas (i.e., "A, B, and C" rather than "A, B and C"), which are also known as Oxford commas, you can search for the word "and" (preceded by a space so that you won't also find all occurrences of *candy* and *pandemonium*). Where necessary, add the missing comma.

And so on. Anywhere your author has used a predictable pattern to state something or to format part of the text provides an opportunity to search for and confirm the consistency of that pattern. Doing this one instance of the term at a time can be tedious when the pattern occurs frequently, but it's the only way to ensure consistency if two or more potentially correct alternatives exist. In the section *Global Search and Replace Operations* later in this chapter, I describe a more efficient way to perform such changes, as well as the necessary precautions, when you are certain the same change must be made in every instance.

If you only need to compare the text with a short list of consistency items that could fit in one small window, you can display that list beside the main document window. (See the section *Juggling windows* in Chapter 4 for details on how to do this efficiently.) As you work through the main document, glance at the reference document whenever you come across something that you must check. For example, in some of the manuscripts I edit, the author introduce a dozen or more unfamiliar acronyms. To understand what they're trying to explain, I need to repeatedly look up each acronym until I've got them memorized. I could use the search tool to repeatedly find the original definition of that acronym, or jot down notes on a scrap of paper, but it's easier to display those acronyms in a window that remains visible as I edit.

> **Don't rule out paper:** I'm a strong advocate of *onscreen* editing, but I nonetheless keep paper and pens beside my keyboard for jotting notes. Sometimes it's most appropriate to type these notes in a word processor file—but other times there's no substitute for paper.

Distractions and Getting Lost

The power of the search tool creates two serious risks: the risk of distraction (losing your train of thought), and the risk of getting lost and forgetting where you began your search. Both risks result in wasted time: in the first case, you need to re-establish your train of thought, and in the second case, you need to remember where you started your search. Let's look at those problems in order.

When you're focusing on substantive editing, such as following a complex argument to its conclusion to confirm that it makes sense and is consistent with the rest of the text, try to carry that process through to the end. Interruptions force us to start the process over again or make it take longer than necessary. Interrupting substantive editing to fix relatively minor consistency problems disrupts concentration and makes it harder to return to that previous mental state. At worst, you can lose a subtle yet important understanding that's dangling right at the edge of comprehension, thereby eliminating your understanding of that point (*satori*, or perhaps a slowly developing *gestalt*) and preventing you from using it to improve the communication. If you're going to use the search function to begin a consistency check, complete your current thought process first. If necessary, jot a note on a scrap of paper to remind you what aspect of consistency you suddenly felt a need to check.

If the issue is as simple as a question of spelling rather than as complex as the correct use of a word in two different contexts, add it to your style sheet and move on; you can always check it later. It's more efficient to do certain kinds of checks, such as reviewing the style sheet entries discussed in Chapter 9, in a single step after you've completed the main edit. On the other hand, if the issue that you've suddenly perceived is complex and will affect all subsequent editing, it may be necessary perform the consistency check immediately.

In each case, it's important to be able to return quickly to where you paused before beginning the consistency check. It's always possible to remember (perhaps with some effort) the last section you were working on, but it's better to get there with the minimum waste of time and effort. There are several ways you can do this:

- You can scroll through the manuscript, a page at a time, until you recognize your starting point. That's slow, but it works *in extremis*.
- If you remember the last few words you were editing, you can search for those words. (This works best for uncommon search terms. Searching for *and* is rarely productive; searching for *it is the beating of his hideous heart!* is more useful.)
- If you remember (or noted on a scrap of paper) the page number where you paused, use the Go To function to return to that page. See Chapter 5 for details on how this function works in Word.
- If your software provides a bookmark feature, use that. Bookmarks are generally invisible unless you set Word to display them, so remember to remove them before you return the manuscript to the author. Add a note on paper or in your style sheet so you won't forget!

These all work, but there's a simpler and faster method: type a pair of special characters that won't appear in the manuscript, such as [ ], as a bookmark. This works in any software, and you can find the bookmark quickly using the search tool. Because most search tools highlight the search term, you can then press the Delete or Backspace key to remove the bookmark. Moreover, because the bookmark is unlikely to legitimately appear anywhere in the text, even a careless proofreader should spot and remove it should you forget. This method uses the computer the way technology should be used: to make life easier. Nonetheless, it's worthwhile to learn about the other options, since one or more may suit your work style better under some circumstances (e.g., recording the page number when you're proofreading). Sometimes comfort is more important than theoretical efficiency, since you'll use something comfortable more readily than something that is extraordinarily efficient but uncomfortable.

For most consistency checks, I recommend starting from the beginning of the manuscript, since this lets you see the search term in its first context, and that context sets the tone for all subsequent instances. However, that's not the only way to proceed. If the search term appears in the current sentence and you use the search tool to begin making changes from that point onwards, the search function will eventually reach the end of the file and ask whether you want to continue from the start of the document. Say yes, and the software will eventually return you to your starting point and then display a note saying that the search is complete.

Refining Your Search

Most search tools offer myriad options that let you do more than match a specific sequence of numbers or letters. Unfortunately, these options may be hidden. For example, by default, Word's Find and Replace dialog box shows only the most basic options, presumably to avoid intimidating new users. Unfortunately, my teaching experience suggests that many editors never learn of these options. If you can't see the full range of possibilities, expand the dialog box: in Word 2010, click the More button, and in Word 2011, click the small downward-pointing triangle at the bottom left side of the dialog box.

In this section, I'll present the most commonly available options. Later, in the section *Advanced Find and Replace*, I'll discuss some extremely sophisticated (but correspondingly complex) options for narrowing your search to an exquisite degree. That being said, the most common searches fall into two categories: matching patterns and finding special characters.

> **Keyboard shortcuts in Word 2011's search dialog box:** There are several keyboard shortcuts for selecting (and then deselecting) dialog box settings. Press Command followed by E to open the Special menu, G to select the Go to tab, I for Highlight all items found in..., K to select Sounds like (Japanese) if you've installed Japanese language support, M (more options) to display the advanced options if they're not already visible, O to open the Format menu, P to select the Replace tab, S for Sounds like, U to select Use wildcards, and Y to select Find only whole words.

Matching patterns

Early search tools were hopelessly literal, and if you didn't precisely specify the search term, you wouldn't find it, even if the term was clearly present. Modern software is more sophisticated. Among other things, it typically provides the following options, which I'll illustrate using Word's conventions:

- **Wildcards (variants):** This option lets the software seek variants of a word or phrase that contain any single character or range of characters at one or more positions within a longer search term. Most commonly, you'll see ? used to stand in for a single character and * used to represent a series of characters. For example, searching for s?ng would find *sing*, *song*, *sang*, and *sung* (i.e., the question mark would be replaced with any of the single characters *i*, *o*, *a*, and *u*, respectively). In contrast, searching for s*ng would find those words plus *stetting* and *searching*. Select the checkbox for **Use wildcards** so Word knows that you don't want to search for the question mark (?) or asterisk (*) characters.

- **Matching case (capitalization):** This option lets you find only text that has a capitalization pattern identical to what you specified in the **Find what** field. For example, this would let you search for *Red Death* without also finding instances of *red death* and *RED DEATH*. If you use this option and type replacement text in the **Replace with** field, Word will use the capitalization in the replacement text to replace the found text; for example, if you search for *red*, select the option for matching case, and type *Red* as the replacement, Word will change *red* (but not *RED*) to *Red*. Invest a few minutes learning how your software handles this option.

- **Homophones ("sounds like"):** This option helps you find phonetic misspellings of the search term. It isn't particularly accurate, but when it works, it works surprisingly well; for example, searching for *masque* would also find *mask*. It's worthwhile trying this option if you only vaguely remember the spelling of a word.

- **Whole words only:** This option lets you narrow your search to include only whole words rather than parts of words. For example, searching for *beat* with this option selected would not find *beating heart*.

- **Word variants ("Find all word forms"):** This option lets you find related forms of a word, such as *laugh*, *laughed*, and *laughing*. (That is, it searches for verb forms. To find noun forms such as *laughter*, use the wildcards option instead.) For example, if you're trying to use a particular verb in the present tense throughout a manuscript, this option lets you find other forms of the verb so you can decide whether to change each to present tense.

- **Location (Word 2010, "Find in"; Word 2011, "Highlight all items found in"):** This option lets you constrain the location to the main document, the footnotes, or the comments. You can also define the direction of a search—forward from the cursor position to the end of the document, or backwards from the cursor position to the start. Some software, including Word, also lets you select a section of the text before you start the search. The software then confines the search to the selected text instead of searching the whole document. This can be very useful if (for example) you want to confine your search to a section such as the bibliography.

- **Formatting:** Most software also lets you search for characteristics of the text such as its font (e.g., Times New Roman 12 point), format (e.g., boldfaced), style (e.g., the Body Text paragraph style), alignment (e.g., flush right), and language (e.g., Canadian French). In Word, display these options by clicking the Format button. Each of these categories has many additional options. For more information, see the section *Advanced Find and Replace* later in this chapter.

Finding special characters

Most software lets you search for a range of special characters. These include the unique symbols and letters in foreign languages, of course, but also many of the specific codes the software uses to define formatting or provide special features such as cross-references. In general, you can search for these characters by selecting them from a special menu or by typing codes that represent them (referred to as *control codes* in Word) into the search box. If you're not sure what a character is or how to type it yourself, try copying it from the text and pasting it into the Find what field. Although Word lets you copy and paste text into both the Find what and the Replace with fields in this dialog box, you lose formatting information (e.g., boldface), and you're limited to about 255 characters.

When Word's Find and Replace dialog box is expanded to show all the options, you can gain access many special characters. First, position the cursor in the Find what or Replace with field. Next, click the Special button and select the desired special character from the list of available options to insert it into that field. Word displays the character as a control code, which is represented by the caret character (the ^ that appears above the 6 on most keyboards) followed by a letter or symbol that defines the specific control code. If you learn these shortcuts, you can type them yourself without having to make a separate trip to the Special menu, so it's worthwhile learning the codes for characters you search for often.

With none of the option checkboxes selected, Word lets you choose from among the following special characters:

Special character	Control code
any single character	^?
any single digit (number)	^#

Special character	Control code
any single letter	^$
carets	^^
column breaks	^n
comment markers ("annotations")	Word 2011 only: ^a
contents of the clipboard (only for the Replace with field)	^c
em dashes (—)	^+
en dashes (–)	^=
endnote markers	^e
fields (used to perform certain automated functions)	^d
footnote markers	^f
graphics	^g
manual line breaks	^l
manual page breaks	^m
non-breaking hyphens	^~
non-breaking spaces	^s
optional hyphens	^-
paragraph markers	^p
section breaks	^b
tab characters	^t
white space (multiple spaces or tabs)	^w

Finding comments: If your version of Word no longer uses ^a to find comments, create keyboard shortcuts (see Chapter 4 for details) for the NextComment and PreviousComment commands. You can also select the Find dialog box's Go To tab and select Comment, or use the icons in the Ribbon's Review(ing) tab.

Note that the letters in these shortcuts must all be lower-case; you cannot, for example, search for ^P if you want to find the end-of-paragraph marker. You can combine these control codes with other search terms, including other control codes. For example, if you wanted to search for the word *editing* at the start of a paragraph rather than in the middle of a paragraph, you would search for ^*pEditing*; this pattern tells Word to search for the end of a paragraph (^*p*), then check whether the first word at the start of the next paragraph is *Editing*.

Also note that the available options change if you make certain selections elsewhere in the dialog box. For example, if you select the option Use wildcards, Word provides options such as characters within a range such as 1 to 3 or characters that appear at the start or end of a word. Exploring these options is a great way to learn new search tricks.

> **Can't find a paragraph marker?** For reasons too complicated to explain here, Word defines two different kinds of paragraph marker. When you can't find a paragraph marker that you know is present, try selecting the Use wildcards option, and then search for [\^13]If that also doesn't work, deselect Use wildcards and search for ^u13.

Be extremely cautious if you try to *replace* any special characters that the software uses to perform a calculation, look up information, or insert information from another location. For example, you could delete all graphics in a document by specifying ^g (any graphic) as the Find what pattern, and leaving the Replace with field blank; this translates into an instruction to "find all graphics and replace them with nothing".

> **Using Go to to find something:** Word lets you search for some control codes by name, type, or number. For example, the Find and Replace dialog box's Go to tab lets you jump directly to a specific instance of some code rather than the next instance. Word lets you specify which instance to find: By name works for bookmarks and other named objects such as text boxes. By type works for fields. By number works for numbered items such comments, endnotes, equations, footnotes, graphics, headings, lines, pages, sections, and tables. You can also move ahead two or more instances at a time by adding a + or − followed by a number. For example, +2 moves two items ahead, whereas −1 moves to the previous item.

Finding Characters and Symbols

The easiest way to find an obscure symbol or letter from a non-English alphabet is to copy and paste the character into the Find what field. Unfortunately, Word won't always be able to find it. However, if you can discover the secret code that Word uses to define this character (its "ASCII value"), you can force Word to search for it. The following macro will reveal that number (see Chapter 11 for details of how to create macros):

```
Public Sub GetCharASCII()
MsgBox "CharCode is: " & Asc(Selection)
End Sub
```

Select the problem character, then run this macro to reveal its number. To search for the character, type the caret character (the ^ above the 6 on most keyboards) followed by the character's number in the Find what field.

Most computers now use what are called Unicode fonts. Unicode is a newer standard that has expanded the outdated ASCII character codes to include a much broader range of symbols. If you need to search for a particular Unicode character and Word won't let you copy and paste it into the Find and Replace dialog box, you can use the following trick. First, find the character in Alan Wood's handy Unicode lookup list. For characters not present in Alan's list, consult the complete official list of these codes at the Unicode Organization's Web site. (Both are accessible from this chapter's Web page.) Word can search for the decimal code for the character, which Alan provides. The Unicode site presents the hexadecimal numbers for characters, which Word won't recognize. To convert them into decimal format, search the Web using the keywords "hexadecimal to decimal conversion" (without the quotes). For example, try EasyCalculation.com's hexadecimal to decimal converter.

Finding the code for a character: Word 2010 (but not Word 2011) can tell you the Unicode value for any character: place the cursor to the right of the character and then press Alt+X. Repeating this keystroke restores the original character. If you receive a file from someone who has used a font that doesn't exist on your computer; any character that Word can't display will typically appear as an empty box. Once you know the mystery character's Unicode value, you can look up its identity using the FileFormat.info Unicode Character Search tool. Replace the mystery character with the correct character.

Once you know the code, Word lets you search for Unicode characters. To do so, type ^u followed by the character's decimal number. For example, you can find the Greek letter alpha (α) using the search text ^u945.

Unfortunately, you can't use this trick in the Replace with field. That's not a problem if you can copy and paste the character into that field. If you can't, try this instead:

- Cut or copy the character to the clipboard.
- Open the Find and Replace dialog box.
- In the Find what field, specify the search term.
- In the Replace with field, type ^c (Word's control code for "replace what you find with the contents of the clipboard").

An exception for the Macintosh: Certain Macintosh ASCII characters differ from those used by Windows, so wildcard searches don't always work the way you'd expect. If you need to use an ASCII code, try enclosing it in square brackets and adding a \ before the caret; for example, [\^013] will find the end-of-paragraph marker. In some versions, you may need to use a four-digit version of the code, often by adding a zero at the start of the number; for example, 013 would become 0013. Confused yet? Blame Microsoft.

Replacing Text One Instance at a Time

Confirm the cursor location: It's tempting to specify sophisticated options in the Find what and Replace with fields. Before you do, double-check that the cursor is in the correct field; it's easy to inadvertently set the options for the wrong field, forcing you to undo the search and replace operation and start over.

It's often possible to replace all instances of a search term in a single step—an operation called a *global* search and replace. (For details, see the section *Global Search and Replace Operations* later in this chapter.) However, if you haven't specified the search term sufficiently carefully, you may end up replacing many instances of the search term that shouldn't be replaced, such as part of a larger word, a quotation, or the title of a bibliographic reference. (Yes, I've done all of these. Oops!) Such a "blind" approach also doesn't provide a chance to confirm whether each instance of the search term should really be changed; in many cases, a single term can be legitimately used in two ways in the same manuscript. Thus, many types of search and replace are best handled one instance at a time. This takes considerably longer than replacing every instance in a single step, but it's safer and can be more effective if the same search term may appear correctly in one context and incorrectly in another. In that case, accuracy is more important than raw speed.

If you leave the Find and Replace dialog box open, you can use it to find the next instance of a search term by clicking the Find Next button, and either replace that instance by clicking the Replace button or leave that instance unchanged and move to the next instance by clicking Find Next again. This works well, but the dialog box has significant limitations:

- First, it tends to obscure surrounding text that provides context that would help you decide whether to replace that instance. (Sometimes it even obscures the search term itself.) If you have two monitors or a large screen, you can drag the dialog box to a position where it won't obscure the manuscript. But if you don't have that much space (e.g., you're working on a small laptop computer while you travel), that won't work.

- Second, you can only copy and paste about 255 characters, including spaces, into the Replace with field. Moreover, to retain that text's format, you must remember to first copy the text to the clipboard. You can then type ^c in the Replace with field to tell Word to use the (formatted) contents of the clipboard.

- Third, you can only replace the search term; you can't make any additional changes, such as revising the format, adding a missing comma, or inserting a comment.

Deleting all occurrences of a search term: To delete all instances of the search term, leave the Replace with field empty, then click the Replace all button. In effect, you're asking the software to replace what it finds with a blank (i.e., with nothing).

To solve these problems, try closing the dialog box and working from the keyboard. The key to this method is noting that when the search function finds the search term, it highlights that text so you can spot it more easily. This highlighting also means that the term is selected. If you start typing, most software will replace the highlighted term with whatever you type. (If this doesn't happen and you're using Word, change the settings for Insert key behavior option, as described in Chapter 4.)

To delete the highlighted term, simply press the Delete or Backspace key. But if you need to replace the search term occasionally, and particularly if the replacement text is long, copy the most likely replacement text (a word, phrase, or sentence) to the clipboard before you begin your search (Control+C for Windows, Command+C for the Macintosh). You can now paste this copied text into the document (Control+V for Windows, Command+V for the Macintosh) every time the replacement is necessary, thereby replacing the highlighted text. (If not, simply move to the next instance.) If you didn't think of this before you began your search, type the replacement text the first time you need to use it, and then copy it to the clipboard for use in subsequent replacements. This is a fast way to work through a document one instance of a search term at a time and replace only some instances.

Pasting with minimal fuss and bother: If you're using Word and have selected the Use smart cut and paste option (see Chapter 4 for details), Word will helpfully insert spaces around any text that you paste into the document. Often, this saves you the effort of inserting that space yourself. But if you're trying to add a prefix or suffix to a word, this feature creates *more* work: you have to delete the space. You could perform another search operation to find all the erroneous spaces and delete them, but you'll find it easier to replace the whole word with a revised version that includes the correct prefix or suffix, or to temporarily disable smart cut and paste until you need it again.

This approach also makes it quick and easy to implement a series of minor changes that might otherwise require considerable cursor movement or that might be difficult to elegantly perform using a global replace operation. Consider, for example, a mistake I must often correct in the science manuscripts I edit. Many of my authors cite multi-author works as follows: "Poe, et al., 2005". The comma before the year is required by many journals, but I've never seen a journal that wants a comma before "et al." One option would be to globally find and delete the spurious comma (i.e., to replace ", et al." with " et al."), but if I'm tracking revisions, that would track each instance of the search phrase as a deletion and create too much visual clutter. A simpler solution would be to turn off revision tracking, do the global search and replace, then turn on revision tracking again and insert a note explaining what I've done. (This is precisely the kind of change that authors should not be required to approve.) But there's an alternative that both minimizes the tracked changes (i.e., deletes only the comma) and that can be used in many other circumstances:

- Search for the recurring pattern that you want to fix, but ensure that you start or end the search term with the character that you want to delete. In the comma example, that search term would be ", et al" (but typed without the quotes).
- Find the first occurrence of this error, then close the Find and Replace dialog box.
- Because the search function highlights the entire phrase, pressing the left or right arrow key moves the cursor to (respectively) the beginning or end of the highlighted text. In this example, use the left arrow key to move to the position before the extraneous comma. You can now perform the necessary correction with a single keystroke: insert text, delete text, or, in this specific example, delete the problem comma.
- Use the Find next keyboard shortcut (Control+PageDown for Windows, Command+PageDown for the Macintosh) to move to the next occurrence of the problem.

Find next stops working in Word 2011 for the Mac: Word 2011's keyboard shortcut for Find next isn't reliable. If it stops working, leave the Find and Replace dialog box open. Because this dialog box behaves like any other window, you can use the "switch to next window" keyboard shortcut (Command+`) to change between the dialog box and the document window. Make any necessary changes, then press this shortcut again to return to the dialog box. Press Enter to find the next instance of the search term. Repeat as necessary.

A little thought will reveal many other ways to use this approach to speed your editing when a global search and replace isn't safe. For example, it's particularly useful when you need to turn a word into a phrase by adding one or more words before or after the search term.

Global Search and Replace Operations

In the previous section, I described how to search through a manuscript to find individual instances of a search term so you can decide how to deal with each instance. But sometimes it's more efficient to perform the replacement throughout the manuscript (*globally*) in a single step. For example, it may be necessary to italicize every instance of a particular word, or to replace a particular deprecated word with an approved word. To do this, specify the search term and its replacement in the Find and Replace dialog box, then click the Replace all button.

If you decide to replace a word or phrase everywhere, be exquisitely careful: it's remarkably easy to change both what you intended to change and a great many additional instances you didn't. *Never* attempt to replace anything globally at the end of a long and stressful day or at any other time when you're too tired or stressed or otherwise preoccupied to think straight, as might be the case if your name is Fortunato and you're completing a rush edit over a cask of Amontillado; at those times, concentrate on more mechanical forms of editing that you can do safely with less conscious effort. Injudicious definition of the search term can create a huge problem for you—worse yet, for the author—to correct. The possibility of creating problems for the author suggests that as a general rule, you should never try a global replacement if you won't have time to read through the entire document one last time to spot any problems.

Restricting searches and replacements to part of a document: Most software lets you limit your search or changes to a specific part of the document. For example, you may need to use consistent wording in the main text but not in the bibliography, where an alternative word may legitimately appear in some titles. In Word, select the part of the document you want to affect *before* you open the Find and Replace dialog box. When the replacement operation is complete, Word displays a dialog box asking whether you want to extend that operation to the rest of the text. Carefully click the No button to avoid undoing your efforts to affect only the relevant text.

One type of problem arises from *stemming*: when you specify a search word that forms the "stem" of other words, the search word *and all other words that contain the stem* will be changed by a global replacement. For example, a colleague once replaced all instances of *day* with *night* to correct a timing problem in a conference schedule, but forgot to type a space in front of *day* in the search term. As a result, she changed all days of the week to nights, so that (for example) *Friday* became *Frinight*. (In Word, selecting the Whole words only option would have prevented this problem.)

Another problem results from the complexity of the search dialog box. With all the checkboxes, switches, and options available, it's easy to miss something you selected in a previous search that is no longer relevant. It's also easy to apply the correct setting, but in the wrong field. Pay attention to which field the cursor is in before you apply any setting, and double-check all search parameters before you start any global replacement operation.

Tracking global replacements—or not

Whether to track global changes is an issue you should discuss with the author. For some kinds of global changes, such as applying a publisher's paragraph style definitions, correcting obvious typos, or replacing all double spaces after a period with single spaces, there's no need to force the author to review and approve each change. Indeed, the author may not have the right to reject such changes. When you're confident this is the case, and the author has agreed to let you make such changes, turn off revision tracking before you perform the global search and replace. Then insert a comment to remind the author what you've done and why, then turn on revision tracking and continue working.

For most other changes, it's wiser to make all global changes with track changes on. This makes it easier for you to spot any errors during subsequent passes through the manuscript, and gives the author a chance to see and correct any errors you failed to notice. If you're working on a manuscript long enough to benefit from the creation of a style guide, create a list of all global changes you made in the document as a separate section in the style sheet that you'll send to the client. If you perform a global replacement before you begin editing to comply with a client's style sheet, you can fix any problems that resulted from these changes during your first editing pass. If you develop an additional list of global changes that will be necessary during your first pass, make those changes before your final pass so you'll have an opportunity to fix any errors during that final pass.

Highlighting all instances of a search term

One interesting alternative to actually replacing text throughout a manuscript would be to apply highlighting to the search term. To do this, all you need to do is specify the type of highlight formatting that you want to apply in the Replace with field of the search dialog box. Here, the goal is to apply a highly visible format that you won't easily miss so that when you encounter the highlighted term, you'll remember to check your style sheet to decide whether a change is necessary. Because you will be removing the highlight before you return the file to the author, there's no need to track this change, so turn off revision tracking.

Word offers a convenient highlighter marker tool that you can apply automatically to all instances of the search term:

- Select the desired color from the menu beside the highlighter marker in the Ribbon's Home tab.
- Open the search and replace dialog box, and define the search term in the Find what field.
- Click to position the cursor in the Replace with field.
- Open the Format menu (expand the dialog box if necessary), and select Highlight.
- Click the Replace all button.

Turn on revision tracking again and continue editing, but pay attention to the highlighted text and fix any problems. When you're done, remove the color highlighting: turn off revision tracking, select all of the text (Control+A for Windows, Command+A for the Macintosh), then click the color No color (Word 2010) or None (Word 2011) from the highlighter icon's color palette. Turn on revision tracking again before you return the file to the author.

If you don't like the highlighter colors or if you're not using Word, you can achieve the same effect using any other available format. Double underlining works well because it's visually prominent and won't appear in most manuscripts. You could also use the Format menu to apply other formats, such as a visually distinctive font (typeface + size) or text color. Choose an option that's easy for you to see or that you can easily find again using the search function.

Word offers a Reading highlight option that differs somewhat from the highlighter marker. Predictably, it works differently in different versions of Word:

- **Word 2010:** In the search dialog box, specify the search term, open the menu Reading highlight, and then select Highlight All. It's not necessary to click any other button: Word immediately applies a yellow highlight color. Use the same menu to remove the highlight format: select Clear all highlighting. Unlike applying highlighting manually, this highlighting is not marked as a change if you are using revision tracking.
- **Word 2011:** In the search dialog box, specify the search term, select the checkbox beside Highlight all items found in, select Main document if it isn't already selected, and then click the Find All button. Word temporarily highlights all instances of the search term: although you can scroll through the document and use Word's menus or Ribbon icons,

clicking the mouse cursor anywhere in the document or pressing any key causes the highlighting to disappear. Because this highlighting is temporary, it is not tracked as a change.

Predicting or spotting problems

The problems caused by a careless search and replace operation can result from surprisingly subtle causes. For example, I once caused myself a fair bit of unnecessary work when I decided to fix page ranges globally in a bibliography. The author had formatted the ranges without a space after the "p.", so that they appeared as (for example) "p.1–3". I tried to add that space globally in a single step by replacing "p." with the same term followed by a space, forgetting that many of the author names in the bibliography looked something like "P.J. Fortunato"; this publisher's style required no space between the initials. Since I didn't notice the problem until after it was too late to undo the problem (Control+Z for Windows; Command+Z for the Macintosh), I had to search through the entire bibliography to find all names that contained this error.

There's one more *gotcha!* to beware: capitalization and formatting. Software is very literal about following your instructions, and will use the exact capitalization pattern you specified when you typed the replacement text. Older versions of Word tended to replace the original text with the new text you specified, but retained the original capitalization pattern (e.g., all caps, all lower-case, only the first letter capitalized); more recent versions replace the original text with the capitalization specified in the Replace with field. Thus, you may need to carefully constrain the capitalization used in the search term (and select the Match case option in the Find what field) so that you can do a separate search and replace operation for each capitalization pattern.

If you do perform a global replacement, there are several steps you can take to protect yourself from potential problems and recover more easily if you should err:

- *Always* save the document and create a backup copy *before* you make the change, especially if the change is complex. If you've made a mistake you can't easily undo, and don't notice it for a few minutes, open the backup copy and start over, but this time define your search parameters more carefully.
- Look for patterns that will restrict your changes. For example, if you don't want to change text in quotations and know that all quotations

are italicized, you can specify that the Find what pattern will only match search terms that are *not* formatted as italic.

Specifying simple font formatting: In the Windows Find and Replace dialog box, you can specify certain basic formats without opening the Format menu: for example, press Control+B for *boldface*, press the same keystroke again to change the format to *not boldface*, and press it a third time to remove any mention of boldface.

- Consider waiting until after you've completed your first pass through the document. The knowledge you've acquired by reading the whole document permits a better-informed decision about whether a search term is being used in only one way or might be used in several alternative ways that should not be changed. Record any potential problem in your style sheet, then make the necessary changes globally before your final pass through the document.
- Use the find function to locate many instances of the search term and examine the first dozen or so to decide whether a global change is safe. Alternatively, use the "highlight all" trick I described in the previous section to find all instances of the search term. This offers a chance to detect instances where the replacement would cause problems.
- If you see a significant problem after performing the global change, undo the change immediately: open the Edit menu and select Undo, or use the keyboard shortcut (Control+Z for Windows; Command+Z for the Macintosh). Most software reports the number of changes it made (in a dialog box or status bar at the bottom of the window); if this number is higher than you expected, stop editing and read through the document to see whether any of the changes are incorrect.
- Consider applying highlighting as part of the replacement format. This will help you focus on the changes during a subsequent pass through the document.
- *Always* leave time for a final pass through the manuscript. Search and replace errors are often obvious or can be detected by spellchecking.

Advanced Find and Replace

Earlier in the chapter, I provided general guidance on how search tools can help you narrow down your search; for example, I described searches for sound-alike words and variant spellings, and the use of wildcards to find similar words that differ in one or a few characters. However, these tools provide somewhat generic solutions because programmers cannot anticipate every possible thing you might want to search for. For those cases when they failed to anticipate our specific needs, it's worthwhile learning to create your own search solutions. These solutions may be referred to as *advanced search and replace*, *pattern matching*, or *regular expressions*, depending on the software; the online help will provide details on how the search tools are implemented. All of the options I'll discuss in this section are available through Word's Find and Replace dialog box, and have more or less powerful equivalents in other software.

A word of warning: Advanced search and replace operations can become quite complicated because it can be difficult to correctly describe the pattern you want Word to search for. Don't worry if you don't understand the details. You can survive quite well as an editor by learning nothing more than what I've already described in this chapter. But when you're ready to tackle really difficult challenges, the details in the rest of this chapter will help.

Mastering the complexities of search and replace: Although I've tried to be thorough, there's no better place to learn the details than from the master: Jack Lyon's *Wildcard Cookbook for Microsoft Word*.

Find and replace options

One of the most powerful ways to refine searches is to specify the formatting of the search term and the formatting you want to apply each time you replace that term with new text. For example, in a book that contains a search term both in the text and in quotations that have been formatted in italics, you might want to find only the instances outside the quotations, since you should never alter the wording of quotations other than to correct transcription errors. Similarly, it might be necessary to find all instances of a given foreign word that are not already italicized and italicize them—a common style choice. Word's search tool can perform these and many other formatting changes. To do so, fully expand the Find and Replace dialog box and click the Format button to display a menu of the available formatting options. You have options in the following categories:

- **Font characteristics:** These options let you search for any format you can specify using the Font dialog box (e.g., typeface, point size, boldface, italics, underlining). For example, you could search for all instances of Microsoft and apply italics, the correct corporate font, and the correct corporate color to each one.

- **Paragraph characteristics:** These options let you search for any characteristic available in the Paragraph dialog box (e.g., alignment, spacing, initial indent). For example, you could search for any paragraph that has a hanging indent of 0.5 inches (a mistake that might be caused by selecting the wrong paragraph format setting).

- **Tab settings:** These options let you search for any of the tab settings that can be defined in the Tabs dialog box. For example, you could search for all decimal-aligned tab stops so you can decide whether a right-aligned tab stop is required instead.

- **Language:** These options let you confine your search to text that was defined to use any of the languages (e.g., U.S. English) that are available in the Languages dialog box. For example, in a document containing many foreign words, you could globally change their language setting to the correct language. Subsequently, Word will use the dictionary for that language during spellchecks. (See Chapter 10 for more details on spellchecks and language options.)

- **Frames:** These options let you search for frames with certain characteristics (e.g., formatted to use text wrap). For example, you could use this option to apply a consistent style and size of text wrap to frames throughout the document.

- **Style:** These options let you search for text formatted using any of the paragraph or character styles (e.g., Body text, Heading 1) available in the Styles dialog box or palette. For example, you could use this option to move through the document, one heading style at a time, to ensure that the capitalization is consistent. Or you could replace all Heading 1 headings with a publisher's heading style.

Find one format, and replace it with a different format? The format options can be applied independently to the search term and to anything you type in the Replace with field. If you leave the latter field blank, only the format of the original text will change. Unfortunately, the format applies to the whole contents of both fields; you can't apply the format to only parts of what you typed.

- **Highlight:** These options let you search for any text that has been highlighted using the highlighter marker tool or globally apply that format to certain words. Though you could scroll through a long document to find this easily visible highlighting, it's much easier and faster to use the search tool.

Adding power to wildcards

Earlier in this chapter, I introduced basic wildcard functions that are present in most software. In Word, for instance, typing the caret character (^) followed by ?, $, #, and * in a search term will find (respectively) any single character, any single letter, any single number, and any group of characters at that position within the search term. Though you can accomplish quite a bit with these options, more powerful options are available for complicated pattern matching. If you select the Use wildcards checkbox that Word offers, the following additional options become available:

To find	Type	Description and example
Grouped characters	( )	The round brackets ask Word to treat the enclosed text as a single unit. This is useful in replacement operations (see the next section, *Replacement options*) if you want to treat each group separately or in defining search terms that appear at the start or end of a word. • Example: Searching for *(copy)(editor)* would let you globally change *copyeditor* to *substantive editor* without affecting *copyediting*. This example is trivial because you could perform the same change without grouping.
Any character in a list	[ ]	The search will find words containing one of the characters listed between the brackets at the indicated position. Note: don't separate these characters with spaces or punctuation. • Example: Searching for *wr[io]te* would find both *write* and *wrote*.

To find	Type	Description and example
Any character in a range	[-]	Ranges must be defined between the square brackets in ascending order (i.e., smallest number first or in alphabetic order). These ranges are case-sensitive, so *A-Z* would find only capital letters, whereas *a-z* would find only lower-case letters. • Example: Searching for *[1-3]* would find any instance of *1, 2,* or *3* in a document.
Beginning of a word	<	• Example: Searching for *<copy* would find *copyeditor* but not *photocopy*.
End of a word	>	• Example: Searching for *write>* would find *rewrite* but not *writer*.
Exclusion (*not*)	[!]	When the *not* character (!) occurs inside square brackets, it means that words containing any of the characters inside the brackets will not be found. • Example: Searching for *[!copy]edit* would find *editor* and *creditor* but not *copyeditor*.
At least one occurrence	@	Finds any text in which the character or group of characters before the @ occurs at least once. • Example: Searching for *(ing)@* would find both *sing* and *singing*
A specific number of occurrences of a pattern	{ }	This search pattern specifies how often the character or group of characters preceding the brace brackets should occur. You can search for: • an exact number of occurrences of a character: For example, *i{2}* would find both *Hawaii* and *skiing.* • at least the specified number of occurrences of a character: For example, *9{2,}* would skip *9*, but would find *99* and *1999*. • a range of occurrences of a character: For example, *0{1,3}* would find *0, 0.01, 0.001, 0.0001,* and *1.00001*

To find	Type	Description and example
Special characters used in wildcard searches	\	Special measures are required for characters such as *, #, and ? that are used as a wildcards; to do so, type a backslash (\) before the character. • Example: Typing \? will let you find question marks as part of a wildcard search—a useful trick when you're editing one of those authors who insists on using !!! to exclaim loudly or ??? to indicate extreme puzzlement.

Finding text that _isn't_ formatted with a specific style: Word can't apply the _not_ wildcard operator, [!], to a paragraph style. But you can find text that _isn't_ formatted using a certain style in two steps: First, do a global find and replace to apply highlighting to all text that is formatted using that style. Second, search for all text that is not highlighted: in the Find what field, select Highlight twice to change the pattern description to Not highlighted (i.e., everything that doesn't have the specified style applied). When you're done, select all the text (Control+A for Windows, Command+A for Macintosh) and apply the No color or None highlight to remove the formatting, as described earlier in this chapter (_Highlighting all instances of a search term_).

Replacement options

Most of the patterns, formats, and special characters you can find using the search tools can also be specified for the replacement text—although there are frustrating exceptions. For example, you can find all underlined text and change it to italicized text in a single search and replace operation: to do so, specify Underlined as the Find what pattern, and specify Not underlined plus Italics as the Replace with pattern.

Some versions of Word before Word 2010 have a quirk related to how they perform such changes in searches that use wildcards: To replace the found text with the same characters, but formatted differently, you must type ^& (the control code that means "use the same text that the search found") in the Replace with field. For example, to boldface all numbers in a document, you would use the following search specifications:

• Select Use wildcards.
• In the Find what field, type [0-9].

- In the Replace with field, type ^& and then, with the cursor still in that field, click the Format button, select Font, and then set the style to Bold.

Replace the search term with itself

Use the ^& code to indicate that you want to retain the found text. For example, to replace all instances of *file1, file2, file3, ...* up to *file9* with *oldfile1, oldfile2, ... oldfile9*:

- Select Use wildcards.

- Type *file[1-9]>* in the Find what field. This means "find the word *file*, followed by any number from 1 to 9 at the end of the word".

- Type *old*^& in the Replace with field. This means "add the word *old* before the search term (^&)".

Note that it isn't necessary to use ^& if you're only applying formatting to each search term that is found.

Replace the search term with the clipboard's contents

Use the ^c control code to tell Word to use the clipboard's contents as the replacement text. This is useful if you want to replace the search term with a chunk of text that is too long to fit in the Replace with field. In that case, copy the replacement text to the clipboard before you begin. For example, you might be editing a document before some crucial text, such as a legal disclaimer, is available. While you wait, you can insert a placeholder such as "/legal disclaimer/". Note that in this example, I added forward slashes on both sides of the placeholder to ensure that I don't inadvertently replace these words where they should *not* be changed, as in a situation where the phrase "consult the following legal disclaimer" appears before this placeholder. When the lawyers provide the actual text, copy it to the clipboard and use it to globally replace the placeholder.

Assuming that we chose an appropriate placeholder, the ^c control code would let us insert the final warning statement in only four steps:

- Cut or copy the replacement text to the clipboard.

- Open the Find and Replace dialog box, and type the placeholder text in the Find what field.

- Type ^c in the Replace with field.

- Click the Replace all button.

A useful alternative: If this feature won't work in your version of Word, or if you're not using Word, you can achieve the same effect using the method I described earlier in this chapter (*Replacing Text One Instance at a Time*).

Also note that when you create placeholders, you should avoid characters that might appear in a wildcard search if you think you might need to use a more complex replacement pattern based on wildcards. For example, we could use *[warning]* as the placeholder, but because the *[* and *]* characters are special characters used in wildcard searches, we would need to tell Word to find the actual brackets. We can do this by adding a \ character before each bracket, but that makes the search pattern unnecessarily complicated.

Replacing subsets of a search term (groups)

What if the text we're seeking comprises two or more groups of characters and we need to perform a separate action on each group? To do so, we must first distinctly identify each group in the Find what field. Word does this by adding parentheses (round brackets) to define each group and a special code (the \ character followed by the group's number) to define the group number. (Group numbers are defined moving from left to right in the field that contains the groups.) In this context, *group* can mean a single character, a range of characters, or a specific pattern of characters—in short, any search term enclosed in parentheses to tell Word that you are treating that term as a group.

Consider the following example: If we were looking for all combinations of a lower-case letter followed by a number so that we could reverse their order, we would specify the search pattern as *([a-z])([0-9])*. The first set of parentheses defines group 1 as the set of lower-case letters and the second set of parentheses defines group 2 as the numbers from 0 to 9.

- To identify these groups in the Replace with field, type a backslash (\) followed by the group's number; thus, *1* would represent the first group (in this example, the letters) and *2* would represent the second group (in this example, the numbers).
- To switch the position of the letter and number, we would type *([a-z])* *([0-9])* in the Find what field and type *2**1* in the Replace with field. The meaning is "replace group 1 followed by group 2 with group 2 followed by group 1".

Remember not to add a space or punctuation between the two group designators: any characters that you type in addition to the group codes will become part of the search term or the replacement text. For example, let's say that we're once again looking for letter–number combinations, but this time, in addition to reversing their order, we want to add some text. We might need to do this in a manuscript in which the author used only letter–number combinations to refer to each graphic, even though the publisher's guidelines require authors to add the word "Figure" in front of these combinations and to place the number before the letter. Here's how we'd accomplish this:

- Type *([a-z])([0-9])* in the Find what field.
- Type *Figure* \2\1 in the Replace with field. (Note the single space I've added after the word *Figure* because I want a space after that word.)
- This code translates into the following instruction: Find any letter (group 1) followed by a number (group 2), reverse their order (\2\1), then add the word *Figure*, followed by a space, in front of the two groups.

Although groups can't be formatted separately in the Replace with field (settings such as italics in that field apply to all groups), there's a workaround that lets you accomplish this. For example, if we want to use the search term *(copy)(edit)* to find *copyedit* and italicize only the first part of that word (*copy*edit), we can accomplish this in two steps:

- Search for *(copy)(edit)* and replace it with \1^&, with the italics format selected for the Replace with field. In this example, \1 refers to the first group (the word *copy*) and ^& refers to the entire search term, namely *copyedit*.
- Click the Replace all button to replace all instances of *copyedit* with *copycopyedit*. Note that *copy* is duplicated at the start of the word and that the entire word will be italicized.
- Next, search for all occurrences of *copyedit* and change those to *edit*, with the replacement formatting specified as No italics.

As this example shows, you can often outsmart Word and work around its limitations if you can think of clever ways to use its strengths to overcome those limitations.

Really powerful searches: Grep, the *general regular expression parser*, is a standard UNIX program that permits remarkably complex (and correspondingly powerful) search and replace operations. Versions are also available for the Macintosh and Windows. However, Jack Lyon's MegaReplacer utility for Windows Word (part of Editor's Toolkit Plus) can do much of this work for you.

Chapter 9. Developing Style Sheets: a Tool for Consistency

Web: http://www.geoff-hart.com/books/eoe/eoe3/eoe3.html
Note: Word 2010 is for Windows; Word 2011 is for the Macintosh

Consistency is something readers never notice—until they trip over an inconsistency. That's why our efforts to impose order on chaos don't belong to Emerson's category of *foolish* consistency.

As I noted in Chapter 8, we often face a considerable challenge when we attempt to impose consistency on manuscripts. Many authors don't understand why consistency is important, and note with some justice that readers are pretty good at detecting and resolving inconsistencies. And after all, they note, "shouldn't challenging material be challenging to read?"

No, it shouldn't. Neither the assumption that readers can easily detect discrepancies nor the assumption that they can easily resolve problems stands up to careful analysis. At best, it's a discourtesy to force our readers to do this extra work; at worst, we may do more than provide a minor intellectual challenge—we may confuse readers and fail to communicate. This is doubly true in an increasingly international world: many of our readers have English as a second or even third language. (Of course, if you're not editing in English, the manuscript also may not be written in the reader's first language.) Texts should be challenging because the concepts are difficult, not because the writing makes the concepts more difficult than necessary. Consistency is important, and sometimes even crucial, because it removes one of the many obstacles between the reader and understanding.

That being the case, we're always responsible for imposing consistency on manuscripts. The important inconsistencies—those that would confuse readers—must be eliminated, even in a fast-turnaround edit. Other consistencies remain important, but if they don't significantly inconvenience readers, and particularly if they're the kind of thing the average reader would never notice, then perhaps they can wait for our second pass through a manuscript, if time permits that additional pass.

Long or complex manuscripts introduce myriad things that we must keep consistent, and the more of these things we must remember, the harder the task becomes and the more likely that some inconsistencies will escape our vigilance. The solution, whether editing on the screen or on paper, is to create a reference guide that summarizes the decisions we've made and the things we must watch out for as we review the manuscript—

in short, an editorial *style sheet*. Each time we encounter a possible inconsistency, we consult our style sheet to see how we decided to handle that situation previously, rather than having to search backwards through the manuscript for a reminder. If we haven't already decided what to do about a particular issue, we can propose a solution, add it to our style sheet, and rely on that decision in our subsequent editing.

Recording such decisions relieves the large and growing burden on our working memory that develops as we dig deeper into a long manuscript. If we let the style sheet do the remembering for us; our task then becomes one of staying alert to the kinds of things that are likely to be inconsistent, and remembering to look them up in the style sheet each time we encounter them.

Rules, schmules! The alert reader will note that the guides I've included in the bibliography and many others rarely use the word "rule" or its synonyms in the title. This is not an accident. Most guides are written by editors who are experts in their chosen field and who recognize that few rules apply universally—there are almost always exceptions. As a result, the authors deliberately present their books as *guides* designed to help us find solutions, not as bodies of law. Keep this in mind, and remember that in the end, we must use our judgment to develop solutions appropriate to each unique situation. Style guides should be guidelines that help us make informed decisions, not corsets that squeeze text into artificial and uncomfortable shapes.

Style *Guides* Versus Style *Sheets*

Before diving into an exploration of consistency, it's worthwhile understanding the distinction between style *guides* and style *sheets*. A style *guide* represents a compilation of *best practices* and proven solutions for the common problems encountered by editors who are working in a specific genre. In this context, genres represent fields of study or discussion, such as journalism, literature, and science. Each genre faces linguistic problems that are common to all forms of communication, but also has its own unique set of problems that may not arise in any other genre. As a result, most editors use a different primary style guide for each genre in which they edit. For example, the Associated Press guide is a preferred resource for journalists, the Sun style guide is a common alternative to the Microsoft style guide for those who edit computer manuals, the Council of Science Editors style guide is a common reference for science editors, and the Chicago Manual of Style and the Modern Language Association (MLA) style guide are common references for academic publishing. (I've provided details for each of these in the bibliography.)

Scientific style: My recent book, *Writing for Science Journals*, is aimed at *authors* who will publish in peer-reviewed science journals, but provides considerable useful advice for science editors.

Unfortunately, it's not possible to cover every conceivable English quirk in a style guide. To do so, the authors would have to include an entire unabridged dictionary, a dictionary specific to the genre, a reference book on modern usage, and various other book-sized collections of reference material. This would be less a style guide than a library. As a result, style guide authors summarize their genre's most common problems and leave us to extrapolate from those examples to the entire marvelous diversity of problems we'll encounter in that genre. For large or complex projects, we may need to consult several books in search of guidance, and even in the Internet era, most of us acquire a shelf of reference material to support our work. But despite these resources, each manuscript presents unique problems that require judgment calls—particularly when we must choose between conflicting advice provided by two style guides or must develop our own solution when no style guide describes the particular problem we face.

When this happens, we must use our judgment to reach a decision that is broadly compatible with the overall patterns in the genre and in our style guides. Then, to ensure we won't have to repeat the thought process hours or days later, long after we've forgotten our original decision, we record these *ad hoc* solutions in a style *sheet*. These style sheets represent our appendices to published style guides and become a style guide for the smallest genre of all: an individual manuscript. They in no way replace the larger guides, but rather summarize the exceptions and supplements to those guides for a given manuscript. With small manuscripts, these exceptions and supplements may be sufficiently rare that a few cryptic notes will jog our memory as we edit. But with larger texts and more complex subjects, recording the exceptions becomes considerably more challenging: the number of elements we must keep consistent grows beyond our ability to keep them all in our memory simultaneously.

There are three compelling reasons to create a style sheet:

- It provides a reference that reminds us of our decisions rather than forcing us to repeatedly reinvent a solution. This lets us make the same changes consistently each time the same problem arises. When new problems arise, we research a solution, then add it to the style sheet.

- It provides a checklist clients can review to evaluate our editorial decisions. If they reject a decision, for good reasons or bad, the style sheet provides enough information for them to quickly find and undo any changes they disagree with.

- It helps a publisher's proofreader confirm how to handle any seeming inconsistencies they encounter. A good proofreader will consult our style sheet before making any changes so as to avoid inadvertently introducing inconsistencies in the manuscript.

Onscreen style sheets offer many advantages over their handwritten ancestors. Large or complex projects, and particularly those with multiple authors, typically force us to create and maintain correspondingly large and complex style sheets. If we record these notes on paper, the style sheet soon becomes impossible to use efficiently: for example, a tidy list of spellings that starts out in alphabetical order quickly accumulates marginal notes and new words penciled in between previous entries in the list. The resulting mess makes it difficult to quickly find any given word. Paper, by its nature, prevents us from efficiently fitting new information within existing information and makes it difficult to reorganize and retrieve information; each such reorganization requires recopying the entire style sheet. Moreover, paper doesn't let us use our software's search function to find specific entries, reorganize the style sheet to support specific tasks, or provide a neat final product to the author or their publisher.

Why not print your style sheet? If you prefer to work on paper, you can still take advantage of an onscreen style sheet: simply print a fresh copy whenever you've added enough new entries that the old copy becomes unusable. Simply update the onscreen version and print a fresh copy. This is also helpful should the cat spill your coffee on the printout. And when you need to use the onscreen version (e.g., to copy text or search for something), you can do that too.

Onscreen style sheets make it easy to repeatedly insert new, legible entries in alphabetical order, and to reorder the list to suit different needs. Keeping the style sheet open in a window beside the manuscript makes it instantly available and frees up desk space for dictionaries and other references. Best of all, we can easily find specific entries in large style sheets using the word processor's search function. For example, if you have a section named "Alphabetical list of family names" and need to check a particular name, you can search for the name; if you don't find it, you can search for that heading and then scroll through the list manually, or search for other family names that should occur near the one you're searching for.

To move efficiently to specific sections with long titles, insert a shorter navigation aid such as [Names] after the heading. Using characters such as the square brackets ensures your search will only find your bookmark, not the same word outside of brackets. If your software provides a bookmark feature, you can use that instead. For example, Word lets you quickly move to a bookmark by pressing Control+G (Windows) or Command+G (Macintosh)—the memory aid is G = go to—then typing the bookmark's name in that dialog box.

> **Navigating in long style sheets:** The tips in Chapter 5 make it easier to move around the style sheet efficiently. If you have a large monitor, you can even navigate the style sheet using the Document Map view. See Chapter 4 for details of this view mode.

Another advantage of an onscreen style sheet is that it can store long phrases or even entire paragraphs for reuse (e.g., a standard warning message that must accompany every procedure in a software manual). Simply copy and paste the text from the style sheet into the document instead of having to retype it from scratch. If you're going to edit many manuscripts in a particular genre, you may even want to create these entries as automatic text so Word can do the typing for you. (See Chapter 11 for details.)

Last, and by no means least, a neatly typed word processor document can be spellchecked and sent to the client—unlike a handwritten style sheet, which must either be recopied completely so that it's legible or typed into a word processor.

In the rest of this chapter, I'll describe the many kinds of inconsistencies we must watch for, and provide some tips on how an onscreen style sheet can help you deal with these inconsistencies.

Kinds of Consistency

There are two main kinds of consistency any editor must find and resolve: internal consistency within a document, and external consistency with the real world or the conventions of a larger genre. Style guides help with both forms of consistency, but they are general-purpose guidelines, not the kind of document-specific guidelines we record in style sheets. There are many flavors of inconsistency within both categories. One of the most important involves any statement that refers to something the author said earlier in a manuscript or may say again later: each such statement represents an opportunity for inconsistency. The wise editor learns to take nothing for granted, and verifies every statement the author makes.

The kinds of things we must help our authors to keep internally and externally consistent fall into several broad categories:

Spelling and hyphenation

Spelling must be consistent both with the publisher's preferred dictionary and within the document. For example, both *onscreen* and *on-screen* are legitimate spellings of the adjective form of this concept; I've chosen to use the closed-up spelling in this book.

Use of synonyms

As I noted in Chapter 8, elegant variation is most appropriate in literature and becomes inelegant variation in most nonfiction. In scientific and technical communication, there is usually a preferred term for each concept, and that one term should be used everywhere, with no synonyms allowed unless the goal is to alert the reader to the existence of the synonyms. In the humanities, other rules apply, and the use of synonyms may be acceptable, particularly when there is no broadly accepted standard term.

Verb tenses, voice, and points of view

In nonfiction, verb tenses are relatively straightforward: for the most part, what happened in the past requires the past tense, what remains true in the present or is happening now requires the present tense, and what is expected or hoped to happen in the future requires the future tense. Similarly, the voice may be active or passive, but is always the voice of the author speaking directly to the reader, and that voice defines a consistent viewpoint. In fiction, the problem becomes much more challenging, as authors can forget what they're doing and unintentionally shift tenses, voices, and points of view. It's our job to bring them back on track.

Conclusions and other details

In manuscripts that contain a summary such as an Abstract or Executive Summary at the beginning or a Conclusions section at the end, we must verify that all statements agree with those made elsewhere in the manuscript. Discrepancies often arise if (as often happens) these sections are written before the author has finished writing the rest of the manuscript, and their conclusions or interpretations change during revision of the rest of the manuscript.

Implicit references

An *implicit* reference occurs when the author refers to something presented elsewhere in a document without naming that location, whether in the form of "as I noted previously" or the repetition of a previous conclusion. Each such statement must be examined to confirm that it doesn't contradict statements elsewhere in the manuscript.

Explicit references

In contrast, *explicit* references occur when authors name another location in the document. These include cross-references, literature citations, page references, footnotes or endnotes, and citations of figures or tables. In each case, the description in the citation must match the actual content of the thing being cited. For any of the numbered citations, the number used in the citation must agree with the number of the thing being cited. Authors often number these things manually, and if that number changes during revision, all references must also change.

Definitions

Wherever an author has explicitly defined a term, we must carefully check all subsequent uses of that term to ensure that they comply with the definition. Particularly where interpretations of a term differ within a genre, it's easy for authors to inadvertently depart from their own definition and begin using someone else's definition.

Shortcuts

Authors often create shortcuts, such as acronyms and initialisms, to avoid having to repeat long phrases. Unfortunately, so many TLAs (three-letter acronyms) and longer shortcuts exist that authors occasionally slip up and use someone else's shortcut. This can be confusing if the reader has learned to subconsciously replace the TLA with one meaning, but the author means something different. This problem wears many disguises. For example, scientists often present equations gleaned from multiple sources; in this case, the shortcuts are the letters or symbols the original authors used to represent certain concepts embodied in the equations (i.e., the names of the variables or parameters). Occasionally, different sources use the same letters or symbols in different ways or use different letters or symbols for the same concept. This creates a confusing manuscript in which a single variable has two or more definitions, or a single concept is represented by two or more variables.

Formatting

Although formatting is often a problem left to the publisher's proofreader or page-layout staff to resolve, most editors are also responsible for imposing at least a basic level of consistency on the manuscript. Some are completely responsible for this formatting. In such cases, we must ensure that headings are consistently styled (e.g., capitalization, use of imperative versus descriptive form), and that recurring elements, such as headers and footers, appear correctly throughout a manuscript. Consistency issues may also arise at smaller scales. For instance, we should ensure that bullet points are either complete sentences or sentence fragments and that numbered lists have no gaps or duplications, and that they either do or do not use a period or parenthesis after the numbers.

Sequences

At a broader scale, consistency in sequence means that a manuscript follows the same sequence of all similar manuscripts in a series. In most peer-reviewed journals, for example, each paper begins with a title, followed by author information and an Abstract. At a finer scale, we must ensure that anything numbered (whether figures or numbered headings) follows an uninterrupted sequence, with no gaps or repetitions, and that anything presented alphabetically (such as a bibliography) has been correctly alphabetized. Often, we must also ensure that information occurs in chronological sequence rather than jumping around in time.

Numbers

The presentation of numbers raises some interesting consistency challenges. For example, most editors have heard the common advice that numbers smaller than 10 should be spelled out, whereas larger numbers should be expressed using numerals. But there are numerous exceptions. For example, you should ignore this guideline when the author mixes large and small numbers; use numerals for all numbers to facilitate comparisons. Moreover, in the sciences, all measurements are presented as numerals, irrespective of the size of the number. There are also consistency issues related to the number of mathematically significant figures that should be presented and which units of measurement to use.

Learning to be Consistent

As our editorial experience increases, we gradually internalize the need to check many types of consistency, and we begin performing such checks without being consciously aware that we're doing so. Until we reach that level of skill, it's helpful to remember the categories of consistency in the previous section and find ways to remember to check each item on the list. A good style sheet can serve as a checklist for each of these types of consistency. It's perhaps facetious to say we should never trust an author to get anything right, but it's also a conservative statement that serves as a good guide to keep in mind when we're checking for consistency. Authors err through simple human inattention more often than through outright incompetence, but whatever the reason, err they do—and frequently.

Components of a Style Sheet

An effective style sheet should contain three main components:
- Identification of yourself and the project.
- A list of the standard references you followed.
- A list of your decisions where standard references proved inadequate.

Identify yourself and the project

Start every new style sheet with information that identifies you and that defines the various components of the project. Provide at least the following information:
- the name of the project
- any relevant reference numbers (e.g., a contract code, a report number)
- the date, particularly if you'll edit different editions of the same document (e.g., an annual report) over a period of several years
- the name of your client or contact person (e.g., the manuscript's author, the manager who awarded you the contract)
- your name and contact information
- a list of file names (and formats, if necessary) for each manuscript and all other material (e.g., graphics files) included in the edit

Without this information, a busy client who is juggling multiple projects, such as the editor of a university press, can't easily determine which style sheet accompanies each project. Worse yet, authors who work with you through an intermediary, such as a publisher's acquisitions editor, may not know who to contact with questions. This information remains important for smaller projects and less busy staff; if the project staff changes due to maternity leave, a long vacation, sabbaticals, mergers and acquisitions, layoffs, promotions, or other inconvenient facts of corporate life, the new project manager will need this information to understand what was done and who did it. This is a specific example of the larger concept of maintaining a good relationship with the author and their colleagues.

If you do many jobs that require style sheets, use your word processor to create a standard style-sheet template that contains all the information you'll submit to each client. This includes a list of any of the standard information described in this chapter; you can always delete items that don't apply to a specific project when you create the initial style sheet for that project. This approach eliminates the need to retype this information for each project, and ensures that you won't miss anything important when you begin a new style sheet.

List the standard references you followed

Client-specific guides: If a client has specific requirements, including standard references they want you to follow (e.g., the *Chicago Manual of Style* instead of the Council of Science Editors style guide; U.S. instead of British spelling), add these to your style sheet.

Clients often specify the sources of information you should consult when they negotiate your contract. When they don't, propose references that you believe are suitable for the manuscript's genre (e.g., science vs. literature). Once the client accepts your choices, or proposes alternatives, add them to your style sheet so that everyone is working based on the same understanding. This discussion and negotiation provides a specific example of a broader principle: it's wise to subject your style sheet to a reality check by the client. After you've spent enough time working on a manuscript to get a good feel for the types of issues you'll be facing, send the client a working draft of the style sheet and ask them to review your proposed solutions. If they accept these decisions, you can continue to use them; if not, you've saved yourself the unpleasant discovery at the end of the project that you'll need to make another pass through the manuscript to undo many of your changes and redo the edits according to the client's preferences. Although you should certainly confirm major additions to a style sheet, you shouldn't send overly frequent updates. Ask your client what frequency they consider appropriate.

List any standard references you used for the overall project, including subject-specific style guides and dictionaries,. Add any non-standard references you consulted. Nowadays, these often include useful Web sites such as online glossaries for terminology, library databases for literature citations, government legislation, and so on. If you consult any people, such as subject-matter experts who work for your client or a colleague who is a recognized authority in a field, add their names and contact information.

Even when a client specifies the style guide you should follow, stay alert for signals that they aren't the final authority. For example, if a different organization (e.g., a big New York publisher) will be doing the final production work, including page layout and proofreading, ask for permission to contact their project manager to confirm that everyone agrees on what style guidelines to follow. Some publishers have no preferred style guide, and only ask that a document be internally consistent, not necessarily consistent with their other publications. Other publishers have rigorous standards they expect their authors to follow, and failure to follow these guidelines or to obtain permission to choose your own guidelines can lead to significant problems for the author after they submit the manuscript to the publisher. (The author's problems often become your problems, so it's in your self-interest to avoid creating problems for the author.)

Just as you confirmed the acceptability of your style sheet with the client, you should also run it past the publisher for a reality check. Better by far to resolve any disagreements before you get too far into the work, and to avoid problems from the start, than to be forced to fix these problems later. Even if the publisher will fix them, you don't want to gain a reputation as someone who creates extra work for others, particularly since page layout and proofreading occur late in the project, when deadlines are approaching and everyone's a bit frazzled. A publisher who appreciates your efforts to make their life easier may become a future client.

List your decisions

The heart of any style sheet is a comprehensive list of all decisions you made that are not inherently obvious (e.g., correcting typos) or that aren't covered by the standard references you agreed to use during your edits. For example, routine spelling decisions can be handled by consulting the dictionary specified in your list of references. Once the client agrees to use that dictionary, you no longer need to itemize the spelling of words that appear in the dictionary. When you encounter an exception, however, add that exception to your style sheet.

Types of decisions to include

The types of decisions you'll need to add to a style sheet typically fall into several broad categories:

- Problem words or phrases: List these alphabetically, with each entry followed by a brief explanation of your decision and logic. Include hyphenation decisions and formatting issues, such as the use of italics for foreign words and phrases or the use of a different font to indicate menu choices in a computer manual.

- Explanations of how you resolved unusual spellings: For example, Chinese words can be transliterated using the modern *pinyin* system of romanization, or the older Wade–Giles system. In addition to specifying the system, record any exceptions, such as quotations from authors who used a different romanization system.

- Bibliographic entries whose titles are in non-English languages: Decide whether to provide English translations, and how to distinguish between translations provided by the original publisher and those provided by the manuscript's author or by you. For languages with a standardized romanization, will you provide a romanized version (e.g., in pinyin)?

- Your choices in situations with two or more valid approaches: Different style guides or authorities may recommend different solutions to a problem. In each case, explain the choice, concisely justify your decision, and cite any relevant authority to support that decision.

- Special-purpose sections that are unique to the manuscript: For example, if a manuscript contains complex footnote, endnote, or citation schemes, includes large amounts of foreign text, includes many quotations, or uses many numerical values, briefly describe the approach you took in formatting or styling each of these elements. Computer books often require complicated systems to communicate menu choices, dialog box names, and so on.

Specifying the locations of stylistic issues

Using your style sheet to indicate the locations of specific problems and inconsistencies will help the author review your solutions, but it's helpful to support this by inserting comments in the text to highlight instances of a problem. (See Chapter 7 for tips on the use of comments in onscreen editing.) These comments eliminate the need to search through the manuscript to find a problem that is only described in the style sheet.

Unless you're proofreading a near-final document that has already been laid out and paginated, it can be difficult to concisely and clearly define the location of changes. In particular, you'll have to unlearn the habit of referring to page and line numbers to locate problems. Despite increasing standardization of fonts, different computers, word processors, and operating systems may use slightly or significantly different *metrics* for the fonts—the parameters that define character size and spacing—or may process these metrics differently. Page and line numbers also differ among view modes (e.g., Draft vs. Print Layout in Word) and depend on whether the author is displaying or concealing tracked changes. The result is that the page and line numbers you cite in the style sheet won't always match the numbers the author will see. In manuscripts being reviewed after heavy editing, the problem is worse because the comments quickly drift away from their original position. For example, if the author accepts a 10-line deletion early in the manuscript, the positions of all subsequent revisions move up by 10 lines. Thus, use your style sheet to describe general problems and your solutions, but describe specific problems directly in the manuscript.

Managing and maintaining your style sheet

As your list of decisions lengthens, add simple, helpful navigation aids such as headings and subheadings. Use white space effectively to facilitate skimming; for example, add generous space above headings, indent text below subheadings, use bulleted lists, or group information in tables. This is particularly effective if you don't know what will happen after a manuscript leaves your hands. Clients whose manuscripts will be subsequently revised by a publisher and the publisher's staff who will prepare the manuscript for publication sometimes receive printed copies of your style sheet rather than the onscreen version, and your simple courtesy in trying to make their lives easier will be greatly appreciated.

> **Make things easy for the author and their publisher:** Such small kindnesses as submitting a tidy, helpful style sheet help clients and publishers see you as someone who cares about their needs. The more they appreciate your efforts, the more likely they are to hire you again or refer other clients to you.

When to implement style decisions

The list of decisions in a style sheet lengthens as we work. We commonly tolerate certain problems rather than solving them immediately until we suddenly develop an irresistible urge to figure out a solution. Sometimes, we implement a temporary solution that suddenly stops seeming reasonable. Sometimes we encounter a solution to a particular unsolved problem relatively late in the manuscript, and discover the solution has implications for parts of the text we've already edited.

When this happens, it pays to pause and add the new decision to the style sheet, and then decide which of two strategies will be most effective:

- If pausing to fix the problem will disrupt your concentration, simply record the problem in your style sheet and plan to fix it in a subsequent pass through the manuscript. During substantive or developmental editing, for instance, intense focus may be required, and stopping to fix a simple style problem would disrupt this focus. Finish your current task before you set out to solve the problem.

- If fixing the problem will solve more problems than it creates, record your current location in the file and pause to fix the problem everywhere before continuing to edit. (Chapter 8 provides an extensive description of how to use the search tools to apply a consistency check and make the necessary changes throughout a document.) For example, if you encounter a precise definition for terminology that the author used previously in a generic sense, it's worthwhile returning to the start of the manuscript and searching for any uses of the terminology that contradict the precise definition. This ensures that when you return to the manuscript, you'll have already made the terminology consistent, or have inserted comments to remind yourself of the problem.

Repeating definitions: For frequently used terminology, add a definition the first time a term appears to provide context for all subsequent uses of the term. In large manuscripts such as books, consider repeating the definitions in each chapter or creating a glossary of key terms. Readers who consult only a single chapter may never encounter the initial definition. Whether you decide to repeat the definition or to present it only once per manuscript (e.g., in a glossary), record this decision in your style sheet.

Pausing to make a frequent change globally can save you considerable time because all the changes you made based on a style decision will stand out from the original text. (When you use revision tracking, you can specify the color and format of your edits to make them easily visible. See Chapter 6 for details.) This lets you see at a glance, without having to consult the style sheet, whether you already fixed a particular problem. Moreover, because you implement all the changes as a single editing task, the changes will be consistent. If you decide that your original solution wasn't perfect, it will be easy to find all those changes (because they're identical!) and revise them all the same way. If you prefer to edit with your changes concealed so you can focus on the results of your edits rather than on the details of each change, you can still indicate that you've already fixed a particular problem by highlighting the changed text. (See Chapter 8 for suggestions on how to highlight changes.)

If a change will be relatively simple, and you're confident you can safely make that change everywhere in the manuscript in a single step, consider making the change globally using the Replace all function provided by the search tool. Chapter 8 provides some recommendations on how to do this safely, but it's worth repeating a cautionary note here: always leave time to ensure that you haven't introduced any errors. If you're not comfortable making a global change because there are many legitimate exceptions to a given style choice, Chapter 8 (the sections *Replacing Text One Instance at a Time* and *Global Find and Replace Operations*) provides detailed suggestions for how you can accomplish this goal with less risk.

You can combine these approaches for many types of consistency check, such as determining whether an acronym was already defined. If you encounter an unfamiliar acronym, your style sheet will tell you at a glance whether it's defined earlier in the manuscript. If not, move to the start of the document and search for the acronym; you may have defined it earlier in the manuscript but have forgotten to add it to your style sheet. If the acronym doesn't appear earlier in the manuscript, define it and add the definition to your style sheet. You can then replace all other instances of the longer text with the acronym throughout the manuscript—either manually, one instance at a time, or using a global replacement. Similarly, if you've confirmed the spelling for (say) a complicated foreign word or a technical phrase that you're having difficulty remembering, use the search tools to find variant spellings and highlight them to remind yourself to confirm the spelling. Should you encounter any similar-seeming wording that *isn't* colored, you'll know that something is wrong with the spelling or that you haven't yet checked that term and added it to your style sheet.

If you're working on a multi-file project, such as a book, continue your consistency check in each of the other files. This helps to minimize your work later in the editing process, when you'll review your style sheet to ensure that you've made the same changes in all files.

Cleaning up the manuscript

When you're finished editing, remember to remove any special formatting that you applied purely for your own use (e.g., highlighting certain terms as a reminder to check them). The author shouldn't have to deal with this formatting. The simplest way to accomplish this is to use the search tool to reverse the formatting change; for example, if you applied yellow highlighting using the highlighter marker, use the search tool to globally find and remove this highlighting, as described in Chapter 6. Alternatively, if you've also used highlighting to remind the author to check certain words or phrases, you can set Word to display only formatting changes (as described in Chapter 6). Then, using the revision tracking tools, you can move through the document, one format change at a time, and reject any formatting that is only for your own use.

Using a Style Sheet

As I've noted previously, a style sheet provides an ongoing reference while you're editing a manuscript for the first time. But its true power becomes apparent when you perform your final edit: You can now use the list of decisions, supplemented by your word processor's search tools, to ensure that you haven't missed any instances of a particular problem.

To support you in this final consistency check, create a table that lists all the consistency checks you must perform based on your style sheet. This table is exclusively for your own use; because it's nothing more than a checklist to help you ensure that you applied all your style decisions consistently, there's no need for clients to see it. The table should include one row for each consistency check, and one column for each file (e.g., the chapters in a textbook, the manuals in a documentation suite) that must be subjected to that particular check. Here's a simplified example of what such a table might look like:

	Ch. 1	Ch. 2
Computer terms		
Change "click on" to "click" for buttons	✓	✓
Change "right mouse button" to "right-hand mouse button"	✓	✓
Change "select the [name] menu" to "open the [name] menu"	✓	✓

Formatting	✓	✓
Heading 1: all caps	✓	✓
Heading 2: only initial caps	✓	✓
Heading 3: only first letter capped	✓	✓
No punctuation at end of headings	✓	✓
Structural/sequence		✓
All tables numbered sequentially	✓	✓
All figures numbered sequentially	✓	✓

Once you've completed your preliminary editing, work through the table one line at a time, and add a checkmark when you're done. For example, the first line reminds me to replace *click on* with *click*. To ensure that I've made this change consistently, I would search for the word *click* throughout a file to find examples where the word is *not* accompanied by the word *on* but *was* accompanied by the name of the object being clicked. (Note that searching for *click on* would not find instances of *click* that were not followed by the name of the object being clicked. These should be rare, but moving text around and cutting and pasting without sufficient care sometimes cause words to appear or disappear.)

Simplifying style sheet checks: Checking every consistency choice in a long style sheet can be tedious. Fortunately, you can automate this process to some extent: try Jack Lyon's Editor's Toolkit Plus or Daniel Heuman's PerfectIt for Windows versions of Word.

If you're doing this work manually, you can either work on one *item* (e.g., capitalization) at a time, and complete that specific check for all documents, or you can work on one *document* at a time, and work through all checks in sequence for that specific document. The first option offers an efficiency advantage because practice should make you faster at performing the check and any associated corrections, but it requires more opening and closing of files. Neither approach is inherently superior. Try both to see which you prefer!

Note that the example table includes two typical headings (terminology and formatting) that you'll see in most style sheets, and a third heading (structure and sequence) that only applies to documents that contain tables, figures, and other numbered items. To ensure that you don't miss anything, each section in your style sheet should have a corresponding heading in the table. Although you can accomplish much the same effect working only with the style sheet, the table makes your progress clearer (it emphasizes what remains to be accomplished before your deadline) and reduces the risk that you'll miss something. If you're only working on one large file, an alternative would be to create a copy of your style sheet, and delete an entry from the style sheet as soon as you complete that check.

Though you can print the table and only display the file you're editing, keeping the table on your computer can be more productive, particularly if you also keep the style sheet open in another window. This requires some window juggling, but offers some persuasive advantages over paper:

- It can be difficult to find desk space for large style sheets or tables, and repeatedly turning your head to consult the list may cause neck strain.
- You can copy text from the style sheet or table and paste it into the search dialog box or the manuscript, thereby eliminating the need to repeatedly retype the same text. For long style sheets, unfamiliar foreign words (or genre-specific jargon), and long phrases, this can save substantial amounts of time and typing and greatly reduce the risk of errors.
- Any text you find using the search function is highlighted automatically. If you specify the search term carefully (see Chapter 8 for details), then pasting the replacement text into the document replaces the original text with the correct replacement in a single keystroke. This eliminates many presses of the Delete key.
- If you've carefully checked the wording and spelling in your style sheet, copying and pasting that text minimizes the risk of error. The first time you do this copy/paste, pause and check the results carefully; if you spot an error, you can fix the problem before you repeat that error throughout the manuscript.

Always conclude your final editing pass with a spellcheck. Nobody's perfect, and any changes we make during our final edit may introduce typos. That's doubly true when we're working through the consistency table, since that's usually the last major step in cleaning up a document before we return it to the client. A single typo may be forgivable, but if you've changed a word or phrase globally or if you're typing a correction once and then pasting it into the text many times, a single error can propagate dozens of times in a long document.

Clean Up the Style Sheet Before the Client Sees It

Even on a computer, style sheets can become quite messy. Cleaning up the style sheet as you work through it will make it easier for the client to review your style sheet, which you should send them with the final manuscript. The goal is to ensure that it is an efficient tool for the client and their proofreader, but also something that provides a good impression of your professional skills. A messy style sheet filled with typos won't give the client much confidence in your editing skills. A happy client is a repeat customer, and a clean style sheet is one of those little details that contributes to their happiness.

So run through the style sheet and do a quick edit to ensure that cryptic notes to yourself will be clear to the client, that there are no typos, and that you've eliminated notes or miscellaneous philosophical musings that seemed worth recording at the time but that aren't appropriate for the client. In addition, take one last look at your decisions; what seemed logical at 2 AM the morning before you return the manuscript to the client may seem less reasonable once you've caught up on your sleep. Spotting a problem lets you fix it so the client will never see the error.

Going Beyond Style Sheets

Not all style sheets resemble the examples I've described thus far. Some take different forms or take advantage of different tools. But each has the same purpose: helping you to impose consistency on a document. Here are a few examples of tips that most editors find useful at one time or another:

Memory aids and related tricks

Keeping your style sheet open beside the manuscript is a good way to impose consistency, but you can also add useful notes and reminders, such as definitions of key terms or explanations of complex concepts, so that you don't have to figure them out each time you encounter them. I find this helpful when I'm grappling with a complex scientific manuscript: if a term or complicated process simply refuses to stay put in my mind, I type an explanation or summary so I can quickly consult that explanation and refresh my understanding. Similarly, I can record the author's conclusions or key points as I encounter them, and refer back to those points. This is a great way to ensure that the author's conclusions at the end of the manuscript match the results they reported earlier in the manuscript, and that all the key results appear in the Conclusions section. You'd be surprised at how often this trick reveals inconsistencies ranging from minor differences in numbers to major contradictions or omissions.

A little thought will reveal other creative uses of this trick. For example, if you need to consult half a dozen Web sites to look up various categories of facts (e.g., one site to search a library database, another to confirm the correct names of metric units of measurement), leave those pages open in your Web browser or create a job-specific collection of bookmarks. Modern browsers let you display dozens of tabs or windows simultaneously, so you can open each page in its own tab or window each time you start work, thereby eliminating the need to search for and reopen these pages. Anything you may need to look up can be kept close at hand.

Consistency through concordances

In previous editions of this book, I discussed the possibility of using concordances to improve your consistency. In its most basic form, a concordance is a list of all the words that appear in a manuscript, usually including the number of occurrences of each word. The advantages of a concordance become clear if you consider the world's biggest concordance: the database used by any Internet search engine. Textual researchers use a constrained version of this approach when they examine a *corpus*—a collection of works in a specific language or subject area, or by a specific author.

Basic concordances are free of context. For example, the concordance for a 1000-page biography of Benjamin Franklin would probably list the word *Franklin* on every page, with no indication of which instances referred to his birth, death, or other events in his life. Similarly, the concordance for a software manual would reveal the word *menu* on most pages, with no indication of which menu. A more useful tool is a "keyword in context" (KWIC) concordance. KWIC concordances resemble the results of Web searches and the indexes of books because they provide enough context (usually the surrounding words) that they help you understand how the word is being used.

Concordances are less useful as an editing tool now that software such as PerfectIt is available to support the way editors work. Such large-scale consistency checks are difficult to do manually, but PerfectIt puts the computer to work doing things that computers do better than we can: automating tedious, repetitive tasks in ways that greatly reduce the possibility of human error. Nonetheless, concordances remain useful for two tasks:

- A basic concordance lists all words used in the manuscript, in alphabetical order. This can reveal variant spellings accepted by the spellchecker. If the concordance indicates the frequency of each spelling, this can help us decide which form is most likely to be correct.

- KWIC concordances reveal the multiple contexts in which a word or phrase appears, each of which should be addressed in our style sheet.

Consider, for example, how we might use the basic concordance in which the words are sorted alphabetically. Jack Lyon, author of the wonderful *Editorium Update* e-newsletter, provides the example of *manger* and *manager*: unless the author is satirizing the eating habits of managers, *manger* probably doesn't belong in the same manuscript, but it's an easy typo to miss during editing, and the spellchecker won't help unless you've added the word to an *exclusion dictionary*. (See Chapter 10 for details.) Similarly, consider a manual on Internet technical specifications. We might expect to find both TCP (the Internet's "transmission control protocol"), but not necessarily TCL (a "tool command language"). Are both legitimate acronyms in this context, or is TCL a typo? (P and L lie close together on the keyboard. It could happen!) Scanning the concordance would reveal the problem; using the search function would let us examine each instance of TCL and, if necessary, change it to TCP—perhaps via global search and replace if TCL doesn't belong in the manuscript. A concordance in alphabetical order can reveal such close cousins that would slip past the spellchecker, since they will most often occur close together in the list.

Other concordance tricks can improve consistency. For example, most concordance software can sort words based on their frequency. Words with the lowest frequencies may represent errors such as *manger* that we should find and correct using the search function. A concordance in alphabetical order provides a useful tool for editing an index, particularly if you're not a professional indexer. The concordance cannot itself be used as an index, since it cannot replace the human indexer's insights into the context of each use of a word. But the word list can help us ensure that the indexer covered every important word. And we can do better: a KWIC concordance would let us substantively edit an index by confirming that the index covers all instances of key contexts of a keyword. In the abovementioned Franklin example, we might find no index entry for the Franklin stove—or a misplaced reference to Aretha Franklin.

Concordances can also help us check *statements* for consistency. Let's say we're working on a really long geography manuscript in which the author may have made inconsistent statements in two or more places about (for example) the size of a certain region. We know one word associated with that detail (the region's name), but we don't want to use the search function to work through hundreds of instances of that keyword so we can check each one. But a KWIC concordance will concisely display all instances of that keyword alongside the accompanying context. We can scan through the concordance to identify each mention of the region's size and correct the size, if necessary. If there are many discrepancies, we can insert a comment at each location to report the contradiction and ask the author to confirm the correct alternative.

If you work with translators, you can use a concordance to check the quality of their translations, even if you don't know the second language particularly well. (Ideally, clients should hire an editor with expertise in the second language, but I've heard many technical writers complain that this isn't possible.) In this case, a different form of KWIC concordance can help. *Parallel* concordances show documents side by side so that you can compare the wording at each location; for example, Biblical scholars might use this approach to compare an English version of the Bible with the source of that translation (e.g., in Greek or Aramaic). By examining each instance of a word or phrase and its corresponding translation, we can identify inconsistencies (different wordings for the same concept). This kind of check is less necessary for translators who are using mature translation memories (software that compiles lists of preferred translations for standard phrases), but remains useful for "free" translations performed without such aids. Even when we don't know the second language, this technique can reveal inconsistencies that we can ask the translator to check.

Speaking of foreign languages, concordances are a useful tool for improving consistency in software—both in the interface and in the underlying programming code. Teams of programmers can use concordance tools to track all the references to a particular entity (such as the name of a variable or a subroutine) within a single long program or across the many files of a project. This is useful for documenting the program code and eliminating certain kinds of errors (e.g., using the same variable name to mean different things in two places, or calling the wrong subroutine). But the approach is also useful for editors: if we can gain access to the file that contains the text in the software's interface (e.g., dialog box titles, button names), a concordance will reveal terminological inconsistencies we can ask the programmers to fix.

Concordances have also been used to teach the subtleties of English. For example, prepositions and adverbs challenge many writers, such as engineers and other folk who have English as their second language. (The engineer's first language? *Tech.*) A concordance can reveal variations in preposition use with a given word or within a specific phrase, as well as variations in the positions of adverbs. An editor could use this list as a tool to correct exceptions to word patterns, but authors themselves can use it as a learning tool to help them write better. Two researchers (Gaskell and Cobb; see the bibliography) recently reported that concordances summarized sentence-level errors in a way that helped less-skilled writers learn to recognize patterns of error in their writing. Better still, the students they tested generally found this approach helpful.

Creating and reviewing concordances for long documents would be a time-consuming way to improve consistency; the resulting word lists can be huge. But this might still be useful when many of the words are unfamiliar or difficult to recognize; examples might be (respectively) a programming language reference with many code words. After reading the original article on which I based this chapter, one colleague gleefully reported his plans to use a concordance to impose consistency on the kind of nightmare editing job many of us dread: a government policies and procedures manual thousands of pages long.

Concordances have many theoretical uses in textual research and education, many of which are discussed at the ICT4LT Web site. If you want to play with concordances and you use Microsoft Word, Jack Lyon's *Word-Counter* utility provides a simple way to create a tabular concordance. Similarly, Alan Wyatt of WordTips offers a useful macro for determining word frequency by creating a word frequency list; the macro also sorts the words into alphabetical order so you can find specific words (and words with similar spelling) more easily. This process can be slow, even on a fast computer. Building a concordance is inherently computationally intensive, but the more serious problem is that Word isn't optimized for this work. For a faster alternative, have a look at the free Simple Concordance Program, which is available for both Windows and the Macintosh. The Concorder Pro software for Mac is also free and worth a look. For commercial products, Windows users should check out the Concordance software. Such dedicated tools will be much faster than any word processor, and will offer considerably more flexibility.

The Wikipedia article on concordances provides a more complete discussion of this subject, and lists some useful programs, but it's not comprehensive. If you have a better concordance resource, please tell me so I can add it to this book's Web page.

Simplified English and controlled vocabulary

In some industries, it's not feasible to translate every manuscript into every target language. For example, in the aerospace industry, the documentation required to safely and correctly maintain a modern airliner is prohibitively long and complex. Even though many phrases would have standardized translations, the difficulty of ensuring that translations in potentially hundreds of languages are good enough to save lives is too high. Until such time as technology improves sufficiently to make translation possible, the industry's solution has been to create a single, rigorously edited and reviewed English version of the documentation. By tightly controlling the word choices used in this documentation, they are able to produce a single documentation set that can be used around the world.

The people who deal with this tightly controlled language need help with consistency, particularly when they must conform to a prescribed standard vocabulary. For example, the Aerospace and Defence Industries Association has developed the ASD Simplified Technical English specification. Techscribe has released a free tool, the Term Checker for Simplified Technical English, that can help implement this vocabulary. Other industries may have similar tools. (If you use one, please contact me with details so I can add it to the book's Web page.)

Publisher- or association-specific style guides

Publishers look for ways to help their authors achieve consistency with the publisher's other publications. One of the most common ways involves the distribution of word processor templates that contain all the desired styles, predefined for ease of use so that (at least in theory) authors can impose consistency on their manuscript right from the start. If you'll be working with an author who plans to submit their manuscript to a certain publisher, check the publisher's Web site or contact their representatives to learn whether such a template is available. If so, you can ask your author to start with the template, or you can import their manuscript into the template and enforce consistency during your editing.

The process of applying consistency will increasingly be integrated with the software that authors use to create their manuscripts. For example, the Associated Press Style guide is commonly used by journalists, and the StyleGuard software has been developed to help writers apply the correct styles as they write. Similarly, StyleEase helps with formatting of Microsoft Word manuscripts to follow the American Psychological Association (APA), *Chicago Manual of Style* (CMS), Modern Language Association (MLA), and Turabian styles. More such tools will emerge over time, so if you do a lot of work for a certain publisher or use a specific style guide, periodically search the Web to see whether someone has released a tool that would make your life easier. (Again, if you use such a tool, please contact me with details so I can add it to the book's Web page.)

Chapter 10. Spelling and Grammar Checkers

Web: http://www.geoff-hart.com/books/eoe/eoe3/eoe3.html
Note: Word 2010 is for Windows; Word 2011 is for the Macintosh

Ask anyone what an editor does for a living, and most will say that we fix spelling errors and correct faulty grammar. Ask an *editor*, on the other hand, and you'll hear how much more we do, particularly if we work primarily as a substantive or developmental editor. Indeed, many editors are insulted by authors who feel we're nothing more than glorified spellcheckers and grammar technicians, and devote considerable effort to correcting that misperception. That being said, no editor's work would be complete without careful efforts to eliminate typos and grammar errors (grammos?). Those two tasks are the subject of this chapter.

Spellcheckers are the most obvious editing tool—so obvious, in fact, that they're about the only part of this book most editors feel they already know thoroughly. Yet because of this belief, many editors never go beyond learning how to launch the spellchecker. Some even forget the limitations of these tools: they can't yet tell when a correctly spelled word is entirely inappropriate for a given context, or which of two correctly spelled words is better for a given context. They also can't catch the homophobes (oops! *homophones!*) that even human editors sometimes miss. The grammar checkers provided by most word processors should help, but they rarely interact with the spellchecker in any useful way, and even the best ones remain oblivious to context, let alone to problems such as notional accord. (English is a uniquely flexible and slippery language that sometimes makes it difficult to parse sentences.) Nonetheless, like spellcheckers, a grammar checker can be useful once you understand its limitations.

> **Caution:** In using either tool, retain an appropriate skepticism. Both tools can *support* our sense of what is right—but cannot *replace* that sense. Both tools miss many errors that only a human mind will catch.

Spellcheckers and grammar checkers also cannot perform the kind of consistency checks that I described at great length in Chapter 9: they can't tell when a word used correctly in a given context is also used elsewhere, correctly or incorrectly, in a different context. (Daniel Heuman's PerfectIt can do this to some extent.) Neither can they tell whether two immaculately written statements are contradictory, misleading, or meaningless.

Some editors like to set the spellchecker to work continuously in the background as they type. In Word, the spellchecker then highlights any suspicious words with a squiggly underline. By all means, try this to discover whether it works for you. (See Chapter 4 for details on how to find the option Check spelling as you type.) I find that all the additional lines that appear on and disappear from the screen are distracting and create so much visual clutter that it becomes difficult to focus on the text. A compromise might be to turn off this option during your first pass·through the document, then enable this option for your final pass, when you've already fixed most spelling problems and it will be less distracting.

Efficiency tip: Perform your spellcheck *only once*, after you have finished your editing. Checking before you begin eliminates typos that might break your concentration, but won't save you from the need for a final spellcheck. Every editor introduces an occasional typo during editing. In addition, you won't know anything about the manuscript until you've been through it once, and won't know which word choices are appropriate. Why fix spellings for words that you're going to delete or that are correct, in context? Use the time you save for more demanding work.

Defining Languages

You might be wondering how the spellchecker knows which dictionary to use when it examines words in search of typos. The main way a word processor does this is by examining the properties of the character and paragraph styles that are used to format the text; these properties include the language or language dialect for the text. (See Chapter 4 for details about working with styles.) The most effective way to perform a spellcheck is to ensure that all character and paragraph styles have the correct language settings. (Some older or less sophisticated word processors may define the language only once, for an entire document, so check the documentation for your word processor to see how it handles spelling dictionaries. In this chapter, I'll focus on Word's implementation.)

After I published the 2nd edition of this book, Microsoft added a feature to Word that attempts to automatically recognize the correct language, but as of Word 2010 and 2011, I've found it more annoying than helpful. Part of the problem is that English has adopted words from most living languages and many extinct ones, and has evolved into several distinctive and somewhat incompatible dialects; my minimalist installation of Word 2011 contains 4 versions of English, and my ancient installation of Word 2003 included dictionaries for 17 English dialects. Which version of English should Word use if it has to guess? Automatic recognition will undoubtedly improve as the programmers become more sophisticated, but currently it's very much a work in progress.

What about authors who include many words from other languages in their manuscript? Although we can resign ourselves to repeatedly telling the spellchecker to ignore these words, we have better alternatives. First, as I noted in Chapter 8, we can use the search tools to find each instance of a word and apply a character style that has the correct language setting. Second, as I'll discuss later in the present chapter, we can add these words to a supplementary (*custom*) dictionary that can be specific to a single manuscript or applied to all of our editing projects.

Word 2010 displays the language settings for the current position of the text cursor in the status bar at the bottom of the screen. Unfortunately, this useful feature was removed from Word 2011. To learn the language setting for a word, sentence, or paragraph, select the word or position the text cursor in the sentence or paragraph, then:

- **Word 2010:** Ribbon > Review tab > Language icon > Set Proofing Language
- **Word 2011:** Tools menu > Language

If you select text before you open the dialog box, you can apply the correct language from this dialog box. If the language settings are broadly incorrect for a document, edit the language properties of the character and paragraph styles, then reapply those styles to solve the problem.

> **A note about reapplying styles:** Word correctly assumes that if you manually applied a style such as a language setting to one or more words, you want to preserve that formatting. Thus, it will not remove manually applied formats unless you force it to do so: select the word or paragraph, then press Control+Spacebar or Control+Shift+Z (Word 2010) or Command+Shift+Z (Word 2011).

The ability to use multiple languages in a document by defining styles with different language settings is a powerful tool for efficiency in multilingual documents: you can define language-specific character styles (for words and phrases) and paragraph styles (for whole paragraphs) and apply them to words, phrases, and entire paragraphs; for example, we could define Body Text French and Body Text English styles for French and English paragraphs, respectively, in a bilingual document. Subsequently, Word will use the specified dictionary in spellchecks, thereby eliminating the need to repeatedly tell Word to ignore that spelling when it can't find a French word in its English dictionary or vice versa. In addition, this will increase the likelihood of catching typos in unfamiliar languages. Failing to use styles in this way can waste an unacceptable amount of time and energy.

If, as sometimes happens, you're running Word's spellchecker and spot something else that needs fixing (e.g., a missing word), you don't necessarily have to stop the spellchecker so you can fix the problem and then restart the spellcheck from the start of the manuscript. If you don't want to interrupt the spellcheck, record the problem phrase on a notepad or in another program so you can return to it when you've finished the spellcheck. If you prefer to solve the problem immediately, click your mouse to position the text cursor inside the document window, correct the problem, then click the spellcheck dialog box again and click the Resume button to pick up where you left off. If you want to accomplish the same trick from the keyboard, you can press Alt+Tab (Word 2010) or Command+[`] (Word 2011) to switch from the spellcheck dialog box to the document window, then the same keystroke to return to the dialog box.

If you'll be working on a long manuscript, review the language settings for the main styles used in the document before you begin your spellcheck. Confirm that these agree with the language or languages that should be used. Authors rarely know how to use the language features correctly, and even if they do, they often use a template (e.g., provided by a conference organizer) with the wrong language settings. Sometimes they copy text from other manuscripts with different language settings; the latter is particularly common during international collaborations among authors.

AutoCorrect or *autocorriger*? Word uses the Balloon Text and Comment Text paragraph style to format the contents of inserted comments. Because AutoCorrect shortcuts (see Chapter 11 for details) depend on the language defined for a style, these shortcuts won't work if the settings of these styles specify a different language. To restore the shortcuts, redefine the styles to use the language for which you defined the shortcuts. Also note: if correctly spelled words in your carefully edited comments are flagged as spelling errors, the language setting is a common source of this problem.

If you need to apply the correct language settings throughout a manuscript and don't have time to edit and reapply each character and paragraph style, there's a shortcut: select all the text in a file (Control+A for Windows, Command+A for the Macintosh), or the subset of the text you want to modify, and then apply the correct language:

- **Word 2010:** Ribbon > Review tab > Language icon > Set Proofing Language
- **Word 2011:** Tools menu > Language > Set Language

Whenever possible, resist the temptation to use this method. Because you will be overriding the language settings defined by the character and paragraph styles, you will lose the new language setting as soon as someone changes any of the properties of these styles and reapplies the changed styles to the text. You'll eventually need to correct all the styles, so it's better to budget some time to do the job correctly so that you won't have to redo it. Note that this problem can also occur if the software has been configured to automatically update the styles in a document to reflect changes in the underlying template; whenever someone opens the document, those style settings will be reapplied.

What dictionary am I using? During spellchecks, Word displays the dictionary being used in the title bar of the dialog box. This will change as you move from word to word if the language setting applied to a word differs from the language of the surrounding words.

Word offers a useful trick that has the unfortunate side-effect of preventing spellchecks from behaving as you'd expect: you can specify that certain words should not be checked. In older versions of Word, you could select No proofing from the list of languages displayed in the Languages dialog box; in Word 2010 and 2011, there's a checkbox labeled Do not check spelling or grammar that accomplishes the same function. Although this is useful for text such as mathematical equations that should not be spellchecked, authors sometimes inadvertently apply this setting to text that *should* be checked. To find such text, use the software's search tool and specify this language choice:

- Open the Find and Replace dialog box. If necessary, expand the dialog box (as described in Chapter 8) to display the search options.
- From the Format popup menu, select Language.
- **Word 2010:** Select Do not check spelling or grammar.

- **Word 2011:** Deselect the checkbox Do not check spelling or grammar, then select (no language) from the list of languages. Unfortunately, there's a bug in the software that sometimes forces you to select a language (e.g., U.S. English) before you can do this.

Using the Spellchecker

In the first edition of this book, I incorrectly assumed that readers already knew how to use the spellchecker and didn't provide details. To remedy that omission, I've added this section to describe the basics for Microsoft Word. Most other software offers similar features, and uses a similar approach.

> **Checking only part of the text:** If you only want to check the spelling of part of the text (e.g., a word, sentence, or paragraph), select that text before you start the spellchecker. When Word finishes, it will offer you the chance to check the rest of the document. Click the No button if you're done with the spellcheck.

Before you begin, spend a few moments customizing the spellcheck options so they work the way you want them to work. (See Chapter 4 for details.) In particular, decide whether you want to review a document's grammar while you check the spelling. That's generally a poor choice, since the grammar checker isn't particularly good. Also, focusing on spelling can distract you from properly considering grammatical issues. In my experience, the grammar check works best in a separate pass if you're going to use this feature; I'll discuss how to use it most efficiently later in the chapter. To start the spellchecker:

- **Word 2010:** Ribbon > Review tab > Spelling & Grammar icon
- **Word 2011:** Tools menu > Spelling and Grammar

> **Checking spelling from the keyboard:** If you don't want to use the mouse to start the spellcheck, use the keyboard instead: For Word 2010, press Alt+T (which used to open the Tools menu), then press S; for Word 2011, press Command+Option+L.

The spellchecker dialog box has three main areas: At the top left, under the heading Not in dictionary, Word displays the word that it believes to be a typo, highlighted amidst the surrounding text. Below that, under the heading Suggestions, Word displays a list of possible corrections. Below the suggestions, the Check grammar checkbox lets you begin checking grammar during the spellcheck if you change your mind and decide you want to do this. At the right, Word displays the buttons you use to tell Word what to do with the ostensible typo:

- **Resume:** This button is present only if you return to the spellcheck dialog box after clicking the mouse inside the document window to fix an error. Click Resume to continue the spellcheck.

- **Ignore once:** If the word is a variant spelling you want to preserve, or an error that should not be corrected (e.g., in a direct quotation or article about common spelling errors), but you may want to correct the word elsewhere (where it really is an error), click this button.

- **Ignore all:** If the word is correctly spelled, but is not part of Word's spelling dictionary, click this button.

- **Add to dictionary:** If the word is correctly spelled and you want Word to ignore it in future spellchecks, click this button. This option adds the word to your custom dictionary, which I'll discuss shortly.

- **Change:** If the word is incorrect, and Word suggests a correct spelling under the Suggestions heading, select that spelling then click this button to make the correction. You can also double-click the correct spelling to replace the highlighted word without having to click this button. If Word doesn't offer any useful corrections, click inside the highlighted word under the heading Not in dictionary, make any necessary corrections (use the arrow keys to scroll through the text if necessary), then click the Change button to implement the change.

- **Change all:** If the spelling is wrong everywhere, select the correct spelling, then click this button (e.g., to change *color* to *colour* to reflect British spelling).

Text too small to read during spellchecks? The font Word uses to display potential typos inside the spellcheck dialog box is too small for easy reading. You can't change its size, but there's an alternative: before you begin your spellcheck, increase the size of the text in the document window. (Use the Zoom feature that I described in Chapter 4.) You can now reposition the spellcheck dialog box so it doesn't obscure the manuscript. Word also highlights the word in the document window, which remains clearly visible behind the dialog box.

- **AutoCorrect:** This button is similar to the Change All button, but automatically fixes spelling errors based on Word's list of AutoCorrect items. This eliminates the need to manually fix a long list of common errors during a spellcheck. However, Word's AutoCorrect items aren't always correct or useful. Use this option only if you're confident the AutoCorrect list contains no changes that Word shouldn't make. I'll discuss how to review and edit this list in Chapter 11.

Word sometimes flags correctly spelled words as errors. There are several possible causes of this problem:

- The word may have the wrong language assigned to it. To fix this, manually reapply the correct language setting.
- The word may have been added to your exclude (exclusion) dictionary. To fix this, remove the word from that dictionary (as described later in this chapter).
- Authors who use non-Roman alphabets often substitute look-alike characters (e.g., the number 1 instead of lower-case L, the number 0 instead of capital O). You can spot such problems using the search function: in Word, the pattern ^$^# or ^#^$ will find number-for-letter substitutions. See Chapter 8 for details on other potentially useful search patterns.
- An obscure setting in the Windows registry (HKEY_CURRENT_USER\ Software\Microsoft\Shared Tools\Proofing Tools\1.0\Override) can fool the spellcheck; deleting this entry will solve the problem. Caution: don't mess with the Windows registry if you don't know what you're doing, and always (i) backup the registry before you begin and (ii) write down what you did so you can undo that change.

Sometimes Word skips over words that are clearly incorrect. As I noted earlier in this chapter, one common cause is that the text has been formatted using the No proofing or Do not check spelling and grammar language setting. However, the most common reason is that Word is trying to be helpful and to save you time by not checking text that it believes you've already checked. To force Word to recheck the entire document (except for words that you specifically told it to ignore):

- **Word 2010:** File menu > Options > Proofing tab > Recheck document button
- **Word 2011:** Word menu > Preferences > Spelling & Grammar tab > Recheck document button

If Word won't check the spelling even after you clicked the Recheck document button, this is most often due to text that has somehow been set to No proofing: Word does what this setting tells it to do and skips these words. To solve this problem, turn off revision tracking and perform a global search and replace (see Chapter 8 for details): In the Find what field, open the Format menu, select Language, and then select (no language), which should be the first option in the language list; in the Replace with field, repeat these steps, but choose the language you want to use in the spellcheck. Click the Replace all button. Turn on revision tracking again. If the document should contain words from only one language, there's an easier way: select all of the text (Control+A for Windows; Command+A for the Macintosh), then apply any new language (as described earlier in this chapter). Select the text again, but this time change the text to the correct language. This second change usually tricks Word into resetting the spellchecker.

Special Dictionaries

If you use the spellchecker without modifying its settings, you're only taking advantage of the standard dictionaries. These are the ones you'll use most heavily, because even in a jargon-heavy or multilingual manuscript, these dictionaries contain the words that bind the jargon and foreign words together. But there are two spelling features many editors never discover, or discover but fail to take advantage of: *custom* (*personal*) dictionaries that contain lists of nonstandard words that you use frequently, and *exclusion* (*exclude*) dictionaries that tell the software to flag certain correctly spelled words that you want to examine more closely. Most spellcheckers first look for a word in their main dictionary, then consult these other dictionaries to see whether the word can be found there.

Custom or personal dictionaries

Most word processors and most desktop publishing programs ship with generic spelling dictionaries for each language that are adequate for a general audience. That audience is typically imagined by the software's developer to be office workers or general readers. Unfortunately, these dictionaries often have surprising gaps even for those audiences, and are hopelessly inadequate for editors who work in specialized genres. If there were no way to teach the spellchecker new words and their correct spelling, we'd waste enormous amounts of time forcing Word to ignore these words every time we edited manuscripts in such genres. Worse yet, we'd have to manually correct typos in these words.

Custom or *personal* dictionaries let us store these unusual words for reuse. Better software, such as Word, lets us create multiple dictionaries, including one overall dictionary that works for all documents written in a given language, and additional custom dictionaries that can be attached to specific documents and used only for those documents. During a spellcheck, the software searches first for each word in its standard dictionary for a given language. If it can't find that word, it then looks in any custom dictionaries that are specified as being available for the current document. If the word is present in one of these dictionaries, the spellchecker moves on; if not, and if the word appears to be a typo for any of the words in these dictionaries, it proposes alternative spellings from these dictionaries.

If a word is spelled correctly, you can simply ignore the supposed error, but if you expect to see that word many more times, it's better to add the word to your custom dictionary: spending a couple seconds doing this once will save you countless more seconds in your future work. In Word, simply confirm the spelling, then click the Add to dictionary button in the spellcheck dialog box. Gradually adding new words as you encounter them will eventually create an entire specialized dictionary of jargon for the genres in which you edit. Most editors know that this option is available; fewer know that Word lets you create a custom dictionary for each genre and add these dictionaries to the spellcheck, as needed. The good news is that this is a powerful feature. The bad news is that Microsoft keeps changing how you access this feature. To accomplish this in two recent versions of Word:

- **Word 2010:** File menu > Options > Proofing tab > Spelling & Grammar > Custom Dictionaries button
- **Word 2011:** Word menu > Preferences > Spelling and Grammar tab > Dictionaries button

Selecting, adding, removing, and creating custom dictionaries

In the Custom Dictionaries dialog box, Word lists all dictionaries that are available for use. The standard custom dictionary is named CUSTOM. DIC in Word 2010 and Custom dictionary in Word 2011. To make a dictionary available for use with the current document, simply select the checkbox beside its name. Conversely, deselect the checkbox to deactivate a dictionary so that it will no longer be used. The following additional options are available:

- **Add a dictionary to the list:** Click the Add button and navigate through your files until you find the correct dictionary. Adding a dictionary only makes it *available* for use. You must still select its checkbox to begin using it. Note that if you're moving to a new computer, you can copy your old dictionary to the new computer, then use the Add button to make it available to Word on the new computer.

- **Remove a dictionary:** If you no longer need a dictionary, select its name and then click the Remove button. Removing a dictionary does not delete the dictionary; it only makes it unavailable until you add it again. Removing dictionaries is useful if you reach the limit on the number of dictionaries you can use with a given manuscript. (See the section *Limitations on dictionary number* later in this chapter for information about limits on the number of dictionaries.)

- **Create a new custom dictionary:** First, select the language that you want the custom dictionary to be used with (e.g., English U.S. versus French Canada), then click the New button. Note that for a dictionary of specialized terminology that will remain constant in all languages (e.g., HTML keywords), Word 2010 lets you choose All languages as the language; that option doesn't seem to be available in Word 2011. Give the dictionary a memorable name, and if you want to use it in multiple projects, save it in the same location as your other custom dictionaries. Alternatively, save it in the directory containing a project's files if you will only use the dictionary for one project.

Where are my custom dictionaries? Microsoft, presumably bored with the old locations, periodically moves the dictionary files to new locations. The easiest way to find them is the Custom Dictionaries dialog box. In Word 2010, look below the list of dictionaries, in the File path field; this is typically C:\Users\[your name]\AppData\Roaming\Microsoft\UProof. In Word 2011, the dialog box doesn't display the full path, but if you click the Add button, Word opens a standard file selection dialog box: click the menu at the top of the dialog box to display the full path, which is typically Users\[your name]\Library\Application Support\Microsoft\Office\Preferences\Office 2011.

- **Revise a custom dictionary:** Select the dictionary, then click the Edit button. (You can also open the dictionary file directly in Word and edit it in Word rather than in the cramped dialog box that the Edit button displays.) If you include a word containing a typo or a word you won't often use again, edit the word list to solve the problem.

Limitations on words in a custom dictionary

In Word's custom dictionaries, word length used to be limited to 64 letters, and words in the dictionary could not contain spaces and could only contain standard ASCII characters rather than the full Unicode character set. These limitations appear to have been removed, but I could not find reliable information on whether other limits apply. If you try adding a word that the dictionary won't accept or that causes the custom dictionary to malfunction, the solution is to remove that word; you've almost certainly discovered an undocumented limitation of the dictionary software.

Word's custom dictionaries also used to be limited to around 5000 words and a maximum file size of about 64 kb (kilobytes), but this restriction has been removed in current versions. The main limitation seems to be that an unusually large dictionary will slow the spellcheck due to the large numbers of words that must be compared with each word in the manuscript.

Free, but really long, custom dictionary: John Petrie, a long-time scientific editor, provides freely downloadable U.S. and U.K. custom dictionaries of science terminology with more than half a million words. If you know of any other dictionaries that you'd like to share, send them to me and I'll add them to the book's Web site.

If you do manage to run out of room (which seems unlikely) and Word won't let you add new words to an existing custom dictionary, simply create an additional custom dictionary, as described in the previous section.

Limitations on dictionary number

Word limits the number of custom dictionaries you can have active simultaneously; as best I can tell, the limit appears to be 10. If you need more than this number of custom dictionaries, activate only the 10 most relevant dictionaries for a given project. Use the procedure described earlier in this chapter to temporarily remove the least relevant dictionaries and add the most relevant ones. If you need to do this dictionary shuffling fairly often so you can use different groups of dictionaries for different projects, learn how to record a macro that will do the repetitive work for you. (See Chapter 11 for more information on macros.)

Back-up your dictionaries! The time you spent creating a custom spelling dictionary is valuable. To protect that investment, include the dictionary in your ongoing backups. To learn the file location, see the note box "Where are my custom dictionaries?" earlier in this chapter.

Exclusion dictionaries

Correctly spelled words that are perfectly acceptable in one context can be embarrassing or inappropriate in other contexts. For example, *pu-*

bic is one of those words that cause nightmares for newspaper editors because it's a common typo for *public* and is likely to appear in inch-high type in headlines, where only the poor copyeditor could possibly have missed it. In my work as a science editor, most of my clients are not native English speakers, so they create many phonetic spelling errors that are correctly spelled but entirely the wrong word. And there are certain common typos (e.g., *form* versus *from*) that my unaided eye tends to skip over.

Fortunately, Word offers an *exclusion* dictionary that lets you force the spellcheck software to highlight such words, thereby providing an opportunity to confirm their correctness, in context. The word *exclusion* comes from the fact that the spellchecker will *exclude* these words from the list of correct spellings and identify them as potentially incorrect. Unfortunately, Microsoft's terminology for this feature varies both between and within versions of Word: sometimes they use "exclude" and sometimes "exclusion". Try both terms if you're consulting the online help or searching Microsoft's Web site and can't find what you're looking for.

Your software doesn't offer an exclusion dictionary? If your software doesn't offer this feature, or does, but you don't like how it works, see the section *Simulating an exclusion dictionary* later in this chapter for some suggestions on alternatives.

In addition to highlighting potentially embarrassing gaffes, exclusion dictionaries let us compensate for personal blind spots related to certain words or to frequently confused word pairs. Once we've added them to the exclusion dictionary, each spellcheck offers a chance to confirm that they're used correctly. Several categories of words can be usefully added to an exclusion dictionary:

Category	Reason to add to exclusion dictionary
Personal preference	We all have preferences for certain spellings. For example, I prefer to use *metre* rather than *meter*; it is, after all, the metric system, not the *meteric* system. Even though *meter* is correct in U.S. English, I want my spellchecker to give me the option of changing that spelling.

Category	Reason to add to exclusion dictionary
Variant spellings	If there are two correct spellings for a word, adding both to your custom dictionary would lead to both spellings being treated as correct. For example, research *centers* in the U.S. become *centres* in the U.K. Adding both words to my exclusion list reminds me to confirm that I've used the correct spelling for each region.
Pairs of similar words with different meanings	This category includes words such as *economic* and *economical*; the first refers to the science of economics, but the latter means inexpensive or cost-effective. Adding these words to the exclusion dictionary reminds me to check whether I've used the right word in each case.
Pairs of dissimilar words with different meanings	Adding words such as *which* and *that*, which many editors use to distinguish between non-restrictive and restrictive clauses (respectively), offers a second chance to confirm that you've used the correct word for the job.
Overused words	Words such as *very* and *really* are meaningless filler that can generally be removed. Where precision is important, it's better to use a precise term that communicates the actual magnitude. Similarly, each of us has a few favorite words we overuse, and we tend to be blind to that overuse. Adding such words to an exclusion list (once we're alerted to their existence) reminds us to reconsider their use.

Creating exclusion lists in Word

To ensure that Word will highlight both lower-case and capitalized versions of these words during spellchecks, enter all excluded words in lower-case spelling. To get you started creating your own exclusion list, copy the list provided on the book's Web site and paste it into your word processor. Delete any words that aren't relevant in your work, or add missing words that are. (If you have any words you think everyone should include in their list, please send them to me and I'll add them to the file so that other editors can benefit from these words. Contact information is available on the book's Web page.)

Single characters excluded: Unfortunately, Word exclusion dictionaries can't include single-character words. The solution is to create a macro that uses global search and replace to highlight all instances of a single-character word so you can check them manually.

In Word, exclusion dictionaries can be created for each language, since they are specific to the language defined for any chunk of text. To create an exclusion dictionary in Word:

Word 2010:

The exclusion files already exist, and you must edit them rather than creating them from scratch:

- For Windows 7, look for these files in the following folder: C:\Users\ [your name]\AppData\Roaming\Microsoft\UProof.
- The file will have a name similar to the following: ExcludeDictionary-LanguageCodeLanguageLCID.lex. For example, the English exclusion dictionary is ExcludeDictionaryEN0409.lex. The four numbers at the end of the name represent the location code (LCID). To learn the code for a given language, search the Web or Microsoft's Web site for the phrase "Locale identification numbers".
- You can't edit the file directly within Word's dictionary dialog box, but Word can open the file easily enough. Select the abovementioned file. If Word asks whether to convert the file format, click No.
- Edit the file (add, delete, or correct words), pressing Enter between words so that each word occurs on a separate line.
- Save your changes. If Word asks you to specify a file format, choose Plain Text.
- Close and restart Word.

Word 2011:

For this description, please thank my Australian colleague Matt Stevens, who found a way to get this feature working despite Microsoft's best efforts to the contrary:

- The first time you begin working with a new exclusion dictionary, start by creating a new blank document.
- To define the file format the dictionary should use, you can't rely on the Save or Save As dialog boxes. Instead: Word menu > Preferences > Save tab > Save Word files as menu > Speller Exclude Dictionary (.dic). Click OK to close the dialog box.
- Save the file immediately using the Save function in the following folder: \Users\[your name]\Library\Preferences\Microsoft.

- Give the file a logical name such as "English exclude dictionary". No filename extension is required for the Macintosh. There appears to be no way to define the language, and you can only have one exclude dictionary active at a time.
- Change the default file type back to the original setting (usually .docx) so you can use that format instead of the dictionary format for subsequent files: Word menu > Preferences > Save tab > Save Word files as menu > Word Document (.docx).
- Enter your list of words; press the Enter or Return key after every word, including the last one, so that each word is on a separate line.
- Now that the dictionary has been created, you can open it, edit its contents, and save the file as you would for any other file.
- Quit and restart Word so these changes will take effect.
- If you need to use multiple exclude dictionaries (e.g., for different languages), close Word, move the old dictionary out of the folder that contains it, and move the new dictionary into that folder to replace it. Having two exclude dictionaries in the same folder may lead to crashes and other problems.

Getting to your exclusion dictionaries in a hurry: The path to the exclusion dictionary is complex. To get there most easily, create a shortcut (Windows) or alias (Macintosh) that leads to their directory and store it somewhere easily accessed, such as your Desktop.

Simulating an exclusion dictionary

If you're having trouble making the exclusion dictionary work, if you find that it simply doesn't meet your needs, or if your software doesn't offer this feature at all, you can achieve much the same results without too much trouble. All you need to do is find a way to highlight all these words by yourself. Note that although you can do this with or without track changes turned on, it's simpler to apply and remove the highlighting with track changes turned off so the author will never see what you've done. Since the highlighting is purely for your own use, this is an acceptable example of doing something without informing the author.

If you use Windows Word and want an easier way: Jack Lyon's MegaReplacer software and Daniel Heuman's PerfectIt can do most of the hard work for you. Unless you're a determined do-it-yourselfer, considering using their software to make the job easier.

Start by creating a list of the words that are giving you trouble. Next, create a macro that will work through your list, one word at a time, and use the find and replace feature to find every instance of those words and apply a format that makes the words stand out; in Word, the easiest approach is to use the highlighter marker to apply a highlight color, since you generally won't have to worry about retaining highlighting anywhere once you're finished. You can also apply a text color, but you'll have to ensure that color isn't required anywhere in the document. (See Chapter 8 for details on how to do this kind of find and replace operation. See Chapter 11 for details on how to record a macro that will do the work.)

Once you've highlighted all the problem words in your list, edit the manuscript as usual, but pay particular attention to the highlighted words. When you're done, remove the highlighting: turn off revision tracking, select the whole text (Control+A for Windows, Command+A for the Macintosh), and then remove the formatting. If you used the highlighter marker, change the color to No color (Word 2010) or None (Word 2011). If you applied a text color, you'll need to repeat the search and replace operation that you used to apply the color, but this time you'll be searching for the applied color, and the replacement color will be Automatic (i.e., the color defined by the underlying character or paragraph style).

Use Clear formatting cautiously: In the previous version of this book, I suggested that you could select all the text and use the Clear Formatting function (Control+Shift+Z for Windows, Command+Shift+Z for the Macintosh). This is only safe if you have not applied any formats such as italics manually rather than using styles. If you have to protect such manually applied formats, use the method described in the previous paragraph instead.

Third-Party Dictionaries

Although you can gradually build your own custom dictionary for each genre you work in, this can take quite some time. Fortunately, others may have already invested this time for you, and you can find a range of special-purpose dictionaries. Searching the Web for *Microsoft Word* plus *dictionary* turns up thousands of options, and you can narrow your search further by adding keywords such as *medical* or *legal*, or the name of a standard dictionary's publisher (e.g., Dorland, Merriam-Webster, Macquarie). Some examples that colleagues have recommended over the years:

- Spellex offers medical, legal, and scientific dictionaries.
- Dorland offers a well-respected medical and pharmaceutical spell-checker that works with Word and WordPerfect.
- Azmanam's chemistry dictionary for Word and OpenOffice Writer.
- The American Geological Institute offers a dictionary for Earth and environmental sciences that also works with WordPerfect.
- Whitesmoke is a general-purpose spellchecker.

Some of the dictionaries you'll find will replace your software's spell-check dictionary but continue to use its spellchecker functions, whereas others are programs that run completely independently of your word processor. An example of the latter is the venerable Spell Catcher, which has been around for more than 30 years and works with most programs for Windows or the Macintosh. If Word's spellchecker frustrates you as much as it frustrates me, consider using an external spellchecker.

Style guides with spellcheck: Chapter 9 lists several programs designed to ensure conformity with a specific style, such as Chicago or MLA, and these programs generally include spellcheckers specific to the guidelines in those style guides.

If you're willing to work outside Word when you need to research a term's spelling, the Internet is a superb resource. For example, the One-Look multi-dictionary search claims to offer access to more than 21 million words from more than 1000 dictionaries. I'll discuss this and other Internet tools for editors in more detail in Chapter 14.

Spelling Surprises

Most spellcheckers have idiosyncrasies that you'll need to learn to live with or work around. For example, older versions of Word couldn't recognize single-character "words" and thus would not protect you from typing O instead of I (adjacent keyboard characters) as a personal pronoun. (Oi!) You can fix some problems by changing the default spelling settings, as described in Chapter 4:

- **Suggest from main dictionary only:** Word won't consult your custom dictionaries.
- **Ignore words in UPPERCASE:** Acronyms won't be checked.

- **Ignore words with numbers:** Word will ignore text such as 1nd (a typo for 2nd).
- **Flag repeated words:** This option will identify doubled words. These often occur while we're editing with tracked changes displayed; it's easy to add a word before a deleted chunk of text and miss the same word right after the deleted text.

As you use the software, keep your eyes open for any unusual behavior that you don't have to tolerate. If you can define a particular type of error as a pattern of text or numbers (see Chapter 8 for details), you can create a simple search and replace macro that will apply a specific pattern (e.g., the yellow highlighter marker) to all instances of that pattern. When you see the highlight, you have a chance to decide what to do about the problem.

Grammar Checkers

The fact that you're reading this book means that you understand something important about human languages: they're sufficiently complex that mastering them requires specialized training and lots of practice. In consequence, only language professionals can reliably spot and fix typical language problems, and sometimes only experienced editors can figure out what to do with the most serious problems—rewriting a sentence from scratch, for instance, rather than trying to patch fatal flaws with a handful of bandaids. Given that most *humans* require editors to straighten out their prose, it's hardly surprising that nobody has yet come up with truly effective grammar-checking software for personal computers. As a result, the current options generally work poorly and provide bad advice only slightly less often than they give good advice. Most editors, after briefly experimenting with a grammar checker, give up in disgust.

Customizing the grammar checker

That being said, most grammar checkers let you disable all or many of their options and force the software to focus on the things it can do well. Each of us has certain blind spots (e.g., overusing passive voice), and once you recognize that they exist, you can try customizing the grammar checker's settings to seek out and highlight that specific type of problem. This strategy can also help you learn to detect such problems on your own by repeatedly drawing your attention to instances of the problem that you missed; over time, you'll learn to spot the problems yourself. Of course, you'll still need to think about the grammar checker's recommendations, since they rely more on pattern matching than on a deep understanding of words and their context. (That understanding will remain *our* job for the foreseeable future.) To customize the grammar checker's settings:

- **Word 2010:** File > Options > Proofing tab > When correcting spelling and grammar in Word heading > Settings button
- **Word 2011:** Word menu > Preferences > Spelling and Grammar tab > Settings button

Current versions of Word provide a surprising range of settings that you can select—or deselect if you find them more trouble than they're worth. Unfortunately, the Windows and Macintosh versions of Word have different interfaces and somewhat different options:

- **Word 2010:** From the Writing style menu, select Grammar only to deselect all of the writing style options, or Grammar and Style to select both the grammar and the writing style options.
- **Word 2011:** Under the heading Writing style, Word offers five groups of settings you can individually adjust (Casual, Standard, Formal, Technical, and Custom).

Here are some useful things that Word can check:

- Comma required before last list item: Checks for missing serial (Oxford) commas before the "and" in a list (A, B, and C).
- Punctuation required with quotes: Checks whether the punctuation belongs inside the quotation marks (American style), or outside (British or *logical* style, with some exceptions).
- Spaces required between sentences (1 or 2).
- Capitalization errors.
- Commonly confused words.
- Hyphenated and compound words.
- Misused words.
- Gender-specific words.

Word 2010 offers 11 grammar settings and 21 style settings you can try out. Word 2011 offers 13 grammar settings and 15 style settings. One editor's hindrance is another's help, so if something seems like it might prove helpful, try it. If it proves ineffective, you've only wasted a few minutes and you can disable that option before you try the next grammar check; if it proves helpful, use that option to save time or reduce the frequency of that type of error. By focusing on only those problems for which you need assistance, you can both improve your accuracy and learn to recognize and solve some classes of problem by yourself.

Using the grammar checker

There is no separate menu choice or clickable icon that will let you check the grammar without also checking the spelling. Thus, you'll need to set Word to check the grammar at the same time as it checks the spelling, then run the spellchecker, as described in the section *Using the Spellchecker* earlier in this chapter. If you spellcheck the manuscript before you check the grammar, Word shouldn't stop too often to report typos, and most of the problems that it reports will be grammar-related.

Disabling grammar checks for certain words or phrases: You can't add new words or phrases to Word's grammar checker, and there's no equivalent to the exclusion dictionary I discussed earlier for spellchecks. You can achieve a similar effect by using the search function to find all instances of the word or phrase you want to exclude and change its language setting to Do not check spelling or grammar (as I discussed earlier in this chapter). Unfortunately, this will exclude the word or phrase from the spellcheck, so carefully confirm the spelling before you try this.

Alternatives to the grammar checker

As an alternative to the standard grammar checker built into your word processor, you might want to investigate special-purpose tools designed to deal with specific aspects of a manuscript's language or structure. For example:

- For AECMA Simplified Technical English, consider Boeing's Simplified English Checker or the Hyper STE software.
- Daniel Heuman's PerfectIt and Rich Adin's EditTools both provide automated forms of consistency checks to detect inconsistencies and help you resolve them. Sadly, both only work for Windows.
- Hemingway Editor for the Macintosh and Windows tries to solve some of the same stylistic problems Word's grammar checker attempts to solve. If you're dissatisfied with Word's tools, try it and tell me what you think.

These tools have the same limitations as grammar checkers: they apply rules mechanically rather than based on a deep understanding of semantics. They nonetheless offer some useful tricks, such as identification of missing articles and problems with participles. The best grammar checkers are still experienced editors, and will remain so for some time to come. Online communities such as Copyediting-L and Techwhirl are great ways to meet human experts who can help you when all else seems lost. For other useful Internet resources, see Chapter 14.

Chapter 11. Automating Your Edits

Web: http://www.geoff-hart.com/books/eoe/eoe3/eoe3.html
Note: Word 2010 is for Windows; Word 2011 is for the Macintosh

An underappreciated advantage of computers is their ability to automate tedious tasks. Though computers have yet to achieve their full potential as labor-saving devices, several promising developments can help you right now. Scripting languages built into your operating system, such as the Macintosh Applescript language and Automator software and the Windows Scripting Host, let you automate many computer-related tasks. (I've provided links to tutorials on both technologies on this chapter's Web page. The bibliography also lists some useful reference material.) With a little research, you can learn how to control most of the software on your computer. The system-level scripting tools are less useful for editing *per se*, but can be very useful for managing associated tasks, such as backing up your files and returning files to an author via e-mail. If you're a real programming whiz, you can even use these tools to develop complete workflow solutions.

Scheduling scripts: Windows users are more likely to replace the default calendar with third-party alternatives, so check the documentation to see whether and how your software can run scripts. Microsoft's article *Task Scheduler Overview* provides an option for all Windows computers. Macintosh users tend to stick with iCal. To schedule an Automator script in iCal , add a new event at the desired time (e.g., every Saturday at 10 AM). Change the alarm type to Custom, and choose Open File as the alarm type. Navigate to the directory where you stored the Automator script, and select the script.

Because the details of scripting languages vary among versions of these operating systems, and because programs vary in their ability to be scripted, I won't provide details on these tools here. For more control and an easier development system, consider third-party tools such as Macro-Express for Windows and Keyboard Maestro for Macintosh. QuicKeys is a proven solution for both Windows and the Mac. You can find a range of other programs, with varying levels of geekiness and user-friendliness, with a little Web searching.

In this chapter, I'll focus on the tools built into your word processor, as these are the tools that most directly support onscreen editing. Most word processors offer at least two groups of automation features:

- *Macros* (also called *scripts*) are simple programs that you can record by setting the software to watch what you do, or that you can write from scratch using the software's built-in programming language.
- *Automatic text* features (also called *autocorrect*) watch what you're typing and automatically perform certain actions, such as replacing a short keyword with a phrase, sentence, or longer text as soon as you reach the end of the keyword or type a specific keyboard shortcut.

To simplify your editing work, you should spend some time creating macros for any multi-step operations that you perform frequently (more than a couple times per manuscript or per day) as well as for any operations that you perform infrequently but that take considerable time to complete because of the number of steps or their complexity. Similarly, you should create automatic text shortcuts for any kind of text that you type repeatedly over the course of a day, or for long text that you may only type occasionally but that takes a significant amount time to type.

Spend a few moments each day monitoring the kind of work you do repeatedly or that costs you time, then spend a few more moments pondering whether this might be something you could automate. If you're not sure, consider asking the question in a forum such as Copyediting-L, where many experienced editors are available to answer your questions. This small investment of time will repay you with significant time savings over the course of the week—and greater savings over the course of a year. The more often you use the shortcut, the more time you save.

It's also important to spend some time researching how your word processor handles these features, since that will determine how you implement and use them. Word, for example, stores its macros in templates, and the macros are available to all files based on these templates. Automatic text shortcuts can be more difficult to pin down, since they're stored in several places and these locations sometimes change between versions of Word. Other software stores these shortcuts in a shared folder available to all software. In Appendix 1, I'll provide details of where current versions of Word hide your automations.

> **Macintosh users beware!** Word 2011 reintroduced the ability to run macros on the Macintosh, but there are vexing incompatibilities with the implementation in Word 2010 for Windows. Most simple macros run just fine in both versions of Word, but more complex macros may need to be reprogrammed from scratch.

Once again, I'll focus on how Word implements these technologies to provide concrete examples of how you can use them. Most modern software provides comparable features, or lets you emulate them using the abovementioned scripting tools and third-party tools.

Run Windows on your Mac? Windows implementation of Word are vastly superior to their Macintosh cousins. Much though I love my Macintosh, I do all my serious editing with Windows. It's easy to run Windows on any recent-model Macintosh using software such as Parallels and VMWare Fusion (for maximum ease of use), or the free VirtualBox software if you're a bit geekier. I've been very happy with Parallels. You'll need a copy of Windows, as well as a copy of Word.

Using Macros Effectively

Word's macros let you capture multi-step procedures such as selecting menu items, customizing settings in the dialog box for that menu choice, then closing the dialog box. They're even more effective for complex multi-step procedures, such as performing a long series of consecutive search and replace operations to correct a variety of problems or to reformat a document to follow a publisher's style guide. Best of all, you don't need to be a programmer to use macros: you can set the software to watch your actions and record them.

Recorded macros can capture just about any menu selection, button click, or typing that you can do using the mouse or keyboard. You don't have to learn computer programming to record macros, although you can develop more sophisticated and powerful macros if you're willing to learn. Just a little knowledge lets you edit recorded macros to fix any glitches or to improve a macro's performance. But the important point is that you don't *need* to do this. You can achieve amazing results just by recording your actions, and for most of us, that's a whole lot less intimidating than trying to learn a programming language.

Macro cookbook: Jack Lyon wrote the wonderful *Macro Cookbook for Microsoft Word*, which provides a simple tutorial on how to use Word's macro features, more details if you're feeling ambitious, and abundant examples to inspire you to create your own.

Creating macros

The easiest way to create a macro is to record one. Before you begin, spend a few moments understanding what you're trying to accomplish and practicing the action or series of actions until you won't make mistakes that would force you to edit or re-record the macro. This is not a question of speed: Word will wait patiently for as long as it takes you to complete the actions, and doesn't record how long each action takes. Word even offers a *pause and resume* feature that lets you stop recording your macro, do a bit of work without recording those actions, and then continue recording. Here's how to accomplish this:

- **Word 2010:** View tab > Macros menu > Record macro
- **Word 2011:** Tools menu > Macro > Record new macro
- Choose a memorable name so you'll remember what the macro does. (The name must be a single word with no spaces, but you can use internal capitalization to clarify the meaning. For example, AcceptEachDeletion is a valid name.)
- Define where to store the macro. By default, macros are stored in the Normal.dotm document template, and are available in any file you're working on. You can also store a macro in the document you're editing, so it will only be available in that document, or in another template, so it will be available in all files based on that template. This lets you create groups of client-specific, genre-specific (e.g., science vs. literature), or task-specific (substantive editing vs. proofreading) macros.
- To assign the macro to a toolbar, click the Toolbars button. In Word 2010, your only option is the Quick Access Toolbar, which appears at the top of the Ribbon, above its tabs; in Word 2011, you can create new toolbars or add the macro to an existing toolbar. See Chapter 4 for details.
- To assign a keyboard shortcut to the macro, click the Keyboard button. If you forget to do this, you can do it later; see the following text box for a summary.

Creating keyboard shortcuts for recorded macros: If you recorded a Word macro but forgot to assign a keyboard shortcut or store it in a toolbar, you can fix this omission using the Customize feature described in Chapter 4. In summary, scroll through the list of command categories until you find the Macros category, then scroll through the list of commands until you find the macro you recorded. Choose a keyboard shortcut for that macro.

- Optional: Add a description of what the macro does. This description defaults to your name and the macro's creation date, but can include useful information such as the conditions under which the macro works—or doesn't work. This description is included in the programming code that Word uses to implement the macro, and you can edit it later.

- Click OK to close the dialog box, and then perform all the steps you want to record: open menus, select options, click buttons, and so on. You can make multiple menu choices and record long, involved procedures. There's a limit to how long a macro can be, but you'll probably never reach that limit. If you do, you can break the macro into two or more parts and run those parts in the correct sequence. (I'll provide an example later in this chapter.)

- **Word 2010:** To stop or pause the recording of a macro: View tab > Macros menu > Stop Recording or Pause Recording. To continue recording after you have paused the recording: View tab > Macros menu > Resume Recording.

- **Word 2011:** Tools menu > Macro > Stop recording. There is currently no *pause* option, so you'll need to complete the series of actions in a single pass, or combine macros created before and after each time you stopped to create the longer sequence of actions.

When you're done, the software translates your actions into program code that Word will understand, and stores this information for future reuse as a macro. Even though the actions you've performed are stored as program code, you need never see or interact with that code in most cases. (If you need to or want to see the code, see the section *Editing macros* later in this chapter for a primer on how to do so.)

Don't procrastinate! I'm my own worst enemy when it comes to reducing my workload. Specifically, I usually wait until I'm completely fed up with some task before I force myself to make time to automate it. Don't be like me!

Running macros

There are several ways to run a macro:
- If you stored it in a toolbar, click its icon.
- Type the keyboard shortcut that you defined.
- **Word 2010:** View tab > Macros menu > View macros. Select the desired macro in this dialog box and click the Run button.

- **Word 2011:** Tools menu > Macro > Macros. Select the desired macro in this dialog box and click the Run button.

Making macros accessible in other documents

If you need to access a macro stored in a specific document or template, you have three options: you can *attach* that template to the current document to replace the original template, you can *add* the template to Word's list of active templates so that all documents gain access to its macros, or you can *transfer* macros directly between documents. (You can use the same approach to gain access to other template-related tools, such as toolbars and style definitions, but here, I'll focus on macros.)

To gain access to the Templates and Add-ins dialog box, which provides the tools you'll use to manage templates and their macros:

- **Word 2010:** First, you'll need to display the ribbon's Developer tab: File > Options > Customize Ribbon > select Developer. In that tab, click the Document Template button.

- **Word 2011:** Tools menu> Templates and Add-ins

The Templates and Add-ins dialog box lets you attach a template to the currently open document, thereby replacing the old template with the new one and making the new template's macros available:

- Click the Attach button, and choose one of the available templates.
- Click OK to exit from the dialog box and apply this change.

You can instead add a template to Word's list of *global* templates, which are opened whenever you start Word so that their macros become available in any open document:

- Click the Add button, then select the desired template. This makes the template and its macros available to Word.
- If the added template does not have a checkmark beside its name, click to select the template.
- If you no longer need the template, either deselect it temporarily (remove the checkmark beside its name) or remove it until you add it again by selecting the template and clicking the Remove button. Note that this does not delete the template.

From this dialog box, you can also transfer various useful things between documents. In Word 2010, you can transfer styles and macros; in Word 2011, you can transfer styles, automatic text, toolbars, and macros. Here, I'll focus on macros:

- Click the Organizer button to display the Organizer dialog box.
- Select the Macro Project Items tab.

- Using the menus at the bottom of this dialog box, select the source document or template that contains the desired macros and the destination document or template that will receive the macros. If either document name being displayed is wrong, click the Close File button to close it; the button name changes to Open File, and clicking the button displays a standard file selector dialog box that will let you navigate to and select the desired file.

- Word displays the list of macros that are available. Select the desired collection of macros from the source document. If a collection with that name already exists in the destination document, and you don't want to replace it, select one of the two names and click the Rename button to choose a new name.

- Click the Copy button to copy the selected macros from the source document into the destination document.

- Unfortunately, you can't select individual macros to transfer. After the transfer is complete, use the Macros dialog box (described in the previous section) to delete any macros that you don't want to retain.

Running macros automatically

It's sometimes helpful to ask Word to run a macro automatically, without your intervention. You can do this by giving the macros names that have been predefined by Microsoft to run under certain circumstances. For these macros to run automatically, they must be stored in a global template (typically, in Normal.dotm) so that the macros are available to any open Word document. The names and the corresponding circumstances under which they run are:

- **AutoNew:** runs whenever you create a new document
- **AutoClose:** runs whenever you close a document
- **AutoExec:** runs whenever you start Word (stored only in Normal. dotm)
- **AutoExit:** runs whenever you shut down Word
- **AutoOpen:** runs whenever you open a document

Because these macros run automatically, they will trigger Word's macro virus warning if they are present in a template that you send to a colleague, so be sure to warn them so they won't fear that you're sending a virus. As always, the behavior in Macintosh versions of Word may not emulate the desired behavior that occurs with Windows versions. Blame Microsoft for shoddy compatibility checks.

Editing macros

Though you can automate almost any Word function by recording a macro, it's helpful to know how to edit macros. This may be as simple as changing the macro's description if you didn't create one when you recorded the macro, or changing an incomprehensible name to something clearer. If you develop complicated macros that require debugging and revision, you may want to add a suffix such as "Final" or "BeingTested" to remind yourself which macros are proven and which ones are works in progress. Editing can also be as complex as fine-tuning specific steps to improve their performance or correct small errors. For example, you may have inadvertently selected the wrong checkbox midway through a long procedure (or it may be selected by default and you forgot to deselect it), and you would rather eliminate that selection than re-record the entire procedure.

Word offers a powerful programming language called *Visual Basic for Applications* (VBA for short) that underlies many of the program's features. Because VBA provides access to just about every function Word can perform, including some that aren't obvious from Word's menu system, you can use this language to invoke these features, alone or in combination. Other word processors have their own macro or scripting languages, of varying degrees of sophistication.

VBA is such a powerful programming language that Word expert Woody Leonard claimed, "Anything you can do in Word... [and many] things you *can't* do in Word, you can do with a VBA/Word program." Unfortunately, the documentation on VBA isn't always in sync with the reality, so it may take some experimentation to make VBA programs behave the way the documentation says they should behave. In the bibliography, I've provided a few references to help you get started with this language.

In Word, you edit macros in the VBA editor, a full-featured professional programming environment that offers many features (including debugging tools) you'll probably never use for simple macros. The online help is particularly useful because it both describes the many commands that are available and explains how to use the VBA editor. For simple editing, all you need to do is type directly in the window that contains the macro, and save your changes. To close the VBA editor, open the File menu and select Quit. It's intimidating the first time you do this, because it seems like you're about to quit Word itself. Don't worry; you're not.

To edit a macro:

- **Word 2010:** View tab > Macros menu > View macros. Select the desired macro in this dialog box and click the Edit button.

- **Word 2011:** Tools menu > Macro > Macros. Select the desired macro in this dialog box and click the Edit button.

You'll now find yourself amidst an intimidating cluster of window panes. Unless you plan to become a full-fledged programmer, the only part you need to worry about is the pane at the right that contains the programming code. Here's an explanation of the code from a typical macro (one that replaces double carriage returns with a single one):

Program code	Explanation
Sub Cleanup() ' Cleanup Macro ' Recorded 8/7/05 by Geoff '	*Sub* refers to a *subroutine* (jargon for the set of commands the macro performs). This is paired with *End Sub* to mark the macro's end. A single quote (') at the start of a line indicates the line is a comment (i.e., not an instruction). This macro is named *Cleanup*. A simple edit might be to remove the line that describes the creation date.
Selection.Find.ClearFormatting Selection.Find.Replacement. ClearFormatting	These lines clear any formatting specifications left over from a previous search.
With Selection.Find .Text = "^p^p" .Replacement.Text = "^p" .Forward = True .Wrap = wdFind Continue .Format = False .MatchCase = False .MatchWholeWord = False .MatchWildcards = False .MatchSoundsLike = False .MatchAllWordForms = False End With	These lines define the properties of the search term between the lines *With* and *End With*. As explained in Chapter 8, ^p is the code for a carriage return; this macro searches for double returns and replaces them with a single return. The other lines define settings such as the fact that the search should continue forward from the cursor position to the document's end, then "wrap" back to the start and continue. The *Match* options define other criteria for the search term: "true" means the option should be used; "false" means it should not.

Program code	Explanation
Selection.Find.Execute Replace:=wdReplaceAll	This line says what to do with the found text: replace every instance of this text with the replacement text defined above.
End Sub	This line concludes the macro.

You can copy and paste any macro code that you want to reuse from another macro; this requires no programming skill. For example, I created one macro that performs many simple translations from French to English by performing a series of several hundred search and replace operations for nouns and other parts of speech whose meaning is fixed (so I can translate them automatically, without knowing their context). This saves me an enormous amount of time because I don't need to translate each of these words manually. When I created this macro, I didn't record hundreds of find and replace operations, nor did I re-record the entire macro each time I needed to add a word pair. Instead, I recorded a single find and replace operation, then copied and pasted the resulting code so I could edit it to contain each new word pair. What did I copy and paste?

- The code that begins with the line *With Selection.Find* and ends with the line *Selection.Find.Execute Replace:=wdReplaceAll*.
- Each time I added new word pairs, I copied this code and pasted it into the VBA editor immediately above the *End Sub* line.
- I then changed the search term following *.Text* to the new search term, and the text following *.Replacement.Text* to the replacement term. Note that it's necessary to retain the double quotes that surround each term.
- Periodically, I edit the list so the search terms are in alphabetical order. This isn't essential, but helps me search through the list.

I haven't made any effort to identify the minimum subset of instructions necessary to create the most efficient macro possible because all my macros run fast enough that I don't feel the need to optimize their code. However, some of the code in this macro is unnecessary. If you want to eliminate a line, simply add a single quotation mark before the line. If the macro stops working, that line was necessary, so delete that quote.

Because I didn't do this revision of my translation macro to make it more concise, I eventually added enough word pairs that the macro was too long to run. The solution was to break the macro into several parts, then instruct Word to run each part in sequence. Here's the macro code that accomplishes this:

Program code	Explanation
Sub Translate1() [long list of search and replace operations] End Sub	This is the code for the first part of my translation macro, *Translate1*. (The parentheses after this name are required by the VBA editor.) Each part of the overall macro starts with such a name and ends with the words *End Sub*. Four more subroutines (*Translate 2* to *Translate 5*) hold the remaining find and replace operations. I haven't shown them here, as they're essentially identical to the code in *Cleanup*.
Public Sub Translate() Call Translate1 ... Call Translate5 End Sub	This is the code that appears after the five parts of my translation macro, and is the actual macro (*Translate*) that I run. It causes Word to run the five individual parts (1 to 5). The *Call* command instructs the macro software to run that named part of the overall macro.

If you need to change identities frequently, as might be the case if you do anonymous reviews in which your identity is concealed from the author (e.g., for peer-reviewed journals), you'll have to change the name you entered in your User Information settings each time. (See Chapter 4 for details of how to do this.) Thus, it's worthwhile recording a macro to accomplish this. *Recording* the macro includes much extraneous code, so I played with the macro to see just how much I could delete. Here's the minimum:

Task	Macro code
To change to a "blind review" identity	Sub Blind() Application.UserName = "Journal Reviewer" Application.UserInitials = "JR" End Sub
To restore your original identity	Sub Geoff() Application.UserName = "Geoff Hart" Application.UserInitials = "GHT" End Sub

To use this macro yourself, simply substitute your name and initials for mine. To add this to your list of macros, open the Macros dialog box, as described earlier. For each of the two macros, type the name of the new macro (*Blind* and *Geoff*, respectively) into the Macro Name field, then click the Create button. Copy the macro text from this table into the VBA editor (it's available for copying on this chapter's Web page) or retype it yourself between the *Sub* and *End Sub* lines that the software provides automatically when you create a new macro. To assign these macros to a keystroke or toolbar, follow the instructions I presented earlier in this chapter, in the section *Creating macros*.

That's as far as I'll go with my explanation of macro editing, since this brief description covers the main things you need to know to get started. You can find more detailed explanations in Jack Lyon's *Macro Cookbook for Microsoft Word*. If you enjoy programming and want to learn more, you'll be able to develop far more sophisticated macros as you master VBA and learn to work directly in the VBA editor.

There are many free sources of instruction and other resources available. Start with the online help in Word and in the VBA editor, which contain detailed information on creating macros. The Electric Editors run the *Grapevine* discussion group, and their Web site provides many free downloadable Word (Macintosh and Windows) and WordPerfect (Windows) macros, each contributed and tested by working editors. Jack Lyon's Editorium Web site is another excellent macro resource that provides many free macros and several powerful macro suites you can purchase that have been designed specifically for editors. While you're visiting, have a look at Jack's newsletter archives for a large selection of free macros accompanied by clear explanations of the details; Jack will teach you how to do a better job of writing your own macros. In particular, have a look at his article on *Using "found" macros* in the 30 May 2001 issue of the newsletter.

Typing text using a macro

If you want a macro to insert a bunch of text, you can't simply type those words into the macro. Instead, you must tell the macro what you want it to do (i.e., type text for you) using the appropriate VBA keywords. There are three main keywords you can use for different circumstances:

- **Selection.TypeText Text:="this text":** This option inserts everything between the quote marks as a single paragraph.
- **Selection.TypeText Text:=MyText:** This option inserts any text you have stored in a variable named MyText (which you must define sepa-

rately). Using variables is an advanced technique I won't discuss in this book.

- **Selection.InsertParagraph:** This option inserts a paragraph mark (an empty line).

Combining the first and third options lets you inserts paragraphs of text that are separated by a carriage return; combining them with the second option lets you insert different text by choosing different variables.

Typical macros

If you spend some time paying attention to what you do as an editor, you'll find a surprising number of things that require multiple mouse actions or keystrokes. Moreover, you'll find yourself performing those actions dozens of times even for short manuscripts, and hundreds or thousands of times for long ones such as books. The movement and selection shortcuts based on finding patterns that I discussed in Chapter 5 are good examples of the latter. Each time you run a macro, you can reduce those steps to the time required to trigger the macro—a fraction of a second if you've bound it to a keyboard shortcut. The longer the sequence of steps and the more often you use them, the greater the savings of time and effort. By the way, that's not just theory; in my 2011 article *Save Time by Mastering the Basics*, I describe how creating just three simple movement shortcuts (to avoid the need to use the mouse) saves me up to 15 minutes per day. The more often you perform a task and the longer the takes, the more time you'll save.

Most editors eventually develop several macros for the kinds of things all editors do (e.g., moving around a document) and at least a few basic macros to meet their unique needs. Just as customizing your word processor's screen display requires close attention to how you work, paying attention to what you do while editing a manuscript will reveal the kinds of actions you perform frequently, or that you perform less frequently but that take considerable time. The key question is whether you'll repeat any of these activities sufficiently often that the time you spend developing a macro (usually only a few minutes) will be less than the time you'll eventually save by using the macro. Surprisingly often, a small investment of time will produce enormous time savings.

If you can't think of any such tasks, find a simple way to record every activity you perform during a day of editing—for example, create a two-column table on scrap paper that lists your actions in the left column, and their frequency in the right column. Each time you do something, add a checkmark in that row of the table. At the end of the day, the activities with the most checkmarks are things you should automate. This simple survey of your working habits will surprise you, since it's easy to ignore boring things we do repeatedly.

The macros you need to develop will depend on your work habits and the nature of the work you do most often. For example, paying attention to my editing revealed many multi-step tasks I was performing dozens of times per manuscript, and often dozens of times per hour. For example:

Reversing word order

Authors with English as a second language often reverse the order of word pairs such as nouns and adjectives. Switching the word order manually takes at least four keystrokes: select the first word, cut that word out of the manuscript, move the cursor after the second word, and then paste the first word into its new location. Recording these steps as a simple macro, without learning VBA, turned this into a one-keystroke operation. Net saving: three keystrokes each time I switch the order of two words, which I do many times for each manuscript.

Fixing formatting problems

Many authors never learn how to format documents using styles, and use multiple spaces or even tabs to indent text; even careful writers sometimes inadvertently introduce spaces at the beginning or end of paragraphs (e.g., by splitting a paragraph) or hold down the space bar too long and enter multiple spaces. To eliminate these problems, I recorded a macro that performed a series of search and replace operations to correct these errors. Each operation only takes a minute or two, but I needed to do them for each manuscript. The macro now saves me those minutes for each manuscript.

Automating translations

Translating one client's French reports into English required careful thought to do the *important* part of the job: converting clear, idiomatic French into clear, idiomatic English. But the *time-consuming* part was to repetitively replace dozens of French technical terms with their English equivalents. To improve turnaround times, I created the translation macro described earlier in this chapter. This macro also converts French typographic rules into their English equivalents (e.g., it removes the space before a colon or percentage symbol), and sets the text's language to English so I can spellcheck the document when the translation ends. After running the macro, I only needed to edit the text so that it flowed smoothly and manually translate any text that wasn't included in the macro.

Industrial-strength automation: If you handle really large jobs using Windows versions of Word, try Jack Lyon's Editor's Toolkit Plus, Daniel Heuman's PerfectIt, and Rich Adin's WordsnSync automation tools. Why reinvent the wheel?

Applying a publisher's styles

Many editors work for publishers that use automated typesetting systems to generate page layouts. To prepare a manuscript for these systems, the word processor's scheme for identifying formats such as headings must be converted into a series of tags, similar to those used to define the structure of Web pages; alternatively, the author's style names may need to be changed to the publisher's style names. Making these changes manually for long documents such as books is time-consuming; as a result, many publishers have developed powerful macros that automate the work.

Copying text into the search dialog box

It's not hard to manually copy text, open the search dialog box, paste the text into the Find what or Replace with field, define the search direction (up or down), click the Find Next button, and close the dialog box. But that takes five keystrokes after you've copied the text. Why not do it in a single keystroke? Here's a macro that will do that (the text is available for copying on this chapter's Web page):

```
Sub FindSelectedText()
' FindSelectedText Macro
    Selection.Copy
' Define selection as variable
    Dim MyFoundText$
    MyFoundText$ = Selection
    Selection.Find.ClearFormatting
    With Selection.Find
        .Text = MyFoundText$
        .Replacement.Text = ""
        .Forward = True
        .Wrap = wdFindAsk
        .Format = False
        .MatchCase = False
        .MatchWholeWord = False
        .MatchWildcards = False
        .MatchSoundsLike = False
        .MatchAllWordForms = False
```

End With

Selection.Find.Execute

End Sub

This macro searches forward through the document. Change True to False in the line that begins .Forward if you want to search backwards. I've bound the two macros to the keystrokes Control+Alt+F and Control+-Shift+Alt+F, respectively. (For the Mac, replace Alt with the Option key.) Since I do this dozens of times per manuscript, even in a short manuscript, this can save me hundreds of keystrokes daily.

You can use this macro to check literature citations more efficiently. In Chapter 8, I described how to check literature citations by copying the References section into a new document and leaving it open beside the manuscript as you work. For long bibliographies, the bibliography won't fit in a single screen, so you'll do much scrolling. To find the cited reference more efficiently, use the abovementioned macro for finding selected text:

- Select the text (e.g., the author's name).
- Press the keystroke (Control+Alt+F) to find the next instance.
- Press the Find previous shortcut (Control/Command+PageUp) to return to where you started.
- Switch to the window containing the bibliography.
- Press the Find next keyboard shortcut (Control/Command+PageDown) repeatedly until you reach the desired reference or find that it's missing.
- If the author's name appears as a coauthor in many references, you may need to press PageUp or PageDown to move past sections where their name appears frequently.

Of course, if this kind of check is a major part of your work, you should record a macro (or edit the one I've provided) to include the repetitive steps, such as returning to your starting point, switching to the window that contains the references, and finding the next instance of the search term).

Macros by real experts

When it comes to developing macros, I'm strictly an amateur. To see the true wizards in action, check out the following sites:

- **The Editorium:** Jack Lyon offers a range of powerful editing aids, many available for free or as a "try before you buy" evaluation copy. Jack's newsletter, *The Editorium Update*, provides regular examples of useful macros that can make life with Word much easier.

- **The Electric Editors:** This site offers many Word (Macintosh and Windows) and WordPerfect (Windows) macros free for the downloading, each contributed and tested by working editors
- **Allen Wyatt's free *WordTips* newsletter:** Advice on all aspects of bending Word to your will, as well as a reader forum that lets you write in with questions.
- **Paul Beverley's *Computer Tools for Editors*:** This free 300-page book offers a ton of macros. Paul also offers training courses.

"Automatic Text" Features

I'm a fast typist, so for longer than I care to admit, I retyped the same questions or comments over and over again while I edited. When I worked under deadline pressure, I often copied previous comments and modified them slightly to address the specific problem that prompted a new comment, but that involved hunting through existing comments to find one that I could reuse—a remarkably inefficient way to work. Although this worked acceptably well for small projects, the first large book I edited taught me how inefficient this approach was. Fed up, I finally took my own advice and began looking for a way to automate the typing.

Most software offers at least basic automated text features. (If yours doesn't, you can often create a macro to do the work, as described earlier in this chapter.) These features may be referred to as "autocorrect", "automatic text", glossaries, library items, or shortcuts. In this section, I'll focus on how Word implements these features. Similar features should be available in other software, or can be added using the scripting software that I described at the start of this chapter.

Why automate the simple things?

If typing a comment and applying any necessary formatting doesn't take long, there seems to be little reason to automate that action. Yet when you perform simple actions repeatedly, the cumulative number of repetitions adds up fast, wasting surprising amounts of time by the end of the day. For example, when I edit scientific articles for journals, I compare the literature citations against the bibliography. In nearly 30 years of this work, I've found that perhaps one author in twenty successfully matches all citations to the references—and many colleagues report lower success rates. For the other authors, many citations are missing from the bibliography, others are present in the bibliography but have not been cited in the text, and many contain mismatches between the author names or publication dates. Even the rare authors who avoid these mistakes often err by omission or commission when they type details of the references in their bibliographies. Publisher details (e.g., name, city) are commonly missing, and authors use "et al." to avoid typing a long list of authors even if the publisher requires that all authors be identified.

In each case, I need to explain the problem and propose a solution. Writing cryptic comments would save time, but as I noted in Chapter 7, terse, telegraphic writing is less effective and less clear than complete, clear sentences. That's particularly true for authors whose native language isn't English. (Indeed, for some of my foreign authors, there's a whole series of language-related comments I need to type in each manuscript.) With some manuscripts, I may retype the same comment dozens of times. Fast though I type, this repetition wastes time better spent on more important things— such as having a life beyond the keyboard. To solve the problem, I created many shortcuts that do the typing for me.

Automatic formatting and text insertion

Word's text automation tools come in three flavors: *AutoFormat*, *Auto-Correct*, and *AutoText* (which was renamed *Building Blocks* in Word 2010):

- **AutoFormat:** automatically applies certain formats as you type, such as capitalizing the first letter of the word that starts a new sentence.
- **AutoCorrect:** automatically corrects common typing errors (such as reversed letter pairs) as you type, but it can also type text for you.
- **AutoText:** Like AutoCorrect, the AutoText feature can type text for you, but unlike AutoCorrect, that text can be very long.

AutoFormat

Although the AutoFormat features are useful, many cause Word users considerable grief because they work behind our back and have an unfortunate tendency to undo some of our changes or introduce changes we don't want or need. For example, e-mail and Web addresses suddenly become clickable hyperlinks, sentences begun with a hyphen suddenly become bulleted lists, and a series of three dashes (often typed to replace an em dash) suddenly becomes a line across the width of the page. Since these kinds of formatting offer little useful editorial assistance, many editors disable most of these features and selectively enable specific useful options. To access these options and disable any that you don't want to use:

- **Word 2010:** File menu > Options > Proofing > AutoCorrect Options button > Autoformat as You Type tab

- **Word 2011:** Tools menu > AutoCorrect > Autoformat as You Type tab

Where did all those styles come from? By default, Word accumulates huge numbers of character and paragraph styles that you *know* you never created. The styles appear because of an obscure setting that causes Word to create new styles whenever you modify text formatted using an existing style. To disable this questionable feature in both Word 2010 and 2011, select the Autoformat as You Type tab, and then deselect the option Define styles based on your formatting.

AutoCorrect

Words monitors your typing, and as soon as you reach the end of a word, it scans its list of rules to find a match for what you've just typed; if it finds a match, it replaces what you've typed with the specified replacement text. To see the standard rules that were provided when you installed Word:

- **Word 2010:** File menu > Options > Proofing > AutoCorrect Options button > Autocorrect tab
- **Word 2011:** Tools menu > AutoCorrect > AutoCorrect tab

Many of these are useful corrections for common spelling errors, such as changing *acheive* to *achieve* and changing (R) to ®, but there are many less useful corrections, such as changing (:) into a smileyface icon. If Word keeps changing something you've typed, and you want it to stop, scroll through the list of AutoCorrect options until you find the problem; select it, and then click the Delete button to remove that entry. If the problem is infrequent, you can undo the change by pressing Control+Z (Windows) or Command+Z (Macintosh) immediately after the change.

Unicode characters: Word 2010 lets you type the four-digit Unicode value for a character and press Alt+X to convert it into the character. Word 2011 doesn't provide that function, but you can simulate it using AutoCorrect. (The same trick works in all versions of Word.) Enter the character using Word's Insert Symbol dialog box, then select the character, open the AutoCorrect dialog box, and create a shortcut for the character (e.g.,]mu for the µ character). If you've spent years memorizing the Unicode values, you can use those numbers as the AutoCorrect shortcut: for example, use]03bc to make Word type µ.

AutoCorrect really shines when you create your own rules. For example, I mistype *please* as *plesae* so often that I created an AutoCorrect entry to solve that problem for me. That saves me some time, but not as much as when I use this feature to type longer phrases. For example, I need to type the following comment in most manuscripts I edit, often dozens of times: "This reference is missing from your bibliography—please add it there." Rather than typing it each time, I created the AutoCorrect shortcut *]mr* (memory aid: missing reference). As soon as I type this shortcut and press the space bar, Word replaces the shortcut with the full sentence. Typing three characters eliminates the need to type 61 characters—a saving of 58 characters each time!

Obtaining correct capitalization with AutoCorrect: Word's AutoCorrect feature doesn't distinguish between shortcuts typed using capital and lower-case versions of the same letter; for example]EOE and]eoe will produce the same result. However, you can define different capitalization patterns for the replacement text. To gain access to these different capitalization patterns, create different shortcuts. For example, create the shortcut]eoecaps for "Effective Onscreen Editing" and]eoelc for "effective onscreen editing".

You can create AutoCorrect entries directly within the AutoCorrect dialog box simply by typing the shortcut in the Replace field and the full text that will replace it in the With field, then clicking the Add button. Unfortunately, you can't format that text in this dialog box and the text will instead take on the properties of the surrounding text when you type the shortcut. To store an AutoCorrect as formatted text:

- Type the text in the manuscript, and apply any desired formatting (e.g., boldface, a paragraph style).
- Select the text.
- Open the AutoCorrect Options dialog box, and select the AutoCorrect tab. The text will already be present in the With field, so you don't need to type it.
- To retain the formatting, select the Formatted text option; if all you want is the words, select the Plain text option.
- Type your new shortcut in the Replace field, then click the Add button to add it to your list of shortcuts.

Did you notice that I used a closing square bracket as the first character of my missing reference shortcut? There are two good reasons for this. First, I'll almost never type a closing square bracket followed by a letter, so I'll rarely type this shortcut accidentally and have to undo it. Second, adding the same prefix before all of my shortcuts causes Word to group them in its (very long) list of AutoCorrect rules, making it easier for me to find and edit my own shortcuts. These reasons are sufficiently compelling that I recommend you develop a similarly standard nomenclature for your own shortcuts; in teaching onscreen editing, I've learned that failing to name these shortcuts consistently causes many problems for my students.

AutoCorrect is limited to a maximum length of 255 characters. For longer replacements, you can create two or more AutoCorrect entries and daisy-chain them: for example, if *]part1* and *]part2* contain the first and second parts (respectively) of a long replacement, you can type them one after the other, or even create an AutoCorrect shortcut named *]part* that Word will replace with *]part1]part2*. Typing *]part* and pressing the space bar would cause Word to automatically expand this into *]part1]part2*; moving the cursor to follow the 1 and 2, respectively, and then pressing the space bar will expand each shortcut into the corresponding replacement text. (A better solution would be to use AutoText, which permits really long replacement text. I'll discuss this in the next section.)

Automatic text depends on the language setting: Word's AutoCorrect rules apply independently for each language. Thus, English shortcuts won't work in (for example) French text. Moreover, shortcuts defined for another language may occur unexpectedly. For example, if you're editing an English translation of a French document, and the translation was done in the same file, the author probably defined the document's styles to use French spelling; every time you type a % symbol or a colon, Word will insert a space before it. To stop this behavior, change the language definition for each style to the correct language (English, in this case). *Voila!* Problem solved.

The kinds of shortcuts you should create depend on the types of comments or insertions you perform most frequently. Thus, you'll need to monitor your editing habits for a few days to learn what these are. After a few years of monitoring, I discovered that I needed the following shortcuts just for asking authors to fix problematic literature citations:

-]mr (<u>m</u>issing <u>r</u>eference) = This citation is missing from the References section. Please add it there.
-]rnc (<u>r</u>eference <u>n</u>ot <u>c</u>ited) = This reference has not been cited in the text. Please insert a citation.

-]aw (author wrong) = The spelling of this author's name (???) differs from the spelling (???) in the bibliography. Please confirm the spelling.
-]wd (wrong date) = The date for this citation (???) differs from the date in the references list (???). Please confirm the correct date.
-]ce (change everywhere) = If you accept this suggestion, make the same change throughout the document.

I've created dozens of additional AutoCorrect entries for many other purposes, including a note that I'm not sure about the meaning and want to propose two alternatives, comments that ask the author to check a particular edit more carefully than the others (because I didn't understand their meaning), and so on. Periodically, I notice myself wasting time retyping some phrase, and after chastising myself for procrastinating, I create a new AutoCorrect entry for that text.

Choose shortcut text you'll rarely if ever type by mistake; for example, because *mr* is also used as a shortcut for *mister*, the] character at the start of the shortcut ensures that I'll only get the "missing reference" admonition when I really want it. Although you can undo undesired replacements easily enough, this grows tedious, particularly if you've already typed several words before you notice the problem.

Autocorrect in Apple's OS X: Starting with version 10.6 of OS/X, Apple has offered the equivalent of Word's AutoCorrect feature in any application. To learn how to use it, consult *MacWorld*'s article *Enable Text Substitutions in Any App*.

AutoText (Building Blocks)

AutoText is designed to handle larger blocks of text, such as the multiple sentences in a standard warning message or the multiple headings and paragraphs in a standard legal disclaimer. To access this information:

- **Word 2010:** Ribbon > Insert tab > Quick Parts icon > Building Blocks Organizer
- **Word 2011:** Tools menu > AutoCorrect > AutoText tab

You can't type AutoText or its equivalent Building Block in this dialog box, so you must type it in the document window instead, apply any required formats, then select the text before you open the dialog box. Once you've added an AutoText to your library, Word 2010 and 2011 will both examine what you're typing, and when they think they recognize the longer text that you're trying to type, will display a popup screentip that contains the suggested replacement text. If Word guessed right, press Enter to insert the full text; if not, keep typing until the screentip goes away.

If you find the screentips difficult to use, you can work around them by creating names similar to those that I described earlier in this chapter for AutoCorrect text: preface each shortcut with] so you can press Enter as soon as you finish typing the shortcut. Word 2010 also lets you press F3 to trigger the replacement. If you want to create your own keyboard shortcut (see Chapter 4 for details), such as to add the missing F3 shortcut in Word 2011, scroll down to the category All Commands, and then scroll down to the command InsertAutoText. Of course, you can also insert AutoText and Building Blocks from the dialog box if you can't remember enough of the start of the text for Word to recognize it.

To remove an AutoText entry you no longer need, open the Building Blocks Organizer (Word 2010) or the AutoCorrect Options dialog box (Word 2011), select the shortcut, then click the Delete button. To move building blocks between templates, use the same Organizer described earlier in this chapter in the section *Making macros accessible in other documents).*

When AutoCorrect and AutoText stop working

If your AutoCorrect or AutoText shortcuts aren't working, there are several possible explanations:

- AutoCorrect shortcuts must be at least 3 characters long, and Auto-Text shortcuts must be at least 4 characters long.
- In the dialog box where you manage these shortcuts, the Replace text as you type checkbox in the AutoCorrect tab and the Show AutoComplete suggestions checkbox in the AutoText tab must be selected.
- The language settings where you're typing the shortcut must be the same as the language for which you defined the shortcut.
- In Word 2010 and 2011, AutoCorrect and AutoText don't work reliably (or at all) when you're typing in the Reviewing Pane. (See Chapter 6 for details of how to use this pane.) The only solution I've found is to type the shortcut in the main document window, then cut and paste the expanded text into the Reviewing Pane.
- The AutoCorrect (Options) dialog box offers an *exception* list when you want to override this feature for certain words (e.g., abbreviations). To access this list, click the Exceptions... button. To stop Word from creating a list of exclusions without your permission, select the relevant tab (First Letter, Initial Caps, Other Corrections) and deselect the checkbox for Automatically Add Words to List. Remove any unnecessary exceptions Word already added by selecting the exception and clicking the

Remove button. There's also an **Add** button that lets you add exceptions you don't want Word to automatically correct.

Transferring automatic text between computers

Word stores AutoCorrect entries in two places: the formatted ones are stored in the Normal.dotm template, and the others are stored in files whose names end in .ACL. If you're moving to a new computer, or want to share your AutoCorrects with someone, you'll need to transfer both files. Building Blocks (including AutoText) are stored in the Normal.dotm template, but may also be stored in Building Blocks.dotm if you've created a *named gallery* to store these shortcuts. The first time you need to find these files, the easiest way to is to use your operating system's search function to find them. The search term will be *.dotm for templates and *.acl for AutoCorrects. (Select the **Use wildcards** checkbox if that option isn't already selected.) However, Appendix I provides details of how to navigate to the correct directories to find these files.

The format of the .acl files used to store AutoCorrect entries seems to have remained unchanged between Word 2003 and Word 2011, which means that if you upgrade from an older version, you can retain your AutoCorrect entries simply by copying the old file and moving it to the new directory. (Keep a backup copy of the file you're replacing, just in case!)

Don't forget: These shortcuts are language-specific, so if you're working multilingually, you'll need to copy the files for all languages in which you've created shortcuts. In addition, if you've created any custom templates for specific types of project, you'll also need to copy any shortcuts stored in those files.

Sharing AutoTexts and other shortcuts within a group: If you create a global template to hold the group's shortcuts, and store it in a shared directory on your network, each member of the group can open that template whenever they need to create a new manuscript. (They can also attach the template to a manuscript that's already been created, as described towards the end of Chapter 4.) All automatic text stored in that template then becomes available. Note that if you adopt this approach, it's wise to appoint one person to manage this file and ask group members to send all proposed shortcuts to that person for implementation.

If you don't have scores of these shortcuts, the easiest way is to store them in a Word file, and (working with that file open) recreate them manually on the new computer. This won't take long, and it offers two advantages: it will remind you of useful shortcuts that you've forgotten you created, and may inspire you to create new ones.

Printing AutoCorrect and AutoText items

Word contains an enormous number of built in automatic text entries, so it can be tricky trying to print only the ones you've created. The easiest way to do this is create a document with a logical name such as "Geoff's automatic text entries" and type all your entries in this document. You'll find it's much easier to revise them if they're in a Word file rather than locked away in a cramped, cumbersome dialog box. Moreover, if you include this file in your backups, you can quickly recreate all of your automatic text if anything horrible happens to your computer. Of course, that assumes that you've established a strong backup routine to protect key files on your computer. See Appendix I for details of how to do this.

You can also coax Word into doing the hard work for you, but if you don't want to waste paper, select the PDF output option first to ensure that you create a file. You can subsequently copy this information into a Word file and reorganize it to suit your needs. To access this feature:

- **Word 2010:** Press Control+P to display the Print dialog box. Under the heading Settings, open the menu that initially displays Print all pages, scroll down to the subheading Document Properties, and select AutoText entries.

- **Word 2011:** Press Command+P to display the Print dialog box. In the menu that initially displays Copies & Pages, select Microsoft Word. From the Print What menu, select AutoText entries.

Back-up your automatic text: Appendix 1 provides details of where current versions of Word hide your automatic text and other customizations. Learn which files to preserve and include them in your regular backup routine. Have I seemingly repeated my plea about backups every three pages? That's because it's important, and many editors never learn to back-up their files without some nagging.

Build your own automatic text features

If your software lacks specialized automatic text functions or if you don't like how Word handles these shortcuts, you can build your own automatic text functions. The easiest solution involves recording a macro that uses the software's find and replace tools to replace all of your shortcuts with the desired text in a single operation. In this approach, simply type all those shortcuts as you edit, without bothering to replace them with the expanded text, then at a convenient moment, run the macro to do the replacements for you. If you don't have many shortcuts, you can do the search and replace operation manually by running through a checklist of all your shortcuts.

If you prefer more control over the replacement process or don't like macros, simply create a file that stores all the shortcuts you plan to use, along with the associated text. Store all your shortcuts in this file, leave it open in a window beside the manuscript that you're editing, then copy the required comments and paste them into the manuscript as you edit. (Chapter 5 describes the keyboard shortcuts for switching efficiently between files and moving within files.)

Last, but not least, you can use many of the scripting or macro programs I listed at the start of this chapter to do the typing for you.

Chapter 12. Editing in Special Situations

Web: http://www.geoff-hart.com/books/eoe/eoe3/eoe3.html
Note: Word 2010 is for Windows; Word 2011 is for the Macintosh

At first glance, word processors seem to be useful only for editing word processor files. After all, if you can't open a file for editing, you can't edit the file, right? Though true, that logic is limited—because most software can save files in a range of formats. In particular, just about any modern program can save or export its files in the Web's HTML and XHTML formats, or as "text" (i.e., with no formatting other than line breaks). Word processors can open these files, and as I'll demonstrate in the rest of this chapter, this means you can edit the files using the software's search tools and revision tracking tools.

Clearly, this opens up a world of editing opportunities. All you need to do is find a way to open the file in your word processor, save it in your word processor's native file format (e.g., .dotm for Word), and edit it with all your changes tracked. In many cases, the author can then review your edits and re-import the edited file into the software they used to create it. Even if they can't, they can at least manually copy your edits into the original software. This makes your word processor a powerful tool for editing more effectively and consistently, and for clearly communicating your edits to the author.

In this chapter, I'll discuss several categories of information you might never have considered editing, and the specific types of editing challenges they create:

- Web pages and other files created using a *markup* language
- desktop publishing files
- databases and spreadsheets
- software interface text

But first, a brief but important digression into the history of publishing to provide some important insights into how editing should fit within any information creation and publishing process.

Edit Twice, Publish Once

In traditional publishing, it was much easier, faster, and less expensive to edit and revise manuscripts *before* layout, so publishers ensured that the heavy-duty editing was performed long before the manuscript was sent for layout and printing (or publishing online nowadays). This was necessary because it used to be difficult to create page layouts with the available tools: When you had to haul a new 10-ton block of marble from the quarry because you screwed up the wording and had to redo several days of hammer-and-chisel work, you had a powerful incentive to figure out what you were doing before you actually tried doing it. Offset printing made things better because the quarry was no longer part of the picture, but you still didn't want to have to reinsert thousands of lead slugs into dozens of wooden galleys to redo the layout of an entire book because the author omitted a paragraph or used a dirty word on page 20 of a 200-page manuscript. Early desktop publishing software, though far more flexible than movable type, was sufficiently primitive that major changes at the layout stage remained difficult and expensive. When I began working with peer-reviewed journals in the mid-1980s, it was still common for journal publishers to charge authors up to US$10 *per line of type affected by an author's correction* after the article had been laid out by the production staff; if inserting a word changed the word wrap in the next ten lines of type, that insertion cost the author US$100.

These problems persist, despite vast improvements in the power and cost of publishing software. Better programs, such as InDesign, are integrated with word processors that let editors and designers work simultaneously on the same publication. That being said, complex layouts still require considerable time and effort, which is wasted if major changes are required late in the production schedule. Even seemingly minor changes, such as renumbering or deleting a figure, have repercussions that ripple like falling dominoes through the rest of the layout. The risk of creating such problems under the pressure of a tight deadline has led to a standard workflow in which the vast majority of the review and revision (including editing) is done long before a manuscript is sent for production.

More sophisticated tools: The software used by high-volume publishers who produce weekly magazines and daily newspapers avoids many of these problems. In addition, technical writers often work with single-sourcing tools that separate the layout or display of information from the information itself. (If you've designed a Web page using cascading style sheets, you understand how this works.) Both groups of tools automatically redo layouts in response to editing—even major edits.

As a kindness to the publication design staff and as a way to avoid creating disastrous errors right before publication, when it's too late to fix them, it remains most productive to edit information heavily before beginning to create a layout. This remains true for all publication types, including Web pages, databases, and spreadsheets, but in these cases, it's even more important to do the editing first. It's so easy to publish this information at the click of a button that it's tempting to publish now and clean up any accidents later. This is generally a poor plan. Moreover, it's entirely unnecessary. Having managed the publication process at various employers for more than 15 years, I can assure you that it's not rocket science to schedule an editing stage between the writing and publishing stages. I'll describe how you can accomplish this in chapters 17 and 18.

Apart from the embarrassment of sharing your stupid mistakes with the world, there's another good reason for editing material before preparing or publishing a final layout: current Web authoring, database, and spreadsheet software offers primitive revision tracking and editing tools compared with those your word processor provides. If you wait until the information is trapped in this software, the collaborative editing and revision process becomes more difficult and less efficient. This is particularly true when information creators, editors, and designers use different and incompatible software.

The solution is simple: just as carpenters proverbially "measure twice, cut once", information creators should *edit* twice and *publish* once. Often, the easiest way to do this is to edit the work within a word processor and transfer it to the publishing software only once it's in near-final form. Even if the information originates outside a word processor (e.g., in a spreadsheet), it may still be helpful to transfer the information into a word processor and edit it there because of the increased accuracy and efficiency this permits.

In Chapter 16, I'll discuss onscreen *proofreading* of documents, which should ideally emphasize a review of the layout, with little or no content editing. In the present chapter, I'll focus on the earlier tasks of developmental editing, substantive editing, and copyediting that should be done long before the proofreading stage. Because graphics represent a special class of problem, I'll deal with them separately in Chapter 13.

Sometimes Light Editing is Possible

If authors have followed the traditional process described in the previous section, we'll probably only have light copyediting to do—work that is almost at the level of proofreading. Then, it doesn't really matter what software is being used to produce the material we'll edit; we don't have to work in that software or import the information into another program. We can simply send the author a list of comments.

For simple edits, all that's necessary is an e-mail message containing such editorial gems as "you spelled my name wrong—it's *Geoff*, with a *G*" and "In the first sentence of the second paragraph under the heading *Editing*, change *revsion* to *revision*". We don't even have to retype the problematic text: we can simply copy it into the e-mail message. We can then explain the problem and how to fix it.

However, as the number of problems increases, the author's job of deciphering and carrying out our instructions becomes increasingly tedious and error-prone. To facilitate this process, consider sending a word processor document containing a table that organizes and presents the information clearly. For example:

Heading	Paragraph	Sentence	Error	Correction
Title	1	1	Jeff	Geoff
Editing	2	1	Typo: revsion	revision

To repeat table headings on each new page: In Word 2010, right-click in the first row of the table, and select Table Properties from the popup menu. In Word 2011, select this option from the Table menu. In both versions, select the Row tab, then select the checkbox for Repeat as header row at the top of each page.

Such a table works better than an e-mail message for two reasons: First, it groups information using navigation aids such as the names of headings that will help the author find the problem. Second, it eliminates the need to repeatedly retype the location description (e.g., "heading"). If we're working with a paginated PDF document, alternative column headings might be Page, Column, and Line number; if we're working on a spreadsheet or a database, the corresponding headings might be the cell coordinates (e.g., row 12, column C) or record numbers, respectively. In each case, the goal is to efficiently and clearly communicate the problem's location and provide enough information for the author to solve the problem. If the resulting table of edits extends over more than one page, repeat these column titles on each page. Most word processors can do this automatically.

Because someone must still implement our edits manually, with the attendant risk of introducing new errors while fixing the old ones, someone must take responsibility for ensuring that our edits were correctly incorporated in the file. Ideally, that should be us, since we're most familiar with the problems we asked the author to solve, and thus best qualified to decide whether they solved them.

Another advantage of using a table is that we can easily add a column for checkmarks to indicate that a change has been made. Whoever is responsible for confirming the results can simply add checkmarks in the table as they work. This makes it easy for the editor or production manager to ensure that all changes were made, and made correctly.

Adobe's PDF file format provides another good option for light edits, particularly since both Windows and the Macintosh let you create PDF files from the Print dialog box of most programs. Authors can therefore create a PDF file from just about any information and editors can use Adobe Acrobat (the PDF-creation software) or Adobe Reader (the reader software) to annotate the information using the built-in editing and commenting tools. Adobe's Acrobat Web Capture tool can even convert entire Web pages into PDF files. Unfortunately, someone must still manually integrate our revisions into the source document, regenerate the PDF file (or republish the Web page), and confirm that the changes were made correctly. Warn your clients to not skip this step! You'd be amazed at how many information creators forget this step, and end up with source files that no longer reflect the contents of the edited PDF file. Thus, all the old errors reappear when it's time to republish the document.

Mastering PDF editing: If you need to do any significant amount of editing of PDF files, it's worth learning from the expert: Adrienne Montgomery, author of the editing blog *Right Angels and Polo Bears*. Her course on this subject will bring you up to speed quickly.

Specialized tools are available for dealing with certain types of files. For example, WebWorks ePublisher (available for Word or FrameMaker) offers professional tools for annotating Web sites. Although this software doesn't appear to offer tools as sophisticated as those in Word and Framemaker for heavy substantive editing, it does work with both programs and presumably lets you use their native revision-tracking tools.

However, it's rare that we will only have to do light editing of a manuscript. More often, managers who don't fully understand the information creation process or who grasp the basics but lack experience, publish their information without editing. This is particularly common in Web publishing, since there's no risk of having to recall an entire print run of a publication and pay for a new printing—thus, there's no perceived cost for fixing errors. (Never mind the irreparable damage that can be done to corporate and other reputations!) In these cases, significant editorial surgery may be necessary, but by this point, the information is stored in special-purpose software, such as a Web site design program (e.g., Dreamweaver) or a database (e.g., FileMaker). Too much work will be required for providing a table of the required changes to be efficient: incorporating the edits manually takes far too long, greatly increases the risk of missing important edits, and risks introducing new errors—which defeats the whole purpose of onscreen editing. Starting from scratch by editing an original word processor document will only work if you have access to that document, and won't work if the information was never in a word processor document in the first place.

Fortunately, we can often move the information into a word processor, use its tools to review and revise the information, and then return it to the software that will be used to publish it.

Many File Types, One Approach

If you can export information from a program (usually via the Save As or Export function) in a file format that your word processor can open, you can edit the file using your word processor's revision tracking tools. At a minimum, the author will be able to clearly see your edits and comments; if you're really lucky, they can implement all your changes in their own word processor and then import the resulting file back into the software that created it.

Because most modern programs can save their information as a text file or as a Web page (HTML), the odds are good you can make this approach work. It won't always be easy, and re-importing the file may create too much work for the approach to be practical. But with patience and persistence, you'll find you can edit a surprising number of types of information. Sometimes, as we'll see later in the case of Web pages, editing in your word processor becomes a truly efficient and practical approach.

There are three things to keep in mind before you use your word processor to edit information created in a different category of software:

- Software such as spreadsheets relies heavily on calculation formulas or other special codes that are closely attached to the words and numbers you'll be editing. For example, many numbers stored in spreadsheets are not actually numbers, but instead conceal calculation formulas such as *sum(c1:c15)*—the Microsoft Excel instruction that adds the contents of cells *c1* to *c15* and reports the result in the cell that contains this formula. This hidden coding typically disappears during the conversion into a format readable by a word processor; most often, the formula is replaced by the result of the calculation. If such coding isn't stored separately from the information it operates on, the author will have to recreate the coding.

- The software used to create the information should ideally re-import the edited file to avoid the need for the author to manually copy our edits into the original file. Unfortunately, some software does a poor job of re-importing the information it exported. In that case, considerable work may be required to recreate the original structure or format of the information.

- Ideally, information formats should be defined once for each category of information (e.g., for an entire column of a database table) rather than separately for each individual piece of information. When formatting is applied to each item, that formatting may disappear during the conversion into a format you can edit in your word processor, and must then be reapplied manually.

You can edit the files in your word processor despite these problems, but you'll have to recognize that the problems exist and develop ways to solve them. This requires the author to think about how to design the information before they create it. For example, storing information separately from the instructions on how to format it (as in the case of Web pages formatted using CSS style sheets) greatly facilitates both content creation and editing.

With these caveats in mind, the overall approach to editing these files follows the same steps for any file format:

1. Extract the information from the software.

Open the File menu, and select Save As or Export. If neither option is available, the Print dialog box should let you save the file in PDF format.

2. Choose the new format.

From the available file formats, choose one your word processor can read. *Rich text format* (RTF) is a good choice for information that is primarily textual, since it retains formatting information such as paragraph styles, whereas *text* may be better for primarily numeric or unformatted information. HTML, XHTML, or XML are better choices for structured information such as Web pages, since they retain the formatting instructions. When text format is your only option, typical options include *text only* and *text with line breaks*. Try both to see which one works best for the combination of programs that you're dealing with.

3. Open the file in your word processor.

Most word processors, by default, list only files stored in their own special format (e.g., .docx files for Word, .wpd files for WordPerfect). If you don't see the file that you want to edit, change this setting. In the Open File dialog box, set the option for Display files of type to All documents (in Word) or equivalent wording.

4. Save the file in your word processor's native file format.

This step is necessary so that you can use the software's version of revision tracking. The codes used to describe revisions are only available in the software's native file format (e.g., .docx for Word), though a subset of these codes will usually be preserved in other formats such as RTF.

5. Edit the file.

Edit the file using revision tracking so the author can see and review your edits.

6. Return the edited file to the author for review.

The author can now review your edits. Ideally, they should use the same word processor you used to perform the edits, since repeated conversions among different formats tends to gradually introduce "artefacts" such as lost or misinterpreted formats. Because most computers now ship with some version of Word, it's a good choice. OpenOffice is also good because free versions are available for Windows, Macintosh, and Linux.

7. Save the file in a format the original software can re-import.

After reviewing your changes and ensuring that no unimplemented edits remain, the author saves the file again in whichever format is easiest for the original software to re-import.

8. Restore the information to its original format.

The author opens the file or imports it into the original software they used to create the information, then performs any necessary cleanup.

Careful inspection is necessary to detect problems such as lost formats or formulas.

Someone must ensure that nothing has been lost, imported into the wrong location, or otherwise messed up. When the software performs programmed actions, such as a spreadsheet's calculations or creating links between a database's tables, these actions must be carefully tested. This step cannot be neglected if you expect to avoid unpleasant surprises. As we'll see in the section on spreadsheets later in this chapter, storing information separately from the codes and formulas that act on that information can mitigate this problem. If you'll be doing large amounts of editing for an author, it's worth discussing how to make that approach to design possible.

Implement a quality-control phase: If you want to use your word processor to edit files created in a different type of program, test this process scrupulously to ensure that it works and to identify problems. This requires a quality-assurance phase: someone with sharp eyes and good knowledge of the expected results must review the re-imported information before it is published. (This is no different than proofreading text after importing a word processor file into desktop publishing software.)

Many authors place files such as spreadsheets and graphics in a word processor document as *embedded objects*; the information is actually stored outside of the word processor and all you see in the word processor is an image of that information. Although this offers certain efficiencies (e.g., tables and graphics in the word processor document can be automatically updated as the contents of the original file change), it's not a useful approach for editing. The problem is that you generally cannot edit the embedded object using the word processor's revision tracking tools. When you click inside the object, the application that created it (here, spreadsheet software) opens. At best, you're restricted to the editing tools provided by that application. At worst, you cannot edit the contents at all.

These general principles apply to any situation in which you'll be using your word processor to edit information created in another type of program. In the remainder of this chapter, I'll present specific examples of how this approach to editing works.

Simple Markup Languages: Web Pages (HTML and XHTML)

Web pages are the most familiar kind of files formatted using a markup language—specifically, the HyperText Markup Language (HTML) and its descendant XHTML. (For simplicity, I'll refer only to HTML henceforth, but my descriptions apply equally well to both formats.) However, markup languages are not new; they were used way back in the dark ages of personal computing. Most computer-based writers in the 1980s (me, for instance) used word processors such as WordStar, in which we manually applied formatting codes that resembled those used in modern HTML. For example, to boldface a word, you'd surround it with codes marking the beginning and ending of the boldface format: <b>boldfaced</b>. WordPerfect represented a breakthrough: it hid these formatting codes until you explicitly chose to reveal them, at which point the markup language suddenly appeared. The ability to inspect these tags was a godsend when it came time to troubleshoot display or printout problems. Microsoft Word ruined everything by hiding the codes, by refusing to reveal them, and by storing the codes in a convoluted proprietary format only a computer could understand and love. Most software now operates similarly.

Other markup languages: HTML is the naïve kid brother of two more powerful markup languages: XML and SGML. I'll discuss them in the next section. If you work with scientists and mathematicians, you may be asked to edit files produced in TeX or LaTeX, specialized word processors designed for typesetting mathematics. Because these programs use their own tag-based markup languages, you can use the approach in this section to edit them too. If you frequently need to edit mathematics files with revision tracking, try the free Lyx software, which is available for Macintosh, Windows, and Linux. If you need to convert Word files into Lyx (LaTex) files, the ever-amazing Jack Lyon has created a handy Word macro (LyXConverter) that will do the job. There's a free trial version, but you should reward Jack for his hard work by buying a copy.

Web pages use essentially the same approach as those old word processors, using pairs of tags such as <em> and </em> (short for *emphasis*) to describe how text should be displayed. These files differ from proprietary word processor formats such as Word's .dotm files, in two significant ways

- The files are in text format so you can edit them without having to convert them from a proprietary format.
- The formatting tags are simple enough that anyone can learn them with a little effort. (Even if you don't want to learn how to create Web pages in HTML, you can quickly learn to recognize the tags.)

The biggest problem lies in the need to sort through all the tags and display the information we'll be editing in such a way that we can focus on the content and ignore the tags. (Here, I'm assuming that as editors, our job is to edit the content, not the tags that describe how that content should be displayed. HTML geeks may be asked to edit the tags too.) However, though we'll want to ignore the tags while we focus on the content, we must minimize the risk that we'll damage any of the tags, since that would prevent the edited Web page from displaying correctly.

While you edit a Web page, pay attention to more than just the individual numbers or words and phrases. The effectiveness of such documents relies on both the information and its presentation, and the two are sometimes inseparable. This is also true in print publishing, but for more dynamic documents such as Web pages, we must also test things such as links and scripts, as well as special effects such as the page's responses to mouse movements (e.g., displaying popup balloons or changing the appearance of a button). Since you're already acting as the reader's advocate when you edit the text, don't hesitate to report usability or comprehensibility problems for the Web page as a whole. Point out problems such as:

- Links whose meaning is unclear.
- Links that go to the wrong destination.
- Unclear structure and navigation schemes.
- Mismatches between the text and any accompanying graphics, whether the problems are objective (outright contradictions) or subjective (an inappropriate style or tone).
- Ineffective or illogical sequences of actions.
- Inconsistency (visual or textual) with other pages that serve similar functions.
- Incomplete content, such as missing contact information or links back to the home page.

Annotating Web sites in your browser: For simple needs, such as communicating design problems to an author, the Scrible software will let you annotate Web sites from within your browser. The drawback is that you're not actually editing the HTML file's contents.

With that in mind, here's how to proceed.

Save the file on your hard disk

If your client has sent you a Web page via e-mail, via "the cloud" (i.e., some form of online storage), or on a DVD or flash drive, simply save a working copy on your computer. If you must work with a page that's already published on the Web, open that page in your Web browser. With the page displayed, open the File menu and select Save As. The options vary among browsers, but typically you should select Web page, HTML only (*.htm, *.html) to save just the text components of the page. If you'll be editing the graphics too, select Web page, complete (*.htm, *.html) or the equivalent option, then edit the graphics separately, as I'll describe in Chapter 13.

Although HTML files are standard text files, most word processors will recognize the filename extension (.htm or .html) and do their best to interpret the HTML codes. Left to their own devices, this means that they'll open and display the file as if it were a Web page (e.g., words meant to be italicized or boldfaced will actually appear that way) and you won't see any of the HTML tags. That's not a good option, because most word processors apply their own formatting and conversion rules to the original HTML tags, and this may change the creator's original formatting. Moreover, since you can't see the formatting tags, you run a high risk of damaging the contents by over-writing existing tags or inserting new ones.

To avoid this problem and ensure that you can see the tags, you have two options. First and easiest, set your word processor to confirm whether it should convert files when it opens them; in Word, select the Confirm conversion on open setting, as described in Chapter 4. When Word asks whether it should open the file as a Web page, just say no. Second, rename the file so your word processor will consider it to be an unformatted text file rather than an HTML file (which it will treat as if it contained formatting because of the markup tags). To do so:

- Make a copy of the file.
- Replace the .htm or .html filename extension of the copy with .txt so your word processor will treat the file as a text file. (That's what it is, but your word processor may not believe you if it sees the .htm or .html extension.)
- Open the file. If you can't see the file in the Open File dialog box, set the software to display All readable files.

Note that this approach leaves the original downloaded HTML file as your backup, so you won't have to create a separate backup copy before you begin editing. You can also use that HTML file to guide your substantive editing; that is, you can open it in your Web browser to see what it looks like, test the links, and so on.

Save the file in your word processor's native file format

The problem with text files is that they can't contain all the fancy formatting your word processor offers, including the formatting codes that implement its revision tracking features. The solution, of course, is to save the text file in your word processor's native file format. To do so, open the File menu, select Save As, and in the field labeled Save as type, select the appropriate file type. For a Word document, that's the .docx format.

Edit the file's contents, *not* its tags

When you open this file, you'll see both the text that you're going to edit and all the tags the creator's software used to describe how that text should appear in a Web browser. These tags pose two problems:

- If you inadvertently delete or modify a tag, you'll change how the page displays in a Web browser. Some deletions or modifications are harmless, but most will have serious consequences for the page's appearance, and the problem may be difficult for the author to find and fix.
- The actual content you're trying to edit may be hidden amidst a thicket of tags, making it hard to see, let alone edit. That's particularly true of documents created in Web authoring software that defines pages as nested groups of tables or other complex hierarchical structures.

The solution is simple: color the tags so they will be less visually prominent than the content you'll be editing, but without making them vanish entirely so that you risk damaging them inadvertently. For example, programmers often change the tags to a color such as green that clearly differs from the surrounding black text. I find that kind of pattern difficult to work with because the colors distract me, and instead use a lighter color such as pale gray. Choose whatever color works best for you. Since you'll be doing this kind of change frequently if you edit many HTML files, and since the change takes several steps, record a macro to do the work for you the first time you go through this process. (If you need help, see Chapter 11 for details on recording macros in Word.) To change the tag color in Word:

- Set Word to begin recording a new macro.

- Name the macro (for example, HideTags), and assign a keystroke if you want to run the macro from the keyboard.
- Open the Find and Replace dialog box. If necessary, expand the dialog box to display the additional search options. (If you need help with this dialog box, see Chapter 8 for details.)
- Select the option Use wildcards.
- In the Find what field, type [<]*[>]. The square brackets mean "look for any of the characters within the brackets", but the asterisk means "any group of characters". This pattern therefore searches for anything that starts and ends with the angle brackets (i.e., any HTML tag). The square brackets are necessary because the angle brackets have special meanings in a wildcard search, and you don't want their special meanings; you just want the actual brackets.
- In the Replace with field, type ^&. The caret (^) character appears above the number 6 on the keyboard. In Word, this code means "insert the search term itself here"; that is, we're not going to delete or otherwise damage the tags, so we'll replace them with themselves.
- With the cursor still in this field, click the Format button and select Font. Select a color that leaves the tags visible, but not so prominently that you can't concentrate on the text. Light gray works well. Don't choose Hidden text as the format and set Word to display only text that isn't hidden; it's too easy to inadvertently delete tags you can't see.
- Click the Replace all button.
- Tell Word to stop recording the macro.

When you run the macro, the file will resemble the text shown here (with a simple edit to show a typical tracked change):

```
<html>
<head>
<title>Example of gray tags</title>
</head>
<body>
<p>This sample text shows the effects of coloring ("ghost-
ing")-the HTML tags so that they appear distinct from the text
that will be edited.</p>
</body>
</html>
```

In this example, I've chosen ghostly gray for the HTML tags, with the text to be edited appearing in the usual black color. I've used boldface plus underlining to indicate an insertion and boldface plus strikethrough to indicate a deletion. Of course, if you'll be editing the tags themselves as part of the job, you won't want them ghosted out. In that case, either don't bother changing their color, or change it so the tags are visually distinct from the surrounding text without being difficult to read.

Edit the content

Because the file is now a word processor document, you can turn on revision tracking and edit the file in the usual way. You'll need to know a bit about how HTML formatting works if you've been asked to review the tags too, and if you're not sure how HTML tags work, it's safer to insert a comment recommending that the author make the change rather than making the change yourself and potentially damaging the structure of the tags. There are two main cautions to keep in mind whether or not you're editing the tags:

- If you move or delete text, ensure that you move or delete *both members* of paired tags together with the text they describe. For example, text contained in a table falls between the <table> and </table> tags, and each row of the table falls between <tr> and </tr> tags. If you move a table to a new position or change the order of rows within the table, move both the tags and the text between the tags to the new location.
- Be particularly careful with find and replace. It's easy to damage key HTML tags if they contain the text you're searching for, particularly for keywords typed in the Head section of an HTML document or named styles or classes in a document formatted using CSS (cascading style sheets). Rather than using a global find and replace, it's safer to replace instances of the search term one at a time. See Chapter 8 for suggestions on how to do this efficiently.

Make the tags reappear

Unless you need to examine (and perhaps edit) the HTML tags, it's not necessary to remove the color that you applied to the text. The author's final step after reviewing your edits will be to save the document in text format once again, and doing so will eliminate all formatting, including the color you applied to the tags. If you must restore the tags to full visibility so you can edit them, or if you want to avoid confusing the author who will review your edits and wonder what happened to the tags:

- Turn off revision tracking.
- Select all the text (Control+A for Windows, Command+A for the Macintosh).

- In the Ribbon's **Home** tab, open the menu beside the **Font color** icon and select **Automatic** as the color. In Word, "Automatic" means that the software should restore the formatting defined by the style that was used to format the text. (See Chapter 4 for a discussion of styles.)
- Turn on revision tracking again.

Review and re-import the file

The author can now review your edits and accept or reject them using their word processor's revision tracking tools. If any of your comments or edits relate to the HTML tags, the author can either edit the tags immediately, or make the necessary changes once they reopen the final file in their Web authoring software. Once they have addressed all your edits, someone (ideally you) should review the file one final time to ensure that no edits were missed, and particularly that no comments were left in the file. Comments created using the word processor's commenting feature may simply disappear when the file is converted back into HTML, since they have no HTML equivalent, but some programs may helpfully add them to the end of the file or insert them at their current position.

Keep a backup copy of the final word processor file, with all edits implemented and all comments removed. To restore the HTML format:

- Open the **File** menu and select **Save As** (in Word) or **Export** in some programs.
- Specify **Text only** as the file type. You'll be warned that some formats cannot be saved in a text file, and asked to confirm whether this is okay. Since your goal is to *remove* all that unnecessary formatting, that's fine: click OK.

> **Don't export *HTML*:** It might seem logical to save or export the file in HTML format, but don't do it! The best you can hope for is that your word processor will add a few useless tags that cause no harm. At worst, your software may rewrite some tags (Word is notorious for this) and cost the designer much time fixing the problem.

- Change the filename extension (usually .txt) to the correct HTML extension (.htm or .html, whichever the author used). Many Web browsers won't recognize a file as HTML until you add the correct filename extension. The author can now re-import the file into the software they used to create it.

The middle step is the one most likely to cause problems, since you usually have two or more options for the text format. To find out which option works best for your word processor, test each one by opening the file with the .htm or .html extension in your Web browser. If the file doesn't display correctly with one of the formats, try a different option. This test will also give you a chance to spot any errors you introduced by accidentally damaging a tag or editing a tag in a way that changes its function.

More Complex Markup Languages: XML and SGML

HTML is a markup language for the masses, and is wonderful for what it does: it presents mostly unstructured information that reflects the casual nature of many Web pages. However, because HTML is designed to facilitate the creation of Web pages rather than to rigorously enforce content and structure requirements, it's not suitable for more demanding applications. Where rigor and consistency are important, a more structured version of HTML called XHTML was developed. From our editorial perspective, XHTML documents are essentially identical to HTML, and can be edited the same way I described in the previous section.

However, XHTML also fails to address key needs of more demanding applications, because it does not inherently control the content and structure of a file. Consider, for example, an online magazine in which each article must start with a title, followed by the author's name and contact information, followed by a short summary of the article, and so on. As the editor, you can certainly impose consistency in this content, but the publisher can't impose this consistency *automatically* during the writing process. In some cases, documents are sufficiently complex that controlling the content and its sequence is essential, and requiring human writers and editors to exert this control is unacceptably burdensome and error-prone.

SGML requires more caution: I haven't personally edited complex XML or SGML files (other than XHTML files). The suggestions in this section were vetted by a colleague who does SGML work for a major aerospace company, so I'm confident the *theory* is sound. The implementation of that theory, however, is left as an exercise for the reader. If you want to test that theory, chapters 17 and 18 discuss how to safely implement onscreen editing. That implementation process is a good way to analyze, plan, test, and implement onscreen editing in an SGML or XML environment.

To provide the necessary control, it's necessary to use a powerful and complex markup language called SGML (the *Standard Generalized Markup Language*). The *generalized* part of that name indicates that the language was designed to be general-purpose, allowing document creators to define their own markup; in a sense, SGML is a tool for constructing custom markup languages that can meet any requirements, such as those of the hypothetical magazine I described. The *standard* part of the name refers to the fact that SGML makes it possible to enforce these requirements and thereby produce a standard document that differs from other similar documents only in its words, not in its structure. The structural requirements are enforced by means of a *document type definition* (DTD) or *schema*, which defines the required and optional sections, and the hierarchy of these sections (e.g., that the author's name must always follow the title rather than coming before the title). In fact, HTML is based on SGML, and differs from SGML primarily in its lack of a strongly enforced DTD. XML, a more recent innovation, is an intermediate approach: it represents an implementation of SGML that combines most of the rigor of SGML with some of the simplicity of HTML.

SGML and XML projects tend to be managed by large organizations such as airplane manufacturers that produce hundreds of thousands of pages of documentation for each airplane, or huge software companies that have large teams of writers, complex single-sourcing requirements (such as the need to create online help and a printed manual from the same source file), and (often) many subcontractors providing documents for their employer's contribution to a much larger overall system. Fortunately, despite their greater complexity, SGML and XML documents are still text files, though it may be necessary to extract them from a database or other central repository before you can work with them. As a result, you can edit them using exactly the same approach you would use with HTML Web pages. Note, however, that although this is possible, organizations that rely heavily on XML and SGML are likely to use specialized software that provides its own editing tools, which represent a better solution.

XMetal Author: Software and Web designers are increasingly recognizing the need to collaborate on documents. For example, XMetal Author lets authors, peer reviewers, and editors collaborate on an XML document over the Web or an intranet using revision tracking tools similar to those provided by Word.

Because the DTDs that govern the structure of XML and SGML documents can be quite complex, the documents can be proportionally more complex to review than Web pages. In addition to the cautions I presented for HTML files in the previous section, keep the following additional points in mind to avoid problems:

- Unless you're using specialized software that tracks changes within its own files, it's crucial that you save the revised document in *text* format. Any other choice guarantees problems because most word processors will revise the tags created by the author's software and damage a carefully designed document's structure.

- XML and SGML documents tend to be more complicated than HTML documents. Even if you don't change the color of the markup tags when you edit HTML documents, consider doing so in XML and SGML documents.

- Unless you really know what you're doing, and have a profound understanding of the DTD, you should never move text or edit the tags; doing so could render the document noncompliant with its DTD, thereby making it unusable without considerable extra work to find and repair the problem. Instead, *suggest* (by inserting a comment) that the author move chunks of text rather than moving the text yourself.

With careful management, this approach should be particularly suitable for situations that involve a large number of subcontractors, each of whom may use a different product to generate the XML or SGML files that will be integrated into the larger project. Rather than requiring each editor or reviewer to own a copy of each subcontractor's authoring software, you can instead edit the files in a word processor if the project manager doesn't provide a better-integrated solution. If you follow the approach outlined in this section, you can simply re-import the final text files into the original authoring software that created them.

If it's not possible to review the XML or SGML documents in your word processor, it may sometimes be possible to edit the files in the original authoring software without tracking your changes. This is a reasonable option if you can use a utility or built-in feature to compare the original and edited files and highlight the differences. For example, FrameMaker includes a document comparison feature that will highlight the differences between any two FrameMaker documents, and also offers the equivalent of Word's track changes feature. Similarly, Microsoft offers a utility called XMLDiff; given any two XML files, XMLDiff will create a third file showing all the differences between them, marked up using XML tags. However, using such a comparison feature has several drawbacks:

- It requires careful file management, since you end up with at least three files at each stage of the review (the original file, the edited file, and a file containing the highlighted differences) rather than a single file containing tracked revisions.
- Such utilities often miss or misrepresent complex changes, particularly when multiple authors review a single document and make contradictory or overlapping changes.
- Such tools are generally less efficient than highly evolved revision tracking features such as those provided by Word.

Nonetheless, a document comparison approach may work just fine if revision tracking isn't available or permitted by your employer or client. In addition, it tends to integrate well with the version-control software used by the types of companies that work primarily with XML or SGML documents.

Desktop Publishing Files

Recent versions of most desktop publishing programs provide an interesting option that greatly facilitates the task of editing a manuscript created in a word processor but that has already been imported into the desktop publishing software for layout. This involves *linking* the layout to the word processor file when the file is first imported, instead of *embedding* the file. The details of linking and embedding vary among programs, but most software observes the following distinction: If you embed the file in the desktop publishing document, all its connections with the original word processor document are severed; in contrast, if you link to the word processor file, the desktop publishing software monitors that file to see whether it has been modified since you began working on the layout, and if it has been modified, offers you the option to update its copy of the text. Linking thus lets you edit the file in the word processor that created it using standard revision tracking tools, review and implement the changes in the word processor, then automatically update the layout of the document without having to manually re-import the word processor file.

Updating of linked files generally works well. For example, if you delete a paragraph in the word processor file or move a sentence to a new location, these changes will be reflected in the layout as soon as you open the InDesign file and update the link. Unfortunately, only some of the work you've done in InDesign will be preserved during the update. For example, if you've flowed the imported text into two columns or broken it across two pages in InDesign, these changes will be retained when you update the link; in contrast, if you manually applied new paragraph styles to each paragraph in InDesign (thereby replacing the word processor's paragraph styles), you'll have to reapply the new styles.

It may take some experimentation to discover the best way to resolve certain problems. For example, if you use the same paragraph style names in your word processor document that you use in InDesign, you won't have to manually reapply paragraph styles when you import the file into InDesign: InDesign will replace the word processor's paragraph styles with its own paragraph styles of the same name. Similarly, if you used character styles to apply formatting, the formatting information should also be preserved. Subsequently, when you update the linked file, you won't have to reapply these styles in InDesign.

Revision tracking in InDesign: InDesign is teamed with an editing program called InCopy, which lets you edit stories in InDesign using revision-tracking tools. Early versions had "issues", but Adobe seems to have gotten the interface right with current versions.

If the linking and updating processes don't work to your satisfaction or if you can't do this at all because your word processor and desktop publishing program are incompatible, there's another possibility. Desktop publishing software often lets you export *tagged* text, which you can then review using an editing process similar to the one described for HTML files earlier in this chapter. For example, Adobe's InDesign lets you export tagged text. The tagged file resembles a Web page created in HTML; that is, you'll see chunks of text surrounded by tags that define how the desktop publishing software sees the information. The software will then use those tags to restore the formatting when you re-import the edited file. If you're careful not to damage the tags, this approach lets you "round-trip" the information: the process of exporting the file for editing and re-importing it for layout creates no changes to the essential formatting information.

Garbage in, garbage out: It's always easier to develop a production process in which the heaviest editing occurs before files are sent for layout. The procedure described in this section is acceptable in the absence of such a process, but it can be a difficult, demanding, and less efficient way to edit a manuscript.

A typical export process creates a number of files—typically one per *story*. (In desktop publishing, *stories* are separate and independent blocks of text, each usually representing a separate word processor file that has been imported and placed in a different *container* in the layout.) Designers typically design publications by importing separate word processor files for each chapter, and sometimes even for smaller chunks such as sidebars. In that approach, each file becomes a separate story, and exporting the publication generates a separate file for each story. It can be challenging to manage all these files and re-import them successfully into their original locations within the desktop publishing program. In addition, if the editing has been heavy, with many insertions or deletions, the text probably won't fit into its original container, and considerable revision of the layout will be required. As I noted earlier in this chapter, doing your heaviest editing before the page layout begins can mitigate this problem.

How to export the tagged text varies among programs. Rather than repeating the relevant sections of the user manual for several programs, I'll present a more general overview of the process. This will be too general to serve as your only road map for developing a review process; you'll have to research the details of exporting and re-importing tagged text in your software's online help, and experiment with a few trial layouts that contain only a few stories until you thoroughly understand how the process works and the kinds of problems you'll encounter. Only once you've gained some experience with how the process works should you attempt to use it in a production environment, particularly under deadline pressure.

Markup languages pose a challenge: If you're editing a manuscript on HTML or another tagging language, you've got a problem: the software may interpret examples of the tags as formatting instructions. Disaster! You'll have to experiment with various combinations of export and import formats to find one that works. One possible solution is to temporarily replace the symbols that define tags from the markup language with new characters that won't be recognized as tags. For example, you could change <em> to *em* before exporting the file, and then restore the original angle brackets once the file has been re-imported.

Here's an overview of a typical process based on the procedures used by InDesign:

- Open the File menu and select Export, then select Adobe Indesign tagged text. If such an option isn't available, XML is a good alternative because it will generate a file containing a standard and robust set of tags. Alternatively, select a file format your word processor can recognize and work with. Rich text format (RTF) typically works well because it preserves most style information.

- If you're asked to choose the text encoding format, choose one your word processor supports. Unicode is a good choice because most modern word processors support Unicode fonts, and this minimizes the risk of special characters being replaced by other characters.

- You may be asked to choose between short (concise) and long (verbose) tags. The main practical consideration is that shorter tags produce less visual clutter (are easy to work around during editing), whereas longer tags may be more likely to preserve all formatting nuances created in the desktop publishing software.

- Don't try to modify the formatting in your word processor unless you fully understand the tagging language and have experience editing its tags. If you're confident a change is necessary, insert a comment to explain that change to the author, and ensure that someone removes all your comments before they re-import the file into the desktop publishing software.

- If the text is difficult to read in your word processor, you can change the font used to display it if the typographic information is contained in the tags. For example, if you see a tag such as <font = symbol>alpha</font> to encode the Greek α, you can change the font used to display the tagged text without affecting how α will appear in the desktop publishing software. Alternatively, zoom in on the text to make it easier to read. (See Chapter 4 for details on managing the view.)

- Test the effects on special typographic features such as ligatures (where two characters merge into a single joined character such as æ), small caps, and alternative characters in an "expert" version of the font that only the desktop publisher may own. If the word processor and desktop publishing program don't define these characters in the same way, you may need to replace them with placeholders. These placeholders could be simple codes such as &ae for the æ ligature; when you reopen the file in the desktop publishing software, search for these placeholders and replace them with the correct characters.

- Edit the file using revision tracking and return it to the author.

- After implementing the edits and ensuring that all comments have been deleted, re-import the file into the desktop publishing software.
- You will generally import the file by reversing how you exported it (i.e., open the File menu, select Import, and choose the same file format and the same encoding you used to export the file). If you see an option such as Read Tags, choose it to ensure the software will interpret the tags as formatting instructions rather than as part of the text.

Databases and Spreadsheets

The modern world runs on data every bit as much as it runs on oil. The quantities of information created and stored each day are mind-boggling, and it would be impossible to make any sense of this sea of information without computer assistance. We use two main tools to manage the chaos:

- *Databases* are designed to store large quantities of textual and numerical data and to retrieve and manipulate (sort, combine, and publish) the data. They may also store more complex information such as graphics and sound files; in case you're feeling jargon-deprived, these are often called *binary large objects* (BLOBs).
- *Spreadsheets* can store text, but are primarily designed to store numerical data, and are optimized to perform calculations on subsets of the data and publish the results as tables or graphs.

Both types of software store data in what appears on the screen as a grid of rows and columns of information. Other aspects of these programs are similar because the software categories have increasingly overlapped: modern spreadsheets provide database tools, and databases provide calculation tools. Both define the information they contain as *data*. For the sake of clarity, I'll treat the two as if they were essentially distinct entities. But because they overlap, they share certain problematic characteristics you must watch for:

Inability to re-import the edited file

Oddly enough, programs can sometimes export files in a format they cannot subsequently re-import without losing information. Always confirm that you can re-import edited files successfully before you implement a process based on exporting information for editing in your word processor. If you can't re-import the edited information, you can at least rely on your word processor to clearly communicate your edits, but you'll need to teach the author how to transfer the edits manually into the original file. Even if the re-importation appears successful, someone must perform quality control on the final database or spreadsheet to spot any problems.

Embedded formulas

Watch for formulas that perform calculations on data obtained from elsewhere within a file or from another file. These formulas are often intermingled with the data on which the formulas operate. Because these formulas will most often disappear when you convert the file into text format for editing in your word processor, you must determine how to find and preserve them. Sometimes this is obvious (e.g., a field is named "total" or "summary"), but sometimes you need the creator's help to learn what formulas they created and where they hid the formulas.

Inefficient design

Just as some authors never learn to use paragraph and character styles, and manually format all text (e.g., increasing the type size and boldfacing the words to create a heading), some database and spreadsheet designers never learn to define formatting and calculation instructions separately from the data. When formatting is manually applied to a specific item (e.g., a single cell in a spreadsheet), you'll lose this formatting if you export the information as a text file for editing; clearly, having to manually reapply those formats will create considerable work for the designer. Similarly, formulas that perform calculations on data pulled from elsewhere in the file are often inserted seemingly randomly amidst the data they use for these calculations. That makes them harder than necessary to find and protect during editing. A more efficient approach separates the data from the formulas that use it or from the formatting instructions that control how it appears on the screen or in printouts.

It's possible to design spreadsheets and databases so that formulas and formatting instructions are mostly separate from the data they work on. This is often done by creating a report template that draws information from a data file, then performs the necessary calculations or applies the necessary formatting only in the report; the file that contains the original data has no formulas and no formats. If your software offers named styles that control formatting, you can apply those styles to individual cells of the report so that when the report is updated, the results of the calculations (but not their format) change; the styles are automatically reapplied.

A corollary to this is that labels should be grouped in one area of the report template, with the calculations grouped in an adjacent area of the template. For example, a sales summary report might have the following structure:

	Q1	Q2	Q3	Q4	Total	Mean
Sales	—	—	—	—	—	—
Profit	—	—	—	—	—	—

Here, the "—" characters represent formulas that pull the quarterly sales and profit information from other files that contain this data, and formulas that calculate the total and mean values of this imported data. As editors, we'll most often be editing the labels that surround these formulas, not the formulas themselves. By grouping the labels around the edges, and grouping the formulas inside the table, it becomes much easier to edit just the labels and avoid damaging the formulas.

An inefficient workflow

As in all the other special situations discussed in this chapter, it's easier and more efficient to edit information *before* you place it in any software that lacks strong revision-tracking tools. The procedures described in the rest of this section are acceptable workarounds for information that already exists in a database or spreadsheet, but are no substitute for a workflow that controls the quality of the information before it is imported into these programs. In the *Editing databases* and *Editing spreadsheets* sections that follow, I'll describe some ways to improve the quality of the information going in, and ways to edit the information when those controls fail.

Editing databases

There are two main types of database we're likely to encounter: *flat-file* databases and *relational* databases. In both types, each chunk of related information within a single file (for example, my family name versus yours) is referred to as a *record*. Flat-file databases usually store all their information in a single file, with recurring items such as a city name in a mailing list database repeated for each record in the file. In contrast, relational databases consist of a linked series of *tables*, each of which contains a subset of the larger database. For example, a simple relational database of your friends' mailing addresses might consist of four files: one that lists the names, street addresses, and postal or zip codes (i.e., information that is unique to each friend), and three additional files that list information likely to be shared by at least some of your friends (cities, provinces or states, and countries). When you generate mailing labels to announce your new book on onscreen editing, the database pulls together the required information from these four files to create an address label for each friend. The advantage of this approach is that any recurring item, such as a city's name, is only stored once (in the file of city names) rather than repeatedly for each friend in that city. This is both reduces file sizes and improves consistency, since you only have to correct typos once rather than once per friend in that city, as would be the case in a flat-file database. (Better flat-file databases now offer similar relational capabilities.)

Editing by exporting and re-importing the data

Both flat-file and relational databases can export their data in a *delimited* format, in which each record is exported as a single line of text, with each item of data for that record separated (*delimited*) from the ones before and after it by characters such as tabs or commas. There is little practical difference between comma-delimited and tab-delimited listings, though the tabbed format is easier to read because it more obviously separates the components of each record. The only case in which you must unequivocally avoid comma-delimited files is when some of the data contains commas; this might be the case in a database of sentences, for instance.

From an editorial perspective, the main implication of working with a flat-file database is that the information is likely to be contained in a single file. That's more convenient than working with several files, but there's a down side: because each record may contain dozens of pieces of data, the exported data can form very long lines. Once the data is in your word processor, the corresponding information (e.g., the city name) for each record no longer lines up in neat columns the way it did in the columns of the original database file. In an address database, for instance, the name, street address, city, province or state, country, and postal code may be long enough that the information for each record wraps onto two or more lines. This makes it difficult or impossible to scan all instances of a specific data type (e.g., city names) in a single pass, moving downwards through the column of names.

In this example, this isn't an intolerable problem because the meaning of each chunk of information is clear, but in complex databases, it's harder to understand what some chunks of information represent (e.g., numerical codes). Since we must understand the meaning before we can edit that chunk, editing becomes more difficult. In addition, we may need to make the same change dozens of times; for example, a complicated city name such as Tenochtitlan might be spelled half a dozen ways. This means we'll need to use the search tool carefully, perhaps supplemented by a style sheet, to find and fix each such problem. (See chapters 8 and 9 for details.)

In contrast, working with a relational database means we'll need to work with several files (one per database table). On the plus side, we'll only need to make certain corrections once; for example, Tenochtitlan will appear only once, in the table of city names, rather than in each address in that city. On the negative side, if we make a mistake once, that mistake will appear in every record that uses the erroneous information; for that reason, we must be particularly careful in our edits. Because most operations that will be performed on relational data are defined using a reporting function that draws data from one or more tables, formulas are not usually stored in individual tables, and that makes it easy to export data from each table, edit it, and re-import it directly into the database. In a well-designed relational database, the nature of the contents of each table is also clear from the table's title; for example, "City names" is unequivocal. This clarifies the context in which we'll be editing the data. Poorly designed or very complex databases may use table names that are more abstract, making the task of editing according to the intended meaning more difficult.

Editing directly in the database

When we can't safely export data for editing, we can edit directly in the database software. (Most of the suggestions described in this section will also work in any spreadsheet software, with appropriate modifications.) The key is to find a way to separate editorial comments from the data. Doing so accomplishes the same goal as revision tracking in a word processor: it makes the edits easy to see because they stand out from the original information.

In a flat-file database, the information is typically stored in a single file. In this case, we can simply add a new column or row to hold our comments, and remind the author to delete this entire column or row after they've finished addressing our comments. Flat-file databases let us add as many blank columns or rows as we need. This makes it easy to type long comments above, below, or to one side of (immediately adjacent to) the editable information. (So long as we're consistent in where we place the comments, authors will learn to use our comments efficiently.) Placing these comments outside the information-containing rows and columns of the database groups the edits in a single place where they're harder to miss and where they won't affect the information we're editing. This reduces the risk that an author will miss comments or that editing will damage information or formulas. Because the comments are adjacent to the information they describe, they're closely tied to that information, and this eliminates much of the need to describe a problem's location, which means less typing for us and easier reading for the author. Apart from ensuring that the edits were implemented correctly, the main quality-control concern is to ensure that the author removes the column or row containing our comments after implementing our edits.

In a relational database, the software manages multiple tables simultaneously. This means that in addition to adding rows or columns, as in the case of flat-file databases, we can add one or more tables that include only our edits. (This is also possible in flat-file databases that offer basic relational capabilities.) For example, if we're editing a database table named *City names*, we can create a matching table named *City names--edited*. Each record in this new table corresponds to a record in *City names*: the first position in the table of city names corresponds to the first position in the table of edited city names, the second positions also correspond, and so on. When we edit the 253rd city name in the original file, we place our edit in the 253rd row of the table of edited names. Needless to say, we must be careful to type our edits in the correct position. This is easier if we display the two tables side by side, with the rows lined up so that it's easy to see where to type our edits. A typical table of comments includes up to three columns: the first (which is not editable by the user) represents the position in the file (i.e., the record number), and specifies the location of the problem; the second is optional, and quotes the problem text or data; and the third describes the problem and how to fix it. The second and third columns can also be combined into a single column that contains only the edited text. This approach clearly identifies the location of the problem, its nature, and the solution.

An advantage of this approach over adding new columns or rows to an existing file is that even if the author doesn't delete the new table, the information it contains won't ever become visible to the database's users. Another benefit is that once the author has finished reviewing our edits and correcting the data in the original table, they can simply delete our table, with no risk of harming the file that contains the corrected data (e.g., by carelessly deleting the wrong row or column).

Editing databases by means of validity checks

It's easier and more efficient to edit material *before* it's incorporated into a database rather than trying to detect and fix errors after they've become part of the data. One way to accomplish this is to implement tools such as carefully edited *pick lists* that force users to select their input from a list of validated information instead of typing it, thereby eliminating the risk of typos. In some cases, we can help the developers implement *validity checks*—rules that constrain what can be entered in each field of a database. When neither pick lists nor validity checks can be implemented, as in the case of data such as family names that are difficult to validate, we can at least recommend a process that sends all newly entered information to someone who is responsible for validating the information manually. In each case, an important editorial role is to identify potentially recurring types of error and work with the database's developers to figure out ways to prevent those errors from entering the database in the first place.

There are several types of data for which pick lists and validity checks can be implemented:

- **A limited range of choices (e.g., country names):** In this case, the data-entry form can list all acceptable choices in a menu, and require users to choose from this list. With no typing, there are no typos! (Of course, it's still possible to select the wrong option from the list, so there should be some way to check this. One common way is to require the user to confirm the information before entering it into the database.) If it's not possible to anticipate every possible choice, there should be a way for users to propose new options (usually by adding an *other* option) and a way for the database to report this new information so someone can check it.

- **Only certain classes of data (e.g., numbers):** Most databases can validate input *as it's being entered* and display an error message if the data doesn't match the specified pattern. For example, programmers can define a pattern such as *nnn-nnn-nnnn* for telephone numbers (where *n* represents a single digit) and warn the user when the typed information doesn't match this pattern. Of course, this validation process must not forbid the entry of correct but unexpected data. For example, many U.S.-based Web sites still won't accept alphanumeric Canadian postal codes, even if the company ships to Canada, because the validity check only accepts numeric U.S. zip codes.

- **Specific patterns that are difficult to constrain:** Where it's not possible to constrain the input data, propose *affordances* (hints or explanations of the nature of the required data) in the data-input forms to guide users during data entry. For example, "Enter the month and day as MM/DD. Type the / character, and type 0 before 1-digit months or days (e.g., type 02, not 2)." That's too verbose for a typical form, but illustrates the kind of details an affordance can provide.

Cautions to keep in mind when editing databases

- If you're editing tab- or comma-delimited files in your word processor, never delete the tabs or commas; these characters tell the database how to organize the data into rows and columns. The database software cannot *correctly* re-import the edited file (and may be unable to import it at all) if the columns of data no longer match the columns in the database.

- Never change the position of information without confirming with the designer that this is acceptable; if you move information to a new position, it may end up in the wrong row or column when it's re-imported into the database.

- Rather than deleting data from a record, propose the deletion using a comment. Simply deleting an item leaves an unfilled hole in the database that may cause significant future problems.

- Confirm that no edits remain before re-importing the file into the database. Different programs handle these remnants differently; for example, undeleted comments may simply be ignored, or may become new records in the database.

- If the database includes formulas, test what happens when you export and re-import the data. See the next section (*Editing spreadsheets*) for more details on testing formulas.

In some database projects, such as library catalogs, the data is updated only occasionally, usually to add new records. In such cases, you should persuade the person who maintains the database to send you all additions in an e-mail message or word processor file so you can concentrate on editing the new information rather than reviewing the entire database, including parts you've already edited, in search of changes. Only once the new information has been edited should it be added to the database. This approach is essential for large, growing databases, since the time required to scan an entire database grows as fast as the database itself. (The phrase "needle in a haystack" doesn't do justice to the problem.) Alternatively, the database developer can use the database's reporting tools to create a file that contains all records that have been added or changed since the last time you edited the database. (This requires the developer to record the date when each change was made. It's not hard to do, but may not be done if you don't ask.) You can then review only those changes.

I've used both approaches successfully, but the first approach is preferable if the data will be published as soon as it enters the database and if incorrect data may be harmful to its users. In this case, the problem must be fixed *before* the data is published. Database owners should accept a slight delay in publishing new data in exchange for the reduced risk of publishing serious errors. Remind them of their potential legal liability if they need any persuasion.

Editing spreadsheets

Spreadsheets resemble databases in many important ways: the data in a spreadsheet are also stored in rows and columns, although these grids of information are referred to as *worksheets* rather than *tables*. Each worksheet may appear as an individual page or tab in the spreadsheet file, depending on the user interface. The collection of worksheets for a given project is often called a *workbook*. Most of the recommendations for editing the contents of databases in the previous section also apply to spreadsheets. (Please review that section before you continue.) That's particularly true when the spreadsheet primarily contains text or numbers, with relatively few formulas or other complications. But unlike databases, which emphasize the management of large volumes of data, spreadsheets emphasize the ability to perform *calculations* on their data. It's the formulas that perform these calculations that create the biggest editing problems.

Older versions of Word could import Excel spreadsheet files directly, without requiring the export process I described earlier in the chapter. As of Word 2010 and 2011, this is no longer possible. However, you can select all the cells you want to edit, copy them, and paste them into Word, where the pasted information will become a Word table. If you have an older copy of Word still installed on your computer, you can directly import Excel spreadsheets and convert them into Word tables. All you need to do is select the file in the **Open File** dialog box and, if necessary for your version of Word, specify the file type as an Excel worksheet, and then tell Word whether you want to import only one worksheet or the entire workbook. When the process is complete, the contents of each worksheet will be a separate Word table. You can then save the file and reopen it in your current version of Word. Where you can't simply copy/paste between programs or open the file, you'll need to export the file into a format compatible with your word processor.

Editing by exporting and re-importing the data

Most spreadsheets define their calculations in a proprietary format that does not translate into text or RTF formats. Although you can often *embed* a spreadsheet in a compatible word processor document, you can't usually edit the spreadsheet's contents in the word processor. When you click on the embedded spreadsheet to edit it, you open the spreadsheet software; if you look closely, you'll see the menus at the top of the screen change to those of the spreadsheet software. This means that you no longer have access to the word processor's revision tracking tools.

The revision tracking tools provided by spreadsheets are primitive compared to those offered by a word processor. Excel's tools are particularly poorly implemented; they're so bad that I won't accept large editing jobs that require me to work in Excel. The tools are clumsy, inefficient, and create an unacceptably high risk that the author won't see an edit or comment and will thereby introduce significant errors into the final file. For example, the following image shows Excel's tiny comment marker and what the messages look like if the author remembers to configure the software to display them:

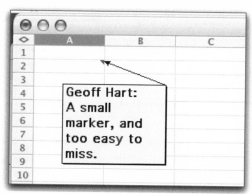

If their copy of Excel isn't configured to automatically display the comments this way, all you see is the tiny red triangle. Inserting comments using the spreadsheet's commenting feature has another risk: many authors who distribute spreadsheets to their colleagues use the commenting feature to provide instructions on how to use the spreadsheet, instructions on what values are permitted in a certain field, and other hints or tips. This may prevent us from inserting a comment in a specific field because one is already present. Furthermore, someone must ensure that the author removes our comments from the file—*without* inadvertently removing their own instructional comments.

If the spreadsheet offers a graphical design mode, it may be possible to create text boxes that float above the rest of the screen and display our comments. These work well as an onscreen equivalent to sticky notes. You can even use the software's drawing tools to link these comments to the problematic text with an arrow. If you can give that box a yellow (or other) background color so that it resembles a real sticky note, it's much harder to miss, thereby reducing the risk of unaddressed comments left in the file.

For light editing, you can use the approach I've described for databases earlier in this chapter and will build on later in this section. But for more demanding work, you'll want to do the editing in your word processor. Unfortunately, exporting and re-importing spreadsheet files will lose the formulas embedded in the spreadsheet. Each combination of word processor and spreadsheet software will require some testing to learn what happens when you pass files from one to the other and back again, and how to deal with any problems. For example, I use an Excel spreadsheet to maintain a running total of my income and expenses and to estimate my taxes. Simple formulas sum the columns and rows, and calculate the total sales tax I've charged and must remit to the government. Exporting this information as tab-delimited text eliminates these formulas and replaces them with the results of the calculations. Were I to re-import that file, I'd have to remember to delete the results of these calculations and recreate the formulas manually. If I failed to do this, these numbers would remain unchanged no matter what new expenses and income I added to the spreadsheet, leading to a nasty surprise at tax time.

If a spreadsheet separates the editable information (headings and other labels, plus the data associated with them) from the formulas, it's possible to copy only the cells that contain information that should be edited and paste them into a word processor file, leaving the formulas safely in place. This works best if the cells containing editable data form a tidy, rectangular block instead of being scattered all over the screen, intermingled with the formulas that will perform calculations using the data. (You'd be amazed at some of the spreadsheet layouts I've seen.) After reviewing our edits, the author can simply copy the edited data and paste it right back into the spreadsheet; selecting the range of rows and columns where it should go before pasting will ensure that the edited data replaces the original data. As long as the author selects the right cells, this process works well. If the spreadsheet software offers the ability to *protect* cells (i.e., prevent their contents from being altered), this protection can sometimes be applied to cells containing formulas to protect them against being overwritten by the pasted data.

In this approach, both the editor and the author must pay close attention to what they're doing to ensure that the edited data returns to its original location; if the person responsible for this step misses the target by even a single column or row, all formulas that refer to the contents of these cells will perform their calculations on the wrong data. In the best case, those calculations will simply fail, and the formulas will have to be re-linked to the new cells. In the worst case, the calculations will proceed using the wrong data, leading to serious errors. Thus, someone must check the results of re-importing the data to detect any errors. This requires careful testing, and for more complex spreadsheets, that testing may prove prohibitively time-consuming and difficult.

Although it's possible to design a spreadsheet to facilitate this process, most spreadsheet designers I've worked with are not professionals (i.e., this is not their main work), are no better at spreadsheet design than they are at writing, and (despite the clear benefits of doing so) have been unwilling to request or listen to my advice. This group tends to perceive the creation of the spreadsheet as more important than editing its contents, and they therefore place little importance on designing the spreadsheet to facilitate editing.

Editing directly in the spreadsheet

When it's necessary to edit directly in a spreadsheet, we can easily add a column of comments to the right of the worksheet's contents, as I described earlier in this chapter for databases. The comments then appear in the same row that contains the problem we're describing, and don't interfere with the contents. Because even the least-organized designer tends to reflexively place the contents of a worksheet close to the left edge of the screen, there's room to add our comments to the right of this area. The result might resemble this:

Cell	Contents	Problem (edit)
B2	300	Didn't we sell 200 units?
B6	Mean monthly sales	Could we add historical data from last year?

Most modern spreadsheets can display multiple worksheets side by side; for those that can't, saving each worksheet as a separate file and opening it in a new window will accomplish the same goal. We can then adopt an easier approach that creates fewer problems: create an entirely separate worksheet that contains the edits and comments. If we enter the comments in the same cell number as the text or numbers we're describing, it's easy for the author to associate the two. A slightly more complex variation of this approach takes advantage of a key feature of spreadsheets, namely their ability to cross-reference the contents of cells at different locations, so that the two cells are linked. Using this approach, we could create a worksheet named "Edits" that contains three columns: the first column contains a reference to the location of the problem (i.e., the worksheet name and the cell name or number), the second repeats the problematic text or numbers or formulas from the original worksheet, and the third column holds our comments. The first column tells the author where to look for the problem; in Excel, for instance, the reference to a cell in another worksheet might look like *Calculator:C12*, where *Calculator* is the name of the worksheet and *C12* is the specific cell in that worksheet. The second and third columns then present the problem and our proposed solution side by side so the author can compare the two and see what we've done.

As in the case of editing relational databases by typing our comments in a separate table, editing in a separate worksheet or a separate file offers two big advantages: First, the author can simply delete the entire worksheet or file once they have addressed all our comments. Second, there's no risk of our comments remaining in the original worksheet.

If we develop a good relationship with the author because they appreciate our editing of their manuscripts, we can often extend that relationship to include spreadsheet design once we establish our credibility in this area. Demonstrating the time savings (thus, the cost savings and increased accuracy of editing) that result from working with a well-designed spreadsheet is a good way to attain that credibility. A few simple design strategies make it easier to export or copy only the relevant data in a spreadsheet. As noted above, the trick is to design the spreadsheet so that, as much as possible, the data is stored separately from the formulas that operate on that data. There are several ways to accomplish this:

- Format the calculation worksheet so its editable parts can be easily extracted. For example, place column titles only across the top of the spreadsheet and row titles only down the left edge, rather than scattering them among the calculation formulas. For example:

<>	A	B	C
1	**Month**	**Sales (units)**	
2	January	200	
3	February	300	
4	March	400	
5		First quarter total	=sum(b2:b4)
6		Mean monthly sales	=c5/3

- Store the data that will be used in calculations in one worksheet, and store the formulas that perform calculations based on that data in a separate worksheet. Because the editable information is completely separate from the noneditable information, it's easy to extract the data for editing with no fear of damaging a formula.

- In any worksheet that requires a mixture of editable data and non-editable formulas, separate the two categories of information as clearly as possible, as shown in the table earlier in this section. Note that in this simplified example, anything in columns A and B is editable, but not the formulas in column C.

These design strategies make it easier to copy a range of cells—possibly even an entire worksheet—and paste it into our word processor without going through the import and export process. Better still, they let us use the same approaches I described earlier in this chapter for editing directly in database software.

Spreadsheet (in)compatibility: Though you may be able to use different spreadsheet software than the author—to use Quattro Pro to edit Excel files, for instance—you'll encounter compatibility problems. That's not to say you shouldn't test this option, but test carefully and implement a quality-control step to detect any problems.

Substantive editing of databases and spreadsheets

The tabular nature of the data in databases and spreadsheets (i.e., the fact that information is arranged into rows and columns) also introduces the possibility of substantive problems that must be fixed in addition to the usual typos and formatting problems. For example, two columns of data that should lie side by side to facilitate comparisons may have been separated by other columns during the design phase, when authors are often still deciding what information belongs in a table or worksheet and aren't yet sure how it all fits together. (Some authors never progress beyond this point, relying instead on various kludges to present the information effectively.) We can point out these kinds of problems and leave it to the author to solve them, but it's more effective if we actually show the author the results of the change. To do so, simply save a copy of the file and use the software's tools to rearrange the columns or rows into a more effective layout. Then submit that sample file (or a PDF of the file) along with our edits so the author can see what we've done and decide whether to adopt our solution.

In addition to simple layout problems, there are subtler and more serious problems related to the underlying logic. It's been said that the computer is a tool for helping us to make more numerous and more significant mistakes in less time than was ever previously possible. That's a *bit* cynical, but only a bit. As editors, our goal has traditionally been to protect our authors from their human weaknesses when it came to writing. But if we're expanding our editorial repertoire to encompass databases and spreadsheets, we should also start thinking about how to protect our authors from substantive errors in this new medium. An example for databases and another for spreadsheets will illustrate the potential problems.

Data in a database is often stored with little indication of its proper context. For example, the data in one table of a relational database may clearly be city names, but without some context, it may not be clear where those names will be used elsewhere in the database. Without that context, it's hard to determine whether data are appropriate. Database publishing, in which software may assemble Web pages, a product manual, or even a newsletter on the fly using information drawn from a database, is a good example. Someone (i.e., us) must confirm that the results are correct and usable, and that they reflect well upon the author. I once owned a GM station wagon whose manual had been created using database publishing. An error in the selection of which records to extract from the database caused the insertion of several chunks of information that were clearly intended for an entirely different car. Similarly, I've seen many catalogs published with wildly erroneous data or even missing data. One clue to the latter is the appearance of text such as *$XXX.XX*—a typical formatting instruction for how to display a price—in place of the product's price. This kind of error is likely to become increasingly common as technical writers continue their move to *single sourcing*, in which documents are assembled from chunks of standard text that can be reused in many different contexts.

Spreadsheets are vulnerable to similar errors, but also to more significant errors of logic (i.e., incorrect calculations). Although we often lack the expertise to review an author's logic, we can usually perform a reality check on *the results* of that logic. Years ago, I read of a study in which researchers provided young students with defective calculators that had been designed to produce wildly inaccurate answers. The researchers were disturbed to discover that few students had enough of a sense of numbers to distrust the obviously defective calculators. More recently, an important client updated the spreadsheet they used to store the work I did for them and calculate payments, but incorrectly defined a formula for calculating totals. I routinely check my statements by calculating an approximate total, and comparing my estimate with their calculated total revealed that their new spreadsheet would have led them to underpay me by several hundred dollars. This kind of problem is particularly severe for spreadsheets, since the numbers may have greater significance than a student's math test—for example, monthly mortgage payments that occur for decades, or the budget for a government program. Many people trust computer calculations blindly; we editors should not.

As editors, we provide a necessary reality check. In proofreading the car manual produced by database publishing, we can note obvious errors such as information for the wrong model of car and subtler errors. In examining the results of a mortgage calculation, we could call a few banks and ask what a typical monthly payment would be for a mortgage of a given size and term, and compare those answers with the spreadsheet's results. In analyzing an invoice or a budget calculation, we might just add up the thousands or millions digits and check whether the result is reasonably close to the calculated total. If so, we can have some confidence the spreadsheet is functioning correctly; if not, we can inform the author that there's a possible calculation error. Authors should, of course, carefully test their formulas to ensure they're correct and bug-free, but some don't, and the ones who do often do a poor job. Sometimes the problem is not that the author isn't conscientious, but rather that the formulas are too complex for easy validation.

In databases and spreadsheets, both the user interface created to help users enter data and the format of the reports or summaries generated by the software must make sense. Just as we can critique a page layout or the structure of a document during substantive editing, we can provide similar criticism to the designers of spreadsheets and databases and can offer advice on how to improve both the interface and the outputs produced using that interface. In fact, *we should do so at every opportunity.* Our role as reader's advocate means we must remember that successful communication involves bridging the gap between author and reader. The only way we can do this for databases and spreadsheets is to actually use the software and report any problems we encounter. This isn't what many designers see as our role (i.e., it goes far beyond simply checking for typos), but just as substantive editing makes our authors look better, it can help database and spreadsheet designers look better.

Editing Software Interface Text

The modern programming environments that are used to create the software we use often store the software's user-interface text buried in the middle of the programming code, but some store this information in a separate file, which is often called a *resource* file. Before the program is compiled (i.e., converted from a form the programmer can understand into a form the computer understands), these files are usually in text format. That means you can open them in your word processor and edit them using revision tracking in a manner similar to my description of editing Web pages and markup languages at the start of this chapter.

Most programmers are reluctant to hand you their programming code, since the risk of damage to the code is high if you don't understand how the interface text is encoded. Accidentally changing some of that code can create problems that take considerable time and expense to locate and fix, and programmers are usually working to solve other thorny problems under unreasonable deadlines. If you point out that you won't be revising the actual code they're working on, and will only use the file to communicate text changes, they may be willing to give you a copy. You can then use your word processor's search tools to find all instances of the markup language that describes interface text and highlight it, as described earlier in this chapter for HTML files. You can then skim through the file and focus only on the interface text.

At a previous employer, the interface text for the software we were developing was stored in a resource file that was independent of the actual program code. The resource file contained simple numeric codes that defined where that text would be displayed after the program was compiled. Because these files were separate from the program code, the programmers were happy to give them to me for editing, since it saved them a lot of time and effort entering corrections for typos or poor word choices. Once I taught them how to use revision tracking efficiently, they loved this approach. An additional bonus was that this produced software that was clearer and easier to use, and much more consistent in its terminology. That made it easier for me to write the documentation and online help.

Quality control: As in the case of all other forms of editing non-word processor files in a word processor, ensure that you include a quality-control phase to ensure that you haven't damaged any of the interface text or the surrounding programming code.

Font Problems: Dealing With Special Characters

From sheer inertia, most authors use the core fonts that are installed with their operating system: this is easier than going to the trouble of purchasing and installing funky new fonts. This is a good thing, because nowadays, the standard fonts are available to anyone with a computer. For example, Unicode versions of Times New Roman, Verdana, and Arial are installed by default along with most operating systems. Many software developers throw in handfuls of additional fonts when we install their software. (Adobe is a notorious example.) Unfortunately, these fonts aren't available to anyone who hasn't installed that software. Developers such as Microsoft also provide core fonts for local languages that contain English characters, but that aren't available on English computers; examples include SimSun for Chinese versions of Word and Mincho for Japanese versions. These can cause problems for editors and readers who don't have those fonts on their computer because the text won't display correctly.

The core fonts may be boringly conventional choices, but using them maximizes the compatibility between computers. Because we have no control over what software and operating system our authors use, we need to be aware of potential problems that result from special characters such as mathematical symbols and non-Roman characters such as those used in Japanese and Chinese. The first time we work with a client who uses a different operating system, word processor, or language, it's necessary to spend some time looking for problems related to fonts. If you're familiar with the subject area in which you'll be editing, you can create a test file that contains the most common special characters you expect to encounter, entered neatly beside their names. You can then send that file to your author so they can review this list and report any problems.

On my Web site, I've provided two PDF files that list the special characters that most often pose problems in my work (primarily scientific editing) and standard keystrokes for inserting them correctly in a document. Neither of these lists includes all the diacritical marks (haceks and the like) that are rare in English but common in central European alphabets, and neither includes non-Roman alphabets other than Greek. If you're working with authors who use these other alphabets, you'll need to test more extensively to identify and prevent any problems.

Though the situation has improved greatly since the 2nd edition of this book, I still occasionally receive manuscripts that contain invisible characters that have been replaced by little white placeholder boxes. Sometimes, if the author has inserted the character correctly, you can simply select the character and change it to a different font, such as Times New Roman; if the character exists in that font, you've solved the problem. If not, asking the author to send you a PDF version of the manuscript often solves the problem, since Adobe Acrobat does an excellent job of maintaining a consistent display across operating systems. If you can see the correct character in the PDF file, you can usually find a way to insert it correctly in the manuscript so it won't cause problems for anyone else. To do this in Word:

- **Word 2010:** Ribbon > Insert tab > Symbol menu
- **Word 2011:** Insert menu > Symbol

When your best efforts won't reveal the mysterious character, the simplest solution is to flag the character with a politely exasperated comment: "Sorry, but I can't see this character on my computer." Of course, the simplest solution isn't necessarily the best.

If the problem occurs with each new manuscript and you can't teach the author how to insert the correct characters in a standard font, it's worthwhile spending some time creating a macro that will find the problem characters for you and replace them with the correct characters. (See Chapter 11 for details on how to record macros.) It's time-consuming to create the macro, but thereafter, you can run the macro each time you receive a problem manuscript, and update the macro whenever you need to add new characters. If the author is using the same software you use, offer them a copy of the macro so they can use it before they send you the file.

Another font-related problem arises from the way that software displays fonts. Authors who write in languages such as Japanese and Chinese often choose to align characters to a grid because it produces tidy and elegantly spaced text; this is analogous to the use of full justification (justification at both the left and right margins) with English text, but using a monospaced or nonproportional English font. The problem arises when these authors use grid-based layout for manuscripts written in English. Recent versions of Word do a good job of displaying these characters legibly, but if you're still using an older version, you may find the text unreadable. Alternatively, you may be able to read it, but you'll find that what you see doesn't match how the cursor behaves. Specifically, the actual position of the cursor within or between words may not match what you see on the screen. Obviously, this makes editing nearly impossible.

There are a few solutions to this problem. I'll start with solutions that don't involve making any permanent changes to your operating system or your Word installation:

- Ask the author to turn off the grid-based formatting and send you a new copy of the manuscript. Unfortunately, this can create a long delay when you're working across time zones, as in the case of North American editors working with Japanese and Chinese clients.

- Provide your Asian authors with an English document template that doesn't use the grid settings, and ask them to use that template when they create future manuscripts for you to edit.

- You can sometimes copy all of the text except the final paragraph marker (¶) and paste it into a new document.

- If you own InDesign, try importing the document into that software (using the Place command). InDesign often handles problematic Word files better than Word itself, and you can now copy the text from InDesign into a new Word file that doesn't use a grid.

- Save the file as HTML to strip out problem formatting, including the grid alignment. This preserves most of the style information from the original document. If necessary, skim the document looking for tags that specify a grid setting and delete them. Then reopen the document, save it as a Word document, and reapply any missing formatting.

- You can create a new document and insert the problem document into it. In Word 2010, select the Ribbon's Insert tab, and expand the document window until the Object icon is visible in the Text group; from its menu, select Text from file. In Word 2011, open the Insert menu and select File.

Note that because your Normal.dotm template automatically defines you as the creator of any new file based on that template (i.e., it inserts the user information that you entered when you installed or personalized the software), you should restore the author's name so that Word identifies them as the creator of the document. To do so:

- **Word 2010:** File menu > Info > Properties summary > right-click on the author name > Edit Property
- **Word 2011:** File menu > Properties > Summary tab > Author field

If you need to work regularly with Asian documents, it may be worthwhile running the software's installer and choosing the option (usually under the heading Proofing tools) to install support for these languages. Consult the online help (or search the Web) for the subjects "Asian language support" or "Enable editing of Japanese text" to find details for your version of Word. Once the installation is complete and you restart Word, you can turn off the grid settings:

- **Word 2010:** Ribbon > Page Layout tab > Page Setup > menu at the bottom of the Page Setup group
- **Word 2011:** Format menu > Document
- In both versions: Document Grid tab > No Grid checkbox > Apply to Whole Document menu choice.

Warning for Macintosh users: Installing Asian language support created several problems with my Word 2011 installation, including changing the way several macros behaved. Your mileage may vary; Word's behavior is unpredictable on the Macintosh. To be safe, don't install Asian language support if you don't have time to reinstall Word from scratch.

Turning off the grid settings fixes the spacing problems and permits business as usual. Because this approach does not change any of the font information in the file, and only deals with the grid-based formatting problem, it's safe to do this. If you're editing in English (the only reason you'd want to turn off the grid), the manuscript can't benefit from the use of the grid, and may even cause problems for others who will read the document, so no harm is done through turning off the grid. (I've been doing this for nearly 10 years, and none of my authors have reported any problems. Still, I insert a comment explaining what I've done, just in case.)

If you don't want to install support for Asian languages, the following macro (see Chapter 11 for instructions on how to create macros) should also solve the problem:

```
Sub TurnOffGrid()
' TurnOffGrid Macro recorded 7/4/2011 by Geoff Hart
With ActiveDocument.Styles(wdStyleNormal).Font
If .NameFarEast = .NameAscii Then
.NameAscii = ""
End If
.NameFarEast = ""
End With
With ActiveDocument.PageSetup
.LayoutMode = wdLayoutModeDefault
End With
End Sub
```

Chapter 13. Coping When Revision Tracking Isn't Available

Web: http://www.geoff-hart.com/books/eoe/eoe3/eoe3.html
Note: Word 2010 is for Windows; Word 2011 is for the Macintosh

I've focused on Microsoft Word in this book for two reasons: First, it's the software I use most often, and I don't want to persuade you to try any approaches I haven't survived and proven to be effective in my own work. (In a few cases, I haven't tried them myself, but they were vetted by experts.) Second, decades of participation in writing-related communities, including the Copyediting-L and Techwhirl discussion groups, has convinced me that Word is used by—or at least familiar to—most writers and editors. I have no objections to other software; I just prefer to teach what I know well and what will be of use to the greatest number of editors.

However, not everyone uses Word, and we sometimes face the challenge of having to work with authors who use different software. Word-Perfect, for example, remains popular with home users, in law offices, and in some government offices; in contrast, Adobe's FrameMaker and Mad-Cap's Flare are popular among technical writers who are responsible for long, complex manuals. The open-source movement has given us OpenOffice and its cousin Libre Office, a suite of tools that is still playing catch-up with these older programs, but that is catching up fast. Last but not least, programmers, some Web designers, and other power users prefer powerful text editors such as BBEdit for the Macintosh or a version of emacs, which is available for most operating systems. (Search the Web using the keywords *emacs* and *download*, followed by the name of your operating system, to find a range of options.)

This diversity is problematic because the notion of a computer *standard* is oxymoronic: even where standards nominally exist for file formats, they may be dishonored more often than they're honored. As a result, whenever we use different software than our authors use, there's no guarantee we'll be able to exchange edited files without creating problems that range from minor annoyances to significant issues. The ideal solution is to use the same software our authors are using, in which case all the tricks I've described for Word in this book should work, *mutatis mutandis*.

Unfortunately, we can't always use the same software as our authors. But with a little creativity, we can often use the solutions I described in Chapter 12 to cover a wide range of situations. As a rule, if we can convert the author's information into a format our word processor can recognize, we can edit it using that word processor's revision tracking tools. If the author can then review our edits and save the results in a format that their software can recognize, so much the better. If not, the tricks I've described in this book will at least let us edit faster and more accurately, while clearly communicating our edits to the author.

When none of the options in Chapter 12 are available, we may need to resort to desperate measures. Sometimes we can ask for a PDF file and use its search tools to impose consistency on the text, then record our comments in the PDF (for relatively simple editing) or in our own word processor (for more complex edits). We can even annotate the PDF file itself using the built-in tools or more sophisticated commercial software. (I'll discuss editing of PDF files in Chapter 16 in the context of proofreading.) Once the file is in PDF format, we can even export it in RTF format so we can open the file in our word processor. *In extremis*, we can always print the manuscript and edit it on paper. But it's a rare situation that would call for this latter approach nowadays.

In this chapter, I'll discuss some last-ditch strategies you can try when all else fails. As you'll see, these are cumbersome and slow compared with modern revision-tracking tools. Before resorting to these measures, have another look at Chapter 12 and ponder how you might use the techniques in that chapter to edit more efficiently. But if you're still stuck, try some of the tricks in the present chapter. I'll briefly discuss the most common incompatibilities, and some ways of solving them, then I'll conclude with some last-ditch solutions: one set for text and the other for graphics.

Incompatibilities Abound

Though there's been much progress since the 2nd edition of this book in overcoming incompatibilities between programs, there's still no universal method for exchanging files between programs without losing any formatting or tracked revisions. HTML, XHTML, and XML probably come closest to a standard format, since the importance of the Web has made it essential for all software developers to let their customers create such files. As a result, you can usually exchange files between otherwise incompatible programs by saving the information in one of these formats, then using the methods described in Chapter 12 to edit the files in your word processor.

Unfortunately, standards for HTML and its related formats evolve over time, and software companies differ in which standards they support and how well they support them. Moreover, there's no standard way to track revisions in such files that works across programs. The HTML format doesn't support all the features offered by word processors and desktop publishing software (e.g., footnotes). XML shows more promise as a standard because of the tight control that document type definitions (DTDs) provide over the content and structure of XML documents; consider standards such as the Darwin Information Typing Architecture (DITA) and the DocBook group's standard, for instance. Needless to say, Microsoft has created its own variant of XML for its Office family of products, thereby continuing their long tradition of partial compatibility. Nonetheless, consider Chapter 12's advice on working via the HTML or XML formats before you try the advice in this chapter.

You'd expect semi-proprietary (thus, controlled) formats such as Microsoft's .docx (Word) and .rtf (rich text format) to be somewhat standardized, but that may be more of a fond wish than a reality. When I was first researching this book, I sent two experienced editors a file I'd edited in Word and asked them to review my edits and add their own in WordPerfect; I also asked them to send me a wholly new WordPerfect file containing comparable edits so I could review their edits in Word. The results, both in .docx and .rtf formats, were not reassuring: there were enough differences that it didn't seem safe to exchange files created in different programs. One or two conversions between programs seemed safe, but if you're going beyond that number, *caveat redactor*! (Since the 2nd edition of this book, I've seen similar problems with files created in OpenOffice and edited in Word, or vice versa.)

Bottom line? If you plan to work frequently for a particular author, you may have to resign yourself to purchasing a copy of their preferred software. Sometimes a client (especially a large corporation) purchases a software license for more copies than they have employees, and you may be able to borrow a copy while you're working on their projects. So long as you don't keep the software or use it for other clients, this should be legal, but ask the client to confirm whether their license covers such use.

If we need to work in a different word processor than the one our author is using, we must carefully test how well our edits transfer and then develop workarounds for any problems. (Producing a PDF file that shows the tracked changes is a good way to accomplish this, since Adobe controls the specifications for the PDF format quite well.) We must also be unusually rigorous in our backup procedures so that if a file becomes corrupted or damaged by repeated transfers between programs, we can revert to a previous version and try to solve the problem. (Appendix I provides details on developing a sound backup strategy.)

Building a software library: Accumulating a software collection isn't impossibly expensive. Companies often offer competitive upgrades to tempt you to abandon your old software. If you own their competitor's software, they'll sell you their software for a large discount. If you're a teacher or full-time student, you can obtain inexpensive educational versions of most programs. (However, you may be unable to upgrade an educational version to a full version. Check the license conditions carefully before you buy!)

Last but not least, it's helpful to learn a few survival strategies that are the modern equivalent of communicating using clay tablets and cuneiform: the communication still happens, but not easily or elegantly. With that discouraging image in mind, here are some potential solutions.

When Revision Tracking is Unavailable

The first goal of revision tracking is to ensure that the meaning of our revisions is clear; thus, the changes must be easy to see. (Ideally, they should also be easy to review and to accept or delete, but the indispensable minimum is that they're clear.) To accomplish this goal, all we need to do is find some form of highlighting that will survive the transfer between programs. However, not all forms of highlighting are equally effective.

Standard text formatting such as boldface, italics, and underlining transfers well between any two word processors I've tested. Thus, an obvious solution would be to identify our edits using these formats. (For cases in which the author uses boldface and italics for other legitimate functions, such as identifying headings and non-English words, adding the rarely used underlining format will distinguish our edits from those uses.) This is efficient for us because there are simple keyboard shortcuts for all three formats: Control/Command+B for boldfacing, Control/Command+I for italics, and Control/Command+U for underlining. You can type these keystrokes before you begin typing new text, or select text (using any of the shortcuts in Chapter 5) and then apply the format. These formats stand out clearly both on the screen and in print, and it's easy for the author to remove them once they've reviewed our edits.

Because both formats use the same color as the rest of the text, they're less easy to see than they could be. Moreover, in documents that already contain large amounts of boldfaced or italicized text, even adding underlining doesn't greatly improve the situation; worst of all, it can be difficult to clearly distinguish our formatting from non-editorial uses of these formats. In that case, it may make more sense to enhance these formats by applying a color to the text. Colors seem to transfer well between some programs. The main drawback is that applying colors to text can require repeated trips to the software's menus or toolbars, or multiple keystrokes. To solve that problem, record a macro that applies all of the desired formatting changes in a single step, then define a keyboard shortcut to invoke the macro or add it as a button in the Quick Access toolbar (Word 2010) or in a custom editing toolbar (Word 2011). See Chapter 11 for details on recording such macros.

The main downside of this approach is that it makes the author's life more difficult: removing the formatting after reviewing our edits can take a lot of steps if they don't know how to create their own macros to remove the applied formats in a single keystroke or click of an icon. Since this chapter assumes that we're using incompatible software, we don't have the option of sending them a macro that would do the work for them. As a result, we must instead teach the authors how to cope with what we've done: for example, we can provide instructions in our cover letter when we return the edited manuscript.

Beware the highlighter marker! Many editors like to use Word's highlighter marker tool to emphasize their edits (see Chapter 6 for details), but that formatting may not transfer successfully between programs. Moreover, you may need to teach authors how to use this feature. Many authors never encounter this tool (in Word, in the Ribbon's Reviewing tab), and have no idea how to remove highlighting. (None of the usual methods work. You have to use the marker tool.)

For a slightly more sophisticated approach, we could create custom character styles (see Chapter 4) such as *Insertion* and *Deletion*. The definitions for these styles can apply any kind of formatting permitted by the software, including a combination of boldfacing or underlining with a color. Style names generally transfer successfully between programs, so this approach is worth trying. Once again, we can bind these styles to a keyboard shortcut or a toolbar icon so we can apply them efficiently during editing. And the author can use search and replace to delete all text tagged with the *Deletion* style if they agree with the deletions. But we'll need to teach the author how to remove the style from insertions and deletions they didn't accept after they've reviewed our edits. If the modified text doesn't include any formats such as boldface and italics, there may be a feature that removes the formatting and restores the surrounding paragraph style in a single keystroke; in Word, that's Control+Shift+Z for Windows and Command+Shift+Z for the Macintosh. This is efficient because it's a single keystroke, and it's easy to learn and use.

Could we use revision tracking to make our lives easier even if the author's software won't recognize this formatting? More importantly, could we do this without making the author miserable? *Maybe*. The answer depends on whether we can figure out what kinds of formatting *will* transfer successfully between our software and the author's software. For example:

- First, use the revision-tracking tools to edit the manuscript.
- Second, use a macro to accept each edit and apply an appropriate format (e.g., boldfaced + underlined) in a single step. Here, "appropriate" means a format the author's software can reliably recognize.
- Third, save the document in a format (e.g., .rtf) that preserves the edit formats and that the author's software can read correctly.

If your software and the author's software can understand each other's footnote and endnote codes, these codes offer another communication option. Typing comments and editorial suggestions into notes separates them from the text, so you don't create puzzle sentences from an uncomfortable mixture of the original text and your edits. This also ties the comments to the correct sentence so that authors don't have to hunt for the location of each change. Authors can usually set their software to display the notes in a separate window or in a separate pane of the document window. This lets them simultaneously see both the original text and your comment, and they can resize and reposition the two windows or panes to suit their preferences. Moreover, they can copy and paste text from the notes to save typing, and can delete the notes as soon as the comments have been addressed. Last but not least, opening the notes window will reveal any undeleted notes that haven't been addressed.

This approach won't work if the manuscript already contains many footnotes because it becomes difficult for authors to separate your comments from the real footnotes. There's also a risk that real footnotes will be deleted by mistake or that some editorial notes will be missed and remain in the final publication, embarrassing everyone. That being the case, if you try this approach, someone must take responsibility for confirming that all editorial notes have been removed and that none of the author's notes have disappeared. This can be a significant challenge in footnote-heavy academic texts; on the other hand, academic authors will rarely use nonstandard software that doesn't provide some form of revision tracking.

It's hard to imagine a situation in which none of these techniques will work. About the only situation I can think of arises when working with programmers and Web designers who insist on writing their code in specialized text editors that permit no formatting other than what's possible using markup tags such as those used in HTML. Though we could use the approach described in Chapter 12 for editing HTML documents to edit the file in Word, such clients are often militant in their refusal to use Word. If we can't persuade them to abandon their principles for the sake of efficiency (usually a compelling argument), we have to encode our edits so that they're both easy to see and easy to understand. In the next several sections, I'll provide some relatively painless ways to accomplish this.

Inserting and deleting text

As I noted in the previous section, it's hard to imagine situations in which the techniques in Chapter 12 won't work. Still, in the interest of completeness, I've retained a shorter version of this section from the 2nd edition of this book. Should you encounter a situation in which you need to use these suggestions—perhaps you've been hired to edit cell phone text messages before they're sent—send me details. I'll include them (with a note of thanks to you) on the Web site and in the 4th edition of the book.

So: let's assume, for the sake of argument, that we need to identify our edits using only the keys available on the keyboard, with no formatting permitted. A simple but effective approach relies on a standard set of character pairs, such as [and], to bracket our edits, thereby making them easy to see—or to find if you're using software that provides a search function. If you're working with the aforementioned Microsoft-averse programmers, text editors, despite their other drawbacks, offer powerful search tools.

With a little effort, we can use such schemes to simulate the effects of using revision tracking. For example:

Before:	`This best of onscreen editing will depend on the author.`

After:	[Delete: This] [The] best [method] of on-screen editing [Delete: will] depend[s] on the author.
Result:	The best method of onscreen editing depends on the author.

Note that I have mostly replaced entire words rather than correcting individual letters. As I noted in Chapter 6, this is easier to read and work with both for us and for the author. However, it still creates a bit of a puzzle sentence because the author must pick through four changes and a comment before they can assemble the final sentence. For this reason, adding the final sentence (labeled "Result") that results from the edits is a kindness to the author because it spares them the effort of having to figure out what that result will be. However, it's considerably more work for us.

If several people will review a document, identify each reviewer so the author will know who to contact with questions about a revision or comment. To provide this information, simply add the reviewer's name or initials. For example:

```
[Change A to B.--Geoff]
```

Always identify such edits using characters that won't appear in the types of files the author is creating; this avoids confusion about which characters indicate our comments and which ones belong in the file. What characters these will be depends on the author's task; for example, don't use angle brackets (< >) in HTML files because these characters mark the start and end of HTML tags. When in doubt, ask the author what characters to use or avoid. For example, Word's VBA programming language uses a single quote (') at the start of a line to indicate that the line is a comment. Thus, when editing VBA text, we could insert lines beginning with a single quote to communicate our edits:

```
' Next line: delete "this"; replace it with "The".
' Is the word "method" missing after "best"?
' Delete "will", then change "depend" to "depends".
```

This requires more typing, but because we can copy and paste the original text, we won't have to retype any of the words we're retaining in our comment. Another advantage of this approach is that if the author misses any edits, they'll remain in the file as comments, where they'll do little or no harm. Since it's still necessary to ensure that all comments have been satisfactorily addressed, it's helpful to tag all comments with our initials or a word such as *Query* that the author can find using the software's search tools. For example:

```
‘ Geoff: Delete this comment when you're done.
```

This approach is suitable for light edits, when we'll mostly be inserting occasional comments rather than heavily revising the text. But even with help from macros or autocorrection tools (see Chapter 11 for details), this approach can be prohibitively time-consuming. Worse yet, as the previous examples show, we may create puzzle sentences or long series of instructions that are difficult for authors to decipher. Instead, try using a line break to place the original text on one line and the revised version plus any necessary comments on subsequent lines. For example:

```
This best of onscreen editing will depend on the
author.
‘ The best method of onscreen editing depends on
the author.

‘ Is "method of..." correct?--Geoff
```

This is an improvement over the previous example because the results of the edit and related comments or questions are clearer; in particular, placing the revised version immediately below the original makes it easier to directly compare the two. Moreover, if our edits are correct, the author can implement the whole series of changes by deleting one line (the original) and then deleting the comment marker from the replacement line. This requires only a few keystrokes—much easier than having to move the cursor repeatedly to several smaller edits and fix each one individually. Also note that I've taken my own advice in Chapter 7 and provided both the solution (the replacement wording) and an explanation of what the author should pay attention to. This slightly increases the burden on the author, since they must figure out what changes I made by comparing the two sentences, but the burden is much smaller than if the text appeared at first glance to be a long series of randomly inserted brackets.

This approach has another advantage—though it may not seem like one at first glance. If we break paragraphs to push the problem text onto a new line, and then insert our comment followed by a blank line, the resulting gap provides a clear visual indication of an inserted comment. The author need only delete the line breaks (¶) to restore the original paragraph. Separating the edits and comments from the original text in this manner reduces the risk that authors will inadvertently delete both our inserted text and some of the surrounding text when they respond to our edits. Best of all, the author can conclude their review of our edits by doing a global search and replace to eliminate the unnecessary line breaks: they will replace the single line breaks with a space (so the sentences don't run together) and the double line breaks with a single line break (to restore the original paragraphs). This requires only three easy steps:

- Globally replace the double line breaks with a placeholder such as ***.
- Globally replace the single line breaks with a space.
- Globally replace the placeholder (***) with a single line break.

Despite these advantages, the approach remains less efficient than using revision tracking, and raises an additional problem: Edits entered in this way are easy to miss because we rely on the author to use the search function to find and review our edits, and authors are notorious for missing things. (The most common cause: they double-click the Find Next button and skip past an edit.) As always, someone must ensure that no unaddressed comments or edits remain in the file for readers to discover.

We can make this process more efficient by obtaining permission beforehand to make certain types of changes without marking them. For example, most authors will let us correct obvious typos, provided we're aware of any unique spelling conventions in the author's genre. As always, ask the author for permission before making any change with potentially broad repercussions, and if you have any doubts, insert a comment that describes the proposed change and asks for confirmation that we made the right choice.

Because each of the approaches described in this section has advantages and drawbacks, I don't recommend any one approach exclusively. Different situations call for different approaches, or perhaps even a combination of approaches. In the next section, I'll present an alternative that may be the best overall solution for inserting lengthy comments. If you combine this approach with the approaches described in the present section for edits that require no explanation, you end up with something that resembles the revision tracking provided by word processors.

Inserting lengthy comments

Comments are a tool we can use to focus the author's attention on proposed changes that might escape their notice or that require justification or explanation of what we've done. In addition, some comments propose multiple options so the author can choose among two or more wordings. (I discuss the basics of commenting in more detail in Chapter 7.) Unfortunately, long substantive comments inserted directly in the text occupy considerable space and make the edited text hard to read: the comments may even be longer than the sentence they describe. In the kind of substantive editing that I do, I commonly insert dozens of such comments even in relatively short documents, and if I had to place these comments directly in the text, my authors would find the result an impenetrable mess. That being the case, we need a solution that is efficient for both editor and author.

My solution adapts a familiar convention used for footnotes and endnotes. Edits that require no explanation can be made directly in the text, as described in the previous section, but longer notes can be compiled in a separate document using numeric codes inserted in the text the comment describes. The process is as follows:

- In the manuscript, insert a number bracketed by special characters that won't appear elsewhere to indicate the comment's location. The result might look like this: [1] or >>1<<.
- Type the comment numbers in a second document. Type your comments after the numbers in this document; the document can be in any format, including your word processor's native format, so long as you can ultimately save it in a form the author can read. *Never* use the software's automatic numbering feature to number your comments, since deleting or inserting comments will force you to manually renumber all subsequent comments in the edited document to match the new numbers in the automatically numbered document.
- Copy longer chunks of the text that will become part of the comment and paste them into the comments you're writing, so you don't have to retype that text (e.g., to rephrase or reposition a sentence). Make the necessary modifications to produce a result the author can simply copy and paste into the original document to replace the problem text.
- When you finish your review, save both the manuscript and your comments in a format the author can use (e.g., text).
- Teach the author how to copy your corrections into the original document and make any required changes.

Again, someone must ensure that no comment markers get left behind. If you miss any, the worst embarrassment you or the author will suffer is the occasional mysterious appearance of a bracketed number in the text—but that's a considerable improvement over leaving a lengthy and perhaps critical comment for all to see.

Editing Graphics

The most obvious case when revision tracking isn't available arises when we're not working with words or numbers—that is, when we're editing graphics. Much of my work involves editing the graphics that accompany an author's manuscript. In such cases, word processors don't provide much assistance, other than as a repository for descriptive comments such as "change the line two inches down from the top right corner and one inch to the left of the right margin from medium blue to dark red and increase the thickness 200%". No matter how clear the description, that's much less efficient than the venerable on-paper approach of circling the problem in red ink and scrawling an illustration of the desired final version. In the rest of this chapter, I'll provide suggestions on how to edit graphics efficiently—an extreme example of things your word processor can't deal with well.

Graphics pose a different kind of editing challenge because (unless we have the same graphics software as the author) we can rarely edit them directly: images are not words, and the word-based tools we've mastered translate poorly to images. We face three main problems with graphics:

- We need to point at the problematic part of an image rather than trying to describe its location with words. Descriptions are too indirect and unobvious to communicate efficiently.
- Even if we understand graphics terminology, it can be difficult to describe many problems in words. If we lack that vocabulary, it's even more difficult to explain the problem. *Showing* is more effective.
- Unless the graphics were created using the word processor's graphics tools, it can be difficult to integrate our comments with the graphic.

If possible, use the same software: As in the case of word processor files, it's best to edit using the same software the author used. Even nominally compatible programs aren't 100% compatible, and using the same software eliminates most problems. If that's not possible, we can at least use compatible software to describe the problem's location and visually communicate the necessary changes. The author can then make those changes in their own software.

Fortunately, there are effective general solutions for each of these problems. Most often, authors or their graphic artist colleagues create graphics using special-purpose graphics software that accomplishes the task faster and better than the primitive tools provided by word processors. This approach also produces graphics files that are more suitable for printing or display on the Web. If we own graphics software that can open the graphic file, the most efficient solution is to insert our edits and comments directly within that file. (If we don't own that software, I'll present some alternatives later in this section.) None of the graphics programs I've used provides tools for tracking revisions and inserting comments, but each provides other options that can be equally effective. In any graphics program, the basic approach is the same:

- Specify the problem's location using pointers, such as arrows drawn using the software's tools. (If you create an arrow once, you can copy and paste it whenever you need to use it again.) This ties the comment directly to the problem, eliminating the need to describe its location.

- Copy, paste, and manipulate individual elements of the graphic to *show* what you mean rather than describing the proposed change. For example, copy a line and apply the desired thickness and color. This lets us use a precise visual image to communicate visual information; moreover, because the new image's properties are displayed by the graphics software, the author or their graphic artist can copy those properties instead of guessing.

- Rather than separating our comments and proposed solutions from the graphic, we can integrate the two in a single visual field.

The problems that arise when we work directly on an image are the same ones that arise in editing spreadsheets and databases, as I discussed in Chapter 12: we risk inadvertently modifying part of the image whenever we insert our proposed corrections, the author may inadvertently delete part of the image when they delete our comments, and some comments may be left behind in the graphic. There are two effective solutions.

First, graphics software often provides a *layer* function. Layers are the software equivalent of transparent acetate sheets laid over the image. Just as we can annotate the acetate without harming the underlying image, we can add an editing layer that contains our comments. We can also copy problematic elements of the graphic and paste them into the editing layer so we can modify them without affecting the original graphic. This approach lets us clearly explain things that can be explained with words using the software's text-entry tools, show the visual aspects of the problem and their solutions using the software's graphics tools, and relate both parts of the explanation to the problematic part of the graphic using an arrow that precisely identifies its location. For example:

Graphics software typically provides text boxes or frames to hold our comments, and lets us reposition those containers the same way we'd move a paper sticky note around a printed page. If the problem involves a change in position, we can extend the arrow from the element that must be moved to our recommended destination for that element. Because our annotations are contained in a separate layer, the author or their graphic artist can simply delete the entire layer after they've made the necessary changes. Some software also lets us define *non-printing layers*; the software ignores these layers whenever it produces a printable version of the image or an onscreen version such as the .gif or .png files used for Web graphics. This offers the additional reassurance that even if the artist forgets to delete the comments layer, our comments won't appear in the final graphic. Of course, the comments will still remain in the original file, so someone should take responsibility for removing them from the file once the corrections are complete.

The second option applies if the graphics software does not offer a layer feature. In that case, we can use the same approach I proposed for spreadsheets and databases in Chapter 12: ensure that all comments lie well outside the image area so they can't affect the image, and so the author can select and delete them without affecting the main image. For example:

		Can we use gray instead?

We can modify these approaches in a range of ways to make them more closely resemble traditional on-paper editing. For example, we can change the color of our comments to the red traditionally used for text edits, or to any other color that clearly differs from the colors used in the graphic. Similarly, we can change the background color of text boxes or frames to sticky-note yellow so they stand out from the graphic's background. Some software even lets us automatically distinguish our edits by offering named styles similar to those used in a word processor or a recordable series of actions like word processor macros. (If not, the scripting tools described early in Chapter 11 may let you accomplish this.) Using a style or a macro lets us format comments with a single click rather than having to manually change multiple characteristics of each comment. Alternatively, we can create a properly formatted comment once, then copy it, paste it in its new location, and revise the text to account for the new situation.

If we don't own graphics software or don't have time to learn how to use such software, Adobe Acrobat and other tools for working with PDF files can achieve an effect similar to that of layers. Because most software used to create graphics can generate a PDF version of the graphics, we can ask the authors to provide a PDF and then use PDF-annotation tools to add comments over the top of the image. (Most of the graphics on this book's Web pages were created this way.) Annotating a PDF file lets us point directly at the elements that must be changed and add a text explanation, but may not let us visually demonstrate a solution; we're forced to describe it in words.

Some authors use the tools provided by their word processor to create their graphics. This isn't the best choice because those tools aren't very sophisticated, and many publishers won't accept such graphics. The advantage of this choice, particularly if the graphic is created in a special *drawing layer* that's separate from the text, is that we can use the word processor's own graphics tools: type a comment into a text box in the drawing layer, move the text box to an appropriate position near the problematic part of the graphic, then connect it to the problem with an arrow.

If we need to describe a visual change, we can copy the problematic part of the graphic, then use the word processor's tools to make the desired changes in the copy. If the graphic was created using graphics software and inserted into the word processor's drawing layer, we can't copy individual parts of the graphic, but we can still use the word processor's drawing tools to create something that looks sufficiently similar to the problem element that we provide a good impression of what we want to achieve. The resemblance doesn't need to be exact; it only needs to be good enough that the author can *see* what we're trying to change.

If the graphics are finalized in graphics software and embedded in the word processor document (the most common case), we can't edit them directly, and it may be cumbersome to use the graphics layer to hold our comments. An easy but inefficient option is to simply type our comments in the manuscript next to the graphic. This forces us to describe the nature and location of the problem and its solution in words, which may be poorly suited to the task. Consider, for example, a description such as "the symbol that looks sort of like a squashed bug—one with six arms, not eight arms—roughly two inches down from the top left corner, and half an inch inward from the left margin, should be half an inch higher and slightly to the left, and in the same slightly lighter gray you used for the squashed bug with eight arms, not six arms"). Fortunately, we can simulate the effects of a drawing layer by creating a table that holds both the graphic and our comments. After inserting a table using the word processor's table tool, we can paste a copy of the graphic (often at a smaller size) into a cell in the table and add comments around it. The result looks something like this:

Comment for top left corner		Comment for the top	Comment for top right corner	
Comment for the left side	\	|	/	Comment for the right side
	—	*	—	
	/	|	\	
Comment for the bottom left corner		Comment for the bottom	Comment for the bottom right corner	

Note my use of simple keyboard characters such as forward and backward slashes, horizontal lines created using em dashes, and vertical lines created using the *pipe* character (|, which is located above the Enter or Return key on most keyboards) to point at the areas that contain problems. These characters can be centered within a cell, as I've done in this illustration, or aligned top, bottom, right, or left so that they point more directly at the problem. If none of the table cells precisely aligns with the problem, it's easy to split existing cells that lie near the problem into multiple cells until one of the new cells aligns more closely with the problem.

This works best for problems that lie near the edges of an image. Problems that lie closer to the image's center are more challenging. Fortunately, word processors that let authors insert graphics also let us *crop* the graphics (eliminate the irrelevant parts) until the problem lies at an edge or corner of the graphic adjacent to one of the table cells. For each such problem, we can repeat this process to create a simplified table that contains only a cropped copy of the graphic and a table cell beside the problem. Of course, when we crop graphics, we must retain enough of the surrounding visual context that the author can easily see which part of the overall graphic we're describing. For example:

Add a lobe?	Make this lobe bigger?	
|	/	
	—	Should we add a lobe on the left?
|	\	
Perfect!	Make this lobe smaller?	

Graphics created in spreadsheets or databases: For graphics created using the graphics tools in spreadsheet or database software, the solutions I described in Chapter 12 for editing text in these programs can be used if you have access to the same software the author used. If not, try the other solutions described in the present section.

For really complex graphical editing, it helps to have some basic skill with graphics software. Personally, I can barely draw a straight line even using the straight-line tool provided by graphics software, but that doesn't stop me from doing the kind of basic editing that I've described in this section. If editing graphics is an important part of your work, I encourage you to become as efficient with the necessary graphics tools as you are with your word processor. The fact that we editors are primarily word geeks doesn't mean we should restrict ourselves to words when it's time to edit the nonverbal aspects of a manuscript.

Editing Multimedia and Video

I'm not aware of any good solution for editing multimedia files such as Flash-based animations or actual videos. However, the approach I proposed in Chapter 12 (in the section *Edit Twice, Publish Once*) is helpful: adopt a traditional workflow in which the heavy editing and review is done before the multimedia is created. Most producers start by developing storyboards, whether on paper or on the screen. A storyboard is a series of graphics (often relatively crude sketches that provide only an overview of the final graphic) and associated text that help the designers visualize the sequence of images and the narration that will accompany them. If the storyboards are produced on paper, which is rare nowadays, they can be scanned into PDF format and you can use standard PDF annotation tools to provide comments. If they are created using a word processor, in a table that presents the image in one column and the accompanying text in the other column, you can use the word processor's revision tracking tools to edit the text, and the techniques described in this chapter to edit the graphics.

I've used this approach with considerable success to design, edit, and revise various forms of instructional video. In most cases, the original storyboard was developed in Word, in the form of a table. In one example, the first column of the table provided a description of the information that would be presented in a given scene, and the second column presented our graphic artist's sketch of the proposed screen layout. In this approach, I could use all of the revision tracking and related tools provided by Word to edit and comment upon the information and the supporting graphics.

Chapter 14. Using the Internet to Improve Your Editing

Web: http://www.geoff-hart.com/books/eoe/eoe3/eoe3.html
Note: Word 2010 is for Windows; Word 2011 is for the Macintosh

In this chapter, I'll depart from my focus on editing using a word processor to discuss things we can do on the screen that don't actually involve editing—but that clearly support editing by answering the questions that inevitably arise while we work. If we're already working on the screen and using onscreen style guides and style sheets, it's not much of a stretch to extend those tools to include the wealth of editing resources available via the Internet. Note that when I use the word *Internet*, I'm not restricting the meaning to Web sites; I'm also including the communities of experts in editing and other subject areas who create the Internet and form its discussion groups. In many cases, humans are the greatest resource of all.

Having spent more than a decade with a high-speed connection, my Web browser constantly ready to respond to queries, I can't imagine going back to paper-only research—and I say that as someone with more than 20 dictionaries living within 10 feet of me, and two bookshelves full of textbooks and other reference materials. Nonetheless, the Internet's research tools greatly improve my editing quality. In this chapter, I'll show how it can do the same for you.

> **Switch to high speed:** Still using a dial-up connection? Switch to a high-speed connection as soon as one becomes available. The two main options are a DSL line from your phone company and a connection from your cable company. (Cable connections tend to be faster and more reliable, but this varies among service providers.) In remote areas, satellite Internet is an option, but tends to be expensive. If you spend enough time online to need a second phone line for phone calls, the cost of a high-speed line is easy to justify.

A Word on Credibility

Internet resources vary in their quality. If your research is important, don't accept the first plausible-seeming answer you come across. The great thing about the Internet is that millions of people freely contribute their knowledge; that's also a bad thing, since many of these people are not qualified to pronounce upon the subjects in which they claim expertise.

Look for the bias: Humans aren't the most logical, objective beings. Anything we communicate is affected to some degree by our hopes, fears, and conscious and unconscious biases. Remember this when you assess the quality of information. Always ask: "What agenda or bias might this source have?" Biased information is not necessarily useless, but recognizing that bias or agenda lets you consider how it might affect the information you find.

As a general rule, prefer sites with clear, rigorous editorial policies for controlling information quality. Dictionary and encyclopedia publishers are not perfect, but they try harder than most. Peer-reviewed journals are a good source of information if you can access their content; most require payment or membership in a group. Government Web sites are also generally credible, since most have full-time editorial staffs and (for the science and medical sites) a peer-review process for additional safety. Standards organizations are similarly reliable, since the material they publish has been subjected to careful, long-term scrutiny. For product information, the manufacturer's Web site is generally a good bet, but many discussion groups provide an unofficial story that the manufacturer won't admit publicly.

The second tier of quality includes university and professional association Web sites. University researchers tend to be experts in their subject, and careful about what they say because they know their colleagues are watching. Nonetheless, universities exert surprisingly little control over what their staff publish, so it's wise to confirm a professor's opinion using other sources, just in case you've found someone with an agenda or significant bias. (University researchers are human too.) Though professional associations are a great source for knowledge of their subject, they tend to be biased in favor of their profession, and often by internal and external politics. Again, a reality check never hurts. Respected authorities in a field (such as Alan Cooper for product design) often maintain Web sites that are great sources of knowledge. However, experts also have biases and preferences. Both university professors and experts from outside academia are also vulnerable to another problem: all interesting fields develop schools of thought, and the combat between rival schools can be intense. Being aware that the conflict exists lets you seek a reasonable middle ground.

The third and lowest level of quality includes Web sites published by individuals with unknown or dubious credentials and the discussion groups in which these and other people participate. You can obtain an enormous amount of high-quality information from these people, since not all experts are festooned with credentials and diplomas—but you'll have to sift through the information carefully to identify the good stuff amidst the background noise. For all such information sources, apply a skeptical eye and seek confirmation. Don't rely on majority opinion unless it's got a solid foundation; the minority often sees truth more clearly than the majority.

One exception to these guidelines relates to what are known as *discourse communities*, which are groups of people who have developed their own jargon or ways of speaking about certain topics. In this case, the interest is not in how dictionary scholars and other experts believe a word should be used, but rather how the words are actually being used. For this purpose, discussion group and newsgroup archives are a useful source of knowledge on the language of that group, how they use that language, and how that usage has diverged from usage by other groups.

The three levels of quality are necessarily general, often overlap, and have exceptions. Communally developed Web resources such as Wikipedia are a case in point. Many articles in this encyclopedia have been written by the world's foremost experts, and have had their content continually refined by criticism and feedback from equally knowledgeable peers, but other articles have a more dubious provenance. The more factual and less political or emotional the article, the more reliable, but even then, you have to keep your brain engaged, looking for discrepancies.

The best advice I can give about using the Web as a source of knowledge is to keep your inner skeptic alert, and never blindly accept a single authority's opinion, no matter how credible, as the final word on a subject. If the opinion seems illogical or contradicts your own experience, seek confirmation. (That's particularly true for politicized topics, such as religion and history.) Two or more compatible opinions from credible sources will always provide more confidence than a single opinion.

With these cautionary notes in mind, how can we use the world's biggest, most eclectic library to improve our editing? In many ways, including:
* investigating word usage
* understanding a subject before we query the author
* consulting online reference material
* consulting online style guides

Investigating Word Usage

Dictionaries

Dictionaries are a beloved source of inspiration and knowledge; I wasn't kidding when I said that 20+ dictionaries lie close at hand, and an unabridged dictionary always sits beside me while I'm working—though it's usually buried beneath piles of other things. But printed dictionaries are limited: they're always a few years out of date by the time they're published, and no printed dictionary is ever truly comprehensive. Moreover, how could any word geek (i.e., any editor) settle for only 20 dictionaries when online resources are so much richer? For example:

- Acronym Finder provides more than 5 million entries for both common and obscure acronyms.
- BusinessDictionary.com provides access to more than 20 thousand specialized business terms.
- Dictionarynet provides lists of dozens of subject categories, each with links to one or more dictionaries.
- The "free online dictionary of computing" provides access to a growing repository of computer terminology.
- Merriam-Webster's unabridged and collegiate dictionaries are available online.
- OneLook has indexed more than 1000 dictionaries.
- Oxford Dictionaries' Wordnik Web site aims to discover "all the words and everything about them". It's off to a good start. Have a look if you've got good enough willpower to not lose half a day exploring.
- The United States Patent and Trademark Office provides a database of registered trademarks and pending trademark applications.

Unconstrained Web searches

If you're not sure how to specify what you're looking for, it's useful to start with a relatively unconstrained search that uses only basic terms related to the subject and then examine the results to see what results are appropriate; adding selected keywords from the results that appear appropriate will help to gradually narrow the results towards your specific subject. The *landing pages* for both Google and Bing (i.e., the pages you see first when you go to those sites) provide a bare-bones interface: a single field in which you type your search term and hope for the best. Both also provide an autocomplete feature that examines what you're typing and suggests similar searches that others have recently performed and that you can click to repeat. This feature often offers good suggestions that spare you the need to figure out your own search criteria. The feature is particularly good at detecting typos and offering to help you fix them; for example, searching for "even is you have money" prompts Google to ask "Did you mean 'even *if* you have money'?" Google's suggestions sometimes turn up profitable leads discovered by other searchers, particularly if you're not sure what to search for. For example, this feature has helped me confirm the spelling of many obscure Latin species binomials where I had only an approximate notion of the correct spelling.

Search the Web from Word: In Word 2010, the free simuSearch utility lets you search the Web (e.g., Google, Wikipedia) without leaving Word. Simply select a chunk of text, click a toolbar icon, and simuSearch sends the text to the selected search engine and displays the results in your Web browser. In Word 2011, this feature is baked into the software: select a word or phrase, and press Command+Shift+L (or Word menu > Services > Search with Google). This saves several keystrokes each time you need to find something; in my work, it saves scores of keystrokes per manuscript.

If you're trying to learn the meaning of a term, it's logical to type *define* or *definition* followed by the term you're researching and see what turns up. Search engines such as Google and Bing go beyond online dictionaries by offering definition searches that scan their entire Web database to find any instance of the search term that appears to be a definition. Even for unusual terms, the search usually finds multiple definitions, allowing you to examine them for differences and commonalities. If a definition search comes up empty, delete the *define* prefix and add related search terms such as *example, explanation, glossary, dictionary, illustration,* or *usage.* If you happen to know synonyms or related words, try adding those words to the search; many online sources compare and contrast related words.

If you're seeking guidance about how a word or phrase is currently being used, searching for this text will provide strong clues about modern usage trends. For example, Google and Bing both report the number of Web pages and other resources (e.g., PDF files) that contain the search term, so you can compare two variants of a word or phrase to see which one is most common (i.e., which one appears to be the most common usage). Since the majority isn't always right, you shouldn't accept such search results uncritically. The less-common phrase may actually be the better bet in certain contexts, such as a specific field of research, even if it's not correct in general use. Adding genre-specific search terms such as *deconstruction* and *criticism* will narrow the results to emphasize that specific genre context. As I noted earlier, the majority vote is important if you want to know how specific discourse communities use language. The criteria I proposed earlier in this chapter will help you decide which of the sources you find will provide the most credible advice for your specific context. Pay particular attention to whether spelling or usage exhibits regional differences, such as those between British and American English.

If you edit in more than one genre (e.g., sciences and humanities), you know that different fields often use the same word in different ways, and you'll need to screen your results to ensure that you're examining usage in the correct genre. For example, the fields of cultural studies and journalism use the term *criticism* quite differently. If you know the genre name, adding that name to your search can reduce the results of an overly productive search by including additional keywords that are likely to occur in that genre. You can also narrow the search by excluding words that are only or predominantly used in other genres (discussed in the next section).

The key to an unconstrained search is that it is iterative: you start with general terms and progressively home in on the specific context you're seeking. In the next section, I'll describe some powerful features that help you narrow your search more rapidly.

Searching within a long page: Many Web pages are thousands of words long, so finding the specific nugget you're seeking can take time. Your Web browser's Find tool will let you search within the page. For example, Firefox lets you start typing the search term and automatically jumps to the first instance of the term, and pressing a keyboard shortcut (Command+G on my Mac) then moves to the next search term. Find and Find Again options are usually available under the browser's Edit menu.

Constraining your search

So much information is now available online that only the most obscure searches will fail to turn up the information you're seeking. On the contrary, the more usual problem is that searches turn up far more hits than you can possibly examine. As I noted in the previous section, the solution is to progressively refine your search by adding keywords. But it's also important to be able to exclude keywords or insist on certain characteristics in the search results. Each search engine provides different options for doing this, and these options change unpredictably, so it pays to periodically revisit the online help for your favorite search sites to see whether they've added useful new options or changed older ones.

For example, Google's bare-bones landing page offers an unlabeled field in which you type your search term. This might lead you to miss the Images button at the top of the screen, which confines your search to images, and a Settings button at the bottom of the screen, which displays a menu that lets you modify the search settings (e.g., how its automatic suggestions function, the number of results per page). This menu also offers an Advanced Search option with many helpful tools:

- Find pages with lets you find pages that contain all of your search words, only exact words and phrases, pages that contain any of the search words, pages that don't include certain words, and pages containing a range of numbers.
- Then narrow your results lets you shorten the list produced by the search to include only certain languages, regions, publication dates, and specific file types.

Reverse image search: Sometimes, rather than trying to find an image, you already have an image but want to know what it is or where it's from. Reverse image search engines use the image as input and try to find its source. In some Web browsers, you can drag and drop an image into Google's search field, but if that doesn't work, the Loud Techie site provides a handful of alternatives.

If you want to access these options from the regular search page, so that you don't have to navigate among the fields in this complex dialog box, Google offers a range of search *operators* that accomplish the same results:

- Add quotation marks around a word or phrase to find only pages that include that exact phrase and spelling. (You used to accomplish this by typing + before a search term, but Google now uses that operator to search for Google+ pages.)
- Add a hyphen (which looks like a minus sign, thus "subtract these words") to *exclude* keywords and eliminate irrelevant results. (This option was not working reliably as I was revising this chapter; some days

it works, and some days it doesn't. Excluding words from a search is still available via the Advanced Search page.)

- If you need to search social media, the @ operator lets you find Twitter users and the # operator lets you find their hash tags.
- If you separate two numbers by two periods (..), with no spaces on either side of or between the periods, you can search for a range of numerical values.
- The * character acts as a wildcard (a placeholder), and functions similarly to the wildcards described in Chapter 8.
- Add the Site: operator before a Web address, and Google will only search within that site to find relevant information. That's particularly useful for searching huge sites such as Microsoft.
- Add inurl: or intitle: to find only results in which the Web page contains a word in its address (URL) or page title, respectively.

For example, if you want to learn about Charles Darwin's development of the theory of evolution, searching for *Darwin* and *evolution* will return more than 50 million results. Unfortunately, a great many of these will also include a discussion of creationism. Adding −*creationism* to the list of search terms produces a slightly more manageable half million results. You'll clearly need to add and exclude additional keywords to find specific topics within that sea of information. Tara Calishain's written a couple of helpful books you'll want to check out if searching becomes a major part of your editing work. I've included them in my bibliography.

The key in any search is to choose enough keywords relevant to your topic that you'll turn up mostly relevant results, without making your query so specific that you exclude relevant resources or find nothing. Finding an appropriate balance is particularly important early in a search, when it's not always clear what keywords will prove most useful. For example, search for *Geoff Hart* and you'll find my messages to various discussion groups and publications, but also information contributed by several namesakes; forcing the search engine to exclude a few words commonly associated with these people (e.g., movie producer, WYFF news) will eliminate most of their contributions and help you find more of my writing. Similarly, if you're seeking information on male deer (an older meaning for *hart*), I have nothing to say on the subject. Excluding *Geoff* and other keywords that I use a lot (e.g., editing) greatly narrows the number of unsuitable results you'll have to pick through.

Within any set of narrowed search results, look for specific categories of information that might help you further narrow your search. For example, if you need a highly technical discussion of a topic, look for search results that include peer-reviewed academic journals; the words that appear in the first few lines of these results or in the Abstracts of the papers will reveal commonly used technical terms that you can include to further narrow your search. Conversely, if you're seeking a layman's explanation, exclude these technical terms to find less-complex Web pages. The words used in the manuscript you're editing are often good choices; adding those words to your search terms will find manuscripts similar to the one that motivated you to search.

Understanding Before You Query the Author

When the facts or logic of a manuscript seem wrong, but we don't understand the subject well enough to pin down the problem, researching the subject can provide the knowledge we need to identify the problem or propose a solution. When that research doesn't reveal the solution, we can at least frame a more intelligent query that neither insults the author nor demonstrates our own ignorance. Difficult terms or concepts that are missing from a standard dictionary are often explained online by governments, encyclopedias, and expert sources, not to mention journal papers and other published expert material. Increasingly, this material includes scanned or electronic versions of books that have been made available by Google Scholar and other online services to support researchers. The tips provided in previous sections will help you home in on the most useful sources.

Encyclopedias are an excellent source of basic knowledge, and many classics such as the Encyclopaedia Britannica are available in free or subscription formats. The Wikipedia is a great place to obtain an overview of a topic and search for additional reference material. Once you understand the basic information, you can follow links in the Wikipedia article or search for keywords from the article to confirm, correct, or expand your understanding. This is an example of a broader rule, namely that it's often necessary to consult several resources. Some will be too technical or advanced; others will be too basic. But with patience, you'll generally find something at the right level of expertise or something basic that provides enough information that you can understand something more technical.

Don't neglect the possibility of joining relevant e-mail discussion groups that turn up in your search. Much though I love the Web's cornucopia of information, I still find that human experts are my best source of information. If you can afford to wait a few minutes or a few hours for a reply, a quick question posted in a relevant online forum will provide answers tailored to your level of expertise, along with useful links to obscure but important Web sites that only an expert would know about.

Netiquette (etiquette for the Web) suggests that rather than heedlessly interrupting a discussion, trying to get what you need, and never showing your face again, you should spend at least a few minutes observing how a group functions (usually by skimming recent messages in the archives) before asking your question. This decreases the odds that you'll commit some egregious social blunder and increases the odds that you'll get a useful answer. If you'll be asking many questions, consider joining the group and offering the benefits of your own expertise. (If you're a freelancer, this sometimes leads to new clients.)

A rule of thumb that applies to most communities, online or IRL (in real life), is that you'll be received more kindly if you first attempt to answer your own question, perhaps by searching a group's archives to see if it's already been answered and by trying other resources, before you ask someone to do that work for you. This will also help you phrase a focused question that is most likely to provide the targeted answer you need rather than vague generalities. Some groups are far more tolerant than others of dumb or poorly focused questions, but why take the chance?

Online Reference Material

Even the best printed references rapidly become outdated, but their online versions tend to be updated more frequently—both because updating online information is less expensive than reprinting a thick book and because the pressure to keep information current is stronger on the Web. There's no shortage of options. For example, most dictionary publishers have developed online resources to cope with the steady influx of new words, and compile these words until the dictionary's next edition is available. (This assumes that printed dictionaries and encyclopedias will continue to be published. With increasingly pervasive Internet access and with most people having access to a smartphone or tablet computer, the future of printed dictionaries is growing dim.)

Resources abound for just about any kind of reference material you might be seeking. Consider the following examples:

- The Teaching Tips site offers an eclectic gathering of "100 unbelievably useful reference sites you've never heard of", ranging from the eminently practical (online dictionaries, librarian references) to the just plain fun (e.g., *Roger's Profanisaurus*, "the ultimate swearing dictionary").
- For science editors, the BIOSIS Index to Organism Names is a great place to determine official internationally accepted names.
- The U.S. National Institute for Standards and Technology provides an excellent guide to the units of measurement used in the International System of Units (more formally, SI, the *Système Internationale*, but better known as the *metric* system).
- For quick access to the guidelines to authors for the world's peer-reviewed journals, use your favorite search engine to find the journal name plus "author guidelines" or similar keywords.
- Federal, state or provincial, and municipal government Web sites provide legislative, statistical, and other useful information.
- National, state, and provincial archives include all kinds of historical information. And the archivists themselves are a wonderful resource.
- Newspapers and other news organizations often maintain substantial online archives.

There are many more such sites, but I haven't made any attempt to list them; too many that interest me will bore you to tears. In addition, Web addresses change too fast for such lists to remain useful without active maintenance, and new sites are always being added, some of which are better than older ones. Nowadays, I find it easier to locate such sites through a Web search than to maintain a list of bookmarks that I must constantly update. If you prefer not to search, general reference sites such as Refdesk provide curated links to myriad useful references. If you work in a specialized field, search for the names of pre-eminent organizations in your field and visit their Web sites to see what reference material they offer or recommend to their members.

Specialized search engines: With a little persistence, you can find search engines optimized for specific searches. For example, Wolfram Alpha emphasizes calculations based on data obtained from statistical databases, but also has some interesting word and linguistics tools. ChemSpider lets you search for the structures of more than 43 million molecules. And speaking of specialized reference material...

Specialized Reference Material

Understanding the nature of the information you're seeking goes a long way towards helping you find that information, because there are specialized resources that support your search. Consider, for example, the common task of checking literature citations and bibliographic details in a manuscript that provides numerous references to an existing body of knowledge. While editing the bibliography, we may need to confirm every detail of the publication, or simply to confirm our suspicions of an error based on an oddity in the reference. (For example, authors who copy publication details from journal Web sites often forget to delete the footnote letters that follow the author names to indicate their affiliation, but an "a" or "e" sometimes looks like it belongs at the end of a name.) If we can't simply say that something looks wrong and ask the author to fix it, we can help the author fix the problem using appropriate online resources:

- The first and best resource is the actual published manuscript. Most publishers provide this information for their books, and most peer-reviewed journals provide at least the correct citation information on their Web sites. This is particularly useful for new manuscripts that you can't find anywhere else. But many publishers also maintain records on manuscripts that are long out of print, and are willing to provide accurate information because this increases the number of readers.

- Google Scholar can be an excellent resource, since (for example) it presents scans of the interior of many books. Amazon's *search inside the book* feature offers similar information for books enrolled in this program. To use this feature, find the book in Amazon, and scroll down to the heading **Inside this book**. For instructions on how to use this feature, click the **Learn more** link beside this heading.

- Look for large general library databases, such as WorldCat, the U.S. Library of Congress Online Catalog, and more specialized databases such as the National Library of Medicine's PubMed database.

- Major universities often provide full or limited access to their research library or online catalogue. Some even offer the most valuable resource of all: an *ask the librarian* link that lets you contact a human expert in literature searches, who can help you find what you're looking for. (Librarians aren't appreciated nearly as much as they deserve to be.)

- ERIC, the Education Resources Information Center, is a favorite resource for academic researchers. (They also offer an interesting thesaurus.) I've also had considerable luck using the Ingenta Connect service;

though you have to pay for access to the full text of articles, searching for titles and bibliographic information is free.

- The Internet Archive's Wayback Machine provides access to an eclectic collection, including old Web pages that have disappeared, in a range of formats.

- For out-of-print and antiquarian books, try online groups of booksellers such as Alibris and ABEbooks. For something really obscure, try the Antiquarian Booksellers' Association of America, which is home to experts at finding information in very specific areas. Since these people earn their living selling their services, don't expect a free ride; at a minimum, be upfront about whether you're intending to buy something so they can gracefully decline the opportunity to help.

If you can't find the original or a scan thereof, searching for citations of that manuscript often helps. Even an obscure reference is likely to have been cited by a scholar somewhere around the world. If you can find two or three citations that agree in all their details, you can be reasonably confident that those bibliographic details are correct.

If you can't find a specific publication or can find it but can't afford the price to buy access to it, try hunting for the author instead. Many authors have their own Web sites or can be contacted by e-mail, and most are happy to confirm bibliographic details. For current journal and symposium papers, you'll often find full copies on the author's personal Web site. Use this information cautiously, since it often represents *preprint* information rather than the final published text. Details may change by the time the manuscript is published.

Always verify your search results. Any resource, printed or online, may contain typos and other errors introduced during data entry, and as I noted earlier, not every source is equally credible. For example, library collections generally have tighter quality control than personal Web pages, though this is sometimes more true of large university libraries than of small local collections.

If you can't find specific details, your search results can sometimes confirm your suspicion that something is wrong and let you send the author a well-researched query. "I could not find any information about this reference in any library catalog or in a Google search" is a much more compelling statement than "please check this reference".

Online Style and Grammar Guides

After dictionaries, what could be dearer to an editor's heart than online style and grammar resources? Fortunately, a great many of both are available online. Herewith, a short and by no means comprehensive list:

Style guides

- Apple Publications Style Guide.
- American Medical Association style guide
- BBC News style guide.
- Chicago Manual of Style
- Council of Science Editors style guide
- *The Economist* style guide.
- International Committee of Medical Journal Editors style guide.
- Reuters Handbook of Journalism.
- Style guide for NASA history authors and editors.
- The U.S. Government Publishing Office style manual.
- William Strunk's classic *The Elements of Style*.

If you're doing academic or scientific editing, the home pages of key research journals in your field can also provide excellent resources. For a given journal, search for its name (in quotation marks so that the search engine will look for the whole name rather than individual words), plus keywords such as *author guidelines*, *instructions to authors*, or *manuscript preparation*. All the large journal and monograph publishers provide online guidelines for prospective authors. For example, the following publishers have their own Web sites, with links to all the journals they publish:

- Elsevier.
- SAGE journals.
- Springer-Verlag plus the former Kluwer Academic Publishers.
- Wiley (including Blackwell Publishing).

Many journals and commercial magazines also provide downloadable sample articles that you can use to reconstruct their preferred style when the style guide itself is unavailable or insufficiently precise. (As these style guides are often written by non-editors, unhelpful official style guides are more common than you'd expect.)

Grammar guides

- Appleyard, David: Lots of useful stuff, including a British-American glossary for those who work across dialects.

- Brians, Paul: *Common Errors in English Usage.*
- Capital Community College *Guide to Grammar and Writing.*
- Conjugation.com: A multilingual site for learning verb conjugations. This may be particularly useful if you work with authors for whom English is their second language and want to help them learn verbs.
- Oxford Dictionaries offers a concise guide to grammatical terms should you need to out-jargon an author.
- Purdue University's online writing lab offers a great list of online resources for grammar, including basic grammar lessons, a primer on article use, and summaries of the APA and MLA style guides.
- Rensselaer Center for Communication Practices "Resources for Writers" offers a concise but useful guide to the complexities of article usage, as well as summaries of APA and MLA styles.
- Straus, Jane: *The Blue Book of Grammar and Punctuation.*
- *The Tongue Untied.*
- University of North Carolina's Writing Center provides a great collection of resources for writers.

Most large universities have a *writing center* to help their students, and your local university may have its own collection of online resources. Have a look and see what's available! Maybe you can even obtain an invitation to teach at their center or a chance to recruit future clients.

The World's Biggest Library

The Internet is the world's biggest library—or perhaps the biggest flea market, given the dubious quality of much of what you'll find surrounding the occasional real treasures. The tips in this chapter are only an introduction to the many resources you'll find if you spend a little time thinking about the details of what you need to consult. My advice is to invest some time looking for tools that support your specific type of work. When you find a key resource, memorize the keywords you used to find it—or record the address somewhere safe, such as your Web browser's Bookmarks menu, your personal Web site, Pinterest, or Pinboard—so you can find it easily again. If you edit in a wide range of genres, you may not have time to maintain this list of resources. In that case, record the list of search terms that brought you to the site for future use.

Despite the wonders of the Web, the greatest treasures remain the communities of experts and amateurs who gather at Web sites, blog, tweet, and participate in e-mail discussion groups. The Copyediting-L discussion group is a particularly great resource for editors, and if you're a member of the Society for Technical Communication, check out their Technical Editing special interest group. Comparable groups exist for most professions. Though no list of groups is ever complete, Google and Yahoo both curate large lists of discussion groups.

Last but not least, don't neglect a great traditional but now under-appreciated resource: your local librarian. Not everything meaningful is available online, and sometimes it helps to have an older librarian who still remembers the value of printed matter and other ancient technologies help you with your research. For example, enormous quantities of information are available on microfiche (e.g., newspaper archives) and are not yet available online—and may never be moved online, despite heroic efforts around the world to digitize everything that can be digitized.

If you don't have a local librarian, consider contacting the American Library Association, its Canadian equivalent (Library and Archives Canada's Ask Us a Question service), or the equivalent in other countries for assistance. Or try an online version: the British Library's Ask-a-Librarian service or the U.S. Library of Congress' equivalent. Most large universities and most national libraries around the world offer a comparable range of services.

Needless to say, since these are people rather than Web sites, try to solve a problem yourself before you take advantage of their services, and if you do ask them for help, treat them with the respect and gratitude that they deserve.

III. Identifying and Overcoming Barriers

Chapter 15. Developing Safeguards

Web: http://www.geoff-hart.com/books/eoe/eoe3/eoe3.html
Note: Word 2010 is for Windows; Word 2011 is for the Macintosh

In onscreen editing, as in on-paper editing, we must safeguard our work. We may no longer need to worry about the dog eating our homework, but the cat may still knock over a coffee cup, flooding our new laptop and electrocuting our hard drive. Toddlers may not be able to insert slices of processed cheese into the CD or DVD drive, but they can still knock the computer onto the floor, and pet hair can accumulate inside the ventilation system until the fan grinds to a halt, the computer overheats, and we end up with an expensive doorstop. Let's not even mention viruses, trojans, and the other computer malware that infests the computer world.

But sometimes, the most obvious hazards are the many ingenious ways that legitimate software can ruin our day. Indeed, with commercial software that itself sometimes seems just a step or two above a virus, working on the computer can seem riskier than working on paper.

Computer security basics: If you're exchanging files with authors, the minimum computer security you should implement is a firewall (which keeps would-be intruders from invading your computer) and antivirus or anti-malware software (which keeps out viruses and other nasties). Because the threat evolves so rapidly, I can't hope to keep you up to date on the best options. If you're not a geek, you can't go wrong sticking with a proven solution such as the Bitdefender family of products. If you want more control over your defenses, the AV Comparatives Web site provides detailed test results for currently available options for both Macintosh and Windows.

If you've ever spent a day cursing your computer, it's easy to forget that *any* editing process contains opportunities for disaster. I've experienced, seen, or heard of problems even with traditional "safe as banks" on-paper editing. Manuscripts have been stolen, damaged by teenagers during a house party, destroyed by fire or a malfunctioning sprinkler system, drowned by an end-of-day mug of beer, thrown out by the janitor or a malevolent colleague (or the editor, though that's not how the story is told), misfiled by the boss or a secretary (or perhaps the editor?), forgotten somewhere public (usually a coffee shop, library, or commuter train), and yes, even eaten by the dog!

Onscreen editing has its own potential catastrophes, including the aforementioned, and you need to take appropriate precautions: keep a copy of your files somewhere you can easily recover them if the originals are stolen or damaged, keep liquids far from valuable electronics, keep pets out of your office (or, more realistically for those of us who are domestic servants to our pets, keep them off the computer), and pay attention to what you're doing. In this chapter, I'll help you develop an editorial routine that protects you from the perils of modern technology.

Make Ongoing Backups of Your Files

When you start work on a manuscript, retain a copy of the original file and work on a different copy. If worse comes to worst, you haven't been making good backups, and your work file is damaged or lost, you can always start over from the beginning. If you mess up something (e.g., via an injudicious global search and replace operation), you can use the original file to help you undo the damage. If you're working on a long project such as a book, where loss of or damage to the file would require you to repeat a prohibitive amount of work, ask for permission to break up the project into individual chapters to limit the risks created by damage to any one file.

Computers tend to be quite stable nowadays, but that doesn't mean they're foolproof. If your computer has shown any signs of instability, or if you're on a tight deadline and can't afford having to redo work if an accident happens, don't wait until the end of the day to make backups of your files: make ongoing backups. Every hour or so, or each time you take a bathroom break, create a manual backup of your word processor file. Should something unpleasant happen to the current version of the file, you can return to the most recent backup copy and try to figure out how to solve the problem. Here's a simple, standard work routine that doesn't take much effort but provides strong protection against loss and damage:

- Before you start work on a manuscript, make a backup copy of the original file (e.g., Hart--original.docx) and work in a different copy.
- At regular intervals (every hour, or whenever you take a break), duplicate the file and give the duplicate an informative name. For example, *Hart-1.docx*, *Hart-2.docx*, and so on. To duplicate Windows files, right-click on the file's icon and select Copy, click somewhere else in the window, then right-click and select Paste. To duplicate Macintosh files, right-click the file's icon and select Duplicate.

- Copy the file to a storage device (e.g., a USB flash drive) that you can remove from the computer and store somewhere safe at the end of the day. For additional security, e-mail a copy of the file to yourself. Even if your computer is stolen or destroyed, that copy will be available via your mail provider's Web interface.

- None of these copies does you any good if your computer is stolen, destroyed in a fire, or goes the way of all flesh and shuffles off to meet its maker. Consider using an off-site storage solution such as Dropbox that can be configured to automatically copy your files as you work.

If this strikes you as too much effort—and it won't after you've lost your first file—at least turn on some of the automatic protections afforded by your software. I've described several of these options in Chapter 4, and provide a detailed solution for backups in Appendix I. In addition, there are some long-term backups you should make:

- Don't erase old backups before the author has approved your final edits. Ideally, wait until the manuscript has been published.

- Archive these files for at least a year after publication. Storage space is cheap, and clients occasionally lose their copy of a file to accidental deletion, a computer failure, or a virus. Several of my clients have been very grateful I could provide a copy of their old manuscript.

- Magnetic storage is fragile, even today. Consider making a physical copy (e.g., a CD or DVD). Store it somewhere far enough from your computer that you're unlikely to lose both simultaneously. Ideally, choose a different building, but at a minimum, store it far from the computer in a location that won't flood.

The last option may seem old-fashioned, but it offers an advantage none of the other backups provides: once a CD or DVD has been created, its contents can't be modified by a virus or by the increasingly frequent "ransomware" that will encrypt your files and make them unreadable until you pay a ransom for a key that can be used to decrypt the file.

Obtain a Backup Computer

If aliens abducted your computer for nefarious purposes two days before an urgent deadline, what would you do? If your answer is anything other than "be up and running again in 2 hours", it's time you developed a disaster plan. A more realistic scenario is that your computer simply dies without any warning. What's *my* plan? Glad you asked. I periodically use software to *clone* my computer's hard disk to an external hard drive. A *clone* is a complete copy of your hard disk that you can use to restore your working computer if its hard drive fails. Once you install a replacement hard drive, it typically takes less than an hour to copy the clone to the new hard drive. For Windows computers, consider Acronis True Image; for the Macintosh, consider Carbon Copy Cloner or SuperDuper. There are many other options.

Build flexibility into your schedule: If you live more than half an hour's drive from the nearest computer store, you might need to order a replacement computer by overnight delivery. That potentially represents a day in which you're without a computer. Wherever possible, try to build a day of flex time into your schedule to cope with such disasters, not to mention occasional sick days when those mollusks you ate at the clam shack didn't digest as well as you'd hoped.

In an emergency, I can connect that drive to my old laptop, boot from the hard drive, and all the necessary software will already be installed and working. This will keep me going until I can order a replacement. Of course, that won't help if I lose the entire computer. But there's a solution for that problem too:

It's tempting to discard your old computer when you upgrade, or sell it for next to nothing, but that can be a false economy. Older computers usually can't be sold for enough to repay our time—particularly if you consider the time it takes to advertise the computer, deal with phone calls or e-mails, and scrub the hard drive to remove your confidential information. If you're self-employed, consider the advantages of keeping your old computer for a backup:

- You have a stable, proven system you can use to work productively. It may not be as fast as your new system, but it's probably fast enough.
- You can switch to it in the time it takes to haul it out of the closet and plug it in.
- You can't argue with the price.

If your old computer can no longer meet your needs, consider purchasing someone else's old computer. I've purchased many capable computers for my kids for less than $200. A particularly good time to look for old computers is right before the school year begins or after Christmas, when many families upgrade their kids or themselves to a new model and no longer have room for the old one. If you live near a university, another good time is the end of the school year, when many foreign students are preparing to return home and have no economical way to bring their computer. For many, it's simpler to sell the computer, even at a loss.

Safeguarding a second-hand computer: Don't buy a used computer if it doesn't come with the original installation disks for the operating system. Even if you have your own copy you can install, it can be tricky to find all the hardware drivers needed to restore full functionality. Reinstall the operating system from scratch (reformat the hard drive), then run your anti-malware software to clean out any particularly stubborn viruses. (Some can infest the hard drive's boot sector and survive reinstallation of the operating system.)

Buying a backup computer isn't as expensive as it seems. Remember that you're a working professional, and are running a business. As a result, any expenses you incur to protect that business are tax deductions you can write off against your earned income. If you don't have an old computer and can't afford a new one, look for alternatives. Maybe a friend or family member has a spare computer they can loan you for a few days in an emergency. But as soon as you can, start setting some money aside as an emergency fund in case you need to replace your computer with little or no warning.

Update Your Software, But Not Too Frequently

It's easy to fall into a *status quo* mindset: your current software works well, so why risk destabilizing it with an update? The answer requires us to distinguish between *necessary* updates and merely *useful* updates. For example, if software is unstable and prone to crashing, then an update that fixes the instability is essential. In contrast, if the software mostly works just fine and the update only adds a few features of questionable value or fixes bugs we haven't yet encountered in features we never use, it's not worthwhile installing that update. Both Windows and the Macintosh can be set to check automatically for updates and either install them without supervision, or ask you for permission to do the install. The latter is generally a safer choice.

When an update is announced, research it using the search tips described in Chapter 14 to learn what problems the update solves. Then search for user experiences with the update (ideally in your favorite online editing discussion group) to ensure that it works as advertised and hasn't caused any major adverse consequences for those who upgraded. If you're not sure, wait a while until the developer has time to detect and solve any bugs.

Avoid the "bleeding edge": Those of us who are veterans of the early days of personal computing have learned that it's unwise to be the first to update our software, and that it's never a good idea to install version 1.0 of anything. The gruesome phrase *on the bleeding edge* describes those brave souls who feel obliged to always install the newest software.

Except for critical updates, it's generally safe to wait a few days before installing an update. This gives bolder individuals a chance to discover whether the update creates more problems than it solves. If any problems arise, the early adopters will report them to the developer. They will also complain loudly and at length in various online communities until the problem is solved. Such communities are therefore great sources of information about software updates. A discussion group for professional editors or writers is particularly useful, since its members will be using the same kinds of software and facing the same kinds of problems that you are, and such groups tend to be friendly, collegial spaces.

If you discover that there have been problems with an update, you can watch these discussion groups for reports that the bugs have been ironed out. If you must install a problematic update anyway—perhaps it fixes a crucial but broken feature or plugs a serious security hole—members of the community can provide advice on how to mitigate the risk or cope with any problems that result from the upgrade.

Back up your computer before major upgrades: If an upgrade borks your computer, you don't want to have to spend hours reinstalling everything and restoring all the computer and software settings. Thus, clone the hard drive before the installation, as described earlier in this chapter.

If possible, try to retain your existing copy of the software when you upgrade to a newer version. For example, most versions of Microsoft Office let you upgrade to a new version without erasing the old version from your hard disk, though you may need to check the installation options carefully to achieve this. (I currently have Word 2003, 2007, and 2010 on my work computer.) If you can't retain the old version, consider installing it on a backup computer if you have one.

The only exception to my advice to wait a bit concerns your antivirus and anti-malware software. Set this software to automatically download updates, but if it offers the option of not downloading complete new versions, that's a wise choice. Like all software, this category has had occasional problems in which installing a new version caused significant problems. But on the whole, it's better to be safe than sorry. The modern computing environment is too dangerous for working professionals to operate without appropriate protections. Macintosh users should also beware. Whether or not Macs were ever inherently safer than Windows computers, there's now enough Macintosh-specific malware out in the wild that Macintosh users shouldn't be cavalier about computer security.

Keep Confidential Information Confidential

Though most of us work on documents that are only truly important to the author, some of the information we may see is confidential and some special projects may require a high degree of security. In these cases, it's our responsibility to ensure that nobody but the author has a chance to see the information without the author's explicit permission. This is true, for instance, of legal documents, proposals written to secure funding, descriptions of trade secrets, patent applications, marketing plans, and sometimes even the results of scientific or technical research.

In these situations, the author is likely to be fully aware of the problem and should provide specific instructions on how we should handle the manuscript. Unfortunately, some authors are naïve about the importance of their manuscripts. Pay attention to what you're editing, and if you feel that the inadvertent release of this information (e.g., to a competitor) could harm your client, take appropriate precautions.

What are *appropriate* precautions? First, you'll need to protect the information both while it's on your computer and while it's in transit back to the author. For basic security that will keep out even moderately determined snoopers, it's sometimes enough to restrict access to your computer. Set your computer to require a log-in password, and if you're working in a context where many people wander by your office and might be tempted to snoop, set the computer to restrict access and require the password if it's been left idle for more than 10 or 15 minutes. This is usually done through the control panels (Windows) or preference panes (Macintosh) that control the screensaver settings.

Of course, this system is only safe if you choose a strong password and don't tape it to your computer for all to see. The strongest password in the world is useless if a thief can easily find it. A strong password should be at least eight characters long, should not be found in a dictionary, and should contain letters, numbers, and symbols such as the characters above the number keys. Since such passwords are notoriously difficult to remember, some experts recommend using a short and easily remembered phrase such as "my password sure is inscrutable!"; the individual words are easy to guess, but the password is so long it will take a prohibitively long time to guess or crack using software. (Needless to say, and thus needful to say, you shouldn't use that specific phrase.)

Word processors may let you set a file to require entry of a password before the protected file can be opened. For example, to do this in Word:

- **Word 2010:** File menu > Info > Protect document > Encrypt with Password > Encrypt Document. Enter the password, click OK, then re-enter the password to ensure that you typed it correctly. Click Save.
- **Word 2011:** Word menu > Preferences > Security tab. In the Password to open field, enter the password. Click OK, then re-enter the password to ensure that you typed it correctly. Click Save.

Don't lose the password, because if you do, you won't be able to open the file again. Software exists to crack Word's built-in passwords, but it's expensive, slow, and not necessarily reliable. Because sending a password by e-mail is about as secure as taping your house key to the mailbox, you'll need to consider alternatives for providing the password to the author. For example, you can send the encrypted file to the author, then phone them to communicate the password. For clients in other time zones or who don't speak the same language you do, you may need a more involved method, such as e-mailing the password to a different address than the one where you sent the file.

This protection may not be strong enough for truly confidential information. To protect the most important files during transit, you need to be able to encrypt them more strongly. Encryption works in a variety of ways, and is too complex a topic to discuss here in detail. The simplified version is that you encrypt a document by using specialized software to turn it into an unreadable code; you choose a password (called a key) when you encrypt the document, and that password must be provided before the software will undo the encryption and make the file readable again. Clients who need bulletproof security will tell you their requirements. For other clients, consider software such as the open-source AES Crypt software, which is free, available for Windows, the Macintosh, and Linux, and has a generally good reputation. Again, because this is quite sophisticated encryption, don't lose the password! Encryption that will stop your government's top spies from reading your confidential information will also stop *you* from reading it if you lose the password. You can also encrypt your entire hard disk or only parts of it, but if a disk problem develops, it may be impossible to recover the encrypted files.

Protect Yourself Too

Thus far, there's little compelling evidence that computer use inherently causes serious physical damage to our bodies, but there are a few caveats to that statement:

- We must be in good health to begin with, since any kind of prolonged sedentary, repetitive activity can exacerbate existing medical problems. Most of us are far too sedentary, and as we age, we may develop various health problems that computer use can exacerbate.
- We must learn how to set up a computer and work environment that will minimize the risk of injury.
- We must learn to take periodic breaks from our work, even when we're facing a tight deadline. Particularly then, since stress makes us more vulnerable to injury.

Appendix II provides a detailed description of the main steps you should take to protect yourself while you use your computer.

Chapter 16. Onscreen Proofreading

Web: http://www.geoff-hart.com/books/eoe/eoe3/eoe3.html
Note: Word 2010 is for Windows; Word 2011 is for the Macintosh

Many editors are asked to do what clients call proofreading—*proofing* for short. In the classical definition of proofreading, the editor reads through the page layout one last time to ensure that no errors slipped through the previous stages of production—stages that included, at least in theory, a thorough substantive editorial review and a detailed and intensive copyedit before the manuscript reached the layout stage. Proofing should therefore be relatively easy because rigorous quality control has already caught and fixed the most significant problems. In addition, we can use all the tools discussed in previous chapters to support the work, though there should be less work because of quality control in previous steps. (In this chapter, I'll emphasize new things to keep in mind for proofreading.)

Unfortunately, clients often request proofreading of documents that really require moderate or heavy editing. Worse, the client isn't prepared to pay for the time-consuming and expensive service required to produce acceptable quality or is too close to an immovable deadline to provide enough time for that work. As ethical professionals, we don't want to do shoddy work simply because there's no time or budget to do the job right. It's our ethical responsibility to report the problem and request instructions on how to proceed. If the client is unwilling or unable to provide time or money for an adequate edit, and we're willing to accept the work anyway, the methods in this book will help get the job done more efficiently than might otherwise be the case. In this chapter, I'll focus those techniques on the specific tasks of proofreading, including the tasks of proofreading PDF files and the unique challenges of proofreading online information (e.g., Web pages, online help files for software).

Deadlines versus "deadlines": Even the most "urgent" deadlines may be more flexible than they seem. The only way to know is to ask the client when they *want* the work done and when they *need* the work to be completed. The two dates differ surprisingly often.

Before I begin, I want to emphasize the importance of educating our colleagues and clients about the value of editing *before* a document goes to its final stages (layout and publishing) and about the importance of building enough time into their schedule to give us time to do our work. In more than 15 years of managing publication processes for government and private-sector organizations, one of the key lessons I learned was that you *can* teach authors and managers to follow a quality-control process and a schedule; this doesn't completely eliminate rushed last-minute editorial corrections, but it does greatly reduce their frequency.

Of course, some clients never learn, and a little judicious manipulation of reality can work wonders. For example, to deal with one colleague who was always 2 weeks late with their contribution for a newsletter, I moved up the deadline by 2 weeks; as a result, when their contribution arrived 2 weeks late, I still had plenty of time to deal with it.

It's also important to educate clients that if a manuscript isn't in its final form, calling the work *proofreading* is misleading. We have no idea what will happen to the manuscript during layout and production, so we have no proof these tasks will be performed properly. If the manuscript is not in proof form—its final version, as it will be published—it *cannot* be proofread. In the remainder of this chapter, I'll assume that we're in the happy situation of actually doing proofreading rather than a full edit.

Client education: Some clients don't understand the publishing process, and wait until the last possible instant for editing—and then call this emergency quality control *proofreading*. This is another example of why it's so important to discuss editorial work with clients until we fully understand what they're asking of us and they fully understand any tradeoffs implicit in this understanding.

A Word About Production processes

To understand how proofing relates to editing and how both tasks fit into the overall publishing workflow, it helps to understand the production process and its associated language. *Proofreading* means *to read [printer's] proofs*. Printer's proofs were traditionally produced by gathering (*setting*) slugs of lead type into blocks called *galleys*, inking the lead type, then pressing it onto paper. Because the printed page was produced from a galley of type and was used to prove (in the word's original meaning, *to test*) what the reader would see when the manuscript was printed, it was called a *galley proof*. Though production processes have changed dramatically, and lead type is no longer used, you'll still often hear proofreading described as checking galley proofs (*galleys*).

In modern printing, manuscripts are produced on computers, and setting type (*typesetting*) refers to the process of arranging text into its final layout in a word processor, desktop publishing program, or more sophisticated software. To obtain proof of what will eventually be printed, printers use the files created with this software to produce photographic film negatives on a machine called an *imagesetter* or *phototypesetter*, which resembles a laser printer with extremely high resolution. The film negatives are then used to generate photosensitive flexible metal, paper, or plastic printing plates that will then be used to transfer ink onto paper. Because film is much cheaper than printing plates and printing presses are expensive to set up and operate, printers save money by using the films as proof of what the printing press will produce. However, because film negatives are fragile, printers don't want to let them out of their hands; instead, they use the film negatives to produce *positives* by exposing special photographic paper on which the resulting text appears blue. The result is called, logically enough, a *blueline proof* or just *blues*. To ensure that the publication will be assembled properly, the blues are *folded and gathered* into a mockup of the final publication.

Because blues represent a photographically exact copy of what will appear on the printing plate, and because the plate represents an equally exact copy of what will eventually appear on the paper, blues are an economical way to predict what will eventually come off the printing press. If the plates are subsequently used to print an actual paper copy for the client's approval, this copy is called a *press proof* because it's proof (a test!) of what will emerge from the printing press. Modern production processes may eliminate some or all of these stages. For example, with digital printing, it's possible to produce the entire print run using a very-high-quality laser printer or inkjet printer. In that case, the first printout serves as the proof of what the other copies will be. There are also direct-to-plate printers that generate the printing plates right in the press, so again, the first copy that comes off the press represents a press proof.

Because most printing is now done from PDF files that have been prepared to a printer's exacting specifications, the aforementioned imagesetters can produce proofs directly from the PDF files. Because the PDF-based production process has been well established and carefully validated for decades, these printouts are an acceptable alternative to more expensive traditional proofs. Indeed, the PDF files themselves are sometimes treated as the only proof that's required. Because PDF proofs are not physical (*hard*) copies, they're often referred to as *soft proofs*. In my cynical opinion, *soft* also refers to a lack of rigor. I recently received a copy of a glossy, full-color magazine in which someone had clearly forgotten the difference between soft and hard proofs: a two-page spread with reversed type (white text on a black background) that probably looked fine on the screen was unreadable in the printed form. I'll come back to this point.

Many documents also include graphics, whether line art (images formed from solid lines of ink) or halftones (photographs, which are printed using patterns of dots with constant spacing but different sizes). For simple one-color printing, blues or high-resolution laser printouts are adequate for most proofreading needs because all we're looking for is accurate positioning of the lines and dots that make up the letters and images. Things become much more complicated in color printing, because we also need to confirm that the colors are correct (i.e., that no color shifts occur), and that the separate color plates are correctly *registered* (aligned so that the colors blend correctly to produce a crisp result). Depending on the printing process and our budget, we may be asked to check color laser printer, color key, inkjet, matchprint, chromalin, or other proofs.

This simplified description of the production process captures the essential details from an editorial perspective: our goal in proofreading is to look for errors in the computer files by examining the proofs, thereby providing a chance to fix any problems before the printer manufactures expensive printing plates or performs the even more expensive step of printing hundreds or thousands of copies of the final product on their press.

Online publishing (such as Web sites) is simpler: the documents are created on a computer screen, and will stay on the computer screen. Moreover, the process is essentially free because there's no cost to upload a corrected file. The cost of errors comes from the damage done to the publisher's reputation before they're discovered, and (sometimes) damage done to someone who loses information or is hurt as a result of following flawed instructions. We'll come back to online publishing in a moment.

How does this production process relate to the subject of this book, which is *onscreen* editing? First, almost all typeset material is now produced on computers, and transmitted to a printer as PDF files. This means we have the option of performing onscreen proofreading by examining these files instead of traditional proofs. Second, even if we will ultimately work with paper proofs or blues, we have an opportunity to spot major problems before the publisher wastes money producing those traditional proofs. These answers explain why the tools offered by onscreen *editing* are relevant in onscreen *proofreading*.

Of course, documents created on a computer are increasingly destined to be used exclusively on a computer. The most obvious examples are the online help files that ostensibly teach us how to use our complicated modern software and the Web pages we consult when the online help fails us. Proofreading these documents is a different challenge from what we do for printed materials: we still need to eliminate the typos and other errors we'd look for on paper, but we must also ensure that the final product displays and behaves correctly on the reader's computer screen.

One big difference in what we look for arises from how onscreen documents are created. In some cases, the author works in a **WYSIWYG** environment: what they see while they're writing is what readers will see when they open the files. In that case, production problems should be less frequent and less severe, because authors and editors should see them as they're writing and revising the document. Other production systems use compiler software to convert the text and images into a different file format; this is the case for PDF files, Flash movies, and online help files. In this case, the file that enters the compiler may look nothing like the file that emerges, and the compilation process can create significant errors with improperly prepared input files, particularly if the compiler is buggy. Further complications arise from the wide variety of screen resolutions and sizes in an increasingly mobile world that includes smartphones, tablet computers, and laptops.

Despite these differences, proofreading of onscreen documents is more similar to than different from how we proofread print documents: in both cases, the goal is to obtain proof that the information's audience will see exactly what we intend them to see. Thus, proofing includes all the editorial tasks we usually do, but performed at the end of a long production process that should have eliminated most errors before we begin. In addition, we'll be looking for a different set of problems, many of them created by the processes used to produce and publish the information.

In the rest of this chapter, I'll discuss how the techniques you've learned for onscreen editing can make you a more effective proofreader, whatever the manuscript's final format. In keeping with the overall theme of this book, I've assumed that you already know the rudiments of proofreading, and thus, I won't try to teach you those skills. Instead, I'll focus on how you can apply your existing skills to onscreen proofing. To learn proofreading basics, consult a standard reference such as *The Chicago Manual of Style*.

When Proofreading Resembles Light Copyediting

With a properly edited manuscript, proofreading should resemble light copyediting: most significant errors should have been fixed in previous stages. However, new problems can arise from the production process. Specifically, whatever form of proofs we've been given to check, they originated as a computer file. Because most desktop publishing and graphics software can now generate PDF files, and because most printing is now done from PDF files, this means that we can generally ask for a PDF file to proofread. For Web pages, we can instead view the files in our Web browser to check the appearance and behavior of the pages, and use the methods described in Chapter 12 to edit the files using revision tracking. If we own the same desktop publishing software used by the client, or editing software that works directly with that software (e.g., InCopy for files produced in InDesign), we can instead request a copy of the desktop publishing file. Alternatively, we can try to develop a process based on the methods described in Chapter 12.

Our goal is to treat these various file types the same way we'd treat old-fashioned galley proofs: we read them and look for the kinds of problems that inevitably arise when humans are involved. The advantage of using a PDF or a desktop publishing file in place of or in addition to a physical proof is that we can use all the onscreen techniques described in this book to improve our effectiveness.

If the document will be printed, it's appropriate to do at least some proofreading on paper. For example, I often print a copy of pages with graphics or with typical problem areas such as small text overlaid on a shaded background to ensure that they print correctly and are as clear on paper as they appear on the screen. (I'll discuss documents that will only be used on the computer screen, such as Web pages, online help files, and EPUB books, later in this chapter.) To *prove* that the printed publication will be correct, we need to inspect its final form—in this case, paper. (See the section *Replacing Printer's Proofs* later in this chapter for an explanation of when this may not be required.)

Even if it's necessary to proofread a printout from a PDF file, we can still use onscreen editing tools and strategies. For example, if we spot a misused word (e.g., a correctly spelled word that is the wrong word for the context), we can use the search function in the software we used to print the document to find all instances of that problem. If we need to describe a problem, we can use the annotation and commenting tools provided by Adobe Acrobat and Adobe Reader. These tools aren't as efficient and powerful as a word processor's revision tracking, but they work well enough for the light changes typically required during proofreading.

> **Editing in Acrobat:** Acrobat Professional permits substantive editing. If you create a tagged PDF file from Word, you can edit it using Acrobat's tools (which resemble Word's track changes features), and import the edits into Word. This eliminates the biggest problem with editing PDF files: the need to manually transfer the edits into the original file. See Adobe's Acrobat Web page "Importing and exporting comments" for details of how this works. However, it's not clear what advantage this offers over editing the files in Word in the first place. It strikes me as a solution in search of a problem.

Taking advantage of your word processor's tools

In onscreen proofreading, we look for the same things we'd look for in traditional on-paper proofreading: bad line breaks, awkward hyphenation, and inconsistencies such as headings that were accidentally formatted as body text. The key to performing these checks *on the screen* is that most of these problems can be found semi-automatically. For example:

- A spellcheck will spot typos faster and possibly more accurately than would be possible on paper. Each of us has blind spots (typos we're likely to miss), and spellcheckers have different blind spots. These blind spots complement each other, so combining our talents improves the result. As I noted in Chapter 10, a spellcheck should always be the last step in any edit, but that doesn't always happen.

- We can search for hyphens at the ends of lines to see whether a manually inserted line break is acceptable. (In most software, automatically generated hyphens, although visible, aren't actually present in the file, so we can't search for them.)

- We can use the search tools to improve consistency checks, as described in Chapters 8 and 9. For example, we can search for a given heading style to confirm that each instance is correctly capitalized. To find manually numbered headings, we can search for the end-of-paragraph marker followed by the code for a number (e.g., ^p^# in Word). By finding each heading in turn, we can confirm the numbering.

- We can search for recurring patterns such as "Figure", "Fig.", and "Table" followed by a space to check both the numbering sequence (i.e., to find gaps and repetitions) and to ensure that the format is correct; for example, we may want to use *Figure* in text, but *Fig.* inside brackets.

- We can check literature citations to ensure that they match the details in the bibliography, with no missing references and no references that have not been cited. These problems should already have been solved during previous stages, but authors sometimes make mistakes in implementing those edits. Proofreading is our last chance to fix the problem.

- We can look for unacceptably large patches of white space by zooming out (shrinking the size of the page) until white space stands out against the background. Some software even has automated tools for finding and highlighting excess white space.

And so on. In short, most things we can do on paper, we can also do on the screen. When we do spot a problem late in a proof, it's likely that a similar problem occurs elsewhere, and if we were working exclusively on paper, we'd have to reread the entire manuscript to spot any instances of that problem we missed. The search tool provided by PDF reader software is particularly helpful because it generates a list of all locations where a particular search term occurs, letting us quickly go to each location by clicking the corresponding search result. Here's what this feature looks like in Apple's Preview software:

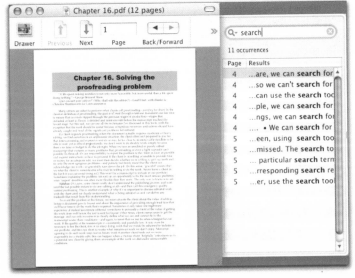

When we proof PDF files, we can also copy the text into our favorite word processor and use all the tools and skills we've developed using that software for onscreen editing; for example, we can use the search tool to look for inconsistent capitalization or formatting. It may still be necessary to annotate the printed copy or the PDF file to communicate the necessary changes, but we at least have recourse to tools that can make the task of determining what those changes should be faster and more accurate.

Extracting text from PDF files: To extract text from PDF files, open the File menu, select Save As, then choose a format such as RTF that your word processor can read. You can instead select and copy chunks of text using the selection tool, but you'll generally have much more cleanup work to do. The more complex the layout, the more manual labor is required to produced a document you can easily edit. You'll have better luck working with the file used to create the PDF.

Trick your eyes into spotting typos

The mind is a queer thing, and sometimes all it takes to see things in a different way is to—*surprise!*—look at things in a different way. One useful tool for spotting typos that you might otherwise miss involves changing the size and shape of the letters during one pass through a document; for example, you can display the text in a new typeface, color, or size, possibly after changing the page width or using a global find and replace to increase the space between words to three or more spaces. Something about the change tricks our eyes into thinking they've never seen the document before and paying more attention.

Obviously, you can't do this in a PDF file, so you'll need a copy of the document used to create the PDF. You won't be able to make such changes without messing up the layout, but you can always copy the text into a temporary file and do your proofreading there; when you find problems, you can subsequently fix them in the original file or insert a comment asking the author to fix the problem. Distributed Proofreaders offers fonts specifically designed to help proofreaders spot common problems, such as mistaking a lower-case L (l) for the number 1.

Proofreader's marks in Acrobat

Current versions of Adobe Acrobat Pro provide built-in tools for simulating Word's track changes feature. See the Adobe Acrobat help topic "Mark up text with edits" for details. With this tool selected, you can click between words or letters and start typing to insert text; you can also double-click or drag to select a word, press Backspace, and Acrobat highlights it with a ~~strikethrough~~ format to indicate deletion. The free Adobe Reader software and the Preview software built into OS X offer similar features.

Mastering PDF editing: If you need to do any significant amount of editing of PDF files, it's worth learning from the expert. Adrienne Montgomery, author of the *Right Angels and Polo Bears* blog, offers a course on this subject that will bring you up to speed quickly.

Traditional proofreader's marks seem to have become a thing of the past, largely because onscreen markup accomplishes the purpose of these marks (clear communication of the nature of a change) more clearly. However, if a client requires you to add proofreader's marks in PDF files, you can also do this manually using Acrobat Pro's **Stamps** tool. It's not a particularly elegant solution, so if you need to do this a lot, Paperlessproofs offers a product that seems more efficient. The plug-in for Acrobat seems to be available only for Windows, but users of other operating systems can try to mark up proofs directly on the company's Web site. For a different discussion of how to use traditional proofreading marks, see John Clifford's 2004 article *Traditional Proofreading in PDF* at the PlanetPDF Web site.

Markup in Apple's Preview software: Preview's built-in tools let you add comments and minor edits to PDF files. To do so, open a copy of the file (because changes are permanent and you don't want to mess up the original file), then: **Tools** menu > **Annotate**. You can highlight and strike-through (but not revise) text, add floating text and notes, or draw ovals and rectangles around words and phrases.

Comparing the Page Layout With the Last Edited Version

Reading against copy (also referred to as *reading to proof*) is an increasingly rare activity. In the old days, when everything was typed and retyped manually, errors were common: typists often missed words, sentences, paragraphs, or even entire pages (when two pages were stuck together), particularly when they weren't given time to check their own work, and someone had to check every last bit of ink on the edited typescript to ensure that it was transferred successfully to the final document. To accomplish this, the proofreader compared that original typescript with the final layout by reading both, side by side, to ensure that both were identical.

> **Side by side proofreading:** Word 2010 (but not Word 2011) allows side by side comparisons of documents so that you can scroll simultaneously through the documents. First, open the documents you want to compare in separate windows. Then: Ribbon > View tab > View side by side icon. If you want the second document to scroll simultaneously as you scroll the first document, click the Synchronous scrolling icon. Click the View Side by Side icon again to cancel this feature.

The two names for this process result from how this proofreading was done: the proofreader would place the original beside the proofs, and read the manuscript *against* (placed beside) the original copy while seeking differences. Sometimes a second person was pressganged into reading the typescript aloud (reading *to* the proofs) so the editor could concentrate on matching the proofs to what the reader was saying. Such proofreading teams developed an entire verbal repertoire for identifying punctuation marks, accents, and so on, and it was entertaining to hear someone proclaiming "periods comma commas comma semicolons comma and exclamation points exclamation point". (Yes, that *does* make sense. Read it again as if you were reading the *names* of the sentence's punctuation.)

Because production work is now done entirely on computers, the risk of lost or misplaced text is lower, so this kind of proofreading is increasingly rare. That's particularly true in high-pressure publishing environments, where tight time constraints often limit us to reading the final text without reference to the original and assuming (or praying!) that nothing has disappeared, been repeated, or been replaced with something of mysterious provenance. It's the proofreader's responsibility to spot accidental insertions by the fact that they make no sense in context, and to spot deletions by the logical holes they leave in the text; although such insertions are usually obvious, holes resulting from deletions may be harder to spot. If we're not given access to a copy of the document that was sent for layout, it's important to clearly inform our client that we can't accept responsibility for fixing all omissions. Nonetheless, we must read with sharp eyes and alert minds to spot as many errors of omission or commission as we can.

One possible way to find major problems involves exporting the text from the final layout into Word (as I described earlier in this chapter for PDF files and in Chapter 12 for desktop publishing files). You can then use Word's Compare documents feature, described in Chapter 6, to compare the two documents.

A broken promise: Fully electronic workflows promise that no information will be lost from the initial draft manuscript through to final production. Alas, this ignores the possibility of human error, such as accidentally deleting text, pasting copied text at the wrong location, or pasting the wrong copied text. Software glitches, though increasingly rare, can also cause problems. In the early days, PDF files often arrived with a single character missing throughout the file; ironically, I encountered this many times in Adobe documents. A similar glitch caused a 2006 issue of *The Magazine of Fantasy and Science Fiction* to be published without a single period anywhere. This so-called "antiperiodical" is now a collector's item—but for editors, it's a cautionary note about the importance of proofreading in the final medium.

Interesting new problems have resulted from how desktop publishing software works. Adobe's InDesign provides a good example of the new kinds of things that can go wrong. The problems begin with how text and graphics are imported into the software. InDesign uses the Place command. For example, when you select a text file to be imported, InDesign changes the cursor into an icon that resembles a paragraph of text:

Clicking the cursor at the margin of the page or column that will hold the text drops the text into that area, which it flows to fill. Alternatively, you can drag the cursor to define a text area, and as soon as you release the mouse button, the text fills that area. The first way this goes wrong happens if something on the page is selected before you place the new material: in that case, the new text replaces the old, just as it would if you paste text into your word processor while a word or paragraph is selected.

The second way involves the Place command's settings. A word processor automatically expands a document, as needed, to make room for new text. Desktop publishing software won't do that by default; it requires us to define layout areas to hold the text. If you haven't specified that text should automatically flow from the current container into the next available container or that it should extend the current container to additional pages if more space is needed, the inflow of new text stops at the end of the current container. To remind us that some text has not yet been placed, the software displays a visual clue. In InDesign, for instance, that clue is a small [+] at the end of the text frame that reminds you that you still need to add that text to the layout:

The screenshot shows that the [+] icon is small and easy to miss. If you don't happen to notice that there's unplaced text, it's easy to forget about it and never add it to the layout. Moreover, if you add new text by typing in the middle of existing text and there's insufficient room for the new and old text to fit in the current container, the excess text will disappear from the screen and that inconspicuous [+] mark will reappear. It's easy to miss this. Of course, if another container is linked to the current one, the text will flow into the second container automatically, but if that container fills up, the problem recurs. Worse yet, since it doesn't occur on the page you're looking at while you work, it's even easier to miss. These unplanned migrations of text cause problems for phrases such as citations of a figure or table using words such as "on the facing page" or other location indicators that are no longer correct.

Importing graphics can cause similar problems: if the text wraps automatically around an imported graphic, then some of the pre-existing text is likely to be pushed off the current page, possibly ending up in limbo. Conversely, if your software is not configured to automatically wrap text around graphics, the text will print on top of (*overprint*) the graphic. Thus, when placing a new graphic in a document, it's necessary to watch for both problems.

Other problems result from how desktop publishing software handles pages. In a word processor, new pages are automatically added as the length of the text increases, but in most desktop publishing software, designers must do this manually. It's easy to add too many pages and leave blank pages within the document. It's also easy to spot those blank pages, decide that you should delete them, and then select the wrong page icon and delete pages that contain text and graphics. The text and graphic generally aren't deleted; they remain in the file as unplaced text, indicated by that pesky [+] icon. If you spot it, you can simply re-flow the text and graphic into the correct locations, though at the risk of pushing subsequent text and graphics off the page and into limbo.

Another problem is that desktop publishing programs control page layouts using templates called *master pages*. Because these must be selected from a menu or from a palette of small page icons, it's easy to apply the wrong master page in documents that use a different master for each chapter or for each type of page. Thus, you must not only confirm that the running headings and other standard features are consistent within a chapter—you must also confirm that they're the correct ones for that chapter.

Cross-references are another problem: if they were generated (manually or automatically) in a word processor, they may need to be recreated in the desktop publishing software. If the links will be associated with *behaviors*, such as launching the reader's Web browser and taking them to a certain Web page (a common design feature for PDF files such as the PDF version of this book), the behavior must be correctly specified. The *continued on page Y* and *continued from page X* lines that are used when stories spread across several pages must also be verified: the continuation line may point to the wrong page, to no page at all, or to a page that was correct until newly added text pushed the target of the reference to a different page. In InDesign, for instance, these links are created manually (not automatically) and must be physically adjacent to their parent text block, which is the text container that precedes a *continued on page Y* line or the text container that follows a *continued from page X* line. If the two text containers don't touch, the link points to the wrong place or to no place. In addition, some cross-references update automatically, whereas others must be updated manually by the designer.

Before you take off: *Preflight* software resembles the preflight checklist pilots use before they leave the gate. It's designed to find a wide range of problems, including many of those described in this section. However, the preflight tools provided by most desktop publishing software can't always find subtle problems, and won't find *any* problems if you forget to use them; a common error is to run the preflight check, make a small change based on its reports, and then assume that the rest of the document was not affected. No matter how trivial the change, always run the preflight software as your last step.

We can read against copy on the screen to ensure that nothing has gone missing and nothing weird has been added: all we need to do is open the original document in the word processor (or other program) that created it, open the layout in the desktop publishing software or display a PDF created from that software, then juggle windows so the original and the layout are visible simultaneously. (The same approach works particularly well for Web pages and online help.) However, this requires a large monitor or possibly even two monitors side by side so we can display enough information to reduce the amount of scrolling required to an acceptable level. Some editors find this uncomfortable and unproductive, and prefer working on paper. That's okay: my goal in promoting onscreen editing is to make your editing faster and more accurate, not to encourage blind allegiance to your computer. If on-paper works better, we should never hesitate to include it in our editing repertoire.

If you're willing to adopt a more technological approach, your computer can facilitate the task of reading to proof by reading the document aloud while you follow along in a printout and mark omissions or discrepancies. This text to speech capability has been built into the Macintosh operating system for many years, and with most Macintoshes, no additional hardware is required; the built-in speakers are adequate for the job. Windows now offers a comparable feature, though you may have to add a sound card and external speakers to a low-end PC before you can use this feature effectively. (And, of course, neither computer will explicitly read out punctuation, as a human proofreading partner would do.)

Talk to me: Windows offers the Narrator utility. For Windows 7, Start menu > All programs > Accessories > Ease of access > Narrator. For details, see the Microsoft article "Hear text read aloud with Narrator". For the Macintosh, the text to speech utility is accessed through the Dictation and Speech preference pane and is available system-wide. In the Text to Speech tab of this preference pane, select the checkbox "Speak selected text when the key is presssed", then choose the voice that will be used to read selected text and its speed. Current versions of Adobe Reader also have a Read Out Loud feature. Bizarrely, it's hidden away under the View menu, but it works surprisingly well, and lets you compare two documents by having the computer read the PDF version of one document aloud while you scan the other version, looking for differences from the narration.

More sophisticated screen-reader software has been developed for blind and visually impaired computer users. Examples include the JAWS screen-reader and Apple's Voiceover software for Macintosh. The Society for Technical Communication's Accessibility special interest group is a good place to turn for more information on such tools, but local societies for the blind will also be a good source of information on this technology.

Replacing Printer's Proofs

If you still produce printed materials, you need some kind of assurance that what you send to the printer is what you'll get when the printed materials return, hot off the press. Except for the problems I discussed earlier in this chapter, which are easy enough to detect once you know that they exist and start looking for them, it's generally safe to assume that the information you see in a desktop publishing file or PDF file won't be lost by any modern production system. Nonetheless, many unfortunate things can happen to that information between your computer and your printer's imagesetter: font substitutions can occur if the printer doesn't have the same fonts on their computer that you have on yours, special characters may disappear for similar reasons, incorrect software settings can produce unexpected results, and a variety of other problems can still trap the unwary and the unfortunate.

Many proponents of fully onscreen production claim that soft proofs (onscreen images) are an acceptable alternative to laser or inkjet printer proofs or blueline proofs, but as I noted earlier in this chapter, I remain skeptical. If everyone involved in the production chain does their job properly, the odds of success are strongly in our favor, and soft proofs are a great way to spot overt problems, such as font substitutions, missing graphics, or incorrect colors. But as I noted earlier in this chapter in my anecdote about the "antiperiodical", subtler problems are easy to miss. Having done on-paper and onscreen editing for nearly 30 years, I still believe that real proofing can only be done accurately in the actual medium that will be used for the final product. We've come a long way even during the six years since the 2nd edition of this book, suggesting that soft proofs are increasingly practical, but the solution remains imperfect:

- **Better gestalt:** Even the largest commonly available monitors can't display two-page tabloid-size spreads at full magnification, but most designers and editors can now afford a monitor capable of displaying U.S. letter and A4 spreads at full size. This lets us see the full effect of a layout (the *gestalt* of a two-page spread) the way that readers will actually see it, and makes it possible to review layouts without prohibitive amounts of squinting, zooming in and out, or scrolling.

- **Legibility is improving:** High-resolution monitors have made it considerably easier to distinguish between similar characters such as commas and periods while displaying large pages at full size. However, small type sizes and light typefaces such as Palatino can still be difficult to read accurately on the screen. It's still necessary to zoom in on the page repeatedly if something appears suspect, or even to add a pass on paper in extreme cases.

Proofreading in the publishing software: If you own or can borrow the client's desktop publishing software, or software such as Adobe InCopy that works with that software, you can ask for a copy of the original files. Even if the client won't let you edit in the production copy of those files, you can still use the software's search tools to (for example) highlight every period in a document so that you can spot a common typo, namely replacing a comma with a period. If the software offers a *story editor* that is separate from the layout view, you can display text in a different or larger font in that editor, in a window beside the layout window. This lets you quickly examine certain parts of the layout without affecting the layout itself.

- **Inaccurate screen display:** The best (e.g., what Apple calls *retina*) displays now provide enough pixels per inch to register even fine details (hairlines, serifs) adequately. However, there are still occasional *display artifacts*—errors in what you see on the screen. For example, PageMaker (now replaced by InDesign) used to display line breaks correctly at 100% magnification, but displayed word and letter spacing within those lines poorly at magnifications less than 200%. To detect spacing problems, you had to zoom in on the page. You only learn about such problems through experience using a particular program.
- **Incorrect color:** Even expensive color-calibrated monitors make it challenging to verify colors on the screen. The problem is that monitors have *color gamuts* (the range of colors that it's physically possible to display) that don't overlap completely with the gamut provided by paper; indeed, different papers (color, texture, finish) have different effects on the perceived color. Thus, what you see on the screen won't match what you see on paper, particularly if the ambient lighting varies. Moreover, even seemingly identical monitors can display colors

differently, and the problem is exacerbated if you move between (say) Windows and Macintosh. Thus, even proofing Web colors can be challenging. Color calibration hardware and software mitigate, but don't eliminate, the problem.

Problems with the color model: Graphic designers occasionally choose the wrong color model. Onscreen color is defined using the RGB (red, green, and blue) color system, which is the default for screen displays. But printed color is defined using the CMYK (cyan, magenta, yellow, and black) color system. The two gamuts don't fully overlap, and sending RGB graphics to a printer will produce unexpected results on paper, even if the colors look fine on the screen.

- **Errors in subsequent production steps:** The first time I printed business cards, I carefully set the PDF options following the printer's instructions—only to receive cards with unacceptably low text resolution. The production staff chose the wrong imagesetter settings. Because I'd followed the printer's instructions, they reprinted the cards at their own expense, but the responsibility for errors isn't always this clear. Printed (paper) or film proofs are the surest way to spot such problems and fix them before it's necessary to redo an entire print run.
- **Low efficiency:** Compared with editing in Word (or with pen and pencil on paper, for that matter), it's still difficult to annotate PDF files. Acrobat's editing tools are bolted onto the software like a Rolls Royce radiator grill on a Lada. More seriously, it's inefficient having to manually transfer the edits into the file used to generate the PDF file after proofreading. Thus, it's unclear to me that editing in Acrobat offers any advantages over transferring files into Word for editing.

Updating the original file: It may seem obvious that someone has to transfer the proofreader's edits into the original file and regenerate the PDF, but you'd be surprised how often amateur publishers (and some professionals) forget this step. Back when I was writing the 2nd edition of this book, it wasn't uncommon to see monthly pleas for help in Internet discussion groups by editors or writers whose clients had deleted the desktop publishing file after generating the PDF file.

- **Font substitutions:** Most publishing software lets you either embed the designer's fonts in the output file (e.g., PDF) or ship them to the printer with the desktop publishing or other files—if the designer remembers to do this. The fonts must also be compatible with the printer's production systems; this isn't guaranteed for artisanal fonts found in dusty corners of the Web. If you use such homemade fonts or older pre-Unicode fonts, paper or film proofs are the best way to ensure the fonts will print correctly.

- **Missing or misplaced graphics:** Publishing software generally checks for broken links to graphics during the preflight process, and if the client transfers the desktop publishing files to a designer or printer rather than sending a single PDF file, the software usually provides a *bundle for the printer* function to ensure that all linked files are included. But again, someone must remember to use this feature. In addition, it's easy to drop the right graphics file into the wrong place, particularly when a bunch of files with lookalike names (e.g., Fig1.png, Fig11.png) are stored in the same directory. Someone must read the text that cites the graphics to ensure the graphic is correct.

- **Embedded files are not updated:** The graphics and other inserted components of a production file are often being modified while the designer prepares the final layout. Thus, it's necessary to update the version of these components that has been inserted in the layout. (This is particularly problematic for tools such as spreadsheets, whose calculations must be confirmed and updated.) Someone must take responsibility for ensuring that only the most current versions of these files have been incorporated in the final layout.

- **Placeholders:** At many high-volume publishers, not to mention amateur publishers, designers insert thumbnails or placeholder text such as the infamous *Lorem ipsum dolor* as they work. Someone needs to scan the entire document to ensure that these placeholders have been replaced with the final graphics and text.

As these examples illustrate, onscreen proofing remains a challenge. None of these problems mean that you should abandon soft proofs entirely. Soft proofs remain useful for spotting obvious problems, and using them appropriately can improve our proofreading effectiveness and efficiency and spare us from costly problems in creating film or printing a manuscript. My point in listing these problems is to convince you that for important jobs, soft proofs should be a *first step* in proofreading, not *the only step*. If you'll be producing your information on paper, you should still consider obtaining a paper copy for your final proof.

As an example of why soft proofs should not be your only means of proofing a publication, consider the article "Printing Goof Nullifies U.S.

Reading Exam" in the 20 November 2007 issue of the *Washington Post*. The company responsible for producing test booklets for the Program for International Student Assessment missed a serious error that occurred at the printer. The original publication design called for text printed on the booklet's inside cover, but when ink on the outside cover bled through onto the inside cover during printing, the printer shifted that text onto the following page and pushed all subsequent text one page farther into the document. As a result, references to text on facing pages no longer made any sense. Though the printer was clearly at fault for changing the layout without the client's approval, traditional publishing would have used blueline proofs or even press proofs that the client could review and approve before printing the booklets. The person responsible for approving the proofs might have spotted the problem, particularly since even-numbered pages would have incorrectly appeared on the right-hand page of each two-page spread.

Proofing Online Information

If your documents will be read exclusively on the screen, then clearly you must proofread those documents on the screen—and confirm that no problems arise when the documents are viewed on different computers or when using different operating systems. In this section, I'll discuss some things to keep in mind when you're proofing documents that will be used exclusively on the screen.

Testing across operating systems: Although Web pages and other online documents generally display similarly on most computers and in most software (e.g., Web browsers, smartphones), it can be challenging to ensure consistency among devices. Although software exists to simulate how an online design will work in a range of viewing environments, it's wise to find ways to test documents in the most common software for a given operating system (e.g., for Web pages, Internet Explorer and Edge for Windows, Safari for the Macintosh, Firefox and Chrome for both operating systems, and variants of all of the above programs for tablet computers and smartphones). Often, gathering a group of colleagues or testers is your best bet.

Most of the things we look for in printed proofs have onscreen equivalents, so we must also include these things in our checklist for proofreading Web pages, EPUB files, and the like. For example, if the software used to create the document requires authors to manually place text (e.g., into a complicated template) or manually select which items should and should not be included in the final product (e.g., for online help files that must be run through a compiler or single-source publishing), there's always the possibility that something will go missing or that the wrong thing will be included. The section *Comparing the Page Layout With the Last Edited Version of the File* earlier in this chapter provides some suggestions on how to account for this.

When we proofread a document that will only be used on the screen, we must account for some idiosyncrasies of the creation process that arise from the nature of the online medium and that aren't a concern with printed documents. These include:

- **Hyperlinks:** One of the advantages of online information is we can jump directly to cross-referenced topics. Just as we would confirm all *see page X* and *see Chapter Y* cross-references in print, we must check their onscreen equivalents to ensure they take us to the correct destination. Whether these links are created manually or automatically (by compiler software), there's always a risk of error. Thus, every link must be tested. Some may have broken (become nonfunctional), and others may lead to the wrong location.

- **Button behavior:** Most onscreen documents have two button types. Standard buttons such as a Web browser's Forward and Back buttons must be tested to ensure they do what they're supposed to do. In online help files, authors often define a *browse sequence* (the order in which readers should move from topic to topic); that sequence must also be tested. If the buttons are created correctly in a template, they should behave correctly in all screens based on that template, but some authors create them manually. Second, custom buttons may be created to produce special behaviors, such as the controls that play a movie or sound file. These must also be tested to ensure that they produce the correct behavior.

- **Consistency of the content:** Just as book chapters may have different text in the running headers and footers but the same style of page numbering, onscreen documents will have both different and similar recurring items. For example, every Web page should have a title in the title bar. Since some Web authoring tools don't require authors to provide a title when they create a new page, Web pages sometimes end up with the inspiring title *Document 1*—or with the same title as a different page if the author copied an existing page rather than creating a new page from a template. Similarly, every Web graphic should have a description (defined using the HTML alt tag) that makes the image meaningful to visually impaired readers using screen-reader software. Some authoring tools (e.g., Dreamweaver) can be set to require this information, but the designer must enable this setting.

- **Visual consistency:** In addition to ensuring that formatting is correct (e.g., that no heading has been defined as body text), we must ensure that related pages (e.g., all online help topics) look similar. If the designer has used CSS (cascading style sheets) to control the appearance of a Web page, we must ensure that they used the same style sheet for pages with similar roles. Similarly, if the interface interacts with the user by (for example) changing the color of a button when the mouse cursor passes over it, or if a pressed button looks different from one that has not been pressed, all parts of the interface must be tested to ensure that they behave as they were designed to do.

- **Correctness:** Just as printed documents must be checked to ensure that chapter titles match the running headers and footers and that the page sequence is correct, so too must we check these elements of online documents. For example, the indexes in PDF files sometimes count page numbers from the start of the PDF file rather than the page numbers that appear on the printed pages (e.g., page 1 is often preceded by unpaginated material).

- **Graphics:** Graphics must be checked to confirm that they are clear and legible. Screenshots are problematic, since different readers may use different screen resolutions when they view documents; what works well on one monitor may be illegible on another. Similarly, when authors compress graphics to save space, we must confirm that the image resolution hasn't degraded unacceptably. Again, testing with colleagues or groups of volunteer testers can detect such problems.

- **Navigation aids:** Every screen of an online document must contain the same navigation aids, unless there's a good reason for one screen to differ from the others. For example, a Web tutorial's welcome screen may only include a Start lesson button, whereas the next screen may be a table of contents with each entry clickable and linked to the corresponding chapter; for the lessons, navigation aids may link to the previous and subsequent chapters by name rather than just *previous* and *next*. But each of these types of navigation aid should be consistent.

- **Fonts:** Most operating systems now include a consistent core set of fonts, and as long as the author or designer used those fonts, display problems should be rare. However, designers often shun the common fonts in favor of more idiosyncratic choices, and for those fonts, it's necessary to test the document on multiple computers to ensure that it displays correctly.

- **Single sourcing:** Technical writers often use *content management systems* that let them use a single source of information (a collection of topics) to generate a range of outputs; for example, the same text may be used to generate printed documentation, help files, and Web pages with largely the same content, but with different presentation formats. Writers who create documents such as catalogs may use a solution such as database publishing, in which they select items from the database that should appear in the catalog. In both types of publishing, someone must proofread the final content to ensure that only the correct information is present, that no information is missing, and that everything is present in the correct form (e.g., high-resolution graphics for printed documents but lower-resolution graphics for Web pages and to support users of tablet computers and smartphones).

Demand Proof!

No matter how we proofread a file, we must remind our clients to ask someone to confirm that all of our corrections have been implemented correctly—and that they were implemented in the source file that was used to generate the PDF file or other document that we proofread. Ideally, we should perform this check, since we're the ones who proposed the corrections and are thus best suited to confirm that the corrections were implemented correctly. Moreover, we have the skills to do the work right, and authors may lack those skills. No matter what time pressures the publisher is working under, someone must perform this final check.

Proofreading will remain an important stage of the publication process as long as humans are fallible and computers remain malevolently contrary. That being the case, it's useful to discuss the importance of this stage with our clients during the early stages of a project. Moreover, we must do some thinking about the most appropriate technology for this work so that we can develop the skills required to use that technology (e.g., learning how to use the editing tools provided by Acrobat). In all types of proofreading, computer tools are a valuable ally in our work. But sometimes we may still need to adopt older technologies such as paper or film proofs or newer technologies such as reviewing a manuscript on multiple computers (e.g., desktop computers versus smartphones). Use the guidance I've provided in this chapter to choose your own balance between the various proofreading options that are available.

Chapter 17. Overcoming Resistance to Onscreen Editing: Coping With the Human Factor

Web: http://www.geoff-hart.com/books/eoe/eoe3/eoe3.html
Note: Word 2010 is for Windows; Word 2011 is for the Macintosh

We humans are a stubborn, recalcitrant, annoying bunch, and each of us is stubborn, recalcitrant, and annoying in our own unique ways. Author–editor relationships bring this observation into sharp focus, and I've emphasized the human aspects of this relationship throughout this book because you'll have difficulty succeeding as an editor if you can't come to terms with the human angle. Authors and editors each bring their own idiosyncrasies to the relationship, making each interaction a challenge in negotiation and consensus-building. Psychologist George Miller had the right idea: "In order to understand what another person is saying, you must assume it is true and try to imagine what it could be true of." None of the solutions I discuss in this book can work if you don't make an effort to understand the author's perspective.

In my experience, people resist onscreen editing for three main reasons: fears, unfamiliarity with the tools, and a combination of prejudices with a desire to protect the status quo. As an editor, you're likely to at least occasionally be dealing with colleagues, co-workers, or clients who hesitate to take the leap. In this chapter, I'll review these potential obstacles to help you understand where their reluctance comes from and how to overcome it. Onscreen editing is so pervasive these days that this chapter may be unnecessary by the time the 4th edition of this book is ready. In the meantime, however...

Fears

As you might expect, there are several fears an author must overcome when you try to encourage them to adopt onscreen editing:
- fear of change and failure
- fear of transgressing the rules
- fear for job or income security

Fear of change and failure

The fear of change is one of the most common fears we face in life and in the workplace. The rapid pace of technological change creates anxiety that we've reached the limit of our ability to cope, and that we'll reveal our incompetence by proving unable to master yet another new technology. This particular fear is compounded by the fear of failure, particularly when our employment and financial well-being are at risk. This book should help you to help your authors overcome their fears; I've lived through or guided this changeover at very different employers, and know the main obstacles and how to overcome them. When authors fear the technology, sharing what you've learned from this book and helping them work through their specific problems is a powerful way to ease their fears. It's important that they know in their heart, as well as their head, that they'll never be alone in trying to master the technology.

This is just one way you can emphasize the *carrot* and eliminate the *stick*. *Carrots* are rewards. They're important because most people won't embrace change unless they believe the change will improve their lives. Your goal must be to give people a reason to try the new technology. It takes some work to understand the people you're working with, since one person's motivator may not interest someone else. Self-interest (e.g., saving half an hour per day) will be enough to persuade some people. Others require more tangible rewards, such as cash bonuses or time off.

Sticks are punishments to be eliminated. They're important because people are more willing to try something new if they're confident they won't fail, or that they won't be penalized and will be allowed to try again if they do fail. Providing the support each person needs reduces the risk of failure, and eliminating penalties acknowledges that we're all human, and sometimes screw up—and that this is okay. Allowing people to fail, to learn from their failures, and to move on removes the most intimidating stick. Knowledge (this book, for instance) is a powerful tool for reducing both the risk of failure and the fear this risk creates. Reminding everyone that you expect implementation to take some time further minimizes this fear.

Employees often find themselves in an ironic situation: on the one hand, their manager truly believes they're intelligent, capable individuals; on the other hand, this suggests they don't need training. (Of course, some managers provide empty flattery in the hope employees won't notice the absence of a training budget.) But no matter how smart they might be, most employees face a full day's work and the pressures of completing that work well and on time. If managers don't reduce this pressure, it's hard to imagine how anyone will be motivated to find time to study something as new and complex as onscreen editing. Managers should provide formal classroom training or informal coaching during scheduled breaks from the daily grind so that everyone has time to learn without sacrificing their other responsibilities. They should also build some flexibility into those responsibilities to give employees the time they need to learn.

Fear of transgressing the rules

Even the simplest and most informal workplace has many written rules that dictate how people work. More intimidating still, many informal or unspoken rules exist simply because everyone agrees that this is how things are done—perhaps because some powerful and vindictive manager has made their preferences widely known. Penalties for breaking a written rule may be clearly spelled out in a policies and procedures manual, but the penalties for breaking unwritten rules tend to be more nebulous, and that makes them considerably scarier. Collectively, these rules create strong barriers to change, since it's natural to avoid breaking rules if this leads to undesirable consequences.

To overcome these fears, it's necessary to start with a clear understanding of what the formal rules allow, and of whether any informal rules change how the formal rules are applied. In particular, you must learn whether and how your proposal to adopt onscreen editing may break any of these rules. If so, you'll need to determine who can authorize you to break the existing rules. For example, if a group of writers has always worked with printouts, most editors will continue to edit their manuscripts on paper rather than risk angering authors or their managers by changing in this approach. It doesn't matter that there may be no written policy that forbids the new approach. Getting a manager's encouragement to proceed removes the fear of earning that manager's disapproval, and may even provide an incentive for their workers to try something new.

If it works... Beware the cliché that *if it works, don't fix it*. Someone may ask you to justify changing a system that has worked well since the first cuneiform manuscript was muddily rejected by the publisher with a suggestion the author hire a good potter. The whole point of this book is that onscreen editing works better. See Chapter 2 for a discussion of why. See Chapter 18 for suggestions about how to minimize risks and take maximum advantage of this technology.

There's an old saying that it's easier to get forgiveness than permission, and though this is often true, it's an unwise strategy if you don't have a forgiving manager. (I've done this several times in my career, but only when I knew my manager well enough to be confident they'd support me.) More importantly, such a strategy ignores the very real fear most people experience when they're asked to bend the rules—let alone break them. Giving the impression that you're trivializing someone's fears by insisting that they break rules is guaranteed to make them resent you, and resentment undermines the sense of cooperation that is necessary for change to occur. Thus, the wiser approach is to recognize that breaking the rules can have serious consequences, and that people are justified in fearing those consequences. To eliminate this fear, work with those who enforce the rules to eliminate any adverse consequences. That's harder than simply proceeding and asking forgiveness later, but far more effective in the long run.

When you want to change the status quo but an author or editor is reluctant, seek a compromise. For example, if an author wants to receive your edits on paper but you want to edit on the screen, do your editing on the screen, then print your edits so they can see what you've done. (Chapter 4 discusses how to customize revision tracking to permit this.) A willingness to compromise preserves or strengthens your relationship with an author, and may open the door to more daring experiments in the future, such as actually reviewing your edits on the screen.

Fear for job or income security

If onscreen editing is so efficient, it's logical to wonder whether we might work ourselves or others out of a job or reduce someone's income by being too efficient. For example, if a department currently employs 10 editors and onscreen editing reduces the time required to complete the work by 10%, a keen-eyed manager under pressure to trim their budget might seize the opportunity to lay off an editor. Nowadays, with short-term budgeting having replaced critical thinking, that's not an idle fear. Similarly, if you're an editor who charges your clients by the hour rather than quoting a fixed price per job, working faster seems likely to reduce your billable hours, and thus your income. Let's look at these concerns in turn.

The first concern is valid if you're working in an overstaffed department where most of the editors have too much free time on their hands and are desperately seeking ways to look busy. In the rare cases where this is true, someone's job security is already at risk, and adopting onscreen editing won't exacerbate the risk. On the contrary, editing more efficiently can turn this risk into an opportunity to preserve an endangered job: it offers the opportunity to do better work in the same amount of time, and seek new clients within the company and offer them your services. For example, I was hired by a former employer primarily to edit their scientific manuscripts. As I became more efficient, this freed up enough time that I expanded my work to cover business letters, funding proposals, annual reports, and PowerPoint presentations, among many other types of editing. By using onscreen editing to greatly increase the efficiency of my work, I accomplished more and better work, thereby demonstrating my value to many more people than I could have reached if I'd continued editing only scientific reports. Increased comprehension of my value *increased* my job security because I became valuable to so many people that laying me off would have significantly disrupted the company's work. (It also made my work much more interesting and diverse, which is not a trivial consideration for most editors.)

Far more often, a company's editors are overworked and must scramble desperately to finish their work without hours of overtime, and the work quality suffers because of the need for haste and the cumulative fatigue that results from unrelenting deadlines. In these situations, editors often resort to editorial triage, fixing only the most serious problems and letting lesser problems go because there's no time to fix them. Such environments guarantee errors, since the faster we work, the less time we have to think carefully about what we're doing, do the job right, and catch our own errors. Increasing our efficiency makes it easier to meet deadlines without working faster or longer hours than is safe, and can thereby increase the quality of our work. That increased quality is often clear to managers, and will be rewarded. Even where it's not clear, authors appreciate it, and that brings different rewards.

The second concern is that income might decrease. For those of us who freelance, the ability to get work done faster can indeed decrease our income if we bill by the hour. (If you're a wage slave, keep reading; there's useful information for you too later in this section.) If you're an established editor and earning a good living, this may not be a problem, because you may find (as many of us do) that time is a more precious resource than money, and anything you can do to free up some time is a priceless benefit. Even if you're struggling to earn a good living, getting work done faster can be a lifesaver when, as commonly happens, all your clients simultaneously send you urgent work with tight deadlines. In such cases, it can be a wise investment to sacrifice some income to ensure that you finish all the work on time without sacrificing quality. That guarantees future work.

But none of this addresses the legitimate concern that you'll earn less money if you bill for fewer hours. The answer, of course, is to stop working on an hourly basis and start quoting a fixed price per job. Peter Kent, whose book I've included in the bibliography, explains clearly how making this change can dramatically increase your income, particularly since clients usually prefer to be quoted fixed prices so they can budget their editing costs more confidently. Here's how this works:

- Estimating a fixed cost by multiplying your hourly rate by the time you estimate the job will take makes it more likely you'll earn your desired hourly rate—if you estimate your productivity accurately.
- Getting the job done faster than estimated (because onscreen editing makes you more efficient) but earning that fixed amount increases your effective hourly rate.
- Increasing your effective hourly rate lets you work fewer hours to earn the same income, or more hours to increase your income.

To successfully adopt this approach, you need to spend enough time tracking your productivity that you can predict how fast you'll work under a range of conditions. There are many published figures on average editing speeds, but these figures are at best misleading. Why?

- These figures are averages for many *editors*, and don't reflect your skills and how you edit. If you edit heavily and with minute attention to detail, you may work far more slowly than these averages.
- These figures are averages for many *authors*, and don't reflect the authors you work with. If your authors are significantly more difficult to edit, you'll take much longer to complete your work than the averages would suggest.
- These figures are averages for *a range of subject matter*, and don't reflect the difficulty of the subjects you'll be editing. If your work is unusually difficult or demanding, you'll take much longer to do the job.

In each case, you can lose significant money if you base the cost of a job on industry-average estimates that ignore your style and skill, your authors, and your subjects. The solution is to track your own productivity with a range of authors and types of work, and use this data to guide your estimates. If you have a scientific personality, you can come up with enormously complex methods of tracking your productivity, such as developing mathematical indices of document complexity and formulas for calculating the influence on your productivity of that complexity, the time of day, and the weather outside. This probably offers a false sense of precision, and simpler measures may work just as well. For example, I maintain separate statistics for manuscripts in the following broad categories:

- The English and French authors at a former employer who are ongoing clients, and whose work is intimately familiar.
- The Japanese and Chinese authors who are currently my main clients.
- North American and European clients for whom I've edited large, multi-author books.

Each group differs sufficiently from the others that I need to record my productivity separately. If I work repeatedly with a particular author, I track their manuscripts separately until I can reliably estimate my productivity for their manuscripts; if I don't do enough work for an author to create such an estimate, I can instead use averages for all clients in a similar category. (If an author is a particular problem, I note this so I can inflate my subsequent estimates.) Over the years, I've collected enough data to reliably estimate my productivity for both long-term and new clients:

- For a regular client, I can use my average productivity for that author.
- For a new author, I can use my average productivity for similar authors (or, if our preliminary interactions indicate significant writing problems, my lowest productivity for that category of author).
- If I won't have a chance to see a job before quoting a price, I can use my lowest productivity in case the current job is a worst-case scenario, and (to sweeten the deal) tell the author I'll reduce the price if I can get the job done faster.

When you're just getting started, or are working with a new client in a new subject area, you won't have such data, but you can still come up with a useful estimate of your initial productivity:

Word (mis)counts words: Word isn't 100% accurate at word counts, but is good enough to rely on. However, you must specifically tell it to include footnotes and endnotes in the count; to do so, select the Include footnotes and endnotes checkbox in the Word Count dialog box. Word also doesn't include text boxes in the word count. You'll have to open each one and count its words individually.

- Obtain a copy of the full manuscript, and skim through it, looking for the most difficult parts.
- Edit a few hundred words in these parts and record how long the work takes. Calculate your productivity in words per hour. (If you select a

block of text before you use Word's word count feature, you'll get a total for just the selected text.)

- Count the number of words in the manuscript. In Word 2010, Ribbon > Review tab > Proofing group > Word Count icon. In Word 2011, Tools menu > Word count.
- Divide the total word count by your average productivity to estimate how many hours the job will take. If the writing quality is highly variable, use the lowest of your productivity values for this estimate.
- Multiply this total time by your hourly cost. Add a fudge factor of at least 10% to account for any unpleasant surprises.

You can and should make these estimates even if you're a wage slave, but then the goal is different: knowing your productivity lets you budget time and other resources effectively. This can save your sanity when a huge editing project is coming, and you need hard data to persuade your manager to hire a contractor to help you through the coming time crunch.

> **Tracking productivity:** I track my productivity using a Word table for infrequent clients and an Excel spreadsheet for repeat offenders. Before starting work, I use Word's Word Count feature. I record the times when I start and stop to calculate how long I spent on a manuscript. My productivity (words per hour) equals the word count divided by that time. Many programs can automate the process. I've listed a few time tracking programs in the *Helpful Internet Resources* section of the book's Web site.

Unfamiliarity With the Available Tools

Unfamiliarity with the available tools arises from three main sources:
- not understanding what the software can do
- ignorance of the ability to customize the software
- lack of practice with the software

Not understanding what the software can do

Many editors feel that their software can't meet their needs, but this is often based on outdated experience with an old version. I once fell into this trap. When I first had the opportunity to begin editing in Word, I had been doing onscreen editing in other software for some time, and was comfortable using that software; moreover, Word had a reputation for difficulty and unreliability, so I vigorously resisted my employer's proposal that we adopt Word. But once the change was forced upon me, I resolved to make the situation as painless as possible, and began exploring the software to understand its power and limitations. I call this my "if life hands you Microsoft Word, make lemonade" experience, because I soon discovered the enormous payoffs from getting past my prejudices and learning the truth. That took time, but one of the most important lessons I've learned over the years is that investing time to make my life easier quickly repays that investment in future time savings and reduced frustration.

Before anyone can use software productively, they must decide that doing so is a worthy goal. Having made that decision, they must invest some time to learn what the software can and cannot do. Talking to other colleagues will reveal what they like and dislike about the software, as well as their tips and tricks for dealing with the problems. If you need to talk someone through this process, encourage them to explore the software rather than letting the gripes of others prejudice their impressions. (It's human nature to remember problems more strongly than the good things, and one person's problem is another person's opportunity.)

This book resulted from this kind of journey, and you get to benefit from the souvenirs and scars I accumulated along the way. If you want to fully comprehend just how much power a modern word processor can offer, you'll have to actually try my advice; there's no better way to learn than actually doing the work and no easier way to appreciate what I'm talking about than by experiencing the benefits firsthand. Then share your knowledge with someone else who's unconvinced so they can benefit from what you've learned. The advice I've provided throughout this book applies broadly to any word processor, not just Word—but you'll have to do your homework to learn how other software implements a particular beneficial feature and how you can take advantage of that feature.

Ignorance of the ability to customize the software

Close behind complaints about the unreliability of computer technology is the complaint that the tools don't work the way we want them to and force us to work in counterintuitive or uncomfortable ways. Computers should adapt to us rather than vice versa, and many complaints about how software works arise from simple ignorance of how extensively we can customize a typical word processor. This widespread ignorance is why I devoted one of the longest chapters in this book (Chapter 4) to describing Word's myriad customizations. It's only a slight exaggeration to describe something as flexible as Word as a kit for building our own word processor. That's particularly true if you discover that you enjoy working with your word processor's macro language; macro experts can redefine just about any aspect of how a program works.

The key to making software fit comfortably is to invest some time exploring its settings. If some aspect of the software annoys us, the odds are good that somewhere, buried deep in the interface, there's a switch that lets us turn off that function or an option that lets us modify how the function behaves. Skim through Chapter 4 looking for settings that solve the "that sure annoys me and I wish I could change it" problem. Then experiment with different settings to see whether they make your life easier or more comfortable. If you're working with an author or editor who has similar complaints, spend a few minutes showing *them* how to change the settings for the behaviors that annoy them most and encouraging them to explore other possibilities. This not only removes their objections to reviewing your edits on the screen; it also builds a relationship in which you're seen as a helper rather than just one more obstacle on the road to publication.

Word processors resemble a new pair of shoes: They look good and seem exciting, but they chafe and cause considerable pain until you break them in. Customizing a word processor is like walking a dozen miles in those shoes: once they conform to the shape of our feet, they stop chafing and we can start enjoying the walk. (Of course, we'll also develop an occasional blister along the way until we adjust the fit properly, and develop calluses from years of friction. The end result is the same: comfort.)

Efficiency isn't enough: What works for me may not work well for you or for someone you're trying to train: if the shoe doesn't fit, don't wear it! Pay attention to your own work or the work of someone you're training, and look for signs of discomfort so you can take appropriate action. Sometimes you'll find a better way to do something—with the caveat that *better* is not defined solely in terms of raw efficiency; a better solution must also be *comfortable*. If not, you won't use it, and you won't convince anyone else to use it either.

Lack of practice with the software

Even when someone understands the potential of onscreen editing, they may think there's no time to learn how to use the tools effectively. The busier they are, the more likely they feel this way, and the greater the payback they'll experience from finding time to try new things and practice them until they get good at each new trick. Unfamiliar tools always appear more difficult than they really are, and the familiarity gained through experience makes them seem increasingly easy.

The trick is to get past that initial hurdle of choosing to invest time now to save considerable time later. If someone is skeptical about this, convince them to start slowly and focus on things with big payoffs. For example, if they write the same text dozens of times per manuscript, teach them to use the software's automatic text features (Chapter 11) to do the typing for them. Encourage them to use the time they save to learn another feature of their word processor, and use that feature to save even more time.

For authors or editors who find it difficult to impose consistency on a manuscript, teach them how to use the search tools (Chapter 8) to find each instance of a term that must be made consistent and how to use the tricks I described to make replacing problem text quick and efficient. In the time they save using search and replace, encourage them to learn another feature that will save still more time.

Repeat this regularly. Each new thing they learn frees up time to learn something new. At some point, they'll find the pressure from deadlines beginning to ease because of their newly improved efficiency, and you can both relax and maybe even schedule time each day to practice new tools and develop proficiency. There's no substitute for uninterrupted practice and exploration when it's necessary to improve proficiency in a hurry.

If you're a full-time editor, you'll become far more proficient with the tools than someone who uses the tools only occasionally. Remember this when you work with your authors. Those who don't have writing as their primary job may only use the tools once or twice per year, and won't be particularly skillful. Be patient, and help them remember. If someone works best with written instructions, write them a concise user guide to help them follow the procedure. For example, download the primer on using Word's revision tracking tools from my Web site and print a copy for your authors, or modify this information to meet your own needs. For my own use, I created a file that lists all the shortcuts I created in Word so I can periodically remind myself of shortcuts I created but keep forgetting to use. Why not create your own list, and share it with your colleagues?

Ask yourself what other tools you could develop. Anything you can do to answer questions and remove the fear caused by uncertainty will make it easier to begin working with the software.

Prejudices and the Status Quo

Each of us has a range of preconceptions, only some of which we're aware of, that prejudice our way of thinking. Some of these derive from attachment to the status quo (the *we've always done it this way* syndrome). Although it's not always possible to identify our prejudices, we can achieve surprisingly effective changes in how we think simply by asking a few questions:

- Why am I reluctant to try a new thing?
- Why is a procedure being done this way?
- Is that the only way to accomplish this goal?
- Is this goal truly useful, or would another goal be more appropriate?
- How can I overcome my fears and learn to accomplish the same goal more effectively, or accomplish a more important goal?

If you're a manager or mentor, substitute someone else's name for the *I* in those questions. The answers may have something to do with fear, and I've discussed how to deal with fears earlier in this chapter. But they may also reveal prejudices—beliefs that lead us to think in a particular way without questioning whether that way's appropriate. Once you've identified the real problem, you can work on solving it.

Organizational prejudices

An organization's *culture* represents the collection of formal and informal practices that have become established over the years and that constrain how people work. Many of these practices do little harm, but when they become overly ritualized, they change from useful into rote responses that have lost touch with their reason for being. When that's the case, it's time to question the prejudice and see whether you can change it into something more useful for the workers and more effective for the organization. Times change; we must change in response.

Inertia—the tendency to continue doing what you were already doing—is a powerful human force. Without a strong reason to change, people tend to keep doing what they're doing. (This is the human equivalent of Newton's first law of motion: objects in motion or at rest will stay in that state until acted upon by an external force. If you're trying to implement onscreen editing, *you* are that external force.)

For example, if you've always worked with printed manuscripts provided by your authors, it's natural to want to keep working with those printouts. Requesting the word processor file used to generate that printout requires you not only to make the leap of faith necessary to try onscreen editing, but also requires you to justify that choice to the author. Doing so may be particularly difficult if you lack a friendly or professional working relationship with the author, in which case it's natural for them to fear that you'll somehow destroy the original file or make changes without giving them the chance to approve what you've done. To allay those fears, you must make a clear case for the change, and reassure the author there are no hidden drawbacks. I persuaded one author to try onscreen editing because we both agreed my handwriting was appalling, and that he would have a much easier time reading my typed comments. Once I'd demonstrated this, the author embraced onscreen editing.

Some organizations separate their authors from their editors, often for ridiculous reasons such as a desire to protect the authors from being disturbed. Such policies clearly make it difficult to build the kind of mutually respectful relationship that leads to effective author–editor collaborations. The solution is to attack the problem (disruptions) in such a way as to make the rule irrelevant. Even the most toxic corporate cultures, which formally discourage and actively interfere with this dialogue during working hours, can't completely prevent dialogue during lunch, while waiting to catch the bus home, during intramural sports, and so on. Each of these opportunities for contact is an opportunity to develop or improve a relationship. Once the relationship exists, you can negotiate ways and times to communicate that won't be disruptive for author or editor. At this point, the no-disturbance rule is irrelevant because you're no longer disturbing the author. Better still, if you've adopted the techniques I've recommended to save the author time, the interaction miraculously changes from a disturbance into a time-saver, and an alert manager who recognizes this may even eliminate the rule.

Some organizations explicitly give authors the authority to overrule edits without discussion. We aren't always right, and authors should certainly have the right to question our edits; it's the attitude that there should be no dialogue that creates problems. An author who respects our expertise and sees the advantages of considering our opinions will learn to ask why we made a change they didn't understand. In any author–editor relationship, it pays to be clear that our edits are *suggestions*, and that we're eager to work with the author to find more palatable solutions if they accept our suggestion that there's a problem that must be solved, but disagree with the proposed solution and feel we can improve it by working together.

One author I worked with early in my career had developed a reflexive dislike for editors and editing based on bad experiences he'd had with a previous editor who didn't understand his work. The first time I worked with him, he coldly announced that he had no intention of paying much attention to my edits because I clearly had no understanding of his writing. Rather than letting that statement go unchallenged, I demonstrated just how well I understood his work, and followed up with several examples of problems with the way he'd tried to communicate his findings. The author, now reassured that I was a peer (if not an equal) overcame his prejudices enough to begin working with me. Eventually, he even learned to call me with questions before he submitted a manuscript for editing, thereby saving both of us time.

Another good example of a traditional practice whose original justification is generally no longer valid is the requirement for a *paper trail*. Some organizations have invested heavily in paper-based workflows, particularly where legal or practical requirements require that they keep copies of all versions of a manuscript. One common goal is to let managers return to earlier versions of a document so they can discover when and by whom errors were introduced; good managers then use this information to ensure that the error doesn't happen again, and bad managers may use it to punish, on the principle that *beatings will continue until morale improves*. Another goal may be to provide legal protection, as in the case of archiving signed releases from technical reviewers to confirm that a manuscript and any changes resulting from the review process were thoroughly reviewed and approved by people with suitable expertise and authority.

Such organizations often resist the change to onscreen editing because (self-evidently) *there's no paper trail*. But given an understanding of the goal, it's clear you can create an onscreen paper trail that works every bit as well as a true paper-based solution: retain copies of each version of the document, and if you don't have digital signature technology to establish proof of the reviewer's identity, print out file copies showing the revisions so reviewers and authors can sign the copies and confirm they approved each version of the manuscript. The paper trail's goal is to provide a record of the process, not to prevent you from editing on the screen; printing copies that were edited on the screen combines the efficiency of onscreen editing with the required paper trail—the proverbial win–win solution.

Personal prejudices

Personal prejudices also may arise from accepting the status quo. A common misperception about onscreen editing is that the low resolution of the computer screen compared with paper inevitably increases the frequency of errors. Modern high-resolution displays make this unlikely, particularly as we gain experience with working on the screen and spend some time customizing the display, as described in Chapter 4. Most editors quickly discover that their editing accuracy improves significantly once they adopt onscreen editing, and also report increased author satisfaction.

Any remaining claims of lower accuracy most likely result from a lack of familiarity combined with a lack of understanding of how to customize the editing environment. When you're doing something for the first time, it's unlikely that you'll be as good at it as you are with something you've been doing well for years, so it's unreasonable to expect immediate proficiency and perfect accuracy. It takes time to get good at anything, and onscreen editing is no exception. This is particularly true if you're an inexperienced editor, and must simultaneously master both the software tools and the intellectual tools you require as an editor.

The solution is simple: combine onscreen and on-paper edits. Editing is never an either–or solution: you can always take advantage of the different things that work best for you in onscreen edits and in on-paper edits. It's been argued that working on paper defeats the purpose of onscreen editing, but that's a spurious objection. There are two common objections to combining onscreen and on-paper editing, and simple reasons why these objections make no sense:

- The approach requires two passes (one on the screen, and one on paper) to do the same job: In point of fact, most editors make at least two passes through a document anyway (once for major issues and a second time to spot anything they missed during the first pass and fix their own errors), so why not do one of those two passes on the screen?
- The approach takes longer: This misperception is based on the assumption that two steps will always take longer than a single step. In fact, onscreen editing generally saves enough time (by fixing the majority of the problems quickly) that the second pass (editing a printout of the revised manuscript) is much faster than it would otherwise be.

If you're new to onscreen editing, it makes good sense to print a copy of an edited manuscript to show the results of your edits. (You can do this by creating a temporary copy of the file in which you've accepted all edits; in Word, you can instead print a copy of the edited file with the tracked changes concealed, as described in Chapter 6.) This gives you a chance to examine the document in a second medium (paper) to spot things you may have missed while working in the first medium (on the screen).

If you discover that you're routinely missing a particular type of problem, you can make a special effort to watch for that problem the next time you edit on the screen. Sometimes you can even use the software's tools to help you. For example, I have great difficulty spotting the difference between a lower-case L (l) and the number one (1) in many fonts, and early in my editing career, several of my authors didn't understand the difference well enough to press the correct keys. Using the search tool lets me find all the cases where a lower-case L has been used in place of a 1 in the text, or vice versa.

Another common myth, fed by the media, is that working with a computer will cripple us with repetitive-stress injuries (*RSIs*), such as carpal-tunnel syndrome. Ironically, writers and editors who once suffered from debilitating writer's cramp and painfully bleary eyes after a day spent annotating low-quality photocopies can be most vocal about this. In fact, evidence for an increased frequency of RSIs among computer users is weak. Editors who complain of eyestrain and cite the greater ease of reading printouts ignore the current optometric consensus that working with properly configured high-quality monitors causes few visual problems—certainly no more than the eyestrain caused by staring intently at printouts all day.

Whether you work on the screen or on paper, editing (or any other kind of repetitive work) can exacerbate pre-existing medical conditions. In contrast, maintaining good health and adequate levels of physical fitness protects against both computer-induced injury and other types of injury and illness. Better still, using a computer permits many forms of automation that can actually reduce the repetition, thereby reducing the risk of RSI.

In researching an article I was writing on RSI (summarized in Appendix II), I found no recent studies that supported the widespread perception that onscreen work increases the risk of injury. The *too long, didn't read* version is that if you take periodic breaks in your work, create an acceptably ergonomic desk and computer setup, and watch for signs of trouble so you can correct problems before they become serious, you shouldn't experience much trouble.

Facilitating the Dialogue

This chapter has a recurring thread you may not have noticed, and that is therefore worth making explicit: it's not sufficient to offer criticism once you detect a problem; you should also offer a solution. Finding the correct solution depends on understanding the other person's viewpoint, because all that's necessary to create a problem is the perception (whether true or false) that a problem exists. Understanding that belief lets you seek a solution that will make that problem, real or illusory, go away.

You can't understand the other person's perception if you can't talk to them about it. This is why dialogue is such an essential part of any author–editor relationship. At some happy point, you may reach the kind of understanding with an author in which they trust your judgment implicitly and know when to ask you for clarification. Ideally, authors should learn to ask us about anything they disagree with rather than rejecting an edit out of hand—or worse, accepting an edit that is wrong because they trust our judgment too much. Sometimes it only takes a simple statement to establish this relationship: "If I misunderstood the sentence, someone else will too. So even if the current wording is technically correct, we can work together to make that correctness more apparent."

If you work in the same building as an author, this dialogue can be conducted face to face, thereby reinforcing the human connections promoted by the dialogue. But many editors, and particularly freelancers with an international clientele, may work through an entire career without ever meeting their authors. In that case, the dialogue occurs through the impersonal medium of correspondence. Even a telephone call to the author is somewhat impersonal, though it at least permits the give and take of human interaction that is so essential in a relationship.

Suzette Elgin, author of *The Gentle Art of Verbal Self Defence*, reported studies of human communication in which researchers found that somewhere between 50 and 90% of the information being conveyed in a conversation was nonverbal. Irrespective of the accuracy of these numbers, their meaning is clear: if you're not talking with an author face to face, you're working at a great disadvantage, and need to make a particularly strong effort to ensure that the author gets the right message.

Chapter 18: Implementing the Theory: a Four-Step Process

Web: http://www.geoff-hart.com/books/eoe/eoe3/eoe3.html
Note: Word 2010 is for Windows; Word 2011 is for the Macintosh

The human and technical barriers to implementing onscreen editing can be formidable, and you can't successfully implement onscreen editing until you solve these problems. Because the journey of a thousand keystrokes is halted by a single *stet*, the first step is to consciously decide that you (personally or collectively) want things to change. Whether you're a manager tasked with managing the implementation for your department, an editor or author working in that department, or a freelancer trying to work with clients on the far side of the world, the steps in a successful implementation are the same:

> **Stet?** The word *stet* comes from the Latin *let it stand*. In editing, it means "don't make this change". Far too many organizations have made *stet* the basis for their organizational culture.

- Obtain permission to try. In a hierarchical relationship, that permission should come from the manager who will suffer the consequences if the change fails or produces undesirable side-effects.
- Propose a test case to demonstrate the benefits of the change. Change is easier to accept once you know it will work.
- Explain how you'll solve *anticipated* problems. Hiding problems or pretending they don't exist undermines trust; in contrast, showing an awareness of problems and having researched potential solutions reinforces that trust.
- Propose how you'll detect and resolve *unanticipated* problems. It's never possible to know everything about a situation, so there will always be surprises. Admitting this, and explaining how you plan to cope, also builds confidence that you're competent to do what you've proposed.

This chapter provides details of each of these steps. My focus will be on the manager who must implement the process with one or more editors and authors, but the same process works equally well, *mutatis mutandis*, if you're a freelance editor who wants to adopt onscreen editing with a client who is tired of on-paper editing and willing to try something more efficient for both of you. The steps are identical; all that differs is the context, and it should be obvious how to modify the steps to account for that context.

Step 1. Get Permission to Try

"Any simple problem can be rendered unsolvable if enough meetings are held to discuss it."—Bill Smith, writing in the Elroy (WI) *Tribune Keystone*

As I noted in Chapter 17, I've been known to go ahead and do something without permission, then ask for forgiveness later if someone objects. And I've escaped with my skin largely intact. But I can't in good faith recommend this approach. Making a change without the permission of the manager who will be affected by the change can be a recipe for bad blood (at best) and could be career suicide if things go wrong. That's particularly true if you haven't tried something before and thus can't be sure you'll succeed. Some managers really do understand the need to take risks, and encourage risk-taking behavior, but they seem to be in the minority. If you're not confident your manager is among the enlightened, it's wiser to take the more difficult step of requesting permission.

An approach that works well in most situations is to propose the change to the manager or managers who will be affected by the consequences of that change. In some organizations, you may need to present a formal business case for the proposal. In others, a reasonable summary of the proposal will suffice. In both cases, the goal is to support your proposal as strongly as possible: you must explain the benefits and drawbacks, list what you know and what you need to learn, and describe how you'll overcome any problems. The two biggest barriers to change are a failure to understand why you want to change something that seems to work and the fear of undesirable consequences.

To succeed, you must break through both barriers: you must demonstrate benefits so tasty (without exaggerating) that the manager can't resist trying, and you must reassure them that you'll either prevent or limit the undesirable consequences. I described the main benefits of onscreen editing in Chapter 2, and describing those benefits in your actual context should be your first step. Chapter 17 describes the most common fears and how you can address them, although again, you'll have to account for the idiosyncrasies of your situation. The rest of the present section will walk you through the process of creating a compelling proposal for change.

Demonstrate the benefits

The first step in proposing any change is to give everyone a reason to keep reading your proposal: answer the question "what's in it for me, my staff, and the organization?" This means that any proposal to implement onscreen editing should start with a discussion of its benefits, ideally in the context of a problem the organization feels it must solve. (At a former employer, the problem was unacceptably long report production times.) It's worthwhile explaining the benefits in Chapter 2 to everyone involved in the publication process. In summary, here's what everyone can expect once the process is up and running:

- increased editing accuracy, thus improved document quality
- decreased editing and revision times, thus fewer missed deadlines and faster times to publication
- decreased repetitive manual labor and duplication of effort
- improved author–editor relationships

Though I've found each of these statements to be true in my own work, that anecdotal evidence won't persuade your manager. Your goal at this stage is to convince them to give you an opportunity to demonstrate that these claims are also true in your specific context. How can you come up with reliable estimates (of saved time and effort, and of increased quality) that your manager will accept, and that you can live up to? Develop the kind of test case I'll describe later in this chapter.

One point is worth repeating: avoid extravagant promises. Implementing any new process takes time, and the initial results won't be as dramatic as they'll become over time as you tailor your approach to the unique characteristics of your workplace and the individuals involved. Allowing yourself some leeway gives you breathing room if things don't go as well as you expect. (That's a particularly important caution if you've just adopted a new version of some software and are still solving its newest bugs.)

Another benefit of estimating the benefits conservatively is that people are generally more impressed when you deliver more than expected. (This is the source of the common business advice to *underpromise and overdeliver.*) Don't work harder than you expect to work in the future just to make the results seem spectacular, because doing so will set a standard you won't be able to meet in the long term; the level of effort required will prove unsustainable.

Eliminate or minimize bad consequences

The second step is to carefully identify the needs of everyone who will be affected by the proposed onscreen editing process. For each need, you must propose a solution that seems likely to meet that need and that provides a means of detecting and solving any problems. Here's an example of how this might look:

Person affected	Needs and solution
Employer (manager)	**No serious problems arise:** The subsequent sections in this chapter explain how to detect and resolve problems. In particular, you'll develop a test case that lets you demonstrate the absence of problems or reveal and solve any problems that do arise.
	A paper trail is kept: Describe how you will retain backup copies of each file, and create signed paper printouts if these are needed.
	Work gets done at least as quickly and accurately as before: Onscreen editing can be faster for both authors and editors, thereby reducing total time. But large time savings are less likely (and delays may even arise) while you and your authors are learning the technology, so your proposal should be scheduled for implementation at a time when any delays won't be critical. Thus, propose that the test occur *after* a deadline or busy period, not before. In addition, plan to collect statistics that will demonstrate improvements in speed or accuracy.
	Accountability is maintained: Describe how the new process will provide the same accountability as the traditional on-paper process. For example, changes can be tracked by date and by the name of the person who made the changes, and you can save ongoing copies of the manuscript so anyone can return to a previous version and investigate what each person did.
	Any adverse changes in work quality are quickly detected and fixed: By performing your second pass on paper, you can quickly determine whether you're missing anything by working on the screen, and can correct anything you did miss. Once you stop finding problems in the paper copy, you can eliminate this step and work exclusively on the screen.

Person affected	Needs and solution
Employer (manager)	**Staffing needs remain constant:** Demonstrating the efficiencies of the process ensures that the manager won't need to request additional staff, but there may be fear that if you're too efficient, someone will be laid off, thereby diminishing the manager's empire. The solution is to make it clear that you are aiming to give the current staff more time to do the job right, particularly under deadline pressure, or to take on more work and thereby eliminate the need to hire contractors during busy periods.
	No damage is done to the human relationships: Emphasize that working onscreen will not mean you never see the authors in person. Instead, make it clear that you will use the new approach to preserve and even improve existing relationships.
Author	**The technology is easy to understand:** I've provided a primer on my Web site that you can give to your authors to help them learn how to use Word's revision tracking. But rather than just delivering a printout and leaving them to their own resources, offer to work with them until they can use the technology effectively. Then ensure that you *do* this; demonstrate that willingness rather than creating empty promises.
	Authors can still review your edits: Teach the authors how to review your edits both with the changes displayed and with the changes concealed. If necessary, teach them how to print a copy that shows your changes so they can do the review on paper.
	Author and editor continue to collaborate: Emphasize that the editing process will remain collaborative, and that no edits will be made without the author's approval. The easiest way to sabotage trust is to make a change *invisibly*, without permission, and to get caught.

Person affected	Needs and solution
Author	**Authors can review and implement edits as least as quickly as before:** Work with authors to demonstrate how much easier it is to read typed comments than hand-written ones, and show them how to incorporate changes using the revision-tracking tools. Also demonstrate the efficiency of copying and pasting typed comments compared with having to retype handwritten comments from scratch.
Editor	**Quality is maintained or improved:** This should never be a problem, since the procedures in this book are designed to make you a *better* editor. But the ability to edit on paper and spot anything you're missing provides the confidence required to proceed.
	The work gets done at least as quickly: A primary goal of onscreen editing is to improve efficiency, which means both accuracy and speed. Collect statistics on your on-paper and onscreen editing rates to demonstrate time savings. Collect data that will show an ongoing improvement as you become more expert in using the technology.
	Relationships with authors don't suffer: Think of yourself as working *with authors*, not with files, and your relationships won't be adversely affected. On the contrary, once authors begin to see the advantages of the new approach, your relationships can improve. (Authors appreciate your efforts to save them time and effort.)
	Managers appreciate the work: If you understand the needs of the managers affected by the new process, you can go a long way towards solving problems they never complained about previously. Ask them about their problems with the current process, then emphasize how your proposal will solve them. (Managers appreciate your efforts to solve their problems without creating new ones.)

Person affected	Needs and solution
Other staff (e.g., secretaries, desktop publishers)	**Other people's work is not disrupted:** If you itemize and address the needs of everyone involved in the publishing process, from the person who formerly typed handwritten edits into the word processing file (often a secretary) to the person who must lay out that information (whether for printed or online publishing) at the end of the process, you can spot any adverse consequences your actions might have for their work. This knowledge lets you avoid the problem or take steps to mitigate it.
	No one loses their job: In the modern workplace, workers rarely have so little work to do that reducing their workload will jeopardize their job. Emphasize that the goal is to free up time for everyone to do a better job of their existing work or perhaps even add to their responsibilities.

Note that this table is *an example*. Though it covers the main points, you should interview representatives of each of the groups of people listed in the table to learn what points *they* consider important. Some of those points will be serious and significant. Others may seem trivial and irrelevant, yet have enormous significance to the people who raise the concerns. Addressing their concerns convinces them you're really on their side, and removes much of the fear that comes from a belief their concerns are not being taken seriously. (Sometimes the consultation process is as important as the results.) If the concerns truly are trivial and irrelevant, they'll be easy to address. But every so often, the concerns prove to be more serious than you thought, and you'll be glad you identified and tried to solve them.

Step 2. Develop a Test Case

"In seeking wisdom, the first step is silence, the second listening, the third remembering, the fourth practicing, the fifth—teaching others."—Ibn Gabirol (ca. 1022–1058)

Managers thrive on numbers and objective data rather than opinions. This is also true of scientists, engineers, accountants, and anyone else who makes a living working with numbers. The only way to convince such people that the onscreen editing offers real benefits will be to collect statistics that demonstrate the improvement. To do so, you'll need to find an author–editor pair willing to work together to test the new system, and willing to record their experience for your benefit and the benefit of those who will follow in their footsteps. You'll also need to pick a few appropriate projects. Next, you'll have to generate numbers from before and after the change to support your case. (That is, you need to collect baseline productivity and error data before you start and then confirm that both improve as a result of the adoption of onscreen editing.) Last, but not least, you'll need to help your test participants work through the project and succeed.

Pick at least one suitable author–editor pair

The human aspect of the author–editor relationship is probably the most important factor in achieving success. Thus, you can only expect your test case to succeed if you can find an author and editor who are willing to work together to test the new process. An ideal author–editor pair has the following characteristics:

- a history of working well together (to minimize the risk of personality conflicts)
- a willingness to try something new (so they won't resent or resist the new process)
- above-average proficiency with the word processor you'll use (so that basic competency with the software won't be a limiting factor; ideally, both must be skilled typists)
- sufficient competence to work quickly and accurately (so any delays will slow them, not bring them to a grinding halt)
- enough free time that they can devote enough time to learn the skills they need to succeed

Your goal will be to work with this team to develop a simple, efficient process that satisfies their needs and identifies any problems that arise so you can resolve them. Because your workplace situation will differ to some extent from every other workplace situation, it's important to emphasize the need to adapt the generic solutions I've proposed in this book to create a custom solution that fits your workplace perfectly. After all, it's human nature to more eagerly embrace a solution you helped to create and proved to be workable than a solution imposed from above, with no reality check to confirm that it's appropriate.

Once you develop a workable process, you'll find it much easier to sell the process to others in the organization. Even inherently recalcitrant authors and editors find their reluctance weakening once their colleagues enthusiastically evangelize the new process—or at least report that it has merit, isn't as bad as they feared, and has been thoroughly debugged. Because your testing should have identified and solved most of the problems the resisters would face, this removes another barrier to implementation: adopters will encounter fewer problems, and you'll solve those problems faster because of your experience with the process.

Although I've concentrated on authors and editors in this section, because these are the two most obvious groups of participants in the new process, don't neglect others who will be affected. For example, if managers and other staff will also be involved, they must be compatible with your test team and willing to work with them. If the manager dislikes the author, and the desktop publisher dislikes the editor, you've added two complications you don't want to have to resolve. In such cases, it's beneficial to pick an author or editor who doesn't meet all the abovementioned criteria perfectly but who interacts well with all the other staff.

Pick appropriate projects

The next step is to pick appropriate manuscripts for your test. A good choice has the following characteristics:

- It is representative of the *typical* range of editing challenges your editors face. This provides an opportunity to encounter and solve most of the problems that will occur in most manuscripts that you will edit.

- It is *not* representative of the worst challenges your editors face. If you start with something that is more difficult than average, you're more likely to run into problems you can't easily solve and to alarm your test participants. You'll have to confront such manuscripts eventually, but try to do so only after you've acquired some skill and confidence in the new procedure. (In short, learn to walk first; try to fly later.)

- It must have a reasonable deadline, with room for slippage. If you encounter unexpected problems, any delays won't cause serious consequences for the author, the editor, or the organization. Adverse consequences can poison people's minds against the new process.

- It must be sufficiently important to justify editing it in the first place, but not so critical that any failures will have serious consequences for the author or the organization. A manuscript that will undergo peer review after editing is an excellent choice, since the peer reviewers can catch any problems; indeed, it's their job to catch these problems.

- A manuscript that will go directly into print or onto your Web site is a poor choice because it offers a chance to display your errors to a large audience, most of whom expect perfection.
- It must clearly demonstrate the potential payback. Short, simple manuscripts fail this test because the time savings will be unimpressive and there may not be enough chances to identify and resolve errors for the exercise to prove useful. For example, a manuscript must be long enough that even small speed improvements produce significant savings: a 10% improvement saves only 2 minutes in a 20-minute edit, but saves an hour in a 10-hour edit. Similarly, a manuscript in which many terms appear dozens of times provides obvious opportunities to improve consistency; a manuscript in which most terms appear only once provides no such opportunity.
- Despite this advice, it may be worthwhile working on a short document purely for the sake of learning how to use the tools. Just don't expect to gather useful statistics from such a document.

You may not find a single manuscript or a series of small manuscripts that meets all these criteria. So long as you understand why each criterion is important, you can make the necessary allowances, such as extending a deadline or combining the times for several small edits to simulate the time needed for one longer edit.

Obtain good numbers

It's difficult to predict what numbers someone will find persuasive; despite our occasional pretensions of objectivity, each of us uses subjective criteria to assess outcomes. That being the case, the way to develop persuasive statistics is to ask the person you're trying to persuade what numbers they want to see. This should be obvious, but my experience suggests that many editors and technical writers believe that quality or improvements can be measured objectively. (These people have never heard of Mark Twain's three kinds of lies: "lies, *damned* lies, and statistics.") The two main types of statistics you can use are completion times and error rates, but as the following examples show, how you collect this information varies:

The metric system: Should you need to use business jargon to persuade someone, call your statistics *metrics*. The meaning is essentially the same, but now you're using the same language as your audience.

Type of statistic	Details
Completion times	It's easy to calculate how long you spent on a particular job, but how can you translate this into a value you can use for prediction? Chapter 17 describes one way. Some managers will ask how much work you accomplished (e.g., how many keystrokes you typed) while you edited those words. Others will want separate times for work on each publication type (e.g., technical reports vs. staff newsletters), for different authors, or even for different levels of difficulty (e.g., rocket science vs. cafeteria menus).
Error rates	Errors can be subjective. Typos are hard to argue with, but what about grammatical problems and subtle logic problems? The subtle problems may be far more important than the typos, since most readers figure out spelling errors and won't be led astray. Moreover, without knowing every conceivable error that existed in the unedited manuscript, how can you possibly determine the number of errors you missed? How do you account for differences between manuscripts? (Some are particularly difficult, others particularly easy, so the expected error rates—both those in the original manuscript and those made by the editor—will clearly differ.) If the person you're trying to persuade is willing to accept a final on-paper edit as a way of determining what you missed while editing on the screen, sometimes that's the simplest proposal.

Since you'll need to demonstrate improvements, you'll also need a benchmark against which to compare the new process. Thus, since you're proposing to replace on-paper editing with onscreen editing, you'll need to collect matching statistics for the on-paper edits you're currently doing. Resist the temptation to inflate your estimates of on-paper editing times and error rates. Apart from the ethics of lying to your manager, you don't want to give the impression that you're not doing a good job already.

How can you come up with numbers that are defensible and reasonable? One of the simplest and most persuasive ways is to pool all your data for on-paper editing. If you don't already have this data, monitor your ed-

iting times over a period of a month or so. (You can do this simultaneously with your test case for onscreen editing, but it takes more organization to
track two different classes of statistics simultaneously.) What you're looking
for is a long-term mean productivity: the number of words per hour you
can edit for all your work combined. If you do enough work to *stratify* your
statistics (e.g., to distinguish between types of work—demanding technical documents and undemanding documents such as the staff newsletter—
or to distinguish between authors), calculate a mean value separately for
each type of work or each author; you'll develop a more realistic mean value. Also calculate some measure of the magnitude of the variation around
that mean: the range from lowest to highest productivity is useful to know,
but more mathematically literate managers may also want values such as
the standard deviation. (Most spreadsheets can calculate these statistics for
you.)

Next, calculate your work times for onscreen editing. First, track the
training time so your manager will know how much training time to budget for. Don't start collecting actual editing and revision data until the participants in your test case have been trained to use the software's revision
tracking tools and have had a chance to practice their new skills. The information you collect should reflect the results of using the tools, not their
learning curve. Ideally, gather data for several edits so you get a better idea
of the range of variation and how fast their speed improves. A single result
is not broadly representative; you want a large enough sample that your results are likely to cover the typical range of productivities.

Your goal is to compare the baseline numbers for on-paper editing and
onscreen editing. If the types of edits used to collect the baseline and onscreen data were similar, you'll see a clear difference, with a greater mean
productivity for the onscreen editing but probably with some overlap of
the two ranges. Ideally, there would be no overlap in the ranges, with the
onscreen editing productivity clearly higher in all cases, but that may not
happen for some time. If you track productivities long enough, you'll see
productivity continue to increase for onscreen editing.

You can use a similar approach to measure accuracy. One useful approach is to assume that one form of editing, whether on paper or on the
screen, produces a final manuscript you can use as your standard for comparison. You can then count and categorize any subsequent corrections to
the other type of manuscript, each of which represents an editing error.
These corrections may be detected by:
• the author, when they first review your edits

- yourself, if you get to edit a manuscript again to catch your own errors
- peer or technical reviewers who examine the manuscript after editing and revision
- proofreaders who have a final look before publication

By counting instances of each class of error (e.g., typo, inconsistency, grammatical error, unclear wording), you can develop statistics on how often each type of error might be missed. Each stakeholder in the process (author, editor, manager, reviewer, etc.) may propose specific types of editing error they want you to track; for example, if a desktop publisher must spend considerable time correcting formatting errors that are missed during editing, this is another category of error that should be tracked.

Statistics 101—a simple test: Statistics software and spreadsheets can test the *significance* of differences between methods. (Statisticians, stop reading now! You know how to do this, and will find my description simplistic.) Keep your test simple: you can demonstrate significance with half a dozen data points, but the test's credibility increases with more data. A dozen data points would be great. Don't have statistics software? Search the Web for the Graphpad online calculation software or use the phrases "two-sample significance test" and "online calculator". Smaller P values mean a greater likelihood your results differ significantly; values <0.05 are good.

Although hard numerical data are persuasive, also collect qualitative, subjective data from the participants. Gathering this information shows you actually care what the participants think, and that's never a bad thing. But subjective impressions also reveal good things you should emphasize when you report the results of your test case to whomever you're trying to persuade. More importantly, subjective feedback sometimes reveals subtle problems you must solve even if they aren't obvious from purely numerical data such as error rates. As I've noted previously, it will be difficult to implement a process that is super-efficient but that nobody wants to use.

Support the author and editor

The goal of the test case is more than just to demonstrate that you can save time and improve accuracy. These are certainly good things to achieve, but there's a less obviously important goal to keep in mind: you want to develop a process that works well enough that others will want to adopt it. Thus, your test case must support the development of a simple process that meets everyone's needs. Because the author and editor may have reservations, and may fear failure—after all, they're the ones in the spotlight—your goal must be to reassure them and provide any support they need to succeed. Spend some time thinking about how you can overcome their fears and motivate them to remain interested:

- Emphasize that the test case is designed to detect and solve problems, that you expect problems, and that they won't be evaluated poorly if problems arise. It's the *process* that you're evaluating, not them.

- Provide a safety net by making it clear that failures will have minimal consequences. If you've chosen appropriate test cases, as described in the previous section, both the risk of failure and its consequences should be small. If the consequences are larger, find ways to protect the participants.

- Offer incentives for all test participants. For some, the intangible and (at this early stage) hypothetical benefits of a reduced time investment, increased ease of creating and reviewing edits, and increased accuracy will suffice. Others will want tangible benefits right away to maintain their interest. Those benefits may be recognition in their next performance evaluation, the chance to leave work early on Friday, or even a financial reward if your situation permits such bonuses.

Since editing is all about human relationships, make an extra effort to protect those relationships and promote their development throughout this process. Be prepared to invest some time asking for feedback on how things are going and listening to complaints. Your willingness to listen to and work with the participants should establish a precedent and a standard for future interactions. That's particularly true if your workplace hasn't already established a culture of cooperation and teamwork. Implementing this process may help you to begin building such a culture.

Provide adequate time

How long will the test case take? There's no way to be sure. In an ideal situation, mastering and applying the techniques I've presented in this book should increase editing efficiency sufficiently to compensate for any initial awkwardness as participants learn to use the technology. Of course, that assumes you can give the participants time to learn those techniques before you actually assess how well they've learned. Once they understand what they'll be doing and how they'll be doing it, the statistics you collect will measure the actual work rather than the learning process. At that point, onscreen editing should take no longer than on-paper editing, and if you know how long the on-paper edit would take, you can use that to predict how long the onscreen edit will take.

Unfortunately, the real world isn't ideal. It's unlikely you'll be able to completely separate an author and editor from their daily work until they complete the test case. Thus, you'll have to budget enough time to allow them to cope with their real job—producing edited manuscripts, not testing a new process. Moreover, you'll have to add some time to design the new process, discuss alternatives, test the alternatives, revise your process, record the data you need to make your case, and analyze that data. You'll also lose time to solving problems, teaching the solutions, and documenting the solutions for future reference. If you have to sell your proposal to one or more managers, you'll need to allocate time for these negotiations too. These small annoyances add up to a considerable amount of time, but you can't neglect them or they'll come back to haunt you.

Moreover, if you're working with more than one author–editor pair, you'll need to consider how to implement the new process across an entire workgroup or even an entire organization once you've proven that it works. You'll need to include time for training, and possibly time and money for computer and software upgrades so everyone can benefit from the new process. Although it's tempting to extrapolate from the learning curve in your test case to the organization as a whole, it's rarely safe to do so. Because you've chosen an ideal test situation (the best people and the most suitable manuscripts), others may not achieve the same results at first. That being the case, consider phasing in the new approach slowly. How long to take will depend on the personalities and competence of your colleagues, on the nature of your workplace, on the time you have available to train your colleagues, and on many other unquantifiable factors.

You'll also have to devote some time to detecting and solving problems, which are the topics of the next two sections.

Step 3. Solve Anticipated Problems

"By three methods we may learn wisdom: First, by reflection, which is noblest; second, by imitation, which is easiest; and third, by experience, which is bitterest."—Confucius (ca. 551–478 B.C.)

I've discussed the various problems you're likely to encounter throughout this book, and have provided solutions or coping strategies for most of them. In this section, I'll summarize the main things you'll need to plan for, and suggest how to deal with the related problems. (I'll discuss the less predictable problems in Step 4.) The predictable problems fall into three main categories:

- organizational and bureaucratic
- human
- technological

Organizational and bureaucratic problems

Organizational and bureaucratic problems are the first class of issues you'll need to address. The main organizational problem is resistance to change, as discussed earlier in this chapter and in Chapter 17. Once companies reach a certain size or have been doing something a certain way for long enough, it becomes difficult to persuade them to try something new. In the worst cases, change can't occur at all without direct intervention from someone powerful enough to impose change. But you can accomplish surprising things if you understand one trick: it's easier to harness the energy of existing processes for your own purposes than it is to stop the processes and replace them with something new and different.

Expressed a bit more directly, you must determine how to accomplish the same goals as the current processes by following that process—but with the relevant changes made, such as replacing on-paper edits with onscreen edits. Given that the goal is to implement a *new* process, this seems counterintuitive until you see how it can be accomplished.

Consider, for example, an organization that requires a paper trail for reasons ranging from the practical (e.g., legal accountability) to the nonsensical (*that's how we've always done it*). With onscreen editing, of course, there's no paper, so managers who require a paper trail may raise this as an objection. Rather than trying to persuade the managers to abandon a paper trail, print each version of the manuscript with all edits visible, add a date stamp, have the person responsible for that version sign their name beside the date stamp, then add the printout to the filing cabinet. (And, of course, make careful electronic backups of each version of the project files, as described in Appendix I.) The result is that you satisfy the manager's need for a paper trail even though most of the work is occurring on the screen. In short, you've used the established practice to provide the source of energy for your new process, rather than fighting those who are invested in the old process over what proves to be an insignificant point.

The organizational and bureaucratic problems you'll encounter fall into several distinct categories:

Problem category	Description and solution
Record-keeping	Maintain a paper trail, whether literal (paper copies) or virtual (backups of each version of a file). If your organization tracks time expenditures on different projects, record the times as you begin to use the new process. The data may be unnecessary in an objective sense, but as I noted earlier, it's wiser to follow existing processes than to fight them. Moreover, this data adds to your body of statistics, and can be used to support your assertions of productivity and quality increases.
Account-ability	Keep careful records of who was responsible for making each change, and who was responsible for accepting or rejecting the change. Teach everyone how to stamp their names on a document, whether literally (with a pen or a rubber stamp on printouts) or virtually (by typing their user name in the Preferences or Options dialog box before they begin using revision tracking).
Work location	Most editors work in their own office, but to discuss edits, you may need to be able to work in the author's office, in a different building (e.g., to compare a user manual with the product it describes), in a library while doing research, and so on. Paper provides maximum portability, and lets editors easily change locations when required, but laptop computers are so affordable there's no reason editors can't carry their computer with them. Tablet computers (e.g., iPads) are even more portable. Bringing the computer to the work location lets you keep your editing on the screen rather than on paper.
Work hours	Managers track times spent on different projects so they can bill other managers for an editor's time, schedule future projects, or justify staffing levels. Fortunately, many programs can help editors track their time; these programs offer the additional benefit of providing data electronically (i.e., no need to retype it). I've provided some suggestions on the book's Web page.

In each case, the solution to bureaucratic resistance is not to fight it, but rather to adopt the existing process, modified to take advantage of on-screen technology. You may still occasionally encounter an unusually recalcitrant manager who resists change purely because that's how they demonstrate their power. But most times, there's a good reason for wanting to follow a certain process. If you can understand that reason and the goal it supports, you can often propose a solution the manager will accept.

Human problems

Human nature represents the second group of problems, and as I mentioned earlier, we humans can be the most difficult obstacle in any implementation process. This means you must anticipate the most common objections people will raise so you can prepare answers to these objections. The following strategies can help you respond to the most common objections in a way that will reduce or even eliminate resistance:

- Provide basic training so people have the intellectual tools to do their work. For those who must master the software (the editors), provide more advanced training and encourage them to use the tools at every opportunity to develop proficiency.

- Teach everyone how to customize the software so it supports the way they work. The more closely the software fits their preferences, the less irritating it will be to use and the less resistance it will raise. Customization also means not insisting that everyone perform every function on the screen or in the same way. Particularly in the beginning, let everyone use the aspects of computerization that provide clear benefits and make the most sense to them, but let them use traditional methods for functions they find easier or more effective on paper. Over time, you may be able to persuade them to move more of their work onto the screen, but even if they don't fully adopt onscreen editing, you'll likely succeed in persuading them to adopt a few tools that make them more productive and effective.

- Provide enough time for everyone to practice using their new tools. You may have to insist that they use the tools for a certain minimum number of hours per day to obtain enough practice to become comfortable with the tools. Initially, the work will be unfamiliar and uncomfortable and slow. But as the work becomes familiar, their comfort will increase and productivity will improve.

- Recognize that authors for whom writing is only an occasional job will use the tools much less frequently than the editors, and will thus require occasional retraining; without ongoing practice, it's easy to forget once-learned skills. Editors should budget time to help authors use the editing and review tools. Use this as an opportunity to strengthen the author–editor relationship rather than considering it unproductive, lost time. In particular, don't grow frustrated with authors who just don't get it; some will never do the work sufficiently frequently to acquire real expertise.

- Some people may initially make more errors while editing on the screen than they would while working on paper. Combining onscreen edits with a final on-paper edit will reassure them that any errors they might miss will still be caught. If you see a pattern of consistent errors, think about how you might solve the problem; my discussion of exclusion dictionaries in Chapter 10 is one example of how you can help authors or editors spot problem words they're missing on the screen. Similarly, the discussions of search tools in Chapter 8 and of automation tools in Chapter 11 show how you can develop tools that help someone overcome their blind spots. Of course, tools alone are not enough; users must be trained to use the tools productively.

- In some workplaces, authors have far more power than editors, and can overrule editors without discussion. There may be physical (geography) or organizational (office politics) barriers that prevent authors from discussing changes with editors. The solution in both cases is to nurture cooperative relationships that slip around or undermine these barriers. Authors must learn that if an editor misunderstood something and felt obliged to change it, other readers will too; thus, the author should consult the editor to learn the cause of the misunderstanding. Where that dialogue cannot take place in person, technology provides alternatives: e-mail works well to exchange questions and answers at the convenience of the correspondents, whereas a phone call or instant messaging (chat) permits interactive, immediate dialogue.

- Because editing work is sometimes very repetitive, editors may fear the computerized approach will take longer than long-practiced paper-based methods. The solution is to help them develop shortcuts such as macros (Chapter 11), and to provide some slack in the schedule until they come up to speed.

- Many people fear that increased computer use will cause repetitive stress injuries (RSIs) such as carpal tunnel syndrome. Provided there are no pre-existing injuries or medical conditions that computer use will exacerbate, this shouldn't be a problem.. That's particularly true if you take measures to create a safe work environment. Encourage people to have regular medical checkups (including their vision) to spot any developing problems before they become serious. Provide good lighting, a comfortable chair, and a high-quality monitor and keyboard. And, as in any other repetitive activity, remind people to take regular breaks. I've provided more information on protecting yourself and your colleagues from RSIs in Appendix II.

These are only the most common problems. It's wise to ask your colleagues what *they* are worried about, particularly once they've begun using the new process. In addition to establishing a precedent for dialogue and ongoing consultation right from the start, and making it clear that you care what your colleagues think, this approach reveals problems you might not otherwise discover. It's always more effective to learn about these problems early and deal with them than to leave them to fester and create bad feelings that will be difficult to resolve later.

Technological problems

I'll conclude this section with a discussion of the technological problems you can expect to encounter at some point and what you can do about them. These fall into several broad categories:

- software incompatibilities
- workflow
- fonts and special characters

> **Beware upgrades!** Rule 1 of software upgrades: they often fail. If the worst-case scenario is that you have to reinstall the previous version, that's not so bad. If you're using downloaded software, create a backup DVD containing the installer before you upgrade. (Include a PDF file that contains the serial number or license.) Always have Plan B ready. As Colonel Jack O'Neill famously wondered in the show *Stargate SG-1*: "Since when does Plan A ever work?"

If you've spent any length of time grappling with your computer, it may seem implausible that technological problems are the *easy* ones to solve, but it's true. It's particularly reassuring that if you've experienced a problem, someone else has probably encountered it, brainstormed or researched a solution, and reported that solution somewhere on the Web.

This book includes many such solutions. You can find solutions to other problems on the Web, with a little help from the search tips in Chapter 14.

What about the really obscure problems that require interactive troubleshooting and possibly virtual hand-holding? For those, you can depend on key online discussion groups; the Copyediting-L group for editors and other large communities of experienced computer users are usually happy to help. (I've included links to several of these groups on the book's Web page.)

Software incompatibilities

Modern word processors remain surprisingly incompatible. Despite various attempts to create a universal file-exchange format, even nominal standards such as HTML aren't fully compatible between programs. Thus, as a general rule, you can minimize incompatibilities by asking everyone to use the same software, and ideally the same version of that software. Even different versions of the same word processor sometimes differ in significant ways; Microsoft, for instance, has been notorious for releasing new versions of Word that aren't fully compatible with older versions, particularly between nominally parallel Macintosh and Windows versions of Word and between Asian and English-language versions. Some editors who work with a wide range of clients retain installations of several versions of their word processor, or several different word processors, to maximize compatibility with their clients' software.

This is probably unnecessary. The version of a word processor immediately before the current release is usually stable and highly compatible across a product line, assuming that you've installed the latest patches. In contrast, the newest version is usually best avoided until the developer has issued at least one major service release to fix the most serious bugs that it's left for users to discover. If you must upgrade to the newer version for compatibility with colleagues or clients, try to retain your older version until the new version stabilizes. Many installer programs provide an option to retain the previous version, though you may need to look carefully for that option. If not, there are two ways to work around that problem:

- Create a new user account on your computer. Each account can have different software installed.
- Install *virtualization* software such as Parallels, VMWare Fusion, or Virtual Box so you can run the new software in a *virtual* computer.

Workflow

Having everyone use the same software is ideal, but such ideals may not exist in the real world. There are practical reasons why some people may need different software. For example, many print publishers produce their publications in specialized desktop publishing software that offers key features that are lacking in word processors, and particularly the ability to describe colors in ways that are meaningful to printers. Word processors typically only understand the computer screen's RGB color scheme, which translates poorly to paper.

If it's possible to edit using team-oriented software, such as InCopy (which integrates seamlessly with InDesign), you can simply move your on-screen editing process into that companion software. This can be pricey. At the time of writing, InCopy cost US$20 monthly, though with volume discounts. If you can't afford such a solution or if no such solution exists for your publishing software, you'll need to work around this problem. Parallel problems arise in publishing other kinds of manuscripts, whether Web pages or spreadsheets. Chapters 12 and 13 describe workarounds. Some of these work surprisingly well, but are nonetheless ways to patch a suboptimal situation rather than truly efficient workflows. A better solution is to design a workflow that lets you edit the contents of a publication *before* layout and final production; editing at those late stages then becomes a more-manageable proofreading problem, as I discussed in Chapter 16.

More thoughts on workflow: In Chapter 3, the section *A standard process* provides some thoughts on effective workflows.

For most editors, the content creators we work with are *writers*, and use word processors to create what we'll be asked to edit. Thus, it makes sense to keep the content in a word processor for as long as possible; this lets us take advantage of the productivity tools I've described throughout this book. Equally importantly, significant changes are generally more expensive at the layout stage than during the writing and revision stage because even relatively simple layouts can require considerable rework to compensate for extensively revised text. But the most important problem is that layout occurs close to a deadline, when there's little time to implement changes and carefully review the results to prevent new errors from being introduced. This latter problem provides the most compelling argument for editing early and in a word processor.

An obvious exception arises when, as is often the case in technical publishing, everyone uses the same software and all layout is done by the writer using that software. This is true, for instance, in companies that use Adobe FrameMaker or MadCap Flare. In such situations, it's necessary to study the software to learn how its tools can be used to permit the same kind of revision tracking offered by Word and other word processors. When these tools are absent or inadequate, chapters 12 and 13 describe workarounds.

Internet publishing is a special case in which workflow considerations are particularly important. The problem with publishing Web pages is that there is no perception of cost: publishing Web pages can be done and undone instantly, with the click of a button, and there's no printer or press proofs to delay the publication. The urge to publish immediately is exacerbated by the mistaken belief that one's Web audience wants information *now* more than they want it to be correct and of high quality. This increases the temptation to publish too soon and the risk of publishing something that will embarrass the publisher before a potentially large audience. Again, editing early in the process (and editing heavily) minimizes the changes required towards the end of the publishing process.

Fonts and special characters

The problems created by computer fonts have greatly decreased since the first two editions of this book. Unicode fonts are now used almost universally, which means that the character sets of most fonts overlap 100%. If you don't have a particularly rare font on your computer, your software generally provides options that let you permanently or temporarily replace it with a font that you do have on your computer and still see the same characters the author saw. Moreover, as long as you're using the same software and version as your author, odds are good that most of the fonts will exist on both computers.

However, nothing's perfect. In an increasingly international world, you're likely to find yourself working with colleagues from distant lands, such as a team of software developers in India or a Chinese scientist hoping to publish in a North American science journal. In such situations, font incompatibilities can still cause occasional problems. In most cases, the solution is simple: agree to use a core set of fonts that exist on both computers. This is one reason, for example, why international peer-reviewed journals commonly specify that authors must use Times New Roman or Verdana in their manuscripts: the journal can be confident that everyone from the author to the reviewers and desktop publishers will see the same text. In many genres, such as the sciences, authors and publishers simply can't afford the risk of having certain special characters replaced by lookalikes (e.g., µ being replaced by u or m).

In some cases, it may be appropriate to permanently replace a colleague's chosen fonts with more suitable fonts. For example, most of my Asian clients occasionally use Asian fonts for certain characters that they don't know how to type any other way. But because they will be publishing their manuscripts in an English journal, with predominantly English peer reviewers and readers who may not have these fonts, I permanently replace the Asian characters with the correct English equivalents.

If you choose to change an author's fonts, do this carefully to ensure that you don't inadvertently change any special characters, such as the math symbols that infest the scientific manuscripts I edit. In such work, it's worthwhile investing some time examining a range of typical documents and creating a list of all the special characters your authors use. You can then create a file containing the names of these characters followed by the characters themselves, and instructions on how to correctly insert these characters. I've created two such aids—lists of Windows and Macintosh character codes for the kinds of characters my clients frequently use. You can download a copy from my Web site for your own use or to share with your own authors.

Ergonomics

Readers of this book can be forgiven for wondering whether computers and software are designed to inflict pain and suffering. Conspiracy theories notwithstanding, computers can cause short- and long-term problems if we don't pay attention. The problem isn't inherent to the technology; more often, it's because we pay inadequate attention to our computer's ergonomics, don't customize our software sufficiently, and are too sedentary, fatigued, or poorly nourished. Moreover, we older editors have accumulated years of damage that our aging bodies aren't repairing so well anymore, which render us more vulnerable to injury. If you'll spend hours each day working on a computer, you need to watch for health consequences.

The solution is to apply the same kind of thinking behind most workplace safety regulations: avoid the problem in the first place rather than trying to fix a problem after it's occurred. The potential for serious injury is clear if you're working with toxic chemicals or construction equipment, but the injuries office workers face are less dramatic and easier to ignore. Back problems, eye fatigue, and carpal tunnel syndrome won't make the evening news, but they're no less disabling to those they afflict. That being the case, and in the absence of protective workplace legislation, take responsibility for your safety and, for managers, that of your employees.

Appendix II provides a detailed discussion of the most common problems and what you can do to prevent them. Here, I'll only summarize the basic principles. The three words in the phrase *repetitive stress injury* each reveal a key part of the problem and the corresponding solution:

- If a *repetitive action* leads to health problems, develop shortcuts such as the macros and automated text features discussed in Chapter 11 to minimize the amount of repetition. You can't develop a *repetitive* injury in the absence of repetition. Remember to take frequent breaks; they interrupt the repetition and give your body time to heal.

- If *stress* causes the problem, eliminate or minimize the stress. For example, buy a comfortable chair and ergonomic keyboard that support your body's natural position rather than forcing you into contortions. If you relieve most of a stress, a healthy body is more likely to cope with whatever remains. In this sense, *healthy* means well-nourished, well-rested, and in good physical condition as a result of regular exercise.

- If an actual *injury* causes the problem, your body will warn you; all you need to do is listen. Apart from exceptions such as falling asleep at the keyboard and striking your head on the monitor, computer-related problems tend to develop gradually. Pain and its cousin, numbness, are warning signs that precede most injuries; fatigue is an early warning sign of pain, as in the case of eye strain. Thus, if you find yourself experiencing fatigue, pain, or numbness by the end of the day, you need to diagnose the cause and fix it before you develop actual injuries.

Step 4. Watch for Unanticipated Problems

Brasington's Ninth Law: "A carelessly planned project takes three times longer to complete than expected; a carefully planned one will take only twice as long."

Murphy's law (*anything that can go wrong will*) applies perniciously to computers. If you're planning to implement onscreen editing and your only experience with the approach is reading this book, expect to encounter occasional surprises; experience is the best teacher, and until you've studied long and hard under that cruel master, you're an apprentice and vulnerable to surprises. Even masters who have progressed to teaching their own apprentices should still expect the unexpected—particularly if enough time has passed between problems that you've grown overconfident. This is particularly true when you're teaching students who aren't smart enough yet to realize that you've already discovered and fixed every possible problem and that it's not possible for them to discover new ones. It's doubly true if you'll be teaching students who *are* smart enough to explore on their own and encounter problems you never imagined.

The key to controlling chaos is to recognize that it exists, and plan accordingly. This means that you should take measures to minimize the frequency and severity of surprises, and should plan how to respond when those measures aren't enough. The procedure is simple:

- Take steps to minimize incompatibilities.
- Adopt an effective workflow.
- Phase in the new process gradually.
- Create paper trails (or equivalents) to spot problems.
- Provide ongoing support.
- Ensure that communication happens.

Needless to say, this simple procedure suffers from the same flaw as all elegant theories: reality doesn't always conform to our simplistic expectations. But this procedure gives you some confidence the inevitable surprises will be rarer and more easily survived than they might otherwise be.

> **Backups 101:** I've mastered the art of sounding sympathetic when friends lose a file to a computer crash and have no backup copy. Should you want to avoid finding yourself in that situation, Appendix I provides full details on how to develop a sound backup strategy.

Take steps to minimize incompatibilities

Step 3 of the implementation described in this chapter provides my case for suggesting that everyone use the same software. That's the single biggest thing you can do to eliminate problems whether you're freelancing or working for a large employer. Unfortunately, this is most likely to be possible when you're working within a single company that has a strong software compatibility policy. Even then, you'll need support from your employer's computer staff when you implement onscreen editing, since it takes significant effort and expertise to ensure that everyone's computer is updated to the same state. When employees have the right to purchase and install their own software or fonts, systems gradually drift out of compatibility. Some companies lock down all computers so only the computer staff can make any changes. Though this ensures ongoing compatibility, it's bad for morale, and if the computer staff is (as is traditional) overworked and under-trained, they may be unable to make important changes such as installing bug fixes in a timely manner.

In many year of working in such situations, the best solution I've discovered is to develop a professional, mutually respectful relationship—possibly even a friendship—with the computer staff. (Unfortunately, computer staff are often too busy and stressed to give you a chance to develop this relationship into a friendship, and some have the kind of personalities that discourage friendship.) One way to get around these problems is to be someone who gives back instead of just taking; for example, I've helped computer techs revise their résumé or create instruction guides that reduced the amount of time they spent explaining things. Friendships make it easier to ask for favors, but owing you a few favors also works in a pinch.

In some cases, you can gain permission to work around a lockdown and customize your computer or your group's computers. Confirming with your manager and the computer staff's manager that you'll take full responsibility for any screwups goes a long way towards getting that permission, particularly if you learn how to create a *disk image* of a stable computer configuration for each computer; if someone messes up a computer, you can restore its original, stable state in minutes by copying the disk image back onto their hard disk. A better solution, since it doesn't look like you're trying to work around the computer staff, is to identify your needs well in advance and schedule solutions so that the staff have time to fit your needs into their schedule; this is such a refreshing difference from the usual panicked, last-minute demands for help that your consideration will be remembered and appreciated.

When you're on your own, try similar solutions. For example, if your ongoing clients use certain types of hardware and software, purchasing compatible hardware and software can remove many incompatibilities. Indeed, some freelancers own both a Windows computer and a Macintosh so they can work on whichever gives them the fewest problems for a given client. I work almost exclusively on a Macintosh, but run Windows using the Parallels software. Though I work exclusively in Word, I have an old copy of WordPerfect I can install if necessary. I also have several older versions of Word installed in case I need to use one of those versions.

Adopt an effective workflow

As I noted toward the end of Step 3 in this chapter, designing an effective workflow is a great investment in peace of mind. Such a workflow is easiest when you're using fully or mostly compatible software. Where significant software incompatibilities exist, you'll need to modify the workflow to account for known problems and to minimize surprises. This is most often necessary when you're part of a publication workflow in which writing is done in one program (such as Word) and design or publishing is done in another program (such as InDesign). In any process, whether you're all using the same software or handing the edited manuscript to someone else for production, it's wisest to do the heavy editing at the start of the workflow, when you have more freedom to take your time and do the job right, not to mention more time to spot and solve any problems.

If you pay careful attention, you'll begin to notice which parts of the workflow tend to cause the most problems or cause specific types of problem. Once you know that, you can begin looking for solutions. For example, at my former employer, we noticed that authors took a long time to produce their first draft of a manuscript. A little investigation revealed the problem: as researchers, their primary job was to do research, not to write, so they'd never received any training in planning a manuscript. Some personal coaching about how to create an effective outline solved that problem. In addition to reducing the time required to produce that first draft, it also greatly reduced the amount of substantive editing required.

Phase in the new process gradually

The easiest way to ensure that onscreen editing will fail is to impose the system without consultation, without training, without enthusiastic support (buy-in), and without testing—in short, to rush through the process without taking the necessary time for everyone to understand the process and grow comfortable with it. Unfortunately, identifying all the problems you may encounter requires careful testing, and there are no shortcuts. A basic approach resembles the following:

• Ask the authors and editors who will adopt the new process, or a representative sample of these groups, to define their needs and the problems they face. Meeting those needs and solving those problems becomes your priority; this provides faster and more satisfying results than focusing on problems you imagine to exist, and creates a workplace culture based on dialogue rather than dictation.

- If you're a manager, you're not one of the people who will be most strongly affected by the change. Thus, you'll have an incomplete picture of their reality. Even if you do similar work, you're only one person, and diverse viewpoints provide a more complete picture.

- Provide formal training, and time for students to practice what they learn. Even skilled computer users who are enthusiastic about learning new tools generally lack sufficient flexibility in their schedule to find time to practice. You may need to plan well in advance to create an opening in their schedules when you can isolate them from the stress of their daily workload and provide time for study and practice.

- If your colleagues aren't eager (or are only cautiously willing) to adopt the new approach, some may sabotage your efforts in an effort to restore the comfortable status quo; others may plod along without making any effort to help you succeed. Identifying these people and finding ways to support them and meet their needs can gain their support. Proving that you value their opinions by accepting some suggestions even if you think you know a better way can gain their support. If you really do know a better way, your task is to convince them to try your solution; for example, promise you'll try their way if your way doesn't work for them, or run parallel trials that test both solutions.

- Compile a list of problems encountered during your test cases, explanations of how to avoid them, and solutions for when you can't avoid them. This reassures adopters who will follow the test case that their colleagues have identified and solved these problems. Each problem solved is one less problem for new adopters to face, so latecomers to the process can adopt a proven, smoothly functioning system rather than having to face the same learning curve. The fewer problems they encounter, the less reason they'll have to oppose the implementation and the more reason they'll have to embrace it.

Create paper trails to spot problems

As I noted in Chapter 17, some organizations require the creation of a paper trail to identify the sources of problems, to provide legal protection, and for other reasons. The first of these reasons provides an opportunity to look for unexpected problems. For example, if you're still producing printed outputs as your final product (e.g., magazines, books), these final paper copies are your proof that the new onscreen editing process works. In contrast, if you check these copies carefully and detect problems, then you've discovered something unexpected and you'll need to backtrack to find the source of the problem so you can find ways to prevent it from happening again. If you've kept a paper trail, whether literally on paper or using the software equivalent, it's generally not too hard to scan back through the sequence of archived documents until you find where the error occurred. The same logic applies to online help files, Web pages, and software interfaces: the proof that a process works is in the final product.

To develop a supportive, cooperative atmosphere, focus this process on identifying and solving problems, *not* on assigning blame and punishing the guilty. If the process becomes adversarial, you raise the level of tension and increase resistance to its adoptions; moreover, tense authors and editors are likely to make more mistakes, not fewer. In contrast, treating the testing process as a means of helping everyone work faster and more effectively, with less stress, can smooth an otherwise bumpy implementation.

Provide ongoing support

One of the truisms of editing is that editors use the editing tools far more often and for longer periods than authors. That's particularly true if you're working with people for whom writing is only a secondary role; for example, scientists primarily do research, engineers develop products, and academics do library research and teach students. All of them write as part of their work, but except perhaps for the academics, it's not their primary role; for some, it may not even be an important role. This has several consequences, most notably that these authors tend to forget how to use the editing tools. They have less incentive than we do to practice and acquire proficiency, tend to forget what they've learned during the long periods between jobs, and generally have many more important priorities.

This means you'll have to provide ongoing coaching to help authors use the tools productively. Although this may seem to be wasted time, that isn't the case if you consider the benefits of developing productive and perhaps even friendly working relationships with your authors. Time invested in nurturing these relationships—here, by helping authors do their job faster and more effectively—is time well spent. It encourages dialogue and cooperation, both of which lower their resistance to being edited and multiply opportunities to work together to develop the best possible solutions for communication problems.

Unfortunately, some authors never do learn to use the tools, despite repeated, long-term coaching and hand-holding. It's not that they're stupid, though it's tempting to leap to that conclusion; things we've learned so well we no longer think about them seem easy, even if they're inherently difficult. Sometimes the problem is a simple lack of motivation, since writing isn't the author's main job. Motivation isn't something we can provide unless we also manage the authors. Because we don't always have time to coach them, despite our best efforts to find time, it's helpful to provide tools that can help authors help themselves when we're unavailable. One such tool is the primer I developed to summarize the key things authors need to know to use revision tracking effectively. Feel free to distribute this primer or to modify it to better meet your specific needs.

Ensure that communication happens

As I've repeatedly noted, the synergy between author and editor only happens if you encourage an ongoing dialogue. This dialogue can occur face to face, in the form of e-mailed questions and comments, or in the form of a telephone call or an instant messaging chat while the document is simultaneously displayed on both your computers so both of you can see what you're talking about and discuss alternatives. If you're working with a wiki or other modern tool for collaboration, you should be able to update the information dynamically as you discuss solutions.

Technology can only support and encourage communication; it is not, in itself, communication. Whether you're a solitary editor implementing onscreen editing with a host of clients, or a manager implementing this process for a department of writers and editors, your goal must be the same: to keep a watchful eye on the author–editor interactions to ensure that people are communicating effectively. Check periodically to confirm that everyone is satisfied their voice is being heard, and if you spot a problem, intervene to solve it before it destroys the dialogue.

Relax a Little!

In this chapter, I've somewhat exaggerated the difficulty of implementing onscreen editing in the workplace by attempting to comprehensively discuss all possible problems. In many cases, you'll encounter few significant problems and can move quickly and painlessly through the implementation process. Follow this four-step approach honestly, demonstrating clear concern for the needs of your colleagues, and it can be surprisingly easy to implement onscreen editing.

If you're working in a high-pressure environment, that pressure can make you feel that implementation must occur immediately and must produce instantaneous, dramatic payback.

Resist that feeling.

To the extent that this is possible, let everyone ease into the process gradually, ideally after going through the preliminary testing that I've described in this chapter so that you can adopt a proven process that addresses all the unique aspects of your specific situation. Expect the full payback to take some time to become apparent, but also make sure that everyone knows what is working well and why that success is important.

I've had good success following the approach described in this chapter at two workplaces (a federal government research center and a nonprofit research institute), and have successfully implemented onscreen editing with several hundred individual clients from every continent except Antarctica and from dozens of different cultures. You can succeed too!

Customized Seminars and Consulting

If you'd like to learn more about onscreen editing, or how to implement the process in your workplace, please contact me at the following address:

Geoff Hart
c/o 112 Chestnut Ave.
Pointe-Claire, Quebec
H9R 3B1 Canada
ghart@videotron.ca / geoff@geoff-hart.com

I'm happy to develop customized seminars to teach you, your employees, or a group of colleagues how to use the techniques described in this book in your own work context and in your own workplace.

IV. Appendices and Miscellaneous Resources

Appendix I. Developing a Sound Backup Strategy

Web: http://www.geoff-hart.com/books/eoe/eoe3/eoe3.html
Note: Word 2010 is for Windows; Word 2011 is for the Macintosh

It's been said there are only two types of computer user: those who have already lost important data to a crash or other mishap, and those who soon will. Although this is a slight exaggeration, it bears an unfortunate grain of truth. Viruses, trojans, spyware, power failures, computer crashes, malfunctioning sprinkler systems, hurricanes, earthquakes, theft, and miscellaneous other disasters can all cause you to lose files. If you're working on a tight deadline, you can't afford that loss, and this means you must develop a simple, robust, reliable backup strategy. The goal of this strategy is simple to describe: to let you get back to work in as much time as it takes to copy your backups to a new hard disk or the hard disk on another computer—ideally no more than an hour or two. Here, I'll summarize what you need to know to create such a system.

The only good backup strategy... is one you actually use. Human nature being what it is, it's better to automate your backups rather than to hope you remember. Check out software such as Backblaze, Carbonite, or Crashplan that will do the hard work for you.

Elements of a Backup Strategy

A successful strategy must:

- protect against losses due to computer, theft, fire, or natural disaster
- let you recover the most recent version of your work
- let you recover earlier versions if the current version is damaged
- offer protection against malware (e.g., viruses)

The goal is to restore as much of your work as possible, as fast as possible. Whether you purchase specialized backup software or archive your files manually, you must accomplish all four goals. It should be obvious that you need to make copies of all manuscripts that you're editing. Less obvious is the need to back up your operating system and software too: it does you no good having a copy of your work files if your operating system and word processor are no longer available. This means you'll need to make a complete backup of your hard disk periodically.

There are two categories of backup. First, *full* backups copy the entire contents of your hard drive; you'll often hear this described as *cloning*, since it creates an exact copy (a clone) of your hard drive. The advantage is that you create an exact copy of your computer, but the tradeoff is that cloning can take considerable time for large hard drives. Second, you can make a series of daily (or more frequent) copies of only the files that changed since the last full backup; these are called *incremental* or *differential* backups. (There are technical differences between these procedures that aren't relevant for the purposes of this appendix.) These are faster to make, since you're copying much less data, but the tradeoff is that restoring your whole hard drive takes longer because the backup software must re-establish its most recent condition by running through all the incremental changes. It can also be challenging to dig through the backups to find a particular file.

Software to clone your hard drive: For Windows, try Acronis True Image. For the Macintosh, Carbon Copy Cloner and Super-Duper are both good options.

Full backups are easiest, but take longer; incremental backups are faster, but harder to work with. A good compromise is to combine both methods with a little manual labor:
- When you finish editing a file, copy it to a convenient backup medium such as a flash drive. Use a different drive for each day of the week, so if one fails, is damaged, or is stolen, you only lose that day's work.
- At the end of the week, make a backup of all the files you worked on that week (i.e., an incremental backup).
- At the end of the month, make a full backup of all files on your computer (clone its hard drive).
- Include both local backups (e.g., stored somewhere in your home) and off-site backups (e.g., using cloud storage such as Dropbox) in your strategy.
- Note: The last two types of backup should follow a schedule that makes sense to you. You may want to do incremental backups daily and clone your hard drive weekly.

Windows and the Macintosh both offer built-in backup software so you can immediately begin making backups without having to buy any new software:
- **Windows:** Start button > Control Panel > System and Maintenance > Backup and Restore

- **Macintosh:** System Preferences > Time Machine

A final word of wisdom before I discuss the details: Always *test* your backups to ensure they succeeded. For example, if you've copied your files to a flash drive, try opening two or three files from the drive. Computer hardware and software are quite reliable, but when they fail, they often provide little warning. If a backup fails and you don't discover this immediately, you may not discover it until you need the backup in an emergency—and then it's too late. If the test fails, immediately take other steps to protect your key data (e.g., e-mail the current work files to yourself) while you repair or replace the backup device. That's not just theory, by the way. Some time ago, I discovered the online backups I was making automatically had stopped working: the backup software showed all the usual signs it was copying and uploading files, but when I went to the backup site to test a few files, the files weren't there! I fixed the problem in a big hurry.

Call UPS to deliver you from electrical problems: To minimize the risk of losing data to electrical problems, use an uninterruptible power supply (UPS). This device offers better protection than a traditional surge suppressor against power fluctuations (both over-voltages that can damage your computer and voltage *sags* that can cause it to shut down). It also provides enough battery power that you can save any open files and shut down your computer safely if the power fails. I wouldn't work without one. You shouldn't either.

Protecting Against Theft and Damage

The best backup in the world is useless if a thief steals the backup along with your computer, if the family dog uses your backup disks as a chew toy, or if a fire or flood destroys both the computer and your backup disks. That being the case, it's important to store your backups where the same unfortunate event that destroys your computer won't affect the backups. When I was a wage slave, I rotated my backup disks between home and work; if the home copies were destroyed or lost, my copies at work (protected by an alarm system, security guard, and fire suppression equipment) were likely to be safe. Conversely, if the copies at work were lost or damaged, I could replace them immediately from my home copies.

A bank's safe-deposit box offers a good alternative if you're working from home, but you could also offer to trade backup disks with a nearby friend.

> **Bank's safe deposit box too small?** Standard safe-deposit boxes are often too narrow to hold a DVD. However, most will hold a portable hard drive; many portables are not much larger than a deck of cards. Portables large enough to back up a full hard drive can cost less than US$50. Flash drives are even smaller, but are prohibitively expensive for cloning a hard drive.

For your most important files, additional peace of mind comes from multiple backup copies stored in different locations. The easiest way to accomplish this is through online (*cloud*) storage. Most services are now available for both Macintosh and Windows systems. Apple's iCloud Drive and Microsoft's OneDrive both start with 5 gigabytes of free storage and offer plans starting as low as US$1 and US$2 per month, respectively, for 50 gigabytes of storage. Google Drive starts with 15 gigabytes of storage and offers 100 gigabytes for US$2 per month. There are many other services, including ones such as DropBox and Carbonite that combine online storage with automated backup solutions. The one drawback to these solutions is that they require an Internet connection. Particularly if you live in a location where your Internet access isn't 100% reliable, online backup should never be your only solution. You need to be able to access your files even when you can't access the Internet.

Of course, if your files are confidential, you'll need to find a means of encrypting them to protect them from prying eyes. If the files are stolen, the thief will still have to decrypt them before they can see the contents. I discuss a few encryption options in Chapter 3.

Recovering the Current Version of Your Work

The most common problem occurs when your computer or word processor crashes and you lose the currently open files. When the crash occurs, you lose any data that hasn't yet been saved to your hard disk, and in extreme cases, the files that were open at the time of the crash may be corrupted beyond hope of recovery. To recover as much of your work as possible, consider making interim backups over the course of the day.

Automated backups

Better-quality backup software has a setting that lets you automatically create ongoing backups of your work at specified intervals. If your software can do this, it's a good option. Word also lets you create a backup copy each time you open a file, and automatically save a version of your open files at regular intervals (see Chapter 4 for details of these settings), and you should enable at least the second of these options. These precautions assume the crash is sufficiently minor you can reboot your computer. For additional protection, create manual backups.

Manual backups

All the automatic backups in the world won't help if a power-surge from the lightning storm that is raging outside your office destroys your computer. The solution is to use some form of removable backup medium that lets you save copies of the file that are physically separate from your computer. While I work, I keep a USB flash drive plugged into my computer, and periodically make a numbered copy of the file I'm working on (copy 1.docx, copy 2.docx, etc.) and transfer it to that device. E-mailing yourself a copy of the file would also work, so long as you remember how to access your e-mail from a different computer.

Recovering Previous Versions of Your Work

Recovering the most recently saved version of your work is a good start, but sometimes that isn't enough. Files can be infected by viruses or slowly corrupted by bugs in the software that created them. Moreover, it's not uncommon to make extensive changes to a manuscript only to discover that these changes were wrong. In some cases, the easiest and fastest way to undo these changes will be to return to a version of the file that predates these changes and start over. (Pro tip: make a backup copy of the file before performing any long, complex series of changes.) Finally, material you deleted from an earlier version of a file sometimes turns out to be valuable, and the only way to recover that information quickly is to find an earlier version that contains it. In each case, you're in trouble if you don't have older versions of the file saved somewhere.

The automatic backups described earlier in this Appendix typically only retain the most recent version of a file. The solution is to retain a series of dated or numbered copies of all files. As I work, I always retain the following copies of the files I'm working on:

- The original file the author sent me. Though you can recreate this file by rejecting all tracked changes, that won't work if the current copy is damaged.
- Today's version of the file on today's flash drive, and yesterday's version on yesterday's flash drive. I use a separate flash drive for each day of the week, but it's generally sufficient to rely on only these two copies because I return most of my work the day after I begin work on a manuscript. When a manuscript takes longer, copies may end up on three or more flash drives.
- Complete weekly backups of all manuscripts. I use one recordable DVD per week for this purpose. (These disks are more stable and last longer than rewritable CDs or DVDs.)
- Ongoing backups of my whole hard disk to an external disk drive. When I'm on vacation, I hide the hard drive somewhere safe.

Beware heat and cold! Modern recording media are quite robust, but they have limits. Don't leave your backups in the car during the summer (or in the winter if the temperature drops below freezing); extreme temperatures can make the information unrecoverable.

Protecting Against Malware

Malware is the general term for software that is designed to damage or steal your information; some software takes control of your computer and turns it into a *zombie* that can be used to distribute spam or viruses, whereas other programs encrypt your hard drive so you can't access it without paying a ransom (*ransomware*). These programs are proliferating at a furious rate, and it's no longer the case that Macs are safer than Windows computers. For your own protection, and to ensure that you don't transfer any malware to a client, you should implement at least two levels of protection: a firewall to keep intruders out of your computer (basic versions are built into both the Windows and the Macintosh operating systems), and anti-malware software. A full discussion of computer security is beyond the scope of this book. If you're not willing to research the topic in any depth or don't enjoy tinkering with your computer, pick a commercially available security suite with a good reputation, such as BitDefender. Here, I'll focus on the implications of malware for backups.

An advantage of DVD-based backups: One reason I like to create backups on DVD is that malware can't erase, encrypt, or change any data once it's been written to the disk.

From a backup perspective, the biggest danger is that malware problems aren't always sufficiently dramatic to alert you. Some malware is slow and subtle, and does its damage progressively over long periods, only revealing its presence after some time has passed and you discover that some of your files are no longer usable. Developers of security software, including antivirus software, are continuously vigilant for new threats, but even when they detect a threat rapidly, it can take some time to develop a solution. During that window of vulnerability between the time a threat is released and the time it's detected and a solution is developed, it's possible to become infected. The only good defense is the long backup history I described earlier; I have weekly DVD backups going back several years. Should a file be infected without being noticed, I can return to those earlier backups to recover it. (This also protects me against those times when I'm not paying attention and delete a file I should have retained.)

Scan your backups too: Some malware leaves parts of itself on your computer to re-establish an infection. Before copying backup files onto your hard disk, scan them using your anti-malware software to confirm they don't contain any malware. It's generally safe to copy infected files to your hard disk and disinfect them using your anti-malware software. So long as you don't run a program or open the infected file, you shouldn't have a problem. If your computer has been infected, disinfect it using your anti-malware software, then make a new backup, free of the infection, and discard any infected copies. There's no sense cleaning up your system, then re-infecting yourself by inadvertently opening an infected file from an old backup.

Protecting Your Word Customizations

If you've followed the advice in this book, you will have created many kinds of useful customizations of your word processor. Again, I'll focus on Microsoft Word. These include templates, building blocks (formerly AutoText), AutoCorrect entries, keyboard shortcuts, macros, and custom dictionaries. Given how much time these save you and how much your productivity would decrease if you lost access to these customizations and had to rebuild them from scratch, it's clearly important to include them in your backups. To do this, you need to know where these files are located both for spur-of-the-moment (i.e., manual) backups and for inclusion in your ongoing (automated) backup strategy.

> **Finding the files:** Microsoft's file locations change unpredictably, seemingly with each new version. If you can't find a given file type, search the Web using your software's version number, the file type, and key words such as *location* that narrow the search. For example: "Word 2016" "Normal.dotm" "template location". In Google, the double quotes ensure that words or phrases appear in the search results. Other search engines may use different syntax.

Word templates

Most of Word's customizations are stored in its template files. To locate these files:

- **Word 2010:** File > Options > Advanced > General > File locations button > User templates
- **Word 2011:** Word menu > Preferences > Personal settings > File locations > User templates
- Select the User templates category, then click the Modify button.
- Word displays a standard file selection dialog box so you can choose a more obvious location for the templates. For example, mine are stored in the folder *Geoff templates* in the same part of my hard drive as my work files, and are automatically included in my backups.

The key file to include in your backups is Normal.dotm, which stores most shortcuts unless you tell Word to use a different repository. Also include any custom templates you've designed. If you haven't moved your template directory someplace more convenient, these files are buried deep in your hard drive. To get to these directories more easily, create a short-cut (Windows) or an alias (Macintosh) to the directory that contains them. Then you can simply double-click the shortcut to go directly to that directory.

Building blocks (formerly AutoText)

Most editors will use AutoCorrect (discussed in the next section) more often than building blocks, but here's where to find any building blocks that you have created:

- **Word 2010:** By default, building blocks are stored in the Normal. dotm template. If you save yours in a *named gallery* (i.e., a special-purpose collection), they'll be stored in Building Blocks.dotm.
- **Word 2011:** AutoTexts are stored by default in Normal.dotm. However, if you create a template and open that template for editing, you can store new AutoText only in that template.

AutoCorrect

AutoCorrect entries are stored in two places: formatted ones are stored in Normal.dotm, and unformatted ones are stored in separate files with .ACL at the end of the name (Windows) or as part of the name (Mac). Note that if you're using Windows, the .ACL part of the file name may not be visible if you have set Windows to conceal filename extensions. Although you can use your computer's Find File function to locate these files, it's simpler to navigate directly to where they're stored:

- **Word 2010:** C:\Users\[your name]\AppData\Roaming\Microsoft\ Office. There's one file per language. If you're working in US English, the file you're looking for is named MSO1033.ACL. For non-US-English ACL files, consult Microsoft's knowledgebase to learn the meaning of the code numbers.
- **Word 2011:** Users\[your name]\Library\Preferences\Microsoft\Office 2011\Microsoft Office ACL [English]. Autocorrect files for other languages include the corresponding language name.

As in the case of building blocks, creating a shortcut or alias will get you to your AutoCorrect files most quickly.

Macros

By default, macros (Chapter 11) are stored in Normal.dotm, but you can also store them in templates that you create for special purposes. In the latter case, be sure to include these custom templates in your backups. To view the code for your macros so that you can copy that code into a Word document as a kind of a manual backup, as I describe later in this appendix), open the Macros dialog box:

- **Word 2010:** Ribbon > View tab > Macros icon > View macros
- **Word 2011:** Tools menu > Macro > Macros

In the Macros dialog box, select the macro you want to inspect and click the Edit button to display the macro in Word's macro editor. You can now copy the text and paste it into a Word document for safekeeping; should you ever need to recreate that macro, copy the text from that document and paste it into the macro editor, as described in Chapter 11. To escape from this editor, press Alt+F4 for Windows or Command+Q for the Macintosh. Don't worry: you're only quitting the editor, not Word!

Keyboard shortcuts

Keyboard shortcuts that you created using the Customize Keyboard dialog box are stored, by default, in the Normal.dotm template. If you chose to store a group of shortcuts in a different template, be sure to include that template in your backups.

Dictionaries

Over time, Word's custom dictionaries and exclusion dictionaries (Chapter 10) accumulate a lot of new words that you don't want to be forced to recreate or to manually add again to the dictionaries. To find these dictionaries, display the Custom Dictionaries dialog box:

- **Word 2010:** Ribbon > File menu > Options > Proofing tab > Spelling & Grammar > Custom Dictionaries button.
- **Word 2011:** Word menu > Preferences > Spelling and Grammar tab > Dictionaries button.

Look below the list of dictionaries for the File path field. In Word 2010, this is typically C:\Users\[your name]\AppData\Roaming\Microsoft\ UProof. In Word 2011, the dialog box is too small to display the full path, but if you click the Add button, Word opens a standard file selection dialog box. If you click the menu at the top of the dialog box that shows the current directory, you'll see the full path leading to that directory. This is typically Users\[your name]\Library\Application Support\Microsoft\ Office\Preferences\Office 2011.

Windows registry files

Thought you were done? Not so fast! If you use Word 2010, you'll also need to include your Windows Registry file in your backups, since Word stores many settings in the Registry. The intricacies of the Windows Registry are beyond the scope of this book, so I'll simply point you to How to Geek's "How to backup and restore the Windows registry".

A manual alternative

I store all of my automatic text, macros, and a list of keyboard short-cuts and customizations that I've created in a file named (logically enough) *Keyboard customizations*. This file gets copied to my DropBox account auto-matically. Should I ever need to recreate these shortcuts and find myself separated from my backups (e.g., while I'm traveling), I can download the file from DropBox and recreate all of my customizations in an hour or so by working diligently through this file, one item at a time. For example, I can copy and paste macro code into the macro editor instead of having to re-record or rewrite the code.

Because I teach writing and onscreen editing in Word, I find this doc-ument useful whenever I install a new version of Word because the act of recreating my customizations reminds me how to teach others to create their own shortcuts. Moreover, I periodically skim this file to see which of my shortcuts I've forgotten and should be using. (You'd be surprised how often that happens.)

Appendix II: Protecting Yourself From Injury While Using a Computer

Web: http://www.geoff-hart.com/books/eoe/eoe3/eoe3.html
Note: Word 2010 is for Windows; Word 2011 is for the Macintosh

The more you use your computer, the greater the risk you'll encounter a repetitive-stress injury (RSI) such as carpal tunnel syndrome. That's not because computers are inherently harder on your body than (say) jogging, but rather because the problems are subtler and develop over longer periods. (Unless you jog 8 hours per day, you also spend more time in front of your computer.) RSI results from overuse of a body part without giving it time to recover, so it's also called an *overuse injury*. Given how much time modern editors spend at the keyboard, overuse is surely a risk. The most common problems fall into three categories:

- aches and pains
- hand and arm problems
- eye strain

This appendix provides the information you'll need to understand these problems and take the necessary steps to protect yourself.

Get professional advice: The original article that formed the basis for this appendix was reviewed by medical and ergonomics professionals, but *it is not a substitute for professional advice*. If you're experiencing a problem, or worried that one may be developing, seek medical advice *now*. Don't wait for the problem to become serious. It's easier and less painful to prevent an injury than it is to treat it.

Aches and Pains

It's unnatural to sit for hours at a time, and computer potatoes can expect their body to suffer. If you contort your body into awkward positions to compensate for a deficient workspace, this exacerbates the problem. The solution is simple, at least in theory: get up and move around or stretch periodically, exercise often enough to keep your body in good shape, and create an ergonomic workspace that minimizes the stress on your body.

The seat of the problem

Sitting for hours compresses your buttocks and upper thighs, thereby reducing blood flow to your legs. Improperly positioned backs and seats on chairs encourage a slumped posture that misaligns your spine and places additional stress on muscles, bones, and connective tissues (ligaments and tendons). If you'll be spending hours in your chair each day, invest in a good one. A good chair has the following properties:

• The cushions comfortably distribute and support your weight, thereby minimizing the pressure on any one part of your body.

• The back rest adjusts to cradle and support your back, and the seat height adjusts: it should be low enough that your legs don't dangle but high enough that your weight doesn't rest solely on your buttocks.

• If the chair has armrests, they must support your arms without creating painful pressure. Hard plastic is particularly dangerous.

Take frequent breaks: Take breaks, particularly when you're facing a tight deadline, so your body's self-repair mechanisms have time to work. Need help remembering? Use software. Any alarm program will do, but specialty software may work better. Try The Ergociser for Windows or Stretchware for both the Macintosh and Windows.

Don't skip the test drive: the only way to tell whether a chair works for your body's unique configuration is to sit in it long enough to understand what it feels like. Test the chair in the store by adjusting it to fit your body, then spend at least half an hour sitting, and at the end of that time, ask a friend to confirm that the chair is encouraging good posture while you're sitting. Bring this book to pass the time!

Chair alternatives: A large exercise ball (*balance ball*) can make a good chair because it adapts to your shape and balancing strengthens your core muscles. They're cheap, thus worth a try. Kneeling chairs are worth trying, but can create significant pressure on your knees. Standing desks became very popular when doctors realized that sitting all day is bad for you. Since they eliminate the chair for at least part of the day, they should also eliminate or mitigate chair-related problems. However, there's little good evidence that they work and that they don't cause other problems. Use them cautiously!

Some people find that a footrest elevates their feet enough to shift some weight to their lower legs and knees, thereby reducing pressure on their buttocks, hips, and thighs. When this works, it improves blood flow to the legs and reduces compression of the leg tissues. However, a too-high footrest can place *too much* weight on the buttocks and their underlying bones. If you buy one, ensure the height is adjustable or that you can adjust the chair's seat height to compensate and pay close attention to whether it improves comfort—or just shifts the pain elsewhere.

Layout of your work area

An ideal desk–chair combination lets your body adopt a natural position, as close as possible to the position your body wants to assume if left to its own devices—but without slumping. While seated:

- Your upper arms should hang straight down from your shoulders.
- Your forearms should be horizontal, and angled slightly inwards (towards your center) in front of your body.
- Your shoulders shouldn't hunch.
- Your neck and spine shouldn't twist.
- Only your buttocks, thigh muscles, and feet should experience significant pressure from your weight.
- Your head should be vertical, not tilted to view the monitor.

The Cornell University Ergonomics Web provides useful information on workstation ergonomics you can use to design your own work area.

Work area problems can be subtle. During my first year of intensive onscreen editing, I began experiencing pain in my right shoulder. The problem was my mouse: the mouse typically lies to the right side of the keyboard, and the additional width of the numeric keypad was forcing my right arm to angle outwards, with my forearm extended away from the center of my body. That small additional stretch put too much stress on an old shoulder injury. Moving my mouse to the left side of my keyboard and learning to use it with my left hand eliminated the pain. By paying attention to my body, I recognized the pain before it became chronic, and solved the problem by eliminating the pain's source.

Mouse alternatives

A standard computer mouse can be difficult or painful to use, particularly if it's a cheap knockoff that came with a cheap computer. Fortunately, there are myriad alternatives, many of which you can test-drive at your local computer store. These include trackballs, vertical mice, trackpads, graphics tablets, and keyboards with integrated pointers.

If you find your mouse difficult to click and scroll, try replacing it with a different device. Alternatively, *add* a new device rather than discarding the old one. Alternating between devices—or using each device only for those tasks it does best or least painfully—is a good strategy, since it lets you stop a specific stress before it becomes harmful, although at the cost of creating different stresses. Graphics tablets are a particularly interesting alternative because holding the plastic stylus is very different from holding other types of pointing device.

Since *repetitive* is the problem at the root of RSI, reducing repetition is part of the solution. Perhaps the best solution is to reduce how much you use the mouse in the first place. Chapter 5 lists many keyboard shortcuts and other tricks for moving around a document from the keyboard, and Chapter 11 provides many tips on how to automate repetitive tasks so the computer does the hard work. Many sophisticated pointing devices come with a handful of buttons that can be programmed to perform various actions with a single click. The X-keys keypads for both Windows and the Macintosh take this to the extreme, with the biggest model offering 128 keys that you can individually program. Combine this with software such as MacroExpress for Windows and QuickKeys for the Macintosh and there's no end to the keystrokes you could eliminate.

Hand Problems

Pay close attention to your hands. Spending a whole day typing is obviously stressful, and carpal tunnel syndrome is just one of many potential consequences. These problems can be difficult to diagnose, and you may need an expert to pinpoint the true problem. Your family doctor is a good place to start troubleshooting your body, but many general practitioners lack the expertise to diagnose RSI problems. Ask to be referred to a specialist who can examine both the unique aspects of your body and how you're using that body to work.

Position your hands comfortably

Many hand problems arise from flexing your wrist too sharply outwards, with your little finger pointing farther towards your elbow than it would with your arm at rest. Bending your wrists at awkward angles compresses the tissues of your wrist enough to cause pain and, eventually, nerve damage. When I first began experiencing hand pain, switching to Microsoft's Natural Keyboard helped; that's the one with the split between the left and right groups of keys and an upward bulge in the middle. The combination kept my arms and wrists straighter while I typed, eliminating much of the stress on my wrists. Logitech and Adesso offer comparable keyboards. More expensive ergonomic keyboards exist, and are worth investigating if you have or are developing serious hand problems. But try the Microsoft and Logitech keyboards first, since they're inexpensive and sufficiently common that you can find one and try it at most local computer stores.

Keep warm: Cold fingers and finger muscles are more vulnerable to injury, and slow the circulation of blood that removes fatigue poisons and delivers oxygen. Keeping your hands warm mitigates these problems. I've used the Handeze gloves, which help, but found an even better solution: I bought a pair of cheap cotton gloves and removed the fingertips. They're more cumbersome, but warmer. If you try such gloves, ensure they're not so tight they cut off circulation. No sense trading one problem for another! Some colleagues use *wristies*, which are like turtleneck sweaters for your forearms. They provide enough warmth to keep your arms and fingers flexible.

Reinventing or replacing the keyboard

Many keyboarding problems originate from the standard keyboard's poor design. The straight arrangement of keys is bad enough, but even ergonomic keyboards create problems from the order of the keys. The traditional QWERTY layout is inherently inefficient, and requires more finger travel than necessary—increasing stress on your fingers. The Dvorak keyboard layout is based on studies of letter frequencies, and minimizes finger travel. Dvorak keyboards are available from many suppliers, but you can instead remap your existing keyboard to use a Dvorak layout; both Windows and the Macintosh let you do this from (respectively) the Languages control panel and the Keyboard preferences panel. If you're still learning to touch-type, consider learning the Dvorak layout.

If your main computer is a laptop, you may have noticed that the keyboard is an ergonomic disaster. Even when the keys aren't too close together, they don't travel as far as a standalone keyboard when you depress them; as a result, your fingers strike the end of the key's motion harder and more often. If you mostly use your laptop at a desk, consider adding a good external keyboard and using that instead. Of course, "different (key) strokes for different folks", as the saying goes: some of my colleagues find a laptop keyboard more comfortable. See what works best for you!

Whatever keyboard you use, avoid jarring your fingers at the end of each keystroke. It's easy to wale on the keys so that each keystroke ends with a jolt to your finger. The resulting vibrations travel up your arm, and are worst if your fingers try to travel farther than the keys permit. Enough of these shocks causes sore fingers and arms. Soft-touch keyboards require less pressure and may cushion the impacts, but some people find them too mushy. No matter what keyboard you choose, try not to pound on the keys.

The least stress comes if you don't strike keys at all, and keyless keyboards have been invented to eliminate finger impacts. For example, a few companies make *projection* keyboards that use lasers or LEDs to project the image of a keyboard on your desk; this lets you *touch* rather than *press* the keys, greatly reducing the stress on your fingers, and some even let you use finger gestures to replace mousing. There are also software keyboards for tablet computers that let you drag your fingers across the screen instead of tapping an onscreen keyboard. These usually offer prediction of common words (similar to autocorrect on a smartphone) so you can tap the correct word as soon it appears. You can even use your tablet computer as a keyboard for your desktop computer using software such as RemoteMouse for Windows and Macintosh and Air Keyboard for your Macintosh.

Dictation software can potentially eliminate the need for a keyboard. As you speak to your computer, the computer translates your voice into words and types those words for you. There's usually a learning curve as the software adapts to the unique characteristics of your voice. Such software is built into Windows and the Macintosh, but you may prefer more polished and mature software such as Dragon Naturally Speaking.

Beware awkward keyboard shortcuts: Many keyboard shortcuts are easy to memorize but painful to use. Watch how you hold your hands when you use them, and if the hand position looks or feels awkward, try choosing a less-painful shortcut.

Rest your wrists?

Some people use cushions, bean bags, gel pads, or other devices to support their wrists while they type. Though less painful than resting your palms and wrists on a hard surface, even the softest supports can compress the tissues of your wrist; worse yet, the cheap plastic wrist rests built into many ergonomic keyboards and the flat decks of laptops are no better than resting your hands on the desk. When I began experiencing hand problems, I purchased a foam-rubber rest, and found myself in more pain at the end of the day than before this experiment. When I watched, I saw myself placing pressure on my wrists in the mistaken belief the rubber was protecting them. Some experts suggest that all wrist rests are unsafe, even the softest gel pads, but as always, let *your* body be the judge.

Ideally, your hands should float above the keyboard, not rest on it— so long as this posture keeps your wrists mostly unbent and doesn't create additional strain on your shoulders, arms, hands, or fingers. Occasionally resting your palms on a soft support won't hurt, but only in moderation.

Eye Strain

Our eyes work best when they move around and focus on objects at varying distances, so spending a day staring at a computer monitor will clearly stress them. Optometrists advise taking frequent breaks to gaze at something more distant than your monitor to stretch and exercise the muscles that help your eyes focus. Taking breaks is easiest if you have a window with a nice view, but even if you work in a cubicle farm, you can walk outside during your coffee break to encourage your eyes to focus on moving objects at varying distances. Here are a few other suggestions:

Visual ergonomics: The Vision Council offers a downloadable PDF guide, *Eyes Overexposed: the Digital Device Dilemma*, that explains some of the problems with the modern digital life, and provides suggestions on some relevant solutions.

Help your eyes focus

Your monitor should generally lie at least arm's length from your body. That's far enough you won't strain to see the whole picture, but not so far you'll squint to see the text. Although no one distance works best for everyone, start with this distance and adjust it until you find a comfortable match for your eyes.

If you wear eyeglasses or contact lenses, ask your optometrist about computer versions optimized to help your eyes focus at the distance of your monitor. Multifocal lenses (e.g., bifocals) let you focus comfortably at a range of distances by looking through different parts of the lens, but not everyone finds these glasses comfortable. If, like me, you rarely look away from the screen while computing, it may be more effective to get corrective lenses specifically designed for computer use. Use a second pair of glasses for distance viewing while you're driving a car or walking around.

Crisp pixels, relaxed eyes

A high-quality monitor is a great investment in protecting your vision. Particularly if you work with small fonts, staring at fuzzy text all day fatigues your eyes, which must work harder to focus. CRT monitors (the deep, clunky ones) provide adequate sharpness, but LCD monitors (the really thin ones) are now a much better bet: the prices are affordable, the resolution is so high it's hard to see the pixels, the screens are much larger than CRTs for the same price, and there's none of the flicker that exists with even the best CRTs. As a result, I no longer consider CRT monitors a good option for most editors, and have mostly removed my description of this old technology from this edition. Ideally, save up enough money to afford an LCD monitor large enough to display two standard pages side by side at 100% magnification. A wide-screen 21- or 24-inch monitor will accomplish this and you'll find yourself working far more efficiently using it.

Large versus multiple monitors: There are distinct advantages to having two or more large monitors connected to your computer, but if space is tight, a single large monitor is a good compromise.

Irrespective of the size and type of monitor you use, experiment with resolutions and display characteristics, as described in Chapter 4, to optimize the display for your eyes. Test the various available typefaces to see which ones display most crisply on your screen. Some believe that certain typefaces (e.g., Verdana) are easiest to read on the screen, but in my experience, the best typeface is more a personal preference than an objective and absolute recommendation. In short, let *your* eyes be the ones to judge which typeface works best for you. Once you've chosen a legible typeface, test different sizes to see which ones are easiest on your eyes; an 11- or 12-point font can cause less eyestrain than the 10-point fonts many people use.

If you'll be doing onscreen proofreading and the type size is fixed by the design specifications, don't assume that you're forced to examine the text at that size. Most software lets you zoom in on the display, thereby enlarging the text without affecting the design. Of course, this works best if you own a large monitor, so this is another reason to buy the biggest monitor you can afford and that will fit on your desk.

Stamp out flicker

LCD monitors don't suffer from the flickering that besets even high-quality CRTs. Nonetheless, check the manual for your monitor to see whether it offers a range of refresh rates (more accurately, *frame rates*). The pixels don't have to be constantly renewed, so the only flickering occurs when you change pixels. In editing, this is most serious when you scroll through a document. The common refresh rate of about 60 Hz is fine for most viewers, but monitors with rates of more than 100 Hz are now available and show less flicker during scrolling. The backlight used to illuminate the screen is more likely to cause significant flicker. Fluorescent backlights suffer more from this problem than LED backlights, so if you can afford the (usually small) price difference, opt for LED backlighting.

There are several features to consider in choosing an LCD monitor:

- **Brightness adjustment:** Higher brightness will be important if you work in a bright environment (e.g., a sunlit room with many windows). But you may also want to decrease light intensity if you find the monitor's default setting too bright. My LG monitor was so bright it hurt my eyes, so I decreased the brightness by about 25%.

- **High contrast:** To make the text stand out clearly from its background, look for a monitor with strong whites and dark blacks. A high contrast ratio (now commonly greater than 1000:1) helps, but because this value isn't based on a standard measurement procedure, don't rely solely on the manufacturer's claims. Look for yourself.

Arrange for suitable lighting

Monitor problems can be exacerbated by traditional fluorescent lights. These flicker slowly enough that many people can see the flicker (me, for instance), and because the light flickers at a different frequency from the monitor, this produces a beating sensation that can strain your eyes further. Traditional incandescent light bulbs don't flicker, but these are fast disappearing. Compact fluorescent lights are a better solution, since they flicker much less noticeably than traditional fluorescents and draw considerably less power, while providing comparable levels of light. LED lights are an even better choice if you can find ones bright enough for your office.

Whatever lighting you choose, arrange the lights and computer to eliminate reflections on the screen from lamps or nearby windows. Reflections create glare that fatigues your eyes by forcing them to work harder to look past the glare. Positioning a screen to face away from windows and lights or adding a glare-reduction filter can help. Sometimes all you need to do is adjust the monitor's tilt so the reflections are directed away from your eyes. Although working in a darkened room might seem a viable alternative, that's usually a bad idea; the excessively high contrast between the bright screen and the dark room can increase eye strain.

If your LCD screen flickers, the most likely cause is that the backlight is failing, that you have a damaged cable, or that you're experiencing power fluctuations. Installing an uninterruptible power supply (a UPS, as described in Appendix 1) can eliminate many power problems, but not ones that originate in the monitor or your computer. Since you should be using a UPS to protect your computer, installing one can help eliminate power fluctuations as the cause of the flicker. Cables are easy to replace and not too expensive; moreover, if the cable is detachable, you can bring it to a friend and connect it to their monitor to see if the cable needs to be replaced. If neither the power supply nor the cable is responsible, you may need to repair or replace your monitor.

Computers aren't tear jerkers

There's evidence that we blink less often while staring at computer monitors, and this probably causes the common complaint of dry eyes at the end of a day of computer use. The solution, of course, is to use nature's own lubricant for your eyes: remember to blink while using your computer, thereby moistening your eyes. Taking regular breaks will help, because you'll blink more often when you're not looking at the screen. Working in a room with appropriate humidity levels also helps. To keep humidity at comfortable levels, grow plenty of household plants in or near your office. In unusually dry climates, consider installing a humidifier.

If your eyes remain dry, consult your optometrist to confirm that there's nothing medically wrong, and ask them to recommend a good brand of eye drops; ideally, ask for a brand without preservatives, which can irritate the eyes. Use a kitchen timer or your computer's reminder program to remind you to periodically moisten your eyes or take breaks.

Solutions

The good news about most overuse injuries is that you can do a lot to protect yourself. See your doctor and your optometrist at least annually so they'll have a chance to detect any slowly developing medical problems you might miss. Between visits, pay close attention to your body so you'll know whether you're beginning to have a problem that you can solve yourself or one that will require professional help. An RSI expert will evaluate more than your symptoms; they'll also ask you about your lifestyle, your work habits and work environment, and various other factors related to the problem. But it's far simpler and much less painful to head off problems *before* they require treatment.

In summary, here are things you should be doing to protect yourself and minimize the risk of problems or their severity if they arise:

- **Invest in good tools:** Your computer equipment and workspace are the tools of your trade. Invest in high-quality tools just as any other professional would do. Set up an appropriately ergonomic workspace, invest in a good keyboard and monitor, and try alternatives to the standard mouse until you find a comfortable pointing device.

- **Improve gradually:** If the cost of building a sophisticated ergonomic workspace is a barrier, improve your setup in phases, concentrating first on the problems that are causing you the most grief.

- **Stay in shape:** Most of us are overly sedentary. Find time in your daily schedule to exercise. A balanced exercise program will strengthen the muscles that support your neck, arms, wrists, and fingers, and will help ward off typical computer-related injuries. Strong muscles keep your body properly aligned. Exercise also strengthens your heart and improves circulation, thereby keeping muscles more limber and removing fatigue poisons more quickly.

- **Talk to your computer:** If you have intractable hand problems, try voice recognition software such as Dragon Naturally Speaking. The software lets you control your computer's operation, and lets you dictate text rather than typing. I haven't discussed voice recognition software because I don't use it, but I've seen a friend demonstrate its power; if you think you might benefit from the software, it's now mature enough I can recommend it. Of course, speech recognition software may also cause RSI problems—for your voice. Pay attention to ensure that you're not simply trading one problem for another.

- **Listen to your body:** Nobody knows better than you do when you're feeling pain. Listening to your body's complaints is the best way to detect problems early enough that you have a chance to fix them; if you have a hard time listening to your body, ask someone to watch you while you work, looking for problems such as hunched shoulders, slumping at the keyboard, squinting, and so on.

Don't forget the *repetitive* aspect of RSI: If you spend long enough doing *anything*, you'll grow tired, and if you push past the point of fatigue, you'll greatly increase the risk of injury. Take a break from the computer and enjoy the other things that life has to offer.

In moderation, of course.

Appendix III: Troubleshooting Microsoft Word

Web: http://www.geoff-hart.com/books/eoe/eoe3/eoe3.html
Note: Word 2010 is for Windows; Word 2011 is for the Macintosh

Troubleshooting any program as complicated as Microsoft Word would require an entire book of its own, and even at book length, it wouldn't be possible to cover all the obscure bugs. The enormous size of Microsoft's knowledgebase (on the order of a million entries last I checked) illustrates the magnitude of the problem. In Microsoft's defense, this problem affects any large program, not just Word.

When in doubt, search the Web: I can't hope to be comprehensive or up-to-date in this book. Each new *patch* and each new version of Word introduces new problems while solving some of the old ones. To obtain the information you need, search the Web for your version of Word (e.g., "Word 2016") followed by a description of the problem. Use the search tips in Chapter 14 to narrow down the results to more manageable numbers.

One problem with any complex program, including Word, is that it grows fatigued over time, and starts to get confused about what it should be doing and how. (Though metaphorical, this really seems to describe what's happening.) Thus, rule number 1 for troubleshooting Word is to quit the program and restart it; it doesn't hurt to reboot your computer too. This computer equivalent of a good night's sleep solves many subtle problems that seem to defy other solutions. Plus, rebooting is easier and faster than many of the other solutions.

That being said, many editors encounter certain known, recurring bugs while using Word. In this Appendix, I'll discuss possible solutions to problems that occur most frequently across versions of Word and that I haven't discussed in previous chapters. They fall into several categories:

- damaged (corrupt) files
- file format problems
- file permission problems
- miscellaneous problems
- numbering problems
- software updates
- template problems

- temporary files
- Word crashes when you launch it

Damaged (Corrupt) Files

Word's old .doc format was complex and fragile, and was therefore vulnerable to corruption. (*Corruption* is the technical term for "bad things happen, then eventually you can't open the file again".) One sign of developing corruption is that the file takes an increasingly long time to open or save even though it doesn't contain any obvious memory hogs such as graphics. You may also see paragraph and character styles not behaving as expected. (See also the section *Numbering problems* later in this appendix.) Eventually, Word may even start crashing after you open the file. The newer .docx format seems to be considerably more stable, but these files can also develop corruption.

> **Corrupted templates:** If Word's Normal.dotm template or other templates have become corrupted, loading them affects all subsequent behavior of Word. Being able to replace the corrupt template with an intact version is another good reason to keep up-to-date backups of all your template files, as described in Appendix I.

To repair a corrupt file, try the following steps (in order of increasing desperation):

- First, turn off the Fast Save option (if you're using an old version of Word) and the Versions option. Then re-save the file under a new name.
- Word 2010 (but not 2011): Open the problem file from the Open File dialog box (Control+O). Select the file, but don't click the Open button. Instead, open the menu beside this button and select Open and Repair. (There's also a Recover text from any file option, but I've never succeeded using that option.)
- Try saving the file in rich text format (.rtf).
- Select all of the file except for the final paragraph marker. (If you can't see that marker, copy everything except the last character in the file or see Chapter 4 for details on how to make it visible.) Copy the text (Control+C for Windows; Command+C for the Macintosh), create a new document (Control+N for Windows; Command+N for the Mac-

intosh), then paste the copied text into the new file (Control+V for Windows; Command +V for the Macintosh).

- Try opening the file in another program. OpenOffice, LibreOffice, and InDesign can often open (and thereby recover text from) files that Word itself can't fix.
- Consider free or commercial software, such as GetData's Repair My Word (Windows only), or try the other programs described in the BetaNews article "Five tools for recovering corrupted Word documents".

Crashes and unsaved files: Word sometimes just disappears suddenly, taking all your work with it. However, Word 2010 may let you recover some of your work even if you can't find a version of the file that contains your most recent work. When you restart Word: File menu > Recent > Recover unsaved files (at the bottom right side of the menu). Should you want to go looking for these files yourself, look in C:\Users\User\AppData\Local\Microsoft\Office\UnsavedFiles.

File Format Problems

The new .docx format that Microsoft introduced with Word 2007 appears to be more stable and resistant to corruption than the older .doc format. Unfortunately, some authors (particularly those in the developing world) still use older versions of Word that cannot read .docx files. In addition, many publishers still (nearly 10 years after the release of Word 2007) don't accept .docx files. In some cases, such as publishers of peer-reviewed journals, the problem is that they use a heavily automated file management system that would be prohibitively expensive to update so that it works with the new format. In such cases, you may need to continue working with .doc files. The good news is that (in my experience) more recent versions of Word have no problem working with files in the older format.

File Permission Problems

Modern operating systems use a complicated system of *permissions* to define which users of a computer are allowed to modify, use, or even see files. The permission settings sometimes change for reasons that aren't obvious; the most common problem occurs when you upgrade to a new computer and the new configuration doesn't precisely match the old configuration; as a result, the system thinks you're someone different. Two common symptoms of this problem are that you are unable to save changes to Normal.dotm or you see the error message Autorecovery save postponed. Both indicate that the operating system is not giving you permission to modify the files or the folders they're stored in.

The solution is to log into your computer as an administrator (if you don't already have administrator access from your user account), and change the permissions of the affected directories. If you don't already know the locations of these directories, open Word's Options (Word 2010) or Preferences (Word 2011) dialog box and inspect the File Locations settings. You can then select these directories using Windows Explorer (Windows) or the Finder (Macintosh) and give your user account the necessary permissions.

Miscellaneous Problems

Can't type symbol characters (Windows)

If the Alt-key combinations that you use to type special characters stop working, the usual problem is that you've inadvertently pressed the Num-Lock key (the top left key in the numeric keypad). Press that key, and the keyboard shortcuts should start working again.

Capitalization is reversed

An obscure bug related to capitalization appeared in Word 2003, and still occasionally reappears. When this bug strikes, typing lower-case letters gives you upper-case letters, and vice versa. Your first reaction may be to press the CapsLock key on your keyboard, and indeed, this solves the problem. Unfortunately, you then have CapsLock turned on in all your other programs, and you need to hold down the Shift key to type lower-case letters—exactly the opposite of what you want. If you switch to other software, capitalization behaves just as expected, so the problem is restricted to Word. Shutting down and restarting Word usually doesn't solve the problem.

Josh Adams solved the problem, and provides a simple solution: Type *Hello* (which will become *hELLO* because of the typing bug), then press the space bar. Word's AutoCorrect feature corrects this capitalization error (resulting in *Hello*) and the capitalization problem is then solved—at least until the next time it happens.

False macro warnings

Even if you delete all macros from a file, older versions of Word may still believe there are macros in the file, and this may trigger Word's warning that the file contains a macro and thus, may contain a virus. The easiest way around this problem is to copy all the contents of the file except the final paragraph marker into a new document that is based on a template that contains no macros.

Normal.dotm template has been changed

Word sometimes gets confused about whether you've modified the Normal.dotm template. If you've set Word to warn you about such changes (see Chapter 4 for details), Word will give you a chance to undo any inadvertent modifications to this template when you quit Word for the day. (This also provides some protection against viruses that can be stored in Word files.) Simply click No if you didn't intend to modify this template, or Yes if you know that you changed Word's configuration (e.g., created new AutoCorrects) and want to preserve the modifications.

If the problem reoccurs, one solution is to open Word, change one of your AutoCorrect entries or keyboard shortcuts, then quit Word and tell it that yes, you really did intend to modify the template. (You can always undo that change the next time you launch Word.) Unfortunately, this doesn't always work in the Macintosh versions of Word, and you simply have to endure the erroneous message until Microsoft solves the problem in a future update.

Slow performance in Word 2011

In early releases of Word 2011 for the Macintosh, Word could be painfully slow. Repeated patches haven't completely solved the problem even as of July 2016, but one possible solution that should improve the functioning of other programs too is to eliminate duplicate fonts. (Microsoft installs its own set when you install Word, and some of these may conflict with Apple's fonts.) To solve this problem, quit all programs, then open the Applications folder and run the Font Book software. Under the Edit menu, choose Select Duplicated Fonts. Reopen the Edit menu and choose Resolve Duplicates. When the software finishes this task, quit the Font Book and restart your computer.

This procedure does not actually delete the fonts; it just turns them off by moving them into a separate folder where the operating system won't load them. If you find that you need one of these fonts, you can re-enable it using Font Book.

Word's "disk full" error

Older Macintosh versions of Word sometimes display an error message that suggests there's no more space left on your hard drive, even if there's really plenty of space. The problem seems to result from Word running out of *file handles*, a jargony way of saying that it doesn't have enough space for the many files it uses to keep track of what you're doing. See the section *Temporary Files* later in this appendix for one possible solution that requires regular housekeeping to clean up Word's detritus.

Sadly, this problem seems to reappear with each new Macintosh version of Word, and it typically takes Microsoft at least one cycle of patches before they admit the problem exists and try to solve it. If this problem affects you, always keep a blank document open behind the document you're working on. If you see this error message, try closing that blank document; this triggers a housekeeping routine that sometimes solves the problem.

The Word MVPs site describes two more sophisticated solutions; search their site for the article "Microsoft's "Disk Full" Error Workaround".

Numbering Problems

Word's automatic numbering feature was badly broken for decades, and involved a sufficiently subtle problem that Microsoft wasn't able to come up with a solution. You'll see this problem arise when midway through a long document, a list that used to start at 1 suddenly acquires a new number, as if it continues a list earlier in the document. Another form of this problem appears when a list that's interrupted by a paragraph of (for example) explanatory text suddenly starts over at 1 after that paragraph. Two solutions seem to work:

- First, don't use Word's built-in automatically numbered styles (List Number etc.). Instead, define your own numbered paragraph style (see Chapter 4 for details about styles), and edit the style's properties so that the Style based on setting is set to None or No style.

- Second, learn to use Word's {SEQ} field codes. David Knopf's article "Autonumbering with RoboHelp and Microsoft Word" provides a clear explanation of how to do so. Ignore the references to RoboHelp (a tool for creating online help in Word) and older versions of Word; the solution should work in any version of Word.

Software Updates

Like any other complex software, Word arrives on your computer bearing a cargo of bugs. Microsoft sometimes tries to fix these problems in a reasonable amount of time, and sometimes they don't. They do periodically releases updates called *patches* or *service packs*, among other names, to solve these problems. If you keep your software regularly patched, most problems will gradually disappear over time. Windows Update (one of the system-level control panels) can be set to watch for new updates, and will automatically download and install them for you. For the Macintosh, Microsoft AutoUpdate (accessed via the Check for updates item under the Help menu) accomplishes much the same purpose.

Microsoft usually does a good job of testing its updates, but also occasionally really messes things up. Thus, a few cautionary notes:

* Unless a new patch is urgent (e.g., a major security issue or a problem that stops you from working), wait at least a week before you install it. This gives more eager users time to discover and report any major problems, and gives Microsoft a chance to fix them.

* Make a backup of all key files (as described in Appendix 1) before installing the update. If your system is basically working fine, consider cloning your hard drive first.

* Always shut down Word before you install any patches. The installer should do this for you, but better safe than sorry.

Template Problems

As I noted earlier, many of Word's customizations are stored in the Normal.dotm template file, which is loaded automatically each time you launch Word. Unfortunately, if Word crashes, the crash sometimes damages open files that have not been saved, including Normal.dotm, thereby eliminating all your hard work customizing Word. Word templates are also a popular target of virus writers. The solution is to include Normal.dotm in your backups. If you customize Word frequently, save a dated copy of previous versions of this template (e.g., *Normal July 2016 backup.dotm*) before you begin each customization session; if you damage anything, you can return to that older version of the template by closing Word, finding and trashing the damaged template, and replacing it with a copy of the most recent non-problematic version of the template, renamed as Normal. dotm.

Temporary Files

Word creates many temporary work files that it uses to keep track of miscellaneous information while you're working on a manuscript. Unfortunately, you can't define where these files should be saved. Some are saved in the same directory as the manuscript (and are invisible because Microsoft doesn't want you mucking about with these files while Word is running); others are stored in the operating system's Temp directory, whose location varies among operating systems and their versions. When you save the file and close Word for the day, Word should theoretically erase the files it no longer needs. In practice, it sometimes forgets—particularly after a crash. If enough temporary files accumulate, Word grows confused and starts crashing. This is less common than it used to be, but you may still need to find these files and manually remove them.

> **More about temporary files:** Microsoft's article "Description of how Word creates temporary files" provides much more detail on these files and their locations. With appropriate modifications, this should be valid for most versions, including Macintosh versions.

It may even be worthwhile adding a recurring monthly note in your calendar program that reminds you to find and delete Word's temporary files. Here's what to look for, perhaps using a search utility such as EveryThing (for Windows) or EasyFind (for the Macintosh):

- Files in the same directories as the files you've been working on: These files will usually have a name that begins with ~ and ends with .tmp. You can find them by selecting the search tool's Use wildcards and Include invisible files options, then searching for ~*.tmp.
- **Windows:** Look in C:\Users\[your name]\AppData\Local, then look in the subdirectories \Microsoft\Word and \Temp

Most of these files can be safely deleted; your computer will stop you from deleting any files that are currently in use by the operating system.

Word crashes when you launch it

If Word isn't launching successfully, or launches and immediately crashes, the odds are good that too many temporary files have accumulated. See the section *Temporary Files* earlier in this appendix for a solution. It's also possible that one of Word's templates has become corrupted, but there are other potential problems, such as incompatible plug-in software. What to do depends on which version you're using, but in both cases, start by quitting Word:

- **Word 2010:** Launch the software in "safe" mode by Start menu > All Programs > Microsoft Office, then hold down the Control key and select Word.

- **Word 2011:** Navigate to Users\[your name]\Library\Preferences\ Microsoft, and drag the Microsoft Word preferences file to the desktop. Word will recreate this file when you launch it again; if this doesn't solve the problem, restore the original preferences file to this directory.

Appendix IV: Word Keyboard Shortcuts (Plus Selected Operating System Shortcuts)

Web: http://www.geoff-hart.com/books/eoe/eoe3/eoe3.html
Note: Word 2010 is for Windows; Word 2011 is for the Macintosh

For clarity, I've used capital letters for all letter-based keyboard shortcuts. However, don't hold down the Shift key unless I have specifically added the word *Shift* to the shortcut.

Accented characters
> See: Type accented characters

Activate the menu bars
> To navigate a program's menus using the keyboard:
> - Word 2010: Press the Alt key, then either type the underlined letter in a menu name or use the arrow keys to move between and within menus.
> - Word 2011: Press Control+F2. Then type the first letter in menu names, the down arrow key to open the menu, and then type the first letter in the menu option's name.
> - For both Macintosh and Windows, press the ESC key to cancel this function.

Boldface text
> Select the text that you want to boldface and press the following keyboard shortcut (or press this shortcut before you start typing new text that should be boldfaced):
> - Windows: Control+B
> - Macintosh: Command+B

Change between programs
> See: Switch between open programs

Change between windows in a program
> See: Switch between open windows in a program

Change font size
> See: Increase or decrease font size

Change keyboard layout (key assignments for different languages)
> This keyboard shortcut can cause considerable trouble if you forget that it exists (e.g., you may suddenly find yourself typing using the French

keyboard). Thus, consider disabling the feature, as described in Chapter 4. If not, the default keyboard command is:
- Windows: Left Alt+Left Shift
- Macintosh: [the shortcut appears to have been eliminated in recent versions of the operating system]

Copy selected text
- Windows: Control+C
- Macintosh: Command+C

Copy or cut noncontiguous text
See: Select noncontiguous text

Create a shortcut (Windows) or an alias (Macintosh) to a file
- Windows: Right-click on the file and select Create Shortcut from the popup menu.
- Macintosh: Select the file and press Command+L, or right-click (control-click) on the file and select Make alias.

Cursor movement
See: Move cursor, Chapter 5

Decrease font size
See: Increase or decrease font size

Delete a word
- Windows: Control+Delete (for the word following the cursor); Control+Backspace (for the word preceding the cursor)
- Macintosh: Command+Delete (for the word following the cursor); Command+Backspace (for the word preceding the cursor)

Diacritical marks, typing
See: Type accented characters

Enable revision tracking
See: Turn on revision tracking

Extend (enlarge) a selection
Hold down the Shift key before using the arrow keys to move the cursor to the end of the desired selection or clicking with the mouse to define the end of the selection.
- Move the cursor with other keys, such as PageDown, to extend the selection faster. See Chapter 5 for details on the many options for moving quickly through a document.
- To extend the selection in Word without holding down the Shift key: position the cursor at the start of the selection, then press F8 repeatedly to select the next word, next sentence, and then next paragraph; at the end of the selection, press Control (Windows) or

Command (Macintosh) plus the period (.) key. See Chapter 5 for more details and options based on this key.

Find text

- Windows: Control+F
- Macintosh: Command+F

Go to

Word's Go to command lets you jump to bookmarks, sections, comments, and other useful locations.

- Windows: Control+G
- Macintosh: Command+G

Increase or decrease font size in Word

Select the desired text. To change the text to the next largest or smallest predefined font size:

- Windows: Control+Shift+> to increase the size; Control+Shift+< to decrease the size
- Macintosh: Command+Shift+> to increase the size; Command+Shift+< to decrease the size

Insert accented characters

See: Type accented characters

Insert copied text

See: Paste copied text

Italicize text

Select the text you want to italicize and press the following keyboard shortcut (or press this shortcut before you start typing new text that should be italicized):

- Windows: Control+I
- Macintosh: Command+I

Keyboard (change key assignments)

See: Change keyboard layout

Menu control from the keyboard

See: Activate the menu bars

Move cursor in Word

- Start of line: Home
- End of line: End
- Start of a paragraph: Control (Windows) or Command (Macintosh) plus the up arrow
- End of a paragraph: Control (Windows) or Command (Macintosh) plus the down arrow
- Up one screen: PageUp

- Down one screen: PageDown
- Start of document: Control+Home (Windows) or Command+Home (Macintosh).
- End of document: Control+End (Windows) or Command+End (Macintosh).

Navigate through a program's menus
See: Activate the menu bars

Open two windows on a Word document
See: Split a Word document window into two panes

Paste copied text
- Windows: Control+V
- Macintosh: Command+V

Programs (switching between)
See: Switch between open programs

Remove manually applied formatting
If you have overridden the formatting instructions defined by a paragraph or character style, and want to return the text to its original, underlying formatting, select the formatted text, then:
- Windows: Control+Space bar or Control+Shift+Z
- Macintosh: Command+Shift+Z

Replace text in Word
- Windows: Control+R
- Macintosh: Command+Shift+H.

Return to your previous position
Either insert a bookmark (using the Bookmark feature or by typing a temporary placeholder such as [ ] that you can search for), or use the Go back function: Shift+F5.

Revision tracking (enable)
See: Turn on revision tracking

Search for text
See: Find text

Select all the text in a document window
- Windows: Control+A
- Macintosh: Command+A

Select a sentence or a paragraph, then extend the selection to include additional sentences or paragraphs
- Hold down the Control key (Windows) or the Command key (Macintosh) and click to select a sentence; to select a paragraph, triple-click without holding down any keys.

- Holding down *only* the Shift key and clicking again anywhere in a subsequent or preceding sentence or paragraph will extend the selection to include the entire sentence or paragraph and all intervening text.

Select noncontiguous text

You can't do this in older versions of Word, but if the goal of selecting is to cut the text to the clipboard so you can move it elsewhere, you can instead use the Spike:

- Select the first chunk of text.
- Hold down the Control (Windows) or Command (Macintosh) key and press F3 to cut the text from the document and add it to the spike (to "spike the text").
- Repeat these two steps (select, then spike, the text) for each additional selection you want to place on the spike.
- When you're done, position the text cursor at the desired destination, hold down the Control key (Windows) or Command key (Mac) and the Shift key, then press F3 again.

In more recent versions of Word, you can select noncontiguous text. To do so, select the first block of text as usual, then for the second and subsequent blocks, hold down the Control key (Windows) or the Command key (Macintosh) before you use the mouse to make additional selections.

***Spike* text**

See: Select noncontiguous text

Split a Word document window into two panes

- Windows: Control+Alt+S
- Macintosh: Command+Option+S

Repeat this keystroke to unsplit the document. Press F6 to move the cursor between the two panes.

Switch between open programs

- Windows: Alt+Tab
- Macintosh: Command+Tab

Switch between open windows within a program

- Windows: Control+F6 in Microsoft Office; Alt+Tab for windows that appear in the Task Bar.
- Macintosh: Command+F6 in Microsoft Office; Command+` (the *accent grave*, on the key to the left of the 1 key on most keyboards) in all programs

Text size (increase or decrease)

See: Increase or decrease font size

Track revisions (edits)/turn on revision tracking
- Windows: Control+Shift+E
- Macintosh: Command+Shift+E

Type accented characters
- Windows: Press Control plus the appropriate accent character (e.g., ', the single quotation mark, for an *accent aigu*), then release both keys and type the letter (for example, typing Control+' followed by *e* produces *é*).
- Macintosh: Press the Option key plus the appropriate accent (e.g., ', the single quotation mark, for an *accent aigu*), then release both keys and type the letter (for example, typing Option+*e* followed by *e* produces *é*).
- For a list of standard keystrokes to create common accented letters for Windows and Macintosh, see the links on the Resources page of my Web site.

Underline text
Select the text you want to underline and press the following keyboard shortcut (or press this shortcut before you start typing new text that should be underlined):
- Windows: Control+U
- Macintosh: Command+U

Undo an action
Not all actions can be undone, but many can, and there's no harm in trying. The standard keystrokes are:
- Windows: Control+Z
- Macintosh: Command+Z

Windows (switching between, with in a program)
See: Switch between open windows within a program

Glossary

Web: http://www.geoff-hart.com/books/eoe/eoe3/eoe3.html
Notes: Italicized words are defined elsewhere in the glossary. Word 2010 is for Windows; Word 2011 is for the Macintosh.

Account: In a computer that requires you to enter a name and password before you can use it, you can establish a separate identity called an *account* for each user. Each account can have different settings and different rights to access the information stored on the computer.

Affordances: Hints or explanations about the nature of the input or response required from the program's user. The best affordances describe the required response concisely, but in sufficient detail that the user need never consult the online help.

Antialiasing: A software technology that lets the video software on your computer simulate the existence of more *pixels* on the screen than the display actually provides. Examples include Microsoft's ClearType and Apple's Quartz software.

Antispyware software: Software designed to prevent computer criminals from installing software on your computer that is capable of spying on your activities. Compare: *antivirus software*.

Antivirus software: Software designed to defend a computer against computer *viruses*. Compare: *antispyware software*.

Archive: Old material stored in a safe place in case you need it again. Also, a synonym for a compressed file. (See: *compression software*.)

ASCII: The American Standard Code for Information Interchange, which was one of the original attempts to standardize the encoding of the characters in *fonts*. Though ASCII did a good job for the characters on your keyboard, it differed between operating systems for characters that aren't on the keyboard, often leading to font display problems when documents were exchanged between operating systems. The *Unicode* standard solves this problem.

Attachment: A file sent attached to an e-mail message.

Audit trail: A series of records used to help an auditor determine what was done to something, when it was done, and by whom. Compare: *paper trail*.

Authoring: Authoring can be the $10 word for the $1 concept of writing or creating. But it's standard jargon in areas such as Web and multimedia development and goes beyond writing to include design roles such as creating an effective structure or creating interactivity.

Backup: A copy of a file stored somewhere safe so you can return to that version of the file if necessary.

Backup medium (media): Any device, from the traditional floppy disk to the currently trendy flash drive, used to store backups.

Blog: Short for "Web log". An online journal maintained by someone who has opinions on a subject and isn't afraid to state them. Blogs range from personal diaries to communities of experts gathered around a respected commentator.

Blues (blueline proofs): A common form of printed proof created by covering a piece of specialized film with the film negatives that will be used to create the metal plates used in offset printing, then exposing the underlying film. The name is derived from the blue color of the resulting image.

Boilerplate: Any recurring element, such as standard copyright statements and corporate logos, that appears in every document in a series. This material is often stored in a template for that series.

Business case: A carefully thought-out proposal that explains what you intend to do, the benefits and risks of doing it, and how you intend to achieve the benefits while mitigating or eliminating the risks. Where money, people, or other resources must be provided, the business case should provide logical, defensible estimates of the quantities of these resources that will be required.

Button: Any *icon* (particularly one that is button-shaped) that you click to make software perform a certain task.

Callout: A way to connect a text comment to a specific part of an image, usually by means of a pointer such as a line with an arrowhead at the pointing end. *Callout* may also refer to the comment itself.

Carriage return: An etymological legacy from the days of typewriters, when the entire carriage that contained the paper being typed upon returned to the start of the next line so you could begin typing on that line. On computers, a carriage return is created by pressing the *Enter* (Windows) or *Return* (Macintosh) keys.

Cell: In a table, each cell represents an information container whose position is defined by a column and row number.

Change bar: A vertical line in the margin of the page that indicates which parts of the text contain editorial revisions.

Character style: A collection of formatting instructions that can be applied to chunks of text smaller than an entire paragraph or heading. Compare: *paragraph style.*

Chat: A synonym for *instant messaging*. The differences between the two terms are of interest only to true geeks.

Clipboard: The name given to the part of your computer's memory where anything that you copy or cut from a document is stored so that you can paste it somewhere else.

CMYK color: The approach used to display color in printed materials. In this approach, cyan (C), magenta (M), yellow (Y), and black (K) inks merge to create a wide range of on-paper colors. A more modern variant of this traditional system, called hexachrome, adds two additional colors—orange and green—to improve color fidelity. Compare: *RGB color*.

Comma-delimited: A *delimited format* in which individual chunks of information are separated by commas. Compare: *tab-delimited*.

Command key (⌘ and ⌘): The Macintosh equivalent of the Windows Control key. On most keyboards, this key appears twice, once on each side of the space bar.

Compression software: Software that uses special encoding techniques to reduce the size of a file without losing any data.

Concordance: A list of all words in a document, as well as (optionally) their frequency and the text surrounding each occurrence of each word. See: *keyword in context (KWIC) concordance*. Compare: *index*.

Consistency: A manuscript is consistent when important words are used identically throughout a manuscript and there are no logical or other contradictions within it (in references, cross-references, statements of fact, conclusions, etc.).

Control-click: A mouse action in which you hold down the Control key before you press the primary mouse button (usually the left-hand button). On most computers and in most programs, this will display a popup menu that allows you to choose among several actions related to the object that you clicked. Compare: *right-click*, *Shift-click*.

Control code: The term used in Word to identify special characters such as paragraph markers or field codes in the search and replace dialog box. The *control* part of the name comes from the fact that the code controls how a feature (in this case, the search function) operates.

Control panel: Software that lets you define a specific aspect of your computer's behavior. For the Macintosh, it's called a *preference pane*.

Copyediting: Editing that focuses on grammar, punctuation, and consistency of formatting and word use, as well as on conformity with a publisher's style guide. Thus, it focuses more on the micro level of sentences and the phrases that make up sentences than on large-scale issues. Compare: *developmental editing, substantive editing.*

Corpus: A collection of works in a given language such as French, in a specific subject area such as geology, or in a specific author's body of work.

Cropping: The process of defining which parts of a graphic should be retained and which should be excluded (cropped out).

CRT: A cathode-ray tube type of computer monitor. Compare: *LCD.*

Cursor: An onscreen indication of where the mouse is pointing (the *mouse* cursor) or where text will be inserted once you begin typing (the *text* cursor).

Custom dictionary: A feature that lets us add new words to the software's main spelling dictionary. (Also called a *personal dictionary.*) Better software lets us create multiple custom dictionaries for special purposes.

Data: In most cases, this is the $10 word for the $1 concept of "information". However, it may also be used to mean information that will be acted on by a program. In that case, it is more nearly equivalent to the input for that action, whereas the result of that action becomes the information that the program's user sees.

Database: Software designed to store large quantities of text and numerical data and to retrieve and manipulate (sort, combine, and publish) the data. A database may also be used to store more complex pieces of information such as graphics and sound files, often referred to as "binary large objects" (BLOBs). Compare: *spreadsheet.*

Database publishing: An approach in which specialized software (or a report template created within a database) assembles a Web page, a product manual, or even a newsletter using information drawn from a database according to specified criteria for what should be included in and excluded from the output.

Default: An initial setting that software uses until you change that setting.

Delimited format: A file format in which each individual chunk of information is separated from the next chunk by a delimiter such as a tab or comma. Commonly used for exchanging information between databases, spreadsheets, word processors, and other programs.

Developmental editing: Editing that helps the author to develop the overall plan for their manuscript, often before they even begin writing. It includes both obvious tasks such as creating an effective outline and less-obvious tasks such as defining what is to be communicated, the nature of the communication's audience, and how to bridge the two to produce an effective manuscript. Compare: *copyediting, substantive editing.*

Dialog box: A window that appears on the screen so you can respond to a question from the software (i.e., begin a dialogue with the computer) or choose from a range of alternatives (most often, the settings that will govern an action that you asked the software to do, such as printing a document).

Dingbat: In traditional typesetting, dingbats were the ornamental characters (such as ☞, ☆, and ❤) that fell outside the usual range of type. The origin of this word is unclear.

Directory: The Windows name for what Macintosh users call a *folder.* Basically, a named location on your hard disk where you can store files (e.g., to group related files).

Disk image: A copy of your hard disk (and particularly of your operating system and programs) created using a special utility so that you can quickly restore your setup if you encounter a hard disk problem or are struck by a serious computer virus.

Dogsbody: See: *editor.*

Double-click: A mouse action in which you press the primary mouse button (usually the left-hand button) twice in close succession. This action selects a word or opens a program in most operating systems. Compare: *single-click.*

Double-click speed: How quickly you must click the mouse button for two consecutive clicks to be interpreted as a single command (e.g., to open a file or select a word).

Driver: Software that controls how a hardware device (e.g., a mouse) or software (e.g., video display software) interacts with you or the computer's operating system.

DTD: A document type definition, which specifies all the required and optional sections in an *SGML* or *XML* document, and the hierarchy of these sections. *HTML* also uses DTDs, but they are not usually enforced by most HTML *authoring* software.

Editor: The neglected, underappreciated hero of the publishing process. The author's knight in shining armor and slayer of the dread dangling participle. See: *dogsbody.*

Encryption: Using software to encode a file or message in such a way that only someone with the correct password can decode and read (or use) the information.

Enter key: A key on a Windows keyboard pressed to enter information into the computer's memory. On a Macintosh keyboard, this is often labeled *Return* instead.

Entity: See: *HTML entity*.

Export: To save information from one program in a format that another program can read. Compare: *import*.

Field: In computer parlance, anywhere in a dialog box that you can type information or select from a popup menu. Compare: *field code*.

Field code: A special code that allows software such as Word to automate certain features, such as inserting the current date, a link to a page number, or the results of a calculation. Compare: *field*.

Filename extension: Letters or numbers added to the end of a file name to help you (and your computer if you use Windows) identify the type of file. For example, .docx files belong to Word, whereas .htm files are Web pages you can display in your Web browser.

Firewall: A software or hardware solution that prevents malefactors from gaining entry into your computer.

Flash drive: A small (finger-sized) storage device that contains flash memory that retains its contents after the power is turned off. These devices are great tools for saving an ongoing series of backups of different versions of a file, and have the additional advantage that you can slip one in your pocket and take it somewhere safe; that way, if anything happens to your computer (e.g., theft or fire damage), you still have the most recent copy of your data on the flash drive.

Flat-file database: A database in which all the information is stored in the rows and columns of a single file (or sometimes a small number of files). Compare: *relational database*.

Folder: The Macintosh name for what Windows users call a *directory*. Basically, a named location on your hard disk where you can store files (e.g., to group related files).

Font: The shape and size information that your computer uses to determine how to display a particular typeface on the screen. Compare: *typeface*.

Font metrics: The parameters that define character size and spacing for a given font.

Font substitution: If someone sends you a file that uses a font that isn't installed on your computer, most software will offer to replace that font (temporarily or permanently) with another font that is installed on your computer. If another font is not substituted, you may be unable to read the text typed using that missing font.

FTP software: Software designed to directly transfer files between two computers without relying on intermediate software such as your e-mail program.

Galleys (proofs): Originally, a printed copy of a page produced by inking the lead type and engravings that were locked together in a *galley* and pressing those materials to a piece of paper to provide a *proof* (i.e., test) of what will be printed. With modern computer typesetting, the term *galley* is typically used for any first-draft proofs of a layout that must be proofread before finalizing the layout and proceeding with printing or online publishing.

Gamut: In the context of color, the gamut represents the full range of colors that a given device can display, whether that device is paper or a computer monitor. Computer monitors use transmitted light, whereas paper uses reflected light, so their gamuts don't fully overlap. See: *CMYK, RGB.*

Gestalt: The perceived whole that is both the sum of its parts and the result of any synergies produced by the interaction of those parts.

Global: Just as *global* refers to anywhere in the world in normal conversation, the computer use of this term refers to anywhere, though the where may be a single document (as in a *global search and replace* operation) or all documents on your system (as in a *global style*).

Global search and replace: A replacement operation that replaces every occurrence of a search term throughout a document. Some software can extend this operation across multiple documents.

Global style: A style that is available in all documents on your computer. In Word, for example, styles that are stored in Normal.dotm are global styles. Compare: *local style.*

House style: The specific style preferences of a given publishing house (i.e., publisher).

HTML: The HyperText Markup Language, which is the system used for defining how the contents of Web pages should be displayed.

HTML entity: A character code used to identify special characters such as accented letters, mathematical symbols, and Greek letters, among many others, in documents that will be published on the Web. Standardizing these codes greatly increased the likelihood that any given Web browser will display the same character.

Hubris: See: *poetic justice.*

Hyperlink: A clickable cross-reference in a computer document that takes you to the location described by that link.

Icon: A small picture intended to serve as a visual reminder of the function of some button or other interface object provided by an operating system or program. Compare: *button*.

Imagesetter: A type of high-resolution laser printer used to create the film negatives that are in turn used to create the printing plates used in offset printing.

Import: To bring information into a program, whether by converting a file in a different format to the format used by that program or by inserting the information directly into an existing file. Compare: *export*.

Index: A list of the locations (page numbers in print, and hyperlinks or page numbers on the computer) of all key terms in a manuscript, including their synonyms. An index should help readers find specific terms or concepts in a specific context. That is, each index entry defines how the term is being used at the specified location, so readers can determine whether the information they are seeking can be found there. Compare: *concordance*.

Insertion mode: A setting in which newly typed characters push existing text aside to make room for themselves. Compare: *overstrike mode*.

Instant messaging: Better known nowadays as *chat*, this technology lets authors and editors establish a link between their computers ("open a session") and take turns typing questions and comments. The instant part of the name refers to the fact that the communication occurs with little or no perceptible delay, in contrast to e-mail messages, which may not receive a response for minutes or even days.

Internet telephony: Using a service such as Skype to conduct a telephone conversation over the Internet (typically using a microphone attached to a computer) rather than using a traditional telephone.

ISP: Internet service provider. The companies that provide us with access to the Internet.

Keyboard delay: How long the keyboard will wait after a key is pressed and held down before beginning to repeat that keystroke. Compare: *keyboard repeat rate*.

Keyboard repeat rate: How fast the computer repeats a keystroke when a key is held down. Compare: *keyboard delay*.

Keyword in context (KWIC) concordance: A *concordance* that also provides the location of each word and sample of the surrounding text (i.e., its context). Compare: *index*.

Kludge: An inelegant workaround used to force the software to do something it would do more elegantly if the designers had spent five seconds thinking about our needs. Such workarounds are described as "kludgy".

Layer: Layers are the software equivalent of a transparent acetate sheet laid over a sheet of paper. Just as you can annotate a printed page without harming the paper by writing on the acetate, you can annotate a graphics file by adding a layer that contains your comments.

LCD: A liquid crystal display type of computer monitor. Sometimes referred to as a flat screen, though this can be misleading because certain CRTs are also referred to as flat screens. Compare: *CRT*.

Lingua franca: Any shared language used as a means of communication among people—or programs—that have different linguistic backgrounds. *Text format* files, for example, are the current lingua franca for file exchange, since most programs understand this format; XML is rapidly becoming the lingua franca of the future.

Local style: A style that is available only in the currently open document. Compare: *global style*.

Macro: A small program that carries out a specified series of actions, saving us the trouble of doing them ourselves. Most often, we create a macro by recording our actions as we do them. More advanced users can learn a programming or scripting language and write their own macros. Once recorded or programmed, the macro can repeat all the specified actions at a single keystroke or mouse click.

Macro virus: A virus in the form of one or more *macros*, usually attached to a Word document. Because Word can run macros automatically when a file is opened (ordinarily a useful feature), a macro virus can infect a computer without requiring any action on the part of the user other than opening the infected document. Once activated, the virus can spread to any other document opened on the infected computer or perform a range of harmful actions.

Malware: Viruses and other programs that can damage the software components of our computer, harvest e-mail addresses, record our keystrokes, and sometimes even steal documents. Suitable protection requires *antivirus software*, *anti-spyware software*, and a *firewall*—all supplemented by a large dose of caution and common sense.

Markup language: A system of codes used to mark text so as to identify its function or format. Common markup languages include *HTML*, *SGML*, and *XML*.

Menu bar: A horizontal bar that runs across the top of the screen and contains a program's most important menus. Compare: *popup menu, ribbon, toolbar.*

Metadata: Literally, "data about data". For example, in a boldfaced word in a word processor document, the data is the word; metadata is the hidden code that tells the word processor to boldface that word.

Mode: A specific manner in which the software operates. For example, in a layout mode, you may have access to special tools for formatting a document and moving text around the screen that are unavailable in the normal typing-only (draft) mode.

Mouse: In this book, I have used the term to mean any pointing device you use to control the position of the cursor. This includes traditional mice, trackballs, trackpads, and other tools.

Mouse cursor: An onscreen indication of where the mouse is pointing. Compare: *text cursor.*

Mouse tracking speed: How fast the *mouse cursor* moves in response to movements of the mouse.

Multi-session CD or DVD: With the exception of -RW (rewritable) formats, CDs and DVDs are designed to be written to only once—that is, in a single session. Modern drives and the software that accompanies them can let us write additional information to discs that have already been written to once (i.e., in a previous session).

Mutatis mutandis: Latin for "the necessary changes having been made". That is, use the approach that I just described, but modify it to account for differences between your situation and the one I described.

Native file format: The standard format used by your software to store all its formatting instructions. For Word files, this is the .docx file format or the *rich text format (RTF)*; for Web pages, this is the *HTML* or *XHTML* file format.

Netiquette: The formal and informal rules of politeness (etiquette) for the 'net (Internet). These rules include trying to help others rather than focusing exclusively on your own needs, and the wise advice given to world travelers: study the culture of a community before diving into it and making a fool of yourself.

Non-breaking hyphen: Most software will split a word that includes a hyphen over two lines when the word occurs sufficiently near the right margin of the text. If you don't want the word to split in this manner, use a non-breaking hyphen instead. The code for typing this hyphen depends on the software you're using, and may not translate successfully between programs.

Non-breaking space: Most software will split an open compound (a phrase that includes a space between the two words that constitute the compound) over two lines if the words occur sufficiently near the right margin of the text. If you don't want the words to be split, use a non-breaking space instead. The code for typing this space depends on the software you're using, and may not translate successfully between programs.

Noncontiguous text: Two or more chunks of text that are not touching; that is, they are separated from each other by intervening text, graphics, or other material.

Nonprinting characters: Special characters that govern how the software performs certain functions, such as displaying text on the screen. For example, Word uses several of these characters as visual cues for the location of such features as tab stops and end-of-paragraph markers to help you understand what you see on the screen.

Object: In computer parlance, an object is more than just something you can point at. Most often, an object is something within a document that has its own settings (e.g., the position of a graphic) or that contains programming that lets you perform actions that are not available elsewhere in the software; for example, a *spreadsheet* object is a spreadsheet file embedded in a Word document that provides access to the tools offered by the spreadsheet software.

Offset printing: A traditional form of printing in which ink is transferred from an inked printing plate onto a rubber pad or other device that then transfers the ink to the paper.

Onscreen editing: Editing using a word processor or similar tool. Note that this definition makes no assumptions about the final destination of the information; that is, it does not apply only to editing materials that will be published online, such as Web pages.

Overstrike (overtype) mode: A setting in which newly typed characters replace (type over) existing text. Compare: *insertion mode*.

Palette: A group of tools gathered into a group (the palette) and presented as clickable *icons* (*buttons*). Palettes most often contain more than a single row of icons, and may be fixed in place or capable of being moved. "Palette" is sometimes used as a synonym for *toolbar*.

Pane: In software that can split a document window into sub-windows, each of those sub-windows is referred to as a *pane*.

Paper trail: A printed copy of every version of a manuscript, usually date-stamped and signed by the person responsible for creating that version. Used as a tool for identifying problems and determining who caused those problems; in a healthy organization, the goal is to find ways to avoid repeating a problem, but some organizations use a paper trail to figure out who to punish. It is sometimes used to show compliance with government or other regulations (e.g., to prove that a particular kind of review was performed), in which case it may also be called an *audit trail*. Some organizations use a *virtual* paper trail (versions of each word processor file); others require a signed printout containing written or typed changes.

Paragraph: In software parlance, a paragraph is all the text between two *carriage returns*, which differs from the grammatical sense of a series of closely related sentences. Thus, a paragraph can be a single-word heading, a grammatically correct paragraph, or a long and rambling collection of loosely related and unpunctuated thoughts. The key point is that the paragraph is treated as a single unit for purposes such as cursor movement and the application of *paragraph styles*.

Paragraph style: A collection of formatting instructions that can be applied to entire *paragraphs* (including headings). Compare: *character style*.

Patch: A small program that the developer of a larger program provides to update that program to solve a problem, such as an incompatibility between two versions of the software. Compare: *service release*.

PDF: The portable document format (or a file in that format) created using Adobe's Acrobat software or various competing programs. PDF files are designed to ensure that the layout of the document and all the information it contains will be preserved and correctly displayed on any computer.

Personal dictionary: See: *custom dictionary*.

Pixel: A picture element (i.e., a dot) on the computer screen.

Poetic justice: The inevitable comeuppance of would-be pundits who become sufficiently confident in their expertise that they dare to write a book on some subject. (cf. *hubris*)

Popup menu: A menu embedded in a dialog box or toolbar (rather than in the *menu bar* at the top of the screen) that pops up when you click on it. Compare: *menu bar*.

Power user: Someone who takes maximum advantage of all the obvious and many of the unobvious features of their favorite software.

Preference pane: The term for a Macintosh *control panel* in OS X.

Proofing: A synonym for *proofreading*.

Proofreading: Editing a manuscript after layout to catch any errors that escaped previous editing stages, to ensure consistency in formatting, and to ensure that the content works well in its final format. Often called *proofing* for short.

Proofs: A sample of the expected final product, whether a printed book or a screen from online help. This sample lets you prove (in the word's original sense of "test") that whatever you submitted for production will appear as you intended (both layout and content) when the final version is published. In short: proofs are your last chance to catch errors before your information is presented to its audience.

Reading to proof (reading against copy): A form of proofreading in which the proofreader reads the original material used to create a laid-out document, and compares it with the document itself to identify any omissions or other errors. Sometimes a second person reads the original material aloud so the proofreader doesn't have to look back and forth between the two documents.

Record: A single set of related information stored in a *database*.

Refresh rate: How fast the image on the screen is refreshed (drawn again). Slow refresh rates can lead to visible flickering.

Relational database: A database in which information is stored in separate tables (often independent files), with related information linked by means of a shared index number or key. Compare: *flat-file database*.

Repetitive stress injury (RSI): Any injury that arises from repeatedly performing an action that causes stress to your body without providing time to recover from that stress; eventually, a significant injury may result.

Return key: A key used to insert a *carriage return* so that you can begin typing on the next line. In most software, this performs the same role as the *Enter key* (i.e., entering information into the computer's memory) and marks the end of a *paragraph*. Windows keyboards tend to use Enter; Macintosh keyboards tend to use Return.

Ribbon: The row of tabs and icons that appeared at the top of the document window starting with Word 2007. Each tab contain one or more groups of related commands. Although this interface resembles a traditional toolbar, the tabs cannot be moved to new positions to become tool palettes.

RGB color: The approach used to display color on a computer screen. In this approach, red (R), green (G), and blue (B) light are merged to create a wide range of onscreen colors. Compare: *CMYK color*.

Rich text format (RTF): A file format developed by Microsoft and supported by many other programs that lets us exchange files between Word and other programs while retaining most formatting information. A handy alternative to Word's own .docx format, particularly since RTF format cannot contain *macros* and is thus a good way to prevent the transfer of *macro viruses* between computers.

Right-click: A mouse action in which you press the secondary mouse button (usually the right-hand button). This action usually displays a popup menu that lists the available options for the object that you clicked. If your mouse only has a single button, hold down the Control key and press that button. Compare: *Control-click, Shift-click*.

Round-tripping: Exporting information from one program into another program for editing, then returning the edited information into the original program with minimal fuss. Rarely as easy as it sounds, but often possible with a bit of planning.

RSI: See: *repetitive stress injury*.

RTF: See: *rich text format*.

Ruler: A visual reference that the software provides to assist in tasks such as positioning text using *tab stops* or specifying the size of paragraph indents.

Screen resolution: The number of dots (*pixels*) that will be displayed on the screen. Screen resolution may be specified as the pixel dimensions of the entire screen, or as the number of pixels per inch.

Script: Another word for a *macro*. A scripting language is the programming language used to create or implement the script.

Search term: The specific character, word, phrase, or pattern that the software's search tool will try to find.

Service release: A fairly major update to software such as a word processor or operating system, provided by the software's developer to solve one or more major problems such as bugs and incompatibilities. Compare: *patch*.

SGML: The Standard Generalized Markup Language, which is a tool for constructing *markup languages* such as *HTML*, but also considerably more sophisticated ones. In particular, SGML allows publishers to require the inclusion of specific information, in a specific order, in each document of a given type. This is done by means of a *DTD*.

Shell account: A software environment in which all commands are sent to the operating system from the keyboard rather than using a mouse combined with icons and menus. Used primarily in the Unix and Linux operating systems.

Shift-click: A mouse action in which you hold down the Shift key before you press the primary mouse button (usually the left-hand button). On most computers and in most programs, this extends the selection from the previous cursor position to the position where you clicked. The result depends on the context. For example, in a word processor document, shift-clicking will select the text between the original cursor position and the position where you clicked, whereas in a window displaying a list of files, one of which is already selected, shift-clicking will select all files between the selected file and the position where you clicked. Compare: *Control-click, right-click*.

Single-click: A mouse action in which you press the primary mouse button (usually the left-hand button) only once. Single-clicking (usually called simply "clicking") positions the text cursor in a document, causes an icon or button to perform the action it was programmed to do, or selects a file, depending on the context. Compare: *double-click*.

Single-sourcing: The creation of two or more outputs (e.g., a printed user manual and a Web page) from the same underlying set of information. This is achieved by designing the information for ease of reuse in each of these multiple contexts, and is often implemented by means of a *database* or a specialized *markup language* such as *XML* that defines which chunks of information belong in each output.

Soft proofs (soft proofing): An alternative to printed *proofs* and on-paper proofreading, in which the person responsible for approving the proofs examines only an onscreen image. (The *soft* part of the name refers to the software nature of the proofs, such as a PDF file, rather than the hardware of paper.) Although this may be a sound strategy for spotting errors before you pay the potentially high cost of real proofs, it's no replacement for the real thing (i.e., printed proofs for materials that will be printed).

Spread: The full image you see when you open a publication and spread out the pages. Most commonly used to refer to a two-page spread that shows the opposing left-hand and right-hand pages.

Spreadsheet: Software designed to store primarily numerical data, and optimized to perform calculations on subsets of the data. Compare: *database, worksheet*.

Spyware: Software designed to install itself surreptitiously on your computer so it can spy on your activities. A form of *malware*.

Standard: To ensure that all computer hardware and software work happily together, developers of these products agree to adhere to a common set of specifications. Before the ink on the agreement dries, they begin creating their own variations on the standard, thereby ensuring that no two programs or pieces of hardware cooperate properly. The word is often considered a one-word oxymoron.

Stet: From the Latin "let it stand", thus the editorial equivalent of saying please ignore that edit or don't change this.

Story: A term commonly used to describe the separate blocks of text (often from separate files) that are imported by a desktop publishing program and placed independently within the layout.

Storyboard: A term used by animation, multimedia, and movie producers to describe how they foresee the sequence of images and associated text that will appear in the final animated product. Traditionally, this was done by illustrating key scenes in the story on art board (similar to cardboard), hence the name. Because animations are expensive, storyboards are used to permit rapid prototyping of the final product, and constitute the equivalent of a blueprint for the final product's appearance. Designers can produce the final product with fewer errors and less need for revision by working from carefully edited and approved storyboards.

Style (text): A named set of specifications for how a chunk of text should be formatted. See: *character style, paragraph style, template*.

Style (writing): The combination of an author's *voice*, word choice, and any guidelines the author followed in creating the manuscript.

Style guide: A compendium of proven solutions to typical difficulties that editors face when editing a manuscript. Since no style guide can ever be fully comprehensive (none, for example, includes a complete unabridged dictionary), editors must also create *style sheets* that extend the chosen style guide. Compare: *style sheet*.

Style sheet: A list of all the decisions we made during our efforts to impose consistency on a document. As a general rule, style sheets primarily include difficulties that are not solved in the *style guide* chosen for a given manuscript. Compare: *style guide*.

Sub-menu: Some menu choices have an arrow at the right edge of the words that indicates the availability of a sub-menu that provides more options related to the main menu:

When you move the mouse cursor over the arrow, a new menu (the submenu) opens to display these options.

Substantive editing: Editing that focuses on the organization, logic, and clarity of the content. Substantive editing also verifies the internal *consistency* of a document and may verify its external consistency with the broader consensus in a field of study. In short, substantive editing focuses on big-picture items. Compare: *copyediting, developmental editing*.

Synergy: When two things produce a more powerful effect together than you would expect from simply adding them, the enhanced result is called a *synergy*. The collaboration of authors and editors is one example of a way to obtain synergy.

Tab (in a dialog box): Most programs now group related functions within a dialog box by dividing the dialog box into sections using *tabs* that resemble the paper or colored plastic tabs used in a three-ring binder. In a dialog box, clicking the name of the tab reveals only the functions grouped under that heading. For example, in the image below, Word's search functions appear on the Find tab, the replacement options appear on the Replace tab, and the Go To tab allows fast movement within a file.

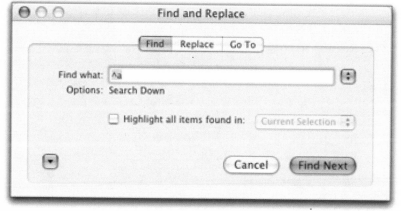

Tab (tab stop): A predefined position to which the text cursor will move whenever you press the keyboard's Tab key.

Tab-delimited: A *delimited format* in which individual chunks of information are separated by tabs (tab stops). Compare: *comma-delimited*.

Tag: A marker or pair of markers that define how a word or chunk of text should be handled by the software. For example, *HTML* uses pairs of angle brackets (< >) to identify its tags, and encloses the text to be handled in some way between a start tag and an end tag (the latter identified by a slash, /); for example, paragraphs begin with <p> and end with </p>.

Template: A collection of standard text and styles that can be used to define the initial content and formatting options available to any document. In software such as Word, templates can also store *macros* and other customizations. See: *character style, paragraph style*.

Text cursor: An onscreen indication of where text will be inserted when you begin typing. Compare: *mouse cursor*.

Text editor: A program designed specifically to manipulate text in *text format* files rather than in the proprietary formats used by word processors. This software may be as primitive as an onscreen typewriter, or may come with bells and whistles that shame your word processor.

Text format: A document format that contains only *ASCII* or *Unicode* characters and that thus does not display any of the special formats provided by a word processor's proprietary format. However, formatting can still be specified in text-format files by using *tags* from a *markup language*, such as *HTML*.

Toolbar: A group of tools gathered into a single group (the toolbar) and presented as clickable icons (*buttons*). Toolbars most often contain a single row of icons, but may be fixed in place or capable of being moved. "Toolbar" is sometimes used as a synonym for *palette*.

Translation memory: A list of preferred translations for standard phrases. Used to improve the consistency of translations.

Triage: From the French word for sorting, editorial triage involves sorting the editing tasks into those that are crucial, those that are important but can wait for a second pass, and those that we can skip—though they would be nice to do if time permits. (The existence of these three categories often leads people to mistakenly assume that the word derives from the Latin "tri", which means three.)

Triple-click: A mouse action in which you press the primary mouse button (usually the left-hand button) three times in close succession. This action selects an entire sentence or paragraph in many programs.

Typeface: The graphical design that characterizes a set of characters (letters, numbers, and other symbols) and makes them appear visually distinct from characters in another typeface. Compare: *font*.

Unicode: A modern version of the old *ASCII* system for defining the characters that make up a given *font*. Unicode fonts are better standardized between operating systems (i.e., there are fewer differences in the character definitions in different operating systems) and provide a much larger range of characters, including those used in many foreign languages. Visit the Unicode Consortium's Web site for more detailed information on the standard.

Uninterruptible power supply (UPS): A device that, like a surge suppressor, protects your computer from sudden spikes in electrical current (e.g., during a lightning storm), but that offers two important additional advantages: better protection against electrical surges, and enough battery power for you to save any open files and shut down the computer if the power fails.

Unix: A powerful operating system used as an alternative to Windows and the Macintosh operating system. Outside corporate and scientific workplaces, Unix is most familiar in its Linux flavor.

UPS: See: *uninterruptible power supply*.

Validity check: A rule or definition that defines the permissible information (what is allowed) for a *field* in a *database* or *spreadsheet*. Validity checks validate information before it is accepted, and ask users to correct errors before they become part of the stored information.

View mode: A specific way of displaying information on the screen; for example, Page Layout mode provides a close approximation of what the document will look like when you print it.

Virtual: Literally, "not real". In practice, used to refer to something stored or displayed on a computer.

Virus: Software designed to invade a computer (possibly to damage its software or steal information) and spread to other computers. A form of *malware*.

Voice: The general sense of what an author "sounds like" that readers gain from reading their writing, as if the author were physically present and talking to the reader. Compare: *style*.

VPN: Virtual private network. Software that sets up a secure "tunnel" between your computer and another computer, making it difficult or impossible to intercept information transferred between the two computers.

Web log: See: *blog.*

Wiki: A Web site or similar online resource that allows its users to add and edit content collectively. The term comes from the phrase "wiki wiki" in the Hawaiian language, meaning "rapidly". The classic example is the Wikipedia, a free online encyclopedia created in this manner.

Wildcard: In many card games, certain special cards can be used as though they were other cards (sometimes as any other card in the deck). Borrowing from this usage, most search and replace tools offer a wildcard function that lets you use a single character (e.g., ? or *) to represent any single character or group of characters. More sophisticated software lets you use wildcards to define character types, ranges or sets of characters, and other useful patterns.

Word: Short for Microsoft Word, word processing software that most editors have a love–hate relationship with. The origin of exasperated phrases such as "Word happens".

Workflow (workflow solution): The flow of work from one stage to the next, such as from writing to editing, from editing to review, from review to layout, and from layout to publication. Workflow solutions are a form of automation that guide their users through the sequence of tasks involved in the overall publishing process.

Worksheet: One page in a multi-page *spreadsheet* file.

WYSIWYG: An abbreviation of "what you see is what you get". In short, the onscreen display closely matches what will appear on paper or what viewers will see in the final onscreen document.

XHTML: A more tightly controlled version of *HTML.*

XML: A specific implementation of *SGML* that provides all of the benefits of SGML, with some of the simplicity of *HTML.*

Bibliography

Web: http://www.geoff-hart.com/books/eoe/eoe3/eoe3.html

Note: On the book's Web page, I have only presented Web addresses for books that are not available in print.

Anon. Apache OpenOffice User Guide. OpenOffice.org.

Anon. LibreOffice Documentation. LibreOffice.org.

Associated Press. 2015. The Associated Press stylebook 2015 and briefing on media law. 536 p.

Beverly, P. 2016. Computer tools for editors. Archive Publications.

Calishain, T. 2004. Web search garage. Prentice-Hall. 264 p.

Calishain, T. 2006. Information trapping: real-time research on the Web. New Riders. 328 p.

Clifford, J. 2004. Traditional proofreading in PDF. PlanetPDF.

Council of Science Editors. 2014. Scientific style and format: the CSE manual for authors, editors and publishers. 8th ed. Council of Science Editors and University of Chicago Press. 722 p.

Dayton, D. 2003. Electronic editing in technical communication: a survey of practices and attitudes. Technical Communication 50(2):192–205.

Dayton, D. 2004. Electronic editing in technical communication: the compelling logics of local contexts. Technical Communication 51(1):86–101.

Dayton, D. 2004. Electronic editing in technical communication: a model of user-centered technology adoption. Technical Communication 51(2):207–223.

Deegan, P. [no date] Office 2010: the real startup guide. Office Watch.

Deegan, P. [no date] Office 2013: the real startup guide. Office Watch.

Deegan, P. [no date] Windows 8.1 for Microsoft Office users. Office Watch.

Deegan, P. [no date] Windows 10 for Microsoft Office users. Office Watch.

Dornfest, R.; Calishain, T. 2004. Google hacks: tips & tools for smarter searching. O'Reilly Media Inc. 479 p.

Einsohn, A. 2005. The copyeditor's handbook: a guide for book publishing and corporate communications. 2nd ed. University of California Press. 560 p.

Fisher Saller, C. 2009. The subversive copy editor. Advice from Chicago (or, How to negotiate good relationships with your writers, your colleagues, and yourself). University of Chicago Press, 148 p.

Friends of OpenDocument Inc. 2007. OpenOffice.org 3 Writer Guide. 3rd ed.

Gaskell, D.; Cobb, T. 2003. Can learners use concordance feedback for writing errors? Département de Linguistique et de Didactique des Langues, Université du Québec à Montréal, Montreal.

Gibaldi, J. 2009. MLA handbook for writers of research papers. 7th ed. Modern Language Association of America. 292 p.

Hart, G.J. 2000. The style guide is dead: long live the dynamic style guide! Intercom, March:12–17.

Hart, G.J. 2001. "Backing up" doesn't mean retreating. Techwhirl.com.

Hart, G.J. 2004. Using Microsoft Word's "track changes" feature: a guide for authors.

Hart, G.J. 2004. Avoiding repetitive-stress injuries: a guide for the technical communicator. Techwhirl.com.

Hart, G. 2011. Uprooting entrenched technical communication processes: process improvement using the kaizen method. Techwhirl.com.

Hart, G. 2011. Save time by mastering the basics: efficient movement within a file. Techwhirl.com.

Hart, G. 2012. Reimagining the review-and-revision process: a case study of improving the speed and accuracy of technology transfer. Intercom February:22–27.

Hart, G. 2014. Writing for science journals: tips, tricks, and a learning plan. Diaskeuasis Publishing. 422 p.

Hart-Davis, G. 2005. Mastering VBA. 2nd ed. Sybex. 736 p.

Hart-Davis, G. 2005. Word annoyances: how to fix the most ANNOYING things about your favorite word processor. O'Reilly Media, 208 p.

Hart-Davis, G. 2010. Applescript: a beginner's guide. 2nd ed. McGraw-Hill. 448 p.

Huettner, B.; Brown, M.K.; James-Tanny, C. 2007. Managing virtual teams: getting the most from wikis, blogs, and other collaborative tools. Jones & Bartlett Publishers. 400 p.

Huggan, C. 2013. Bend Word to your will. Word MVPs.

Huggan, C. 2013. Migrating from Word 2004 to Word 2011. Word MVPs.

Jaszi, P.; Aufderheide, P. 2010. Code of best practices in fair use for scholarly research in communication. American University School of Communication, Center for Media and Social Impact.

Judd, K. 2001. Copyediting: a practical guide. 3rd ed. Crisp Learning. 304 p.

Kent, P. 1998. Making money in technical writing: turn your writing skills into $100,000 a year. MacMillan. 280 p.

Knopf, D. [no date] Autonumbering with RoboHelp and Microsoft Word. Knopf Online.

Leonard, W.; Hudspeth, L.; Lee, T.J. 1997. Word 97 annoyances. O'Reilly & Associates. 338 p.

Lyon, J.M. 2008. Microsoft Word for publishing professionals: power-packed tips for editors, typesetters, proofreaders, and indexers. The Editorium. 632 p.

Lyon, J. 2011. Macro Cookbook for Microsoft Word. The Editorium. 106 p.

Lyon, J. 2015. Wildcard Cookbook for Microsoft Word. The Editorium. 104 p.

McElhearn, K. 2009. Take control of customizing Microsoft Office. 101 p. TidBITS Publishing Inc.

McKenzie, J. 2011. The Editor's Companion. 2nd ed. Cambridge University Press.

Microsoft. 2003. Microsoft manual of style. 4th ed. Microsoft Press. 464 p.

Negrino, T. 2014. Microsoft Office for iPad: an essential guide to Microsoft Word, Excel, PowerPoint, and OneDrive. Peachpit Press. 240 p.

Negrino, T.; McElhearn, K.; Binder, K. 2002. Microsoft Office v. X inside out. Microsoft Press. 1008 p.

Neuberg, M. 2004. Take control of what's new in Word 2004. 73 p. TidBITS Publishing Inc.

Neuberg, M. 2004. Take control of what's new in Word 2004: advanced editing & formatting. 78 p. TidBITS Publishing Inc.

O'Moore-Klopf, K. 2009. Getting started as a freelance copyeditor. KOK Edit, 16 p.

Powers, H. 2009. Making Word work for you: an editor's guide to the tool of the trade. Editorial Freelancers Association. 80 p.

Sun Technical Publications. 2009. Read me first! A style guide for the computer industry. 3rd ed. Prentice-Hall. 464 p.

Thaler-Carter, R.E. 2009. Freelancing 101: launching your editorial business. Editorial Freelancers Association. 48 p.

Ticktin, N. (Ed.) 2007. MacTech's guide to making the transition from VBA to AppleScript. MacTech.com

University of Chicago. 2010. The Chicago manual of style. 16th ed. University of Chicago Press. 1026 p. (plus Web site).

Bibliography

Weber, J. 2002. Taming Microsoft Word 2002. WeberWoman's Wrevenge. 122 p.

Weber, J. 2004. OpenOffice.org Writer: the free alternative to Microsoft Word. O'Reilly Media, Inc. 234 p.

Helpful Internet Resources

Because the addresses for software and Web sites change so frequently, and because they took up so much space in the first edition of this book, I've chosen to present this information only on the book's Web site:

http://www.geoff-hart.com/books/eoe/eoe3/eoe3.html

This way, I can maintain the links more easily and can also provide instant access to the sites for people who bought the print version of the book. Please write to me via the Contacts link at the top of each Web page if any of the links break or if you have suggestions for additional links you'd like me to add.

About the Author

Legend has it that I've been writing and telling stories (both occasionally landing me in trouble) since I was 6, but it took nearly 25 years to realize I could earn a living at this trade. Fortunately, IBM (Toronto) was sufficiently intrigued by the compelling lack of qualifications exhibited by my résumé to call me and ask why I was wasting their time. They hired me that afternoon, suggesting that either (a) I'm very persuasive or (b) they were very desperate. Not long after donning the blue sarariman uniform, I ducked a massive workforce "redeployment" by finding a home with the Canadian Forest Service (Sault Ste. Marie), for whom I toiled happily for the next 6 years. Keeping an ear to the ground led to dusty ears, but helped me duck yet another major "rightsizing" and return to my home town (Montréal), where I worked for the Forest Engineering Research Institute of Canada for the next 10 years. Since 2004, I've been a freelance scientific editor who specializes in working with authors who speak English as a second language, but must nonetheless publish in English.

I've worked as a technical communicator since 1987, during which time I've been onscreen editing (mostly), writing technically, creating online help (enough to know better), translating French manuscripts, audience analyzing, technology transferring, designing Webs, instructionally designing, video scripting, slide presenting, speech-writing, and information designing. I also teach workshops in a range of subjects that occasionally surprises me—including a stint at the United Nations and others in Bangalore and Beijing. I'm pondering adding a hat rack to keep all those hats off my desk, but I'm afraid someone might notice and add more hats.

Somewhere along the way, the Society for Technical Communication noticed all this activity and made me a Fellow. Which goes to show that *maybe I really am that persuasive.*

Photo courtesy of Mathew Stevens

Index

Index

(continued)

Index

(continued)

Index

(continued)

Index

Index

Index

(continued)

Index

Index

Index

Index

X

Z